PEVSNER: THE EARLY

Pevsner – The Early Life

Germany and Art

by Stephen Games

continuum

Published by the Continuum International Publishing Group

Continuum UK, The Tower Building, 11 York Road, London SE1 7NX

Continuum US, 80 Maiden Lane, Suite 704, New York, NY 10038

www.continuumbooks.com

First published 2010

British Library Cataloguing-in-Publication Data
A catalogue record for this book is available from the British Library.

ISBN 978 1 44114 386 0

Typeset by Pindar NZ, Auckland, New Zealand
Printed and bound by MPG Books Ltd, Cornwall, Great Britain

Contents

Introduction   1

1   Home   21

2   Family   32

3   Friends   44

4   Death   54

5   History   67

6   University   76

7   Leipzig   85

8   Pinder   96

9   Dissertation   106

10 Mannerism   116

11 Dresden   129

12 Göttingen   143

13 Interlude   154

14 Modernity   166

15 Hitler   174

16 Dismissal   185

17 England   199

    Appendix   207
    Notes   215
    References   237
    Index   245

To Sophie

Introduction

Fifty years ago, in 1960, Colin McInnes wrote an essay marvelling at 'The Englishness of Dr Pevsner'. In the half century since then, many others have also marvelled at that Englishness. England has a long list of notable Germans who've made England their home, from Holbein and Handel to the Hanoverian kings and Prince Albert, but no one has ever become English and made a career out of England in the way that Nikolaus Pevsner did, and the English have honoured that association by gladly embracing him as one of their own. I remember the first time I saw Pevsner identified as a 'German' scholar in a German reference book and finding the claim offensive, so English did I think of him (and so badly had Germany treated him).

Not everyone in England has been convinced by Pevsner's Englishness, however, and those who pay tribute to him as an Englishman and an English icon have often done so in the face of adversaries who've sought to undermine his authority in the field of English studies by playing up his Germanness. Opinion about Pevsner is polarized, but on this question at least, both his friends and his enemies in England have operated from a shared premise: that his status as an expert working in England and on England has depended on where he was thought to stand as an individual on the spectrum of Englishness. The more English he appeared, the more persuasive he seemed; the less English, the more unwelcome and dangerous. On the one hand, Pevsner, in 1960, passed the nationality test for McInnes. On the other, in 2000, a critic who might be regarded as McInnes's polar opposite wrote: 'Should a man with no English social background have been encouraged so quickly to a position where he could exert an unwise, and, in a very real sense, an "alien" influence?'[1]

It's not for me to challenge the prejudices that lie behind either of these views, pro and con. The English evidently find it important that those who presume to examine and write about them are well accoutred nationalistically. What concerns me is that while everyone has been concentrating on the extent of Pevsner's Englishness, no one has ever given serious attention to the reality of his Germanness. It's true that in the 1950s and 1960s, people who objected to Pevsner and his writing often resorted to stereotypical criticisms, accusing him of German dryness, Teutonic thoroughness and an over-concern for classifying buildings at the expense of a more 'English' sensitivity to their human associations: who'd built them, who'd owned them, who'd lived in them and how they related to the life of the community. John Betjeman, for example, conducted a nasty campaign against Pevsner for many years and made Pevsner's Germanness a focus of his onslaughts. In the introductory essay to his *First and Last Loves* in 1952, Betjeman wrote: 'The Herr-Professor-Doktors are writing everything down for us . . . so we need never bother to feel or think or see again.'[2] Pevsner was sufficiently alarmed by these and other attacks to start collecting research material on the English contempt for foreigners. But the examples most often cited today as evidence of a local aversion to Pevsner – the poems of Peter Clarke of the Victorian Society – were in fact written with affection and have been mischievously misrepresented, especially by Betjeman's biographer, Bevis Hillier. That, however, is a subject for a later volume of this biography.

The object of the current volume is to look at issues of nationality and identity in Pevsner's life, and to do so initially not in terms of what these questions meant for the English when Pevsner was in his fifties and sixties but what they meant for Pevsner when he was in his formative years. Pevsner was born in 1902. He grew up in Germany, thought of himself as German and expected to make a life and career for himself in Germany. He saw the end of the Wilhelmine era and of the Kaiser. He saw the First World War, the rise and fall of the Weimar Republic and the arrival of Nazism. He also experienced conditions and events specific to his family and himself. How was he affected? How did he respond? That's what this book tries to show, using documentary evidence and avoiding the temptation to colour events by reference to what became apparent later. With just a few exceptions – references to marginal characters who won't appear again – the book proceeds on the basis that hindsight is an unwelcome partner in the writing of history.

As Charles Jencks has written, Nikolaus Pevsner was 'a British institution and twentieth-century architecture's last arbiter of taste'.[3] His voice and his opinions formed the centre of a broad cultural consensus in the middle years of the last century; after him, that consensus broke up. The failure of anyone to have looked at such a large figure in the round before now is inexplicable. I can however explain why it has taken me so long to do so.

I first became aware of Nikolaus Pevsner in the summer of 1972 when I read his *Pioneers of Modern Design* and decided on the strength of it to take his teachings and the teachings of Walter Gropius seriously, and study not just design but also architecture, which meant attending two different schools. Nine years later the BBC asked me to make a radio programme in celebration of Pevsner's eightieth birthday in 1982. And in the summer of 1983 I signed a contract with a London publisher to produce Pevsner's biography. That contract, so innocently entered into, gave me just eighteen months to write 80,000 words in time for a hardback to appear in 1985 and a paperback in 1986. This current book, weighing in at 115,000 words, dealing with Pevsner's life only up to 1933 and appearing twenty-five years late, is the first downpayment on that commitment of half my life ago.

How can a book take so long to write? Quite simply, I had no idea what I was getting involved with when I took the project on. I was enthusiastic about

Pevsner during my years as a student in the 1970s because he'd been the single most visible authority in the field of architecture and because I was convinced by many of his beliefs. But I had little grasp of the issues a study of him would throw up, or of the amount of material I'd have to read, or the number of people I'd have to talk to to make sense of him.

I began my student career studying typography and design under Richard Hollis and Anthony Froshaug at the Central School of Art in London, where we were taught that the minutiae of our daily design decisions had some kind of moral energy that would trickle down from us and into the world at large. Outside our own community, design might be unloved and undervalued but the idea was that we knew better and our time would come. Gropius had said so and Pevsner had confirmed it. They were our heroes, and that made us, in their image, also heroic, even if our own individual approaches to design were modulated by other figures.[4] Pevsner was therefore central to how we saw ourselves and I had no thought that he was anything other than a good thing.

I had no thought, either, that there was anything partial about my view of him. What we learnt from Pevsner was that architecture was the mother of the arts and that, for the modern world at least, art was more impressive when it had a purpose than when it was merely decorative. I didn't see that as contentious. And when I read Pevsner, I didn't see him as contentious. I didn't see him at odds with either earlier writers or his contemporaries. I read Pugin and Ruskin and J. M. Richards and Henry-Russell Hitchcock and John Summerson and Ian Nairn and Reyner Banham not for how they contradicted each other but for how they complemented each other and moved the story of architecture forward, and felt sure this was how they saw themselves too. Architectural writing, for my generation of students, seemed to be collegiate. It didn't occur to us that values were in any important respect arguable, or that ideas we thought of as universal were in fact specific to our own field of endeavour.

Reading Pevsner at art school persuaded me that studying architecture provided a necessary framework for understanding all the subsidiary arts, and on this wobbly platform, I went to Cambridge to see if it was true. (It wasn't.) My own route into Pevsner had been through his *Pioneers* book, which dealt with the birth of the Modern Movement (never called 'Modernism' in those days because it wasn't regarded as an 'ism'). At Cambridge I discovered there was another route into him through his historical writings and in particular through his *An Outline of European Architecture*. Architectural history, however, was a quite separate discipline and one we architects needed to know little about. At Cambridge, architects and art historians shared the same building – a row of Victorian houses called Scroope Terrace – but with the exception of one or two shared members of the teaching staff, we had nothing to do with each other. We were scruffy, creative and had long hair; art historians were well groomed and timid. David Watkin, for example, who taught at the wrong end of Scroope Terrace, even wore a neatly folded handkerchief in the breast pocket of his pinstripe, three-piece, Savile Row suit.

Art historians were therefore virtually invisible to us. They were also genu-
inely academic in a way we weren't, though for us this meant they were tragically
divorced from practice. Poor things: they could only document and theorize.
We were doers and almost everything we did was therefore more valuable than
almost anything they did. What we learnt from our two favourite history lecturers, Nicholas Bullock and Robin Middleton, about historiography – comparing
the writings of Semper and Schinkel and Viollet-le-Duc, for example – was never
anything more than intriguing. As for contemporary theory, that came to us as
the pet ideas of whatever architect happened to be invited to our studios each
term. (Sir Richard MacCormac, who went on to build the Ruskin Library at
Lancaster University, seemed to spend most of his time insisting that we align
our plans to double- or Japanese- or tartan-grids.)

Pevsner was not of course an architect but seemed to be on our side in a way
that Cambridge's art historians were not. In fact, we weren't even aware he was
fundamentally an art historian. For us he was simply the champion of modern
architecture, which meant he was our man rather than theirs at Scroope Terrace's
conservative end: politically progressive and forward-thinking and interested in
the next thing, as Ian Buruma would describe him more than twenty years later.
He was 'Pevsner', sui generis – a constant reminder that we were in a privileged
line of succession back to the Bauhaus and that what counted was the rational
and the modest and the practical. That gave me a licence to emulate him and
devote myself to explaining architecture. I was, and remain, massively in his
debt.

By the time I contracted to write about him, Pevsner was only just alive,
terribly reduced by Alzheimer's and incapable of being interviewed. There was
however a huge amount of written material to be found in the archives of
institutions he'd been involved with: universities he'd studied or taught at, committees and other bodies he'd been active on, and publishers who'd brought out
his writings. In addition there were the memories of people who'd known him.
In 1983, having not written a book before, I imagined that if I worked quickly
and comprehensively, I could master the job relatively swiftly.

In my outline to the publisher, I therefore talked merrily about examining
Pevsner's life and raising what I then regarded as the central questions that his
career invited. I'd talk about his work as a historian, critic, academic, editor,
campaigner and broadcaster. I'd look at his involvement with Birmingham
University, the Courtauld Institute, the *Architectural Review*, Birkbeck College,
Cambridge University, Oxford University, Faber and Faber, Penguin, Thames and
Hudson and the Victorian Society. I'd review his contribution to the National
Advisory Council for Arts Education, the National Council for Diplomas in Art
and Design, the Arts Panel of the British Council, the Royal Commission on
Historical Monuments, the Historic Buildings Council and the Royal Fine Art
Commission. I'd write about how he wrote his many books as well as looking in

detail at the two vast publishing enterprises he took on in the late 1940s – *The Buildings of England* and the *Pelican History of Art*. I'd explain the mechanics of how he managed, edited and, in the case of *The Buildings of England*, wrote most of the forty-six volumes that contributed to these. And I'd try to show how he was able to do all of this, as well as broadcasting, dissertation reading, travelling, lecturing and writing elsewhere, alongside his main teaching commitments at Birkbeck in the evenings and once a week at Cambridge, where he served as Slade Professor from 1949 to 1955.

To achieve all of this, I'd talk to his colleagues and assistants and secretaries, asking how he worked and what he expected of those he worked with. On the basis of what they told me I'd try to explain the changes in his methods over forty years. I'd look at what and how he taught, and also whom he'd taught. I'd even draw up a family tree to show who his students had been and what they'd gone on to do, to reveal the extent of his influence worldwide.

Then there'd be the critical or interpretative side of the book where I'd look at Pevsner's ideas, how he'd come by them, what he meant by them, the various problems they gave rise to, the consequences of his view of himself and finally his place in the world of architectural history and criticism today. Even as I signed the contract, I didn't yet realize that this would actually involve rather a lot of effort.

I assumed the work I'd already done for my BBC programme had given me a head start. I'd recorded interviews with nearly a dozen of Pevsner's associates: among them, his former PhD student the architectural historian Reyner Banham, who as a young apprentice had missed a bus while waiting at a bus stop in Bristol because he was so engrossed in Pevsner's *Outline of European Architecture*; Pevsner's colleague at the *Architectural Review* Sir Alec Clifton-Taylor; and Sir Ernst Gombrich, who told me how the Swiss psychiatrist and entomologist Auguste Forel had named a newly discovered ant after the young Pevsner and thereby, in Gombrich's view, introduced the spirit of the ant into Pevsner's soul and made him unimaginably industrious.[5] These and other hour-length interviews had been reduced down to make a forty-five-minute programme, which meant there was much more material I could call on for my book.[6]

The programme had also generated some useful background research. My producer on the programme, Thomas Sutcliffe, had asked the BBC Library to provide us with photocopies of every Pevsner-related newspaper cutting in the BBC archives, which illustrated the conventional view of Pevsner in the British press. That conventional view was made up mainly of recurring anecdotes about his work on *The Buildings of England* – his funny work habits, his funny remarks about buildings, the funny things that happened to him during his month-long tours of English counties, his funny work schedule and his funny attitudes. What was said about his character ran strictly to form. Pevsner was always 'dry', 'precise' and 'perfectionist' but also 'kindly' and 'wry'. He had 'twinkling eyes' and 'only the faintest trace of a German accent'. His apparent formality was only a front. He could laugh at his own reputation as a martinet. He must have been twins because no one man could have done as much in his life as Pevsner did. Ho ho.

In addition to this, there were the facts and opinions, rarely checked, often repeated: that he was a refugee from the Nazis and had come to England in 1933, or '34, or '35. That he'd proposed *The Buildings of England* to Allen Lane after the war because 'he was amazed that the English had no equivalent to the record of German architecture compiled by Dehio' except for the Victoria County Histories and the volumes of the Royal Commission on Historical Monuments, which, at present rates of progress, wouldn't be finished for another 200 or 300 or 400 years. That he'd 'changed the way we look at our buildings' and 'taught the English to appreciate their own heritage'. That he'd saved a century. That he'd seen himself as a general practitioner and not as a specialist or consultant. That he'd taken no royalty, and only a small salary, for his work for Penguin. That he was more English than the English.

The radio programme repeated some of this mythology on Pevsner uncritically. I regret that now. I also regret that we didn't do more to look at the nature of Pevsner's thinking and at revisionist views of Pevsner that had started to develop in the previous ten or fifteen years, especially among American architects and in a wing of Scroope Terrace I hadn't realized as a student was a hotbed of anti-Pevsnerism. What impressed me most, for example, in the making of the programme was a casual observation not by any of the contributors but by Thomas, the producer. Tom pointed out an oddity about the idea of the Zeitgeist – Pevsner's beloved notion of the unifying spirit of the age. Pevsner had commended artists for conforming to the Zeitgeist but had concentrated in his writings on those who'd anticipated it: his 'pioneers'. What, then, was more creditable: to be in advance of the Zeitgeist or to be a part of it? Pevsner didn't raise the issue and nor did we. We should have done because it's a confusion that lies at the heart of his work. It's also a nice example of an art-historical question that doesn't grow out of the laborious apparatus of art history.

We should have addressed it also because it was very much in the wind at the time. The besuited Watkin, for example, had just hinged his reappraisal of Pevsner on the issue of the Zeitgeist, making it the lynchpin of two dangerously seductive branches of Germany philosophy: Hegelianism and Marxism. In *Morality and Architecture* in 1978, Watkin had argued that for 150 years, leading writers and architects had acted like devils or papal inquisitors, forcing dogmas upon innocents, denying them basic freedoms, making them betray their own natures and punishing them when they went astray. And these writers and architects weren't just independent agents acting alone but a succession of diabolical co-conspirators, each building on the depravity of those who'd come before, the last and worst being Pevsner, the Antichrist, engineering the last push that would turn the world into a sort of Bolshevik hell.

Watkin wrote as if architecture necessarily created the political conditions of society. Thus, if architects built buildings in a 'Marxist' way, the whole of society would be become Marxist. He demonstrated this notion by spelling out an intellectual legacy that went from successors of the tyranny of French rationalism (Pugin and Viollet-le-Duc), via the delusional Socialists of the Arts and Crafts movement (Morris to Lethaby), to various European theorists enacting nightmare scenarios of escalating horror in which German romanticism locked arms with Communism to lead the world into the abyss.

Watkin had every reason to want to roast mainstream architecture in the late 1970s: for twenty-five years, even the most sophisticated architects and planners had been blithely putting up buildings of staggering awfulness and congratulating themselves on doing so. One can well understand why an outsider like Watkin should feel, metaphorically, that the profession had been mesmerized by some terrible Svengali. What was interesting, however, about Watkin's wish to challenge this architecture – the motive behind his book – was that while setting out to invalidate Pevsner and his predecessors by exposing the invalidity of their methods, he'd actually copied them.

His belief in a society being shaped by its architecture came straight from Pugin, whose thinking he'd warned against. His idea that the present condition of architecture could be blamed on a succession of influential names – a linear chain of culpability from Pugin to Pevsner – rather than on more complex issues was the mirror image of Pevsner's chain of progress from Morris to Gropius. The internal dynamic that governed that chain was exactly equivalent to the German 'Kunstwollen', a concept he'd ridiculed the use of, alongside the Zeitgeist. The names in his chain weren't free-acting individuals or even real people with minds and motivations of their own but functionaries in a necessary historical process, an approach he'd dismissed as Marxist and intellectually offensive. He'd exercised retroactive moral judgements about what people in the past should or shouldn't have done, even while cautioning against ahistoricism. He'd also warned against dogma in modern life (though not against religious dogma), been selective and misleading in his quotations, relied entirely on published texts without conducting any primary research, and made use of the Zeitgeist to explain the inexplicable but defining grip on architecture at any moment – all against the apparent thrust of his book.

How does one account for Watkin's blindness or lack of self-awareness or hypocrisy? Was it because he'd lived his entire life in one academic institution? Was it because, as a certain type of dry-as-dust professional historian, he didn't like to look beyond the printed page? I don't know; I can only say that I'm still astonished at how easily Watkin's words about Pevsner can be turned back on himself: 'This is an architectural history which disregards the individual circumstances and achievements of individual artists, the alternatives they accepted or rejected, and instead manipulates actors building up to the dénouement of a predetermined drama' – the predetermined drama being, for Watkin, the failure of modern architecture. All this time, Watkin was passing himself off as the

saviour of civilization and a crusader against Pevsner's methodology when he
was in fact his nemesis's incredibly wicked alter ego.

It might have been fun to have had it out with Watkin in my radio programme about Pevsner in 1982 but the engagement would probably not have
been rewarding for the listener. He did in fact take part in a programme I made
about 'post-modern' architecture a couple of years later and turned out to be less
brilliant with a microphone trained on him than when typing at his computer in
his rooms at Peterhouse. And since I'd already taken a pop at him in a review of
his book in *The Sunday Times* in 1978, Tom Sutcliffe thought it was best to move
on. 'The war's over, Stephen,' he'd say when I got worked up about something
I cared about and he didn't. But I don't think it is. Clearly.

After I'd won a contract to write Pevsner's life, the Pevsner family wouldn't
agree to its being authorized and wouldn't let me have his diaries but did give
me a copy of a family history he'd written in 1954 and suggested names of
people I should contact, in Britain and the USA, and in Germany, where some
of Pevsner's in-laws still lived. These and other suggestions gave rise to many
hundreds of inquiries, tracing people who'd known Pevsner in the past and teasing out further contacts. The family also allowed me to read some of Pevsner's
correspondence. Every couple of weeks I'd drive to the mews on the north side
of Hampstead Heath where his children had cottages and I'd take away cardboard
boxes – two or three at a time – of whatever correspondence they thought it
was safe for me to see. Most of the time the boxes contained letters to and from
Pevsner on issues to do with the publication of his books abroad. I read and took
notes on his correspondence with his German publisher, his Dutch publisher,
his Danish publisher, his French publisher, his Hungarian publisher, his Polish
publisher, his Portugese publisher, his Yugoslav publisher, his American publisher
and his Japanese publisher. After a few months, I'd become something of an
expert on questions to do with the appearance of his foreign editions: who was
going to do the translations, when the translations would be done, the quality of
those translations once they'd been completed, how repagination would affect
layout, what new pictures were available and who'd supply them, what the paper
quality would be and what royalties he'd be paid. So that was good.

At the time, no one seemed sure what Pevsner's correspondence might contain but its existence in London, just a mile or two from where I lived, was one
of the things that reassured me I could complete my research and still hold down
a day job. The arrangement of the papers into different themes – publications,
lectures, travel, broadcasts – was also reassuring because it suggested if I worked
methodically through all the papers, I'd eventually have covered the whole of
Pevsner's career. While I was busy on the papers, however, the family decided to
put them up for sale, along with Pevsner's library of 7,000 books, and called in
Quaritch, an antiquarian bookseller in London (founded in 1847 by a German
from a town near Göttingen) to handle the sale. The hope, apparently, was that
the collection would be bought by an institution Pevsner had been closely

connected with, such as London University or Cambridge.

Meanwhile, I was starting to collect some very interesting anecdotal material from people who'd known Pevsner outside his professional life or who had access to archival information they thought I should see. Some of the most fascinating contributions were from Rosalind Priestman, who told me at length about Pevsner's life in Göttingen in the early 1930s, and at about the same time, diary entries and newspaper clippings written by Priestman's aunt, a social activist and writer for the *Birmingham Post*, that I was shown by Fred Wolsey, the aunt's executor. Both added a completely new dimension to Pevsner's popular image that I suppressed because I wasn't yet able to relate it to his life as a whole.

It was now starting to become clear to me that my decision to study ancient Greek at school instead of modern German was not guided by a strong vision of my future needs. I therefore put myself on an intensive language programme, at first on my own and then at the Goethe-Institut in London. Once I'd gained sufficient fluency and made an initial trip to West Germany in April 1984, I asked the British Council for help in organizing a study tour to the two Germanys. The Council put me in touch with the Interior Ministry of the Democratic Republic and the German Academic Exchange Service (DAAD) of the Federal Republic. The Interior Ministry provided accomodation and support in Leipzig, Naumburg and Dresden in the East; the DAAD funded me to visit Berlin, Göttingen, Bochum, Marburg, Frankfurt am Main, Nuremburg and Munich in the West. I'm grateful to all three services for their assistance.

Visiting West Germany in 1984 was highly productive. Pevsner had spent one semester at each of the universities of Munich, Berlin and Frankfurt and had later taught at Göttingen. His sister-in-law still lived in Marburg; her son Franz lived in Bochum. Nuremberg had the art historians' section of the German National Museum. Every stop threw up reams of material. Visiting East Germany was even more productive. Pevsner had been born and brought up in Leipzig and had spent four semesters at its university. Naumburg was where his father-in-law had bought a country estate. Dresden was where he'd got his first job. But visiting East Germany was daunting because it was in the Soviet zone of influence, which meant venturing into one of the most repressive of the Warsaw Pact countries. It was said there wasn't an activity that went on in the GDR that wasn't infiltrated by the Stasi (the Ministry of State Security or secret police). By the 1980s, one person in six was supposed to be either on the staff of the Stasi or a paid informant; 10,000 of its informants were aged eighteen or below. Since East Germany's emergence in 1950, almost a third of its population had fallen victim to Stasi surveillance, detention or torture. It wasn't the sort of place you'd want to go to by choice.

In fact, East Germany was very much the sort of place you'd want to go to: just not under the Communists. Apart from looking for hidden microphones wherever I went (on the advice of the British Council) and inadvisedly talking politics when talking to people I thought I could trust (against the advice of the British Council) and being propositioned by almost anyone who saw I was smoking an American brand of cigarettes (against the advice of my doctor), the trip was a delight. On the instructions of the Ministry, I was housed by Leipzig University – which at the time called itself Karl Marx University – in the beautiful Villa Tillmanns, just next to the Reichsgericht, the Imperial Court of Appeal, where Pevsner's father-in-law had practised. I was able to spend long hours in libraries and official archives where the staff were always helpful and courteous and gave me everything I asked for.

In the evenings and at weekends I'd try to reconstruct mentally the places that Pevsner had known. I made notes and took photographs of the buildings he'd lived in or seen or worked in – even of the gravestones of members of his family. There were many surprises. Before my visit, I'd thought of East Germany as an essentially Soviet creation of characterless post-war apartment blocks. It hadn't occurred to me that anything of the past might have survived British bombing or Soviet rebuilding. And yet the mediaeval church of St Thomas, the Thomaskirche, and its affiliated school, the Thomasschule, where Bach had been choirmaster and which Pevsner and his older brother had attended, still existed. Many of the eighteenth-century Baroque town-houses that Pevsner had written about for his doctoral dissertation on Leipzig still existed. Much of the spacious 'Musikviertel' or 'Music Quarter' where his parents had lived still existed. The Johanna Park, where he'd ice-skated one cold winter in his teens and met the girl who only a few years later would become his wife, still existed. And so did many of the buildings of the university where he'd enrolled as a student in 1921.

There were also the town buildings that had gone up in the years after Pevsner was born and that he would have seen under construction. There was the Neues Rathaus (started in 1899 but not completed until 1905) with its eccentric, Neo-Baroque frontispieces and towers. There was also the strangely curving Deutsche Bücherei (1912), now the German National Library, with its pair of round stair turrets, looking like a chunky version of Gropius's lightweight Deutscher Werkbund pavilion of two years later. Buildings I'd thought were all destroyed still existed.

That's not to say that wartime bombing hadn't done massive damage. The Brühl, the Jewish fur-trading district near the railway station where Pevsner's father had his business premises, had been almost totally destroyed; so had the Neue Gewandhaus[7] (1884), Leipzig's acoustically perfect concert hall, where Pevsner's mother had triumphed as a society hostess. There were also still huge bombsites waiting to be restored, and Soviet-era monstrosities of soul-destroying banality (though no worse than parts of Birmingham), and everything was decrepit and decaying, from the older buildings to the food in the shops. At the Villa Tillmanns where I was staying, the bath didn't work and when I asked when it would be fixed, the concierge told me she'd submitted a request for a plumber the previous year and was confident the authorities would deal with it soon. The sense that this was indeed 1984 – Orwell's 1984 – was everywhere, from the lorryloads of troops that kept coming and going in Dresden to the invocations on posters that read 'Stärken wir die DDR mit höheren Leistungen in Sport und Forschung' – 'let's strengthen the country with greater efforts in sport and research'. Not for nothing was the door to a darkened basement comedy club in Leipzig kept locked and unlit at night.

But in Leipzig, on a sunny July day in 1984, one could still conjure up the age of tramcars and straw hats, of bourgeois confidence and civic wealth. I photographed as much of it as I could – and of Dresden in the rain, and of Naumburg Cathedral with its beautiful and grotesque sculptures, and of the garden-suburb streets of Göttingen with their cutesy, inflated cottages and exaggerated roofs, and when I got back to London I gave the negatives to my publisher at the time for safekeeping. They were all lost.

Far away in Los Angeles, the Getty Trust was just setting up a research institute in art, to soak up surplus money generated by the sale of Getty Oil to Texaco. While I was in Germany, its archivist, Nicholas Olsberg, was sent to London to examine Pevsner's papers and put a valuation on them. He found the material 'extensive, but badly arranged'. There were few photographs and few materials associated with either Pevsner's editorship of the *Architectural Review* or *The Buildings of England*, he noted, and many of the papers were no more than jottings for lectures that would be of little use to other scholars. There was however a box file of references to British architects whose names didn't appear in Howard Colvin's standard dictionary of architects, as well as scattered correspondence with architects and other scholars. Olsberg identified letters and reminiscences from Gropius and van de Velde, research materials related to William Morris, Frank Pick and Charles Rennie Mackintosh, background research for Pevsner's *A History of Building Types* and letters from family and friends.

With Getty executives trawling the world for artists and art historians whose archives could form the core of their new Pacific coast facility, Pevsner's collection was found slightly disappointing in terms of the wonders it might have contained (all the *Buildings of England* papers, for example, remained with Penguin Books and were housed in Penguin's own warehouse), but what existed was essential and the Getty therefore put in a successful shut-out bid. Towards the end of the year, material I thought I'd be able to rely on in London was packed up, together with the best of Pevsner's books, and transferred to California, putting the backbone of my research out of reach. At the time I was told to be grateful the papers hadn't gone to the next highest bidder: the University of Tokyo. And the Getty people did agree to fly me to Los Angeles and host me for a month (supplying me also with a red Mustang), officially so I could advise them on their new collection, unofficially so I could at least take stock of my situation.

At the time the Getty Center was using as its temporary base a new twelve-storey office building on Fourth Street, Santa Monica, and that's where the Pevsner archive was housed. In January 1985 a preliminary effort was made to put it into some kind of order and in February I was flown out to take a look at it: the first outsider to be allowed to do so. By then the Getty had got a better idea of what it had bought: manuscripts, notes, letters and pictures; cuttings of occasional writings; texts of lectures delivered in the USA, Germany, Spain, Holland, Brazil and other countries; scripts of radio broadcasts; notes on buildings around the world; abstracts of books; correspondence and minutes of committees that Pevsner had sat on (the Redundant Churches Advisory Board, the British Academy, the Victorian Society, the William Morris Society, the board of the *Architectural Review*, the Jerusalem Committee and others); teaching notes; annotated copies of books by other authors including Le Corbusier's *Modulor* and Wright's Wasmuth monograph; pocket diaries from 1951 to 1978; Pevsner's student notebooks; his reading notes; his research notes during his period in Dresden; page proofs from his books and magazine articles; samples of wallpaper from the Wiener Werkstätte; and files from the Charles Rennie Mackintosh memorial exhibition of 1933.

All this material has been open for inspection for twenty-five years. In 1985, with no archival searching aids yet available and with the papers still in relative disarray, the state and extent of the material was overwhelming. I was told that the collection took up 140 feet of shelving; with rehousing in different boxes it now 'only' takes up seventy feet. At no point, during my trip to Los Angeles, was I ever able to see the collection in its entirety, however. I was given a list of what was known to be available and invited to request a few items at a time. Among these were numerous diaries – mostly appointment books but some from Pevsner's adolescence, written in shorthand and, I eventually worked out, documenting his dreams and his feelings for the girl who became his wife. For days and days I puzzled over copies of these, on the four-block walk from the motel on Ocean Avenue where I was being housed, past avenues of ridiculously tall and spindly wind-blown palm trees, to the Getty. I'd stay at the Getty until long after dark, and then until late at night in one of various diners on Wilshire Boulevard.

Protected in the Getty offices from the baking heat of a Southern Californian February, I also read letters from Pevsner's mother about the death of his father, and his notes on the Italian Renaissance and the Baroque, and on Geistesgeschichte and the history of science and agriculture and botany, and on art education, and on Ashbee and Voysey. I even found his copy of *Baedeker's Great Britain* from 1930 – an English language edition, heavily used, the index pages and map in tatters, the spine missing but with copious handwritten notes filling in what Pevsner obviously thought were great gaps in what it should have contained. As I worked, inquisitive visitors would come and go. On one occasion, Charles Jencks came by to see what the Getty was all about, and invited me to his newly built blue folly in Rustic Canyon with its Latin mottos and orange trees.

Although I saw much, my month in Los Angeles still gave me only a glimpse of what the Getty's Pevsner archive contained. With only a few days left before I had to get back to London, I realized I was researching Pevsner's life more slowly than he'd lived it – not the best strategy for a biographer. I was also coming across material I wasn't quite comfortable with and couldn't incorporate into the familiar picture of Pevsner I still shared. In spite of that, I held out for nine more months before deciding I couldn't see where I was going and that there was no choice but put the work on hold until my circumstances changed and I could think it out afresh.

Thirteen years went by. During that time the Getty organization bought a hillside in Brentwood from UCLA and commissioned Richard Meier to design a campus on it, not in his trademark white but in sheets of brown marble shipped from the Getty's own quarry in Italy, also bought specially for the purpose. On this 110-acre site above the 405 Freeway, it created, among other things, an art gallery, an institute for conservation studies, a networked catalogue and an accessible database that connected the British Museum, the Louvre, the Prado, the Uffizi and the Met, all for something in excess of a billion dollars.

From 1998 I went back to this wonder of the modern world several times for further periods of study – not only doggedly working through the Pevsner material during the day but teaching myself about German art history, which until then had been a huge gap in my knowledge, in the evenings. For the first time I started to familiarize myself with the great adventure of Kunstwissenschaft, the achievements of Burckhardt and Wölfflin and their successors, those off-putting abstractions like Geistesgeschichte that anglophones always struggle with, and the details of what was at stake in teaching and writing about art history in the Weimar period. I was able to tackle these subjects only because of, once again, the Getty's largesse, its vast resources and its willingness to accommodate me in its huge library, all alone, for many hours after the Special Collections room had closed for the day. Each evening, as I took the Getty's driverless rail shuttle back down the Getty hill to the Getty underground car park, I felt, at last, I was starting to get some context on who Pevsner had been and what had moved him before he'd become English. But it had taken more than fifteen years, there was still a long, long way to go and I still couldn't see how the research process would ever feel complete enough for the writing to begin.

During this time, no rival biography had appeared, in spite of ample material to produce one; in fact, the Getty's Pevsner archive still seems to be relatively unused, even though it provides an unsurpassed insider's view of the evolution of art and architectural history over fifty years, of the history of Kunstgeschichte in the 1920s, of conflicting views of Modernism in the 1930s, of the mission in English architecture in the 1940s, and so forth. It also provides evidence of Pevsner's cast of mind: of his youthful enthusiasm for Spengler, for example, whom the German left regarded as a bogus sensationalist in the 1920s but whom Pevsner can be found writing to as an admiring fan and whose views on the rise and fall of cultures he reproduced – distilled, thank goodness – at the very beginning of his *Outline*. Anyone wanting to see how an individual historian engaged with the vast edifice of art history, architectural history, architecture and conservation need only look at Pevsner's student notebooks and correspondence in the Getty collection. It's far easier to do this now than when I started out twenty-five years ago. Visits can be arranged, research assistants can be hired and the catalogue is viewable online. And yet much of it remains unread.

Also available and unread are copies of newspaper and journal articles that Pevsner wrote when he was still in Germany. In 1970 the American Association of Architectural Bibliographers devoted its seventh volume to Pevsner's writings. The publication listed his journalism as well as his books and book reviews and while there are gaps in the record, most of these early German writings are cited and the Getty has been standing by with copies of them, for anyone who's cared to look, for a quarter of a century. But no one seems to have done so.

After one of these protracted trips to Los Angeles, I reintroduced myself to the Pevsner family and asked once again if I could see Pevsner's diaries. Disappointingly, they still weren't available. As an exercise, however, I decided to test myself and see what I could write without them. To my surprise, I was able to produce 50,000 words in two months on Pevsner's background and early professional training while I was teaching as an adjunct professor for Boston University. Greatly compressed, that writing makes up perhaps a fifth of the present book. It wasn't obvious at the time, however, how to take it further.

What eventually spurred me on was the thought that Pevsner's centenary was approaching and that if I wasn't yet in a position to produce a biography, I could at least bring out a proxy work. In the Written Archives of the BBC in Caversham, outside Reading and just a mile from where I was born, I'd come across more than seventy transcripts of Pevsner's radio talks and two large files of his correspondence over a thirty-year period. Methuen agreed to publish this as *Pevsner on Art and Architecture* in 2002 and, by way of an introduction, I wrote a long essay about Pevsner's relationship with the BBC which my editor at Methuen decided was too long and too candid. He asked me to find another subject.

In the summer of 2001, the Victoria and Albert Museum had held a two-day conference on Pevsner. The following year, Birkbeck College, where Pevsner had taught art history for some twenty-five years, held another two-day conference. Towards the end of the second day, during a question-and-answer session, one of the speakers talked about the art historians whom Pevsner had commissioned for his *Pelican History of Art* and surprised the audience by observing that in at least one case, and possibly two others, his German contributors had had questionable political credentials that, rightly or wrongly, would have ruled them out for many other commissioning editors. The conversation then turned to Pevsner's politics and touched on material I'd been aware of now for almost twenty years but not known how to handle. I decided that if Methuen needed a different introduction to the BBC talks book, it was time to confront this topic. I therefore incorporated it into the first summary of Pevsner's life to take notice of his early years. That book appeared in November of Pevsner's centenary year and was greeted with an angry reception in the UK press. A paperback, slightly revised, appeared in 2003 and an expanded edition is being planned with the original introduction available as a companion monograph.

The publication of the Methuen book didn't provide any clarification about how to complete the biography. In some despair, I offered all my research material – some two shelf metres of interviews and other papers – to Birkbeck College, only to have them turned down by Will Vaughan, Birkbeck's then professor of art history. The spectre of Pevsner was evidently not going to go away. And so over the next five years, while editing four volumes of John Betjeman's prose and broadcast writings, I continued to put out inquiries about Pevsner. Among the most valuable responses was the loan of an entire archive from the son of a Birmingham man who'd tried repeatedly to contact me in 1983 about his memories of Pevsner in the mid 1930s and died just as I was about to arrange a meeting.

And then, suddenly, everything clicked into place. Late in 2008, having just completed work on *Betjeman's England*, I decided to write an account of the reception my Methuen book had got six years earlier. At the suggestion of Kevin Gardner at Baylor University, Texas, I contacted Ben Hayes at Continuum and Ben enthusiastically adopted the book as a personal project. He didn't quite get what he was expecting. After quickly writing a history of what had happened in 2002, I found I had to explain why I'd written what I'd written and before long the entire structure had changed. The book was no longer a review of 2002, which now appears as an appendix here, but, astonishingly, the first volume of the biography proper.

I know whom I have to thank. Once I'd moved all my Pevsner files – all two metres of them – into my study, I was hit by one last wave of anxiety. Could I really compress all this research? It was then that Bea, my wife, pointed out that the files were simply my reference library and that I already knew the story and just had to write it. With that, the logjam was broken. I'm in Bea's debt for that, and for supporting me throughout the writing period. It was a six-month job, demanding and taxing but, thanks to her, never daunting. I'm grateful too to Ben for taking my original pitch to him on trust and standing by me solidly. And to Nick Evans, whose cover design is just right.

For almost thirty years, I've been plagued by the awareness of unfinished business and, as I type this, I look forward to a great sense of relief once it's done. *Pevsner – The Early Life: Germany and Art* is an extension to the alternative introduction that Methuen asked me for in 2002. It looks in detail at Pevsner's upbringing and family background, his university education, aspects of his private life and his professional career as a writer, critic and lecturer. At last I've got this first part of Pevsner's story off my chest. The research process never ends, however, and even with the book now finished, I continue to find new information I would have included if there'd been more time and that would have brought more precision to what I've written. (I'm particularly worried, for example, about whether Pevsner visited the Bauhaus in 1925 or not: in 2002 I thought he did; now I think he didn't.) I therefore have to take refuge in Pevsner's habitual caveat: what I've done was my best stab at a new subject, given what I knew up to the publishing deadline. I'm only too aware of where I could have done more work but there comes a time when you have to stop preparing and start baking. Further volumes in this biography can now follow, I hope, or fear; as for this one, I'll try to correct any errors that come to my attention in later editions.

The number of people I need to thank is so extensive that it would fill a book of its own. Many of the most important contributors are people I talked to and had correspondence with between 1981 and 1986 and people I've talked to and exchanged emails with since 1998. These include members of Pevsner's or his wife's family, former colleagues or students of his, and people who knew him in some other capacity, in Germany or Britain or elsewhere. Many of those contacts are now dead. Those I've quoted directly are listed in the bibliography at the back of the book. (Those still living are quoted in the present tense.)

I've also been helped by friends and assistants, and kindly and sometimes not so kindly librarians and archivists, and people I enlisted to help translate manuscripts for me or check that my own translations were adequate. Of these I need to name, first, Jutta Krug, now at WDR in Cologne, who travelled with me around parts of West Germany in 1984, helping me get to grips with what was still a very foreign culture for me, attending interviews with me (though almost everyone spoke perfect English), helping me navigate the protocols of German university and newspaper archives, especially in Göttingen, and doubling up with me on note-taking when we had to work against the clock. In Birmingham, Christine Penney, then the assistant librarian at the university, was wonderfully and creatively helpful, digging up information and contacts for me with selfless zeal (unlike two archivists in Germany I'd dearly love to name, who only found ways of being obstructive). Those Birmingham contacts will come into their own in volume two of this great project. In London, Asher Rozenberg helped transcribe endless pages of correspondence between Pevsner and his colleagues, as well as other random material. Thanks to him I now know that Pevsner wrote the section on polychromy in the *Penguin Dictionary of Architecture* in 1977 but left gaps for his fellow editors Hugh Honour and John Fleming in Italy to fill, and that he called Louis Kahn in America 'Lou'. That information may yet come in handy one day.

A mist has descended over exactly who helped me when I restarted my work on Pevsner twelve years ago but mention must be given to Fred Wyatt, who was sent to Dachau, the Nazis' first concentration camp, as a political dissident in 1937 before being deported to South America and arriving at last in England. Fred gave me great help in understanding the cultural climate in Central Europe in the 1920s and 1930s from a left-wing point of view, while Henry Morland helped me understand Germany in the same period from a conservative stand-point and loaned me two American PhD theses that proved invaluable: Jehuda

Reinharz on Deutschtum and Judentum (1972) and Carl Rheins on German-Jewish patriotism (1978). Thanks also to Janet Leifer and Ettie Boehm for certain translations in 1998.

Towards the end of this current piece of work, a number of people made great efforts to help me tie up loose ends at a distance. I'm absolutely indebted to Christine Hüper, in Hameln, near Hannover, who traced magazine articles and other essentials that I couldn't locate in London and put up with my incessant requests for more. Her daughter Cosima Bock also helped me while living with us in London, not least in making sense of Thomas Mann's handwriting. Cosi is now studying art history at Göttingen, as is Sarah Schmidt-Petersen, who also stayed here for three months. Anne Lind helped with last-minute translations, Annika Schellbach with last-minute transcribing. Tove Larsson taught me how Swedish works.

Annegret Karge in Dresden deserves special praise. I made extensive notes about Pevsner when I visited the National Archive in Dresden in 1984, where I looked at correspondence and annual reports of the Gemäldegalerie, among other things, but Annegret, in the course of writing an MA thesis[8] that she submitted in the summer of 2009, has penetrated secrets far beyond my reach and I'm grateful to her for her willingness to share them. (If only others in London had been so kind.) For the record, where I've quoted but not cited Pevsner's words about his life in Munich in 1921 and his visits to England in 1930 and 1933, I've been reproducing material that was quoted but not cited at the V&A's Pevsner Conference in 2001. For other citations I particularly wish to thank Tilo Bönicke of the Stadtarchiv in Dresden, Tuvia Pollack and his grandfather Heinrich Pollack in Israel, Josef Keith in the library at Friends House in London, Ruth Frendo at the Courtauld Institute in London, Lee Sorensen at Duke University, North Carolina, Joan Clinefelter at the University of Northern Colorado, and Joachim Whaley of Gonville and Caius College, Cambridge, all of whom have generously kept me supplied with information whenever I've asked for it.

For the production of this book I wish to thank the team at Continuum: my editor Ben Hayes, production editors Alice Eddowes and Nicole Elliott, designer Nick Evans, freelance proofreader Peter Gill and all the sales team; and at Pindar NZ in New Zealand: project manager Kim Pillay and my proofreader Tordis Flath and indexer Richard I. McGregor.

I need, finally, to record my thanks to the Getty Research Institute for funding two of my visits to its holdings (in February 1985 and November 1998) and to the Authors' Foundation for helping to fund my writing in 2009. (I should also say that I'd often have been lost without the help of Google, Multimap and Wikipedia, so often unacknowledged in scholarly writing.) And I very much appreciate Jo Whaley's willingness to read and check this first volume prior to publication and Charles Jencks's willingness to read and endorse it. As for other names, a list will have to suffice and I apologize to the many others there's not been space for or I've inadvertently omitted.

INSTITUTIONS IN THE UK

BIRMINGHAM	Birmingham Central Library, Archive	Rachel Clare
	Birmingham University, Special Collections	Christine Penney, Jenny Childs
DURHAM	Durham University	Michael Stansfield
EDINBURGH	Edinburgh University Library	Grant Buttars, Arnott Wilson
LONDON	Courtauld Institute	Ruth Frendo, Barbara Thompson
	Goethe-Institut	Annemarie Goodridge, Ulla Rieck
	Guardian News & Media Archive	Mariam Yamin
	German Historical Institute	Christiane Swinbank
	Friends House, Library	Josef Keith, Tabitha Driver
	Royal Holloway	Jon Hughes
	Warburg Institute, Archive	Claudia Wedepohl
NEWCASTLE	Newcastle University, Robinson Library	Elaine Archbold
OXFORD	Bodleian Library, Special Collections	Colin Harris
	Oxford University, History Faculty	Jane Cunning

INSTITUTIONS IN GERMANY

BERLIN	Auswärtiges Amt, Politisches Archiv	Gerhard Keiper
	Bundesarchiv	Franz Göttlicher, Kristin Hartisch
	German Archaeological Institute	Patricia Rahemipour
	Humboldt University, Archive	Constanze Haase, Winfried Schultze
	Humboldt University, Archive for Sexology	Erwin J. Haeberle
COLOGNE	Stiftung Rheinisch-Westfälisches Wirtschaftsarchiv	Jürgen Weise
	Wallraf-Richartz Museum and Fondation Corboud	Götz Czymmek
DESSAU	Stiftung Bauhaus	Lutz Schöbe
DRESDEN	Staatliche Kunstsammlungen	Gilbert Lupfer, Kathrin Iselt
	Stadtarchiv	Tilo Bönicke
	Gemäldegalerie	Tom Haasner

FRANKFURT AM MAIN	FAZ Archive	Birgitta Fella
	Johann-Wolfgang-Goethe University, Archive	Christine Bach
GÖTTINGEN	Georg-Augustus University, Archive	Karin Schlote, Ulrich Hunger
	Stadtarchiv	Rolf Lohmar
KARLSRUHE	National Museum of Natural History	Christiana Klingenberg
KASSEL	Stadtarchiv	Sigrid Schieber
LEIPZIG	Gewandhaus	Claudius Böhm
	Grassi Museum	Sabine Epple
	Israelitish Religious Community	Klaudia Krenn
	Sächsisches Staatsarchiv	Petra Oelschlaeger
	Stadtarchiv	Olaf Hillert, Birgit Horn-Kolditz
	Thomanerchor	Stefan Altner
	Thomasschule	Marion Hegewald
	University Archive	Sandy Muhl
MUNICH	Bayerische Staatsbibliothek	Rita Schäfer, Peter Schnitzlein
	Institut für Zeitgeschichte	Klaus A. Lankheit
	Ludwig Maximilian University, Archive	Claudius Stein
	Zentralinstitut für Kunstgeschichte	Christian Fuhrmeister
NAUMBURG	Stadtmuseum	Siegfried Wagner

OTHER INSTITUTIONS

GREECE	German Archaeological Institute, Athens	Joachim Heiden
SLOVAKIA	Forel International School, Bratislava	Zarin Buckingham
SWEDEN	National Archive, Stockholm	Britt-Marie Lagerqvist
SWITZERLAND	Neue Zürcher Zeitung, Zurich	Monika Gadient
	Thomas Mann Archive, Zürich	Gabi Hollender
USA	American Museum of Natural History, New York	Donat Agosti
	Dictionary of Art Historians website and Duke University	Lee Sorensen
	Getty Research Institute, Research Library, Los Angeles	Loisann Dowd White
	Harvard University, Cambridge, Mass	Emily Walhout

While this book does not pretend in any way to constitute an authorized part-biography, it couldn't have been written without the very considerable participation and guidance given to me by the children of the late Sir Nikolaus Pevsner, all of whom knew what I was involved with and what they were contributing to when they assisted me. I'd therefore like to acknowledge with thanks their interest and support for this project in its early days; the interviews, memories, ideas, advice, contacts and materials they supplied me with when my research began; the understanding that I'd be free to draw on what they gave me and make as much use of it as I saw fit; and their continuing indirect support in not having withdrawn that understanding at any time in the years that have followed.

The author would be grateful to any reader of this book for having any errors or omissions pointed out to him in as much detail as possible.

Stephen Games
Muswell Hill, 2009

1

Home

Nikolaus Pevsner was born into a family that had climbed from nowhere to the top rank of Leipzig's bourgeoisie. Fregestraße, the street in which he thought he'd been born, commemorated one of the wealthiest bankers of the nineteenth century, a member of the Frege family of merchants and academics.[1] Ferdinand-Rhode-Straße, where his parents moved to in 1906, was named after Carl Ferdinand Rhode, a businessman who'd made a large endowment to the city of Leipzig five years before his death in 1872. And Schwägrichenstraße, where they eventually settled in 1912, honoured Christian Friedrich Schwägrichen, a Leipzig botanist important in the field of taxonomy and classification. These were notable figures in the German kingdom of Saxony.

The flats that the Pevsners lived in were all to the south and south-west of the Promenade Ring that circled Leipzig's town centre, a district of broad boulevards, built from the late 1880s for the well-off. The Pevsners' flats were in streets with no musical connections themselves but the district was called the Musikviertel, the Music Quarter, because of the many other roads named after composers: Telemannstraße, Sebastian-Bach-Straße, Haydnstraße, Mozartstraße, Beethovenstraße. One of the Pevsners' flats was also just a street away from the Tschaikowskistraße home of their friend Arthur Nikisch, the Hungarian director and principal conductor of the Leipzig Gewandhaus Orchestra and the Berlin Philharmonic.

The Musikviertel was unique in Germany and an indicator of Leipzig's cultural ambition. From the perspective of Britain, where new suburbs of the same period tended to venerate members of the royal family and nobility, popular holiday resorts or the builders of the suburbs themselves, naming streets after composers might seem no more significant than the naming of telephone exchanges after poets in London in the 1920s,[2] a happy coincidence between letters and numbers on a telephone dial. In Leipzig in the 1880s, naming streets after composers was a matter of civic pride. Although Germany felt overshadowed on three sides by France, Italy and Austro-Hungary, in music it was supreme; and Leipzig, the city of Bach, Schumann, Mendelssohn and Wagner, was its apex. In the late nineteenth century, many of the world's most promising young musicians went there to study – Grieg from Norway; Sullivan, Elgar and Delius from England – and so when Leipzig built the Musikviertel, it was broadcasting its role in German culture.

The status of music in Leipzig set a standard that the Musikviertel's architecture tried to emulate in its opulence. The earliest streets consisted of dramatic five- and six-storey apartment blocks in a strict, disciplined, Italian style; around 1900, some seventy-two villas were built in looser, more artistic styles. Both apartments and villas were different from what was being built in London in the same period. Where London terraces tended to be mean and ungenerous, these Wilhelmine buildings were ostentatious in their high ceilings, wide doors, expensive woods and ornamental inlays, with some of the later ostentation a little overbearing and mad. And where London families lived, typically, in homes that were self-contained, narrow and high, their counterparts in Leipzig lived on single floors of communal buildings that were wide and deep.

The streets and buildings that Pevsner grew up in and that would have shaped his ideas about what was normal were therefore quite different from anything an English child would have been familiar with. The Pevsners' apartment building in Fregestraße, for example, was a big stone building on the north side of the street, mainly plain but with classical hood-mouldings over the windows and, slightly out of place, lilies and sunflowers in panels over the oriel and front door. There were ceramic tiles inside the entrance hall, with monstrous heads and languid faces, and extraordinary stone owls, represented in a fashionably morbid style, hinting at their ancient Greek connotations as the symbol of Pallas Athena and hence of wisdom, and at their ancient Roman connotations as the symbol of death.[3] It's not surprising that in his *Buildings of England* guide to London in 1952, Pevsner would say of the stucco terraces of South Kensington – London's closest equivalent to the Musikviertel in the sense of its being a German-inspired cultural quarter[4] – that 'the whole area between Queen's Gate, the Park, Gloucester Road, and Brompton Road is . . . completely devoid of any objects of interest.' South Kensington, by Leipzig's standards, was uniform and dull. (In its favour, though, was its absence of Jugendstil ornament, of which Pevsner had a lifelong horror and which he regarded as sick, deranged and freakish – perhaps because of the morbid owls.)

To the modern eye, late nineteenth- and early twentieth-century Leipzig is a pleasure. The Musikviertel in particular, built by entrepreneurs who grew wealthy during the 'Gründerzeit', the economic boom that Bismarck engineered under the Kaiser, has scale and presence. That doesn't mean that Leipzigers universally welcomed it – especially Leipzigers of the generation that followed those it was built for. According to Ulrich Michel, six years Pevsner's junior at school and the son of friends of Pevsner's parents, Leipzig didn't have a single building of international importance. 'One or two old squares provided a pleasant sight but on the whole the buildings of Leipzig were solid and unremarkable', he wrote.[5] Pevsner also had little to say in favour of German architecture of that period when writing about the nineteenth century in the early 1940s. He noted the emergence of a Neo-Renaissance style in Munich in 1816 and the 1830s, and the growing exuberance of Italianate forms between 1850 and 1860 but damned the later manifestations of this Second Empire style, the equivalent of the German Gründerzeit, as 'so superficial – truly superficial – a conception of architecture', adding that 'in Italy it has disgraced Rome with the national monument to King Victor Emmanuel II'.[6]

Although Pevsner would despise the architecture he'd grown up with, he probably didn't despise the standard of living that went with it. Wilhelmine architecture in the late nineteenth century was accompanied by numerous technical improvements. Beautifully made furniture and fittings, the use of gas and electricity for lighting and cooking, labour-saving devices in the kitchen and decent sanitary-ware in the bathroom were all becoming common. Thanks to his German upbringing, Pevsner could therefore take for granted domestic amenities that in England would still have been regarded as luxuries. With this in mind, he rather amusingly dedicated his 1966 *Buildings of England* volume on the North Riding of Yorkshire to 'those publicans and hoteliers of England who provide me with a table in my bedroom to scribble on' because there were so many other publicans and hoteliers who didn't provide him with any of the facilities he'd grown up to regard as basic. Thirty years earlier, his wife, also from Leipzig, was horrified at the primitive conditions she and Pevsner had to live with in their four-storey Victorian cottage on the edge of Hampstead Heath: the pinched exterior, the rattling sash windows (an architectural feature unique to Britain), the steep and narrow stairs, the terrible plumbing, the cold.

Trying to explain this disparity in the late 1930s, Pevsner blamed the British public for being insufficiently demanding. In Germany, he said,

> If you want your shoes soled and heeled, you still hand them confidently to Herr Muller who does the job conscientiously in his back-room where he works with one journey-man and one apprentice. There is no Branch 26 of a back-in-a-day shoe repairing service to lure you away from the craftsman. The same is true – at least outside Berlin – of the cabinet-maker, the plumber, the locksmith, etc. It is an extremely interesting consequence of this . . . that a cultured public also expects the very best article . . . Hence the successful handweavers, silversmiths, potters, all over Germany, and hence the many Kunstgewerbe [craft] shops in German towns, shops of a kind which scarcely exist in Britain.[7]

In Britain, Pevsner added, 'such shops cannot exist without a demand', meaning that they didn't exist because Britain was in some ways less discerning than Germany – a thought with its roots in his earliest experiences.

Pevsner's father, Hugo, was said to have been wealthy. Records in Leipzig's archives show this wasn't always the case. In the 1890s, Hugo and his wife had lived in fairly mean apartments, moving frequently and at one time giving his workplace on the Brühl, or Brühlstraße, as their only settled address. By the time their first child was born in 1899, they were living on the second floor of an apartment house in Elsterstraße, to the west of the town centre: 'not a poor district but far from posh', a contemporary of Pevsner's wrote later.[8] They were still in Elsterstraße when Pevsner himself was born in 1902. It wasn't until a year later that the family moved to 27 Fregestraße, a slightly smarter location, north-west

of the town centre and near the city zoo. It was this address that Pevsner wrongly
believed to be his birthplace.

A move to 41 Ferdinand-Rhode-Straße, in February 1906, brought more
social caché but the Pevsners' grandest moment came in September 1912 when
they took up residence in Schwägrichenstraße in a grand apartment house
designed by Otto Brückwald, the architect of Leipzig's New Theatre and the man
responsible for overseeing construction of Wagner's Festspielhaus in Bayreuth.
Pevsner recorded years later that the family occupied the whole of the first floor
of this building. His friend, the architectural writer Alec Clifton-Taylor, recalled
Pevsner telling him the apartment had twenty-three rooms;[9] Ernst Ullmann, an
art historian whom Pevsner met on a visit to Leipzig in 1977, remembered him
saying it had twenty-seven rooms.[10]

The Pevsners' apartment at 11 Schwägrichenstraße[11] was luxurious and their
fellow residents were celebrities. On one floor lived the writer Elsa Asenijeff, the
model and long-standing companion of the artist Max Klinger. On another was
a well-known music publisher, while Brückwald, the architect of the building,
lived on the ground floor and ran his office from the basement. Today's *Dehio*
architectural guidebooks, early versions of which inspired Pevsner's future career,
commend the exterior of the building for its painted Neo-Renaissance façade,
central bay and Ionic columns, and the entrance hall for its magnificent decoration, circular vestibule, colonnaded alcoves and double staircase. A marble plaque
over the front door of the building has the Biblical quotation:

Ein jegliches Haus wird von Jemand bereitet; der aber alles bereitet, das ist Gott.
(For every house is built by someone, but the builder of all things is God.)

Because of its odd lettering, this sentence has been mistaken for 'Chr. 3:4'
(Chronicles), as if it were an Old Testament reference to Solomon's building of
the Temple – and, fancifully, as a prophecy of Pevsner's interest in architecture.
It is in fact 'Ebr. 3:4' (Hebrews) and therefore a New Testament reference to the
superiority of Jesus over Moses.

A first cousin of Pevsner's, Heinrich Pollack, now 96, has vivid memories of
the building:

Our relatives, the Pevsners, lived in a well-appointed apartment in Schwägrichenstraße.
Is it just my fantasy that the stairs were made of marble with a red carpet running up
them? It's true that there was no elevator and no central heating in that old-style stately
building but that didn't matter because there were enough servants around. The household was governed by Anna [Pevsner's mother], friendly and good-natured, and helping
her were a cook and a chambermaid. In the winter the coal oven gave off a comfortable
heat. The wide apartment was arranged with fine, original furniture. On the walls hung
paintings, including some modern art. There was even a picture of Jesus who followed
me with his eyes wherever I went in the room and seemed to come from another world.

In the study[12] was a big desk at which my aunt – but not my uncle – wrote letters in clear handwriting.

The music room had space enough for a grand piano and a gramophone, and their record collection contained everything from classical music and operettas to Negro spirituals. Also notable was the library of the house, in which I grew more and more interested as I got older.

How nice it was to be coddled at our visits! My mother [Ida] could relax and so could I, and all my memories seem misty-eyed. Our visits began with an unhurried breakfast. Aunt Annie took her time with us. The servants were called with an electric bell hanging down from the lamp or the ceiling. Crunchy rolls were served in silver baskets. We ate them with soft-boiled eggs, golden butter, jam. The only restriction was that we had to behave. I'd already learned that at home, somehow, but Aunt Annie was strict. I had great respect for her. We learned our good behaviour from her.[13]

Another cousin of Pevsner's, Ellen Dreessen, was evidently less charmed by Annie than Heinrich Pollack had been and remembered that she behaved 'like a duchess. She thought I had terrible table manners and put books under my arms to keep my elbows in.'[14]

In addition to young Nikolaus, who was generally known as Nika (sometimes spelled Nicar), and his mother Annie, whom he called 'Muo', the members of the 'Pewsner' household, as it was correctly spelled, were his father Hugo ('Vuo') – much more tolerant than Annie, recalled Dreessen[15] – and Nika's older brother, Heinrich Wolfgang, known as Heinz. At various times, Heinz and Nika were brought up by a Russian governess called Fräulein Chomse, by cooks and maids, by French teachers male and female, and by Anna Krause, the family's devoted housekeeper. Krause, Pevsner later wrote in a family history, 'came into the house before my birth and attended to all our little needs from nappies to outings'.[16]

Pevsner's childhood was dominated by his mother and her interest in art and music. Annie, he said, 'had learnt to paint as a girl. She also sang and we had plenty of music at home and a grand piano. The music went from Italian opera to negro stuff and the Cake Walk.' Music, as we've seen, was not just an entertainment at that time; it defined German high society. The city subsidized an operahouse, a playhouse and the world-famous Gewandhaus concert hall. 'The Gewandhaus was really the meeting point of Leipzig society', wrote Ulrich Michel. 'To have a subscription to the Gewandhaus, morning or evening, showed that you had arrived and were accepted – and actually, I never listened to concerts with better acoustics in all my life. In the morning on Thursdays was the public rehearsal and in the evening the concert proper, a white-tie affair at which young girls curtsied to their aunts.'[17] For any ambitious family (and Pevsner regarded his mother as socially ambitious[18]), access to this world was vital. Possession of musical skills was also an advantage. All children were expected to have piano lessons and would go to their music teacher, or receive a music teacher in their homes, dressed in their smartest lace collars and patent leather pumps. In Pevsner's case, his mother asked the concert pianist Liez Knauth to teach him – with only moderate success, Pevsner noted, though he and Knauth remained close friends until the end of her life. He later recalled the music room in the Pevsner house 'in which I used to practise on the grand piano – fervently for two hours on end and in a roaring fury because I was so totally devoid of talent. All this my mother tolerated without ever complaining or protesting. She must have much approved the turn of my mind to music.'

Thanks to his mother, Pevsner gained an entrée into Leipzig's most elevated circles and with it the expectation that such access was normal. According to Michel, the basis of this entrée was the 'salon' that Annie presided over as a society hostess. Its figurehead was the charismatic Arthur Nikisch – dramatic black hair in a centre parting, huge moustache with twirled ends – who'd taken over both the Gewandhaus Orchestra and the Berlin Philharmonic in 1895. 'Mrs. Pevsner, small in stature, was a "grand dame" and her word was law,'[19] Michel wrote, and 'many actors and musicians were to be seen [at her parties].' Those who became family friends, in addition to Nikisch, included the writer Franz Adam Beyerlein, the singer Elena Gerhardt, the pianist Paula Hegner (who accompanied Gerhardt whenever Nikisch was unavailable[20]), Hegner's husband the publisher Johann Jakob Hegner,[21] and Consul Alexander Meyer von Bremen, whose father-in-law, the Protestant theologian and Bible scholar Constantin von Tischendorf, had discovered the Codex Sinaiticus. Nika may also have been introduced to Paderewski, the pianist and future Prime Minister of Poland, because he kept as a trophy a personal note from Paderewski with a phrase of music and a signed dedication to 'my little friend, Nicolai Pevsner'.

As a boy, Pevsner was serious and self-contained but quick enough to be found amusing by even the brightest of his mother's stars. They'd chat and play with him and tell him stories when they saw him at Annie's salons, and send him letters and little gifts when they were away. (Ricarda Huch once told him how she'd greeted the Swiss art historian Heinrich Wölfflin one morning with an informal 'Lieber Heinrich, wie geht es Dir?' ('Dear Heinrich, how are you?') after having chatted to him the night before at a party, only to receive a sharp suggestion from Wölfflin that she revert to the more formal 'Ihnen'.) Among Pevsner's papers, a greeting card from 1912 survives on which Nikisch had penned the first four bars of Beethoven's Fifth Symphony (the first commercial recording of which he would make the following year), together with Beethoven's familiar words 'So pocht das Schicksal an die Pforte' ('Thus knocks fate at the door') and the dedication 'den lieben kleinen Nika Pevsner' ('for dear little Nika Pevsner'). The belief that he was a welcome guest among the great and the good was one of the main gifts that Annie imparted to her younger son.

Annie's rise had not been painless. In the early days of her marriage, she'd had a reputation as a flirt. Her friend, Beyerlein, went on to write a short story called 'Like a Feather in the Wind' ('Wie eine Feder im Winde')[22] with a character reputed to have been based on her and whom he described as 'beautiful, kittenish, cruel and covetable'. Her nephew, Heinrich, recalled it being said of her that when she was young, 'she lived for her own pleasure'. (He added: 'I don't know how much of it is real.') She also seems to have burnt herself out. In the family history he wrote in the 1950s, Pevsner noted that when he was three, his mother had suffered a crisis, 'caused perhaps by lack of occupation adequate to her intellectual capabilities, perhaps by dissatisfaction in other ways'. Because of the structuring of his family history, with his separating of his parents' stories into two different narratives rather than intertwining them, Pevsner gave the impression that his mother's crisis was a weakness in her personality rather than a response to a cause. Had he brought his parents' stories together, he might have noted that the crisis coincided with the fact that his father had nearly died from tuberculosis around this time, leaving him with one lung and in need of steady nursing. Pevsner knew this because in mid-August 1905 the whole family had moved to Bad Reiboldsgrün, where there was a sanatorium specializing in TB cases, and they'd stayed there for five months.[23]

Pevsner didn't elaborate about any of this in his memoir but did hint that his mother may have been unhappy in her marriage and that she and his father were ill-suited.[24] In an undated draft he added a handwritten note that merely said 'Alcohol' alongside the words 'Melancholy' and '1908?' 'In any case,' he went on,

> She had a kind of Gemütskrankheit [breakdown] with a deep melancholy and then went to Auguste Forel at Yvorne in the Vaud, just south of the west end of the Lake of Geneva. Forel[25] was a celebrated psychiatrist (his *magnum opus*, perfectly serious, is called *Die sexuelle Frage*),[26] a celebrated ant collector and ant specialist, and an infuriated teetotaller, a very remarkable man. His portrait is one of the best things by Kokoschka, done while my mother was there. We got to know his family well, because Muo [Annie] went again, though we went always a little in awe of Professor Forel himself.

Forel's ground-breaking interest in neural structures and in the links between anatomy, behaviour and social issues had led him in 1889 to found an institute at Burghölzli in Zurich for the medical treatment of alcoholism but he retired prematurely in 1898 and saw patients only privately in his home, first in Chigny près Morges, then in Yvorne. It was in Yvorne that Nika's father bought a second home, 'a former baker's house with an oven' that was 'close to the church' and where the family 'spent several holidays'. It was one of these visits that gave rise to the story about Forel naming an ant after Pevsner that the Viennese art historian Ernst Gombrich first recalled in a BBC programme about Pevsner in 1982:

> [Pevsner] once told us that when he was a little boy, his family went off on vacation in Switzerland by Lake Geneva at Morges.[27] Morges is a place where the great taxonomist Auguste Forel worked. Forel was one of the great taxonomists of ants and he was engaged that summer giving names to any number of new species. And he ran out of names, and

since he liked the little boy he named one of them after Nikolaus Pevsner. And I always say that the spirit of that ant entered into Pevsner's soul [which explains why] he is so incredibly industrious.[28]

Forel had found the ant in question in Venezuela and named it '*Crematogaster distans r. pevsnerae*' in or around 1911, including it in his ant database of 1912.[29] This adds to the evidence that Annie's visits continued after 1908.

Forel's own industry also anticipates Pevsner's in later life. In addition to being the single most prolific describer of ant species of his day, he was as influential and important in early psychiatric thinking as Freud and was Switzerland's first 'sexologist', advocating sexual education and total sexual freedom. He promoted the idea of eugenic breeding, was shortlisted for a Nobel prize for his discovery of brain structure, was active in the anti-alcohol movement, became a Bahá'í, and was pictured on the face of the Swiss 1,000-franc banknote, Switzerland's largest note (which his son objected to on the grounds that as a passionate Socialist, Forel should have been shown on the lowest-value ten-franc note because that was the note of the people). His reputation today has suffered from the eclipsing of his work by more singled-minded specialists and by his views on racial relativism, which have needed some delicate explaining.

Annie's therapy involved her sublimating her personal crisis into a public mission. 'Forel must have convinced my mother that she was capable of both intellectual and social work', wrote Pevsner. 'She turned to teetotalism and started a non-alcoholic restaurant called, after the progressive head of her own school at Leipzig, Auguste Schmidt Haus. It was first in the Inselstraße, then in Dresdnerstraße, sold nice and neat meals for 60 or 70 pfennig, and went exceedingly well.'

Annie's new activity coincided with Leipzig's emergence as a centre for progressive politics and early feminism, though we have to take on trust what Pevsner said about her level of involvement, because it's hard to find evidence for it today. The problem is that the Auguste Schmidt Haus was launched in 1902, which pre-dates Annie's conversion to social work.[30] She seems, however, to have helped to run the institution later and was certainly associated with other women's organizations, serving at various times as vice-chairman of the International Women's Service and as matron of a children's home in Frohberg, outside Leipzig. It's through these activities that she probably befriended Ulrich Michel's mother, a passionate feminist throughout her life, and Michel's father, who in 1911 became editor-in-chief of the Leipzig-based *Brockhaus* encyclopaedia.

Young Nikolai was intrigued by Forel's influence on his mother but also aware of the impact it had on his father: 'They started married life with a cook and a maid and had at first quite a gay and certainly an unsophisticated circle. Some of them later disappeared from my mother's life; others remained as somewhat incongruous survivals.'[31] Annie had apparently already launched herself on a

career as a Leipzig hostess before she met Forel; afterwards, says Pevsner, and as
a result of her new direction,

> Her circle of friends … turned chiefly to men from Leipzig University, both from fields
> of science and art. My father was a little left out of this … My father would perhaps have
> liked better to go on with that [earlier] circle than to change to my mother's later circle.
> He was a great cardplayer, first at Skat and later at Bridge, but never a gambler. Of his
> business friends few came into the house … He did not read much and must have been
> very puzzled by many things in the home.[32]

As a result of Forel's influence, Annie translated into German a French book on
English utilitarian ethics by Jean-Marie Guyau, which she may have worked on
while attending Forel at Yvorne and which was published in Leipzig in 1914.
Already an anglophile, she seems to have been introduced to Guyau's writings
by Ernst Bergmann, a Privatdozent[33] in the philosophy department of Leipzig
University. Bergmann had started teaching at Leipzig in the winter semester of
1911–1912 and, as Leipzig University's records show, became an external adjunct
professor in 1916. His curriculum ranged from the ancient Greek philosophers
to Descartes and Kant; Guyau, a maverick genius of forty years earlier, was a
private passion.

Jean-Marie Guyau, born in 1854, was a French philosopher whose career
was halted by his early death. While still a student in Paris he'd won an essay
competition on the topic of utilitarianism in 1873[34] and, encouraged by Herbert
Spencer, revised and published what he'd written in two volumes, the second of
which – on utility and evolution in English contemporary morality – appeared
in 1879. He went on to write about art, time and religion, and was named as a
source and influence by enthusiasts from Kropotkin to Durkheim.

Guyau was tutored by his mother's cousin, the philosopher Alfred Fouillée,
whom she lived with from 1857.[35] Fouillée was interested in Nietzsche, whom
he promoted in France, and in the new field of sociology, and he introduced
the young Guyau to ancient philology, philosophy, mathematics and music,
eventually becoming the boy's trustee. In 1889, a year after Guyau died, Fouillée
codified Guyau's thought and tried to ensure his intellectual survival in a book
called *La moral, l'art et la religion d'après Guyau*.[36]

One of the first things Bergmann did on his arrival in Leipzig was propose
to a local publishing house, Alfred Kröner Verlag, that Guyau's entire output
should be translated into German. Kröner accepted, perhaps because Bergmann
promised to develop a market for the books by teaching a course on Guyau in
his private seminars. He may also have taught a special course for women at the
Auguste Schmidt Haus, because the publishing project he took on involved an
unusually large number of women. Of the six volumes in the series that came
out between 1912 and 1914, four were translated by women.[37] Annie, whose
notebooks show she was attending improving lectures in and around Leipzig

University at the time, was one of them.[38]

Guyau illustrated what Bergmann and others saw as a crisis in Western civilization. Guyau had argued that the modern age had destroyed the natural unity of reason and emotion (qualities he personified as the 'Theoretical Man' and the 'Practical Man'), leaving these two forces so divided as to lose touch with each other. Of this modern condition, he wrote:

> Modern urban man . . . is entirely brain, entirely intellect, entirely consciousness, plan and intention. He lives without religion, without much morality, and lately even without law. He recognizes no authority . . . His old God-directed world has collapsed and he tramples on its ruins without sentimentality. He is his own highest court of appeal and his own last resort. Yet he is unhappy, however upright and purposeful he may seem . . .[39]

This gave Bergmann two tasks as a philosopher: to bring the message of man's spiritual dislocation to those still unaware of it, and to convince those who were aware of it but too disturbed to do anything about it that they should embrace it, as Guyau had done, so they'd find a measure of balance to compensate for their lost spiritual unity. 'Being unwhole is our fate,' Bergmann wrote.

> We are transitional beings, we have evolved into urban creatures and lost our natural selves. But we have to go on; there is no going back. Perhaps this will give birth to a new wholeness at the end of our human earthly road, a new synthesis of belief and life. Today we are infinitely far removed from it. We are divided and must compromise. Pragmatism defines us. That is how we are, for good or ill.[40]

There are obvious Christological parallels in this writing. For Bergmann, Guyau was not only 'the French Nietzsche' but a secular Jesus, universal, innocent, paradoxical, suffering because of our urban condition (symbolized by tuberculosis, the quintessential urban disease) and dying prematurely at the same age as Jesus. Bergmann rhapsodized him as '. . . a man of the greatest acumen and the richest fund of knowledge. But with the heart of a child and almost the mind of a girl – a real modernist with an almost horrifying disbelief coupled with a religious longing that we find otherwise only in the mystics of the Christian Middle Ages . . . "Intellectual disappointment, moral hope" – thus did I formulate Guyau's code in 1912. It is the code of a thoroughly modern human race.'

Bergmann's message to his audience of bourgeois wives was typical of millennialists down the ages: civilization was at a turning point, self-aware people were cursed with being brainy, irreligious and immoral, and normal laws were being thrown into chaos: bait, perhaps, for anyone who wished to take it.[41] Annie was evidently attracted by this message, not least because of the intellectual respectability it gave to her need for personal freedom. Bergmann repaid her interest. In his introduction to the books, he congratulated her for having 'not shrunk from the great trouble of searching out and quoting from numerous references to English writers, as far as they are available in German translation'. He also ensured that in the first edition of the book she translated for him, her name appeared as 'A. Pevsner' and in the second – a more decorative work – as 'Annie Pevsner'. In neither case did she appear as 'Frau' ('Mrs'), unlike two of Bergmann's other translators.

Bergmann taught Annie about the workings of academic research and the nature of modern life, as he saw it. In view of how their lives later developed, their association in the 1910s seems strange. In spite of sponsoring Guyau, English philosophy, modern existentialism and Annie herself, Bergmann in 1922 became one of the first members of the new Nazi Party and went on to found a Nietzschean movement aimed at setting up an ultra-nationalist Germanic religion to replace Christianity.[42] In 1933 he co-founded the Deutsche Glaubensbewegung (Movement for German Belief), an umbrella group for Aryan groups committed to Teutonic racist pantheism. (He also recommended exterminating 'a million of the human refuse in the large cities' and compulsorily mating lesbians to 'cure' them of their 'masculinity'.) The following year, in a book that provided a popular but eccentric endorsement of Nazism,[43] he described the history of the Church as two thousand years of degeneracy and decadence, revealed that Jesus was Nordic rather than Jewish, and identified Hitler as the messiah. His interests brought him into partnership with a fellow-Leipziger, Carl Peter,[44] who was a confidant of the Nazi secret service chief Reinhard Heydrich. Together they formed what became in 1937 the Vereinigung Deutsche Volksreligion (German Folk Religion Association). Peter quoted Bergmann in *Ernst Bergmann und seine Lehre* in 1941 for such remarks as 'The greatest crime against humanity is the Judeo-Christian belief in sin' and 'If you really want to eliminate the genetically inferior and help produce a super-breed of racial aristocrats, you'll have to give up your Christianity.'[45] In 1945, on the news that Allied troops had taken Leipzig, Bergmann committed suicide in Naumburg, thirty miles away. By chance, Naumburg – home of Nietzsche's mother and of the Nietzsche Archive that Nietzsche's sister created in 1894 – was also where the man who became Pevsner's father-in-law owned a country estate.

2

Family

Leipzig's premier boys' school, the Thomasschule, had a nationwide reputation. Founded as the poor school of a new church – St Thomas's – by Augustine canons in 1212, it was taken over by the city of Leipzig in 1539 and grew famous after Bach became its choirmaster and organist. By 1900 it was serving both sides of Leipzig's upper echelons: Old Leipzig, the upper-class elite who lived mainly in the suburb of Gohlis, and the newer, upper-middle class who lived, like the Pewsners, in and around the Musikviertel. Heinrich Pewsner, Nika's brother, attended the school from 1910; Nika joined two years later, as pupil No. 25 in a class of thirty-three. Both had previously attended a preschool (Vorschule). A third of Nika's classmates had fathers listed as 'Kaufmann' (businessman), as his own father was; the rest included military men, teachers, professors and doctors.[1]

Most pupils in the Thomas School were from Leipzig but sixty others – many of them sons of high-court judges and senior academics from Thuringia rather than Saxony – were choral scholars who boarded and continued in the Bach tradition by singing in the choir of St Thomas's church (the Thomaskirche), with which the school retained an association. Every Friday afternoon the choir gave a concert called a *Motette* that was free to all and had a reputation as a place for unsanctioned liaisons.[2] Religion was no longer central to the school's ethos but there was overwhelming religious uniformity. Most pupils were registered as Evangelical Lutheran (the mainstream Protestant religion in Saxony) while only a dozen boys were registered as Jewish and even fewer as Catholic – a quite different pattern from the demographics of Leipzig as a whole, which was made up of just under 470,000 Protestants, 7,000 Jews and 22,000 Catholics at the time.

The Thomasschule was the oldest of Leipzig's four classical grammar schools and one of the oldest surviving schools in Europe, and boys were admitted from the age of ten. Entry was by examination but it was thought unusual for anyone from a professional family not to gain entry. Ulrich Michel, who became a pupil in 1918, felt the school bred arrogance as much as achievement. Most pupils were expected to go on to university and study Classics. To study science, said Michel, was an afterthought and engineering unheard of.

Schoolboy attitudes were rigidly hierarchical. The boys made friends only within their own social class and regarded other schools as below their status. In the classroom it was not uncommon for boys to pull rank on the staff and the school encouraged or perpetuated this by blocking boys from families regarded as unsuitable.[3] When Nika started there in 1912, at the age of ten, the roll numbered just over 500, which included the choral boarders, who were allowed to stay on after their voices broke.

The only uniform at the Thomasschule was a green cap with two silver stripes. Pupils walked to school or cycled. In winter, the school day ran from 8 am to 1 pm; in summer, from 7 am until midday, with the chance of being sent home at 11 am if the weather was too hot. Latin was studied for nine years, French for seven and Greek for six. English was available but voluntary; so was Hebrew, which was still part of the German classical curriculum and was chosen mostly by pupils who planned to study theology. Lessons lasted forty-five minutes and boys took sandwiches for their mid-morning break.[4] There was voluntary hockey one afternoon a week. There were no prefects, and the head boy, the *primus omnium*, had no duties. In class, everyone sat in pairs according to rank, with the class *primus* in the right-hand desk at the back. Only in their last two years were pupils allowed to sit where they liked and to bring cushions to soften the hard wooden seats.[5]

Several times a year concerts were held at which the school choir sang and where boys, teachers, parents and former pupils came together. One particularly large event was the 700th anniversary of the school's founding, which coincided with Nika's arrival in September 1912. This celebration, lasting several days, brought some 1,800 alumni back to the school and featured, among other things, displays of gymnastics and a performance of Sophocles's *Antigone* accompanied by the popular incidental music Mendelssohn had written for it in 1841.

Pevsner was a diligent and gifted pupil. He began his school career with religion, German, Latin, history, geography, arithmetic and nature; later he added French and Greek but turned down the options of English, Hebrew, drawing and stenography. He regularly came top of his year in his studies but didn't regard himself as a high achiever by his own standards. He felt overshadowed by his mother and the dynamic personalities that she brought into the home – Nikisch of the Gewandhaus and his wife, Richard Heinze, the rector of Leipzig University, and a constellation of visiting writers, artists and performers. He also felt overawed by his older brother, two years ahead of him: popular, dashing, confident, brilliant and in every way a more Promethean personality. By contrast Nika felt plodding and dull.

Nika's personal anxieties were exacerbated by the devastating realization that on a number of counts, he was at a social disadvantage compared with his classmates. Most of these anxieties centred on his father. Although a cousin of his father's was one of the directors of the Zeiss-Ikon camera factory in Dresden,[6] Hugo's line of business – fur trading – was too far down the social register for Nika to feel he could hold his head up high. Writing about his father in his family history forty years later, he still professed not to know how Hugo had got into the fur trade or even what his father actually did. He knew only, he said, that it had to do with fur brokerage or transportation, or something in between, 'for he did not own lorries or goods wagons', and defended his imprecision by adding: 'I am rather vague about this; for the truth is that we, the family, took much too little interest in the business side of life.' Friends and family members were far less prim. Pevsner's sister-in-law, Marianne Kockel, called Hugo 'a fur merchant on commission' and Ulrich Michel described him as a 'forwarding agent for the fur trade'.

The problem wasn't just that Pevsner wasn't interested in his father's business; it was that his father wasn't grand enough to warrant taking an interest in. Where other boys were proud to show off their parents at school events – at the performance of *Antigone*, for example, at the anniversary concert – Nika found his father something of an embarrassment. Even in his fifties, the best Pevsner could say of him was that he had 'a heart of gold', a phrase too sentimental to be convincing. He'd earlier noted, in a rough draft of his family history, that his father was 'good-hearted' and 'handsome' but deleted these points from the finished text in favour of a balder listing of what he saw as Hugo's features and flaws. Hugo, he wrote in his revised text, 'was dark with black hair, black moustache, brown eyes, brown skin, and very large ears, and well dressed'. This lack of enthusiasm contrasts with the warm memories of other members of the family – of the occasion when Hugo, a strong swimmer, was stopped by a swimming bath attendant and told to go to a nonswimmers' pool because the crawl, which he'd learnt in Russia, wasn't then a recognized swimming style in Germany[7] – or of a neighbour's daughter to whom Hugo would always courteously offer a peppermint whenever they met in the street.[8]

A second disadvantage Nika felt was that his father was Russian, as was his mother, at a time when fear of the Tsar's intentions, and of incipient Russian Communism infiltrating the German workers' movement, made Russians in Germany potential objects of suspicion. Nor did his parents provide any kind of pedigree by way of consolation. They were peasants, not aristocrats, and they'd come to Leipzig – Hugo under his own steam in 1890, Annie as a child some time earlier – because Germany offered the possibility of a better life. While other boys could boast about their parents, Pevsner was always pained that, in his own words, Hugo 'never spoke German perfectly. His [Russian] accent was strong and occasionally he made a mistake.' That made him a liability for a boy being schooled alongside other boys from the cream of Leipzig society, all acutely aware of class and status.

The consequence of Nika's father being Russian was that Nika and his brother were also Russians, in spite of having been born in Germany. This became an issue in 1912. Sixteen years earlier, in 1896, Hugo had tried to become a naturalized citizen of Saxony, and hence of Germany, and been turned down. He then seems to have reconciled himself to remaining an alien. It wasn't until 1912 – the year when Nika started at the Thomasschule – that he agreed to try a second time, and it's not impossible that it was Nika who urged him to do so, supported by Annie.

Under pressure from his family, perhaps, Hugo submitted a fresh application, this time attaching references from sponsors who attested to his good name and financial self-sufficiency. They stressed in a letter to Saxony's Ministry of the Interior in Dresden that:

> Pewsner is a friend of the arts, with a lively interest in the local Kunstgewerbe [arts and crafts] museum [also known, from 1896, as the Grassi Museum]. His wife is also a founder of the Augusta Schmidt House, a centre for young women, for which she has accomplished much. The applicant is one of the best-known businessmen of the Brühl in Leipzig and keenly desires to be a full member of the municipality, because he runs his business from here with great success and satisfaction and enjoys the respect of his peers. In particular he'd like his two sons to have an association with Germany in which he, his wife and they are already completely involved.

On 4 April 1913 this application was also rejected, on the grounds that it was 'not particularly urgent'.[9] Then, with rather more attack than in 1896, Hugo sent a complaint to the Ministry, probably penned by Annie, citing a list of items that the Grassi museum had purchased from H. Ball, a dealership in Dresden, and that Hugo had paid for: a seventeenth-century glass with enamel decoration, an eighteenth-century porcelain mother-and-child (possibly by Kaendler), a nineteenth-century Meissen cup and a Baroque frame. He also included a letter of recommendation from the chairwoman of the board of the Auguste Schmidt House and from Pastor Grohmann, a prison chaplain for whom his wife did good works. This time he was successful and on 7 August 1914, just six days after Germany declared war on Russia and three days after Britain declared war on Germany, Hugo, Annie and their two boys became citizens of the kingdom of Saxony, and thus Germans.

What damage Nika might have suffered from not having been naturalized sooner is impossible to know, but his sense of being an alien at a time of intense nationalism must have left him feeling unequal to his peers and less able to participate in what he saw as the great march of German destiny. He may even have experienced xenophobia and bullying from his classmates as significant numbers of pupils and teachers rallied to Germany's cause and enlisted in the armed forces, emptying the Thomasschule and leaving it echoing. John Betjeman, in England, was bullied during the war for having a Dutch name that was thought to be German. Pevsner's names were also foreign. Although he later changed it to Nikolaus, his first name at this time was Nikolai – his given name at birth – and this marked him out at once as not a Wilhelm or a Fritz.

(And Nikolai's other given names were no more reassuring. His second name, Bernhard, commemorated an uncle, Bernhard Perlmann, one of his mother's brothers, who was born in 1879 in Leipzig, had gone to seek his fortune in Port Arthur – also known as Ryojun: now Lüshun Port or Lüshunkou – in China, had contracted a venereal disease there, got into gambling debts and committed suicide. His third name, equally inexplicably, was in memory of one Leon Toker, the husband of his mother's eldest sister Cacilie, known as Sonja, whom Pevsner described later as 'clearly a bad egg', who 'gambled and . . . probably also had affairs [and] deserted his wife and left her with one daughter'. Pevsner's cousin Ellen Dreessen remembered that Toker was a morphine addict and committed suicide.[10])

Technically at least, Pevsner's sense of being an outsider in Germany would have been rectified to some extent by his naturalization. What remained painful to him was that while the stigma of being Russian had been removed, a deeper stigma remained: that of being Jewish. Again, one wonders whether he encountered harassment or bullying at school that intensified his dislike of being Jewish and his desire to prove himself more German, or whether his distaste was merely the distaste of the times. In either case, his heritage was not one that a socially nervous Thomaner could feel proud of, especially when his best friend, Helmut Meyer von Bremen was the son of a consul (though this didn't seem to affect the father's friendship with Nikolai's parents) and would go on to be a composer of church music. Even in later life, his discomfort about Judaism permeated his sense of self and can be seen resurfacing repeatedly in his family history.

Pevsner's mother, Annie Pevsner, was born Annie Perlmann in 1876, he wrote, and he was only able to trace her family history back three generations: not much, by Helmut von Bremen's standards. Her origins, Pevsner thought, were in Russia, 'but from one of those Baltic provinces which were Russian then and are now Russian again' – an odd misapprehension, because she was in fact born in Moscow. He recorded Annie's mother's name only as Jeannette, one of five children born to Leib Blidin, and remembered her as 'small and rather plump'. Her real name was Taube Selde – Jeannette was her less Jewish-sounding pet name – and she was the daughter of a fur trader who'd moved to Leipzig from Sagar, a hundred miles west of Dresden on what's now the German side of the Polish border but was then in Silesia.

In Leipzig, Jeannette had married another fur trader, Saveli Maximovich Perlmann, whom she may have met through her father. According to Pevsner, both the father and the husband had prospered until 1901, which Pevsner describes as a 'disastrous year'.[11] Jeannette's father was wiped out and returned to Sagar. Her husband, who also saw his affairs collapse, became bankrupt. He and Jeannette then left Leipzig, heading first to Berlin, before trying their luck in China, which also exported furs. They finally moved to England and settled in West Hampstead,[12] a late Victorian suburb in north-west London, where Perlmann gave up business and became a writer. Pevsner was taken to visit his grandparents by his mother, possibly with his father and Heinz as well,[13] shortly before the First World War. He remembered them, slightly sniffily, as living in 'one of those innumerable little red brick houses lining in terraces the streets of that part of Hampstead as the streets of so many other English suburbs'.[14] (In his London guide of 1952, he said, even more sniffily, of West Hampstead that it 'need be visited only by those in search of Victorian churches. The streets and houses require no notice.' It certainly wasn't the Musikviertel.)

In his family history Pevsner didn't dwell on his mother's Jewishness. She had little formal interest in religion and put her efforts into other activities, which partly redeemed her for him, even if these activities gave rise to other problems. What else redeemed her was that her father, having taken to writing, could now be described, with some relief, as 'really a scholar more than a businessman', the first member of Pevsner's family to express any academic leanings. In theory, that meant he was no longer tainted by trade; unfortunately his writings were almost wholly concerned with Jewish matters. Perlmann was an early and active Zionist, arguing in favour of Jewish self-determination and against cultural imposition. He was also passionately concerned with the survival of Jewish identity and in one of his several books on China expressed concern that the Jews of Kaifeng had allowed Confucianism to colour their religious practices. His books – all published by Jewish publishers in the East End of London (Mazin & Co., Whitechapel; Hayehudi, Brick Lane; and Israel Narodiczky, the anarchist printer, in the Mile End Road) – were popular enough to be published in German, English and Yiddish versions. They were also published in Hebrew, which was unusual for the time, because Hebrew was only just being reconstructed for modern usage and shows Perlmann's commitment to the idea of a future Jewish state, then still half a century away.

'My grandfather spent much of his time at the library of the British Museum', recorded Pevsner. 'I have several publications of his, the first being one written in China in 1903 and called *Einiges über China* [*Something about China*]. It has a strong bias against the Christian missionaries and their lack of appreciation of Chinese religion and institutions.' He continued:

> In 1908 he wrote a short paper in *The Zoologist*, proving that an animal mentioned in the Bible (Exodus XXV, 3–5 and Ezekiel XVI, 10) and called, in Hebrew, Thakash is not a zebra but the then newly-discovered African animal called okapi. In 1909, Probsthain's published a pamphlet on *The Jews in China* discussing the remarkable fact that the Jewish families in China have developed Mongol racial features without actual mixture of races. In the same year, another pamphlet came out with a new interpretation of Hamlet.[15]

The publisher of *The Jews in China* was in fact Narodiczky and Pevsner's crediting of it instead to Probsthain's, which was merely the bookseller that distributed it, may suggest he wanted to give his grandfather a more respectable English imprimatur, rescuing him from his reputation as a 'Hebraist', as the *Jewish Chronicle* described him at the time.

Pevsner's unease about his grandfather was noted some years later by a cousin, the daughter of one of his mother's three brothers, whose husband had worked for the American Legation in Khabul. On a visit from the USA to London in 1970, she met him with some of her Embassy friends for a walk on Hampstead

Heath. 'He told them he worshipped at the German Lutheran church', she said of Pevsner. 'I asked if he'd forgotten that our great-grandfather had been a Talmudic scholar. He said "So what?" and the conversation stopped immediately. Later I said I wanted to see our grandfather's house in Sumatra Road, West Hampstead. He said "Why do you want to see that ugly little house? There are more interesting things to see." He wouldn't take me. He wasn't interested in him. He said "He wasn't a scholar; he went broke in every business endeavour he tried and decided to spend his last twenty years in the British Museum."'[16] Saveli Perlmann died in 1916. His wife, Jeannette, returned to Germany after the war and lived, until her death in 1928, first with her daughter Ida in Berlin, then with her son Georg and finally with Pevsner's parents.[17]

While Pevsner could trace his mother's family back just three generations, he could trace his father's family back eight generations, though not with any greater pleasure.

> We start with a learned man – *probably, I assume, a rabbi* – who was called Shmuel, lived at Posen first and later in Galicia and wrote a work called *Rosh* . . . His [younger grandson] was called Shmuel Shmelkin, lived again in Posen [and] was very famous (*no doubt as a rabbi*). His son Reb (*rabbi?*) David lived first at Lemberg and later at Mir near Minsk . . . He had a son, Elia Benjamin [whose son] was my great-grandfather *and called himself* Reb Gershen Tanchum Posnen. He lived from 1812 to February 14, 1881 . . . was born at Minsk and married the daughter of Mardochai Goldberg, a wealthy wholesale merchant in drugs and chemicals. This Mardochai wanted his daughter, aged 15, to marry a scholar. He chose Gershen, aged 14, because Gershen had a year earlier read a sensational essay at the synagogue of Minsk. But his father-in-law wanted him all the same to become a merchant . . . As a scholar, or theologian if you like, he was a man of some distinction. I have a Hebrew book of his. There is a story about him and *the great English rabbi Moses Montefiore* which was published in a magazine at Vilna 'by the author of Dybuk', *whatever that may mean* . . .[18] [Author's italics.]

This passage, written in the early 1950s and coming from a historian who was otherwise careful about facts, is remarkable both for its carelessness and lack of charity. Sir Moses Montefiore was not, for example, a rabbi but a banker and philanthropist, probably the most celebrated Jew in England in the nineteenth century after Benjamin Disraeli, knighted in Queen Victoria's coronation year after serving as Sheriff of the City of London from 1837 to 1838. 'Reb' is merely the Yiddish equivalent of 'Mr'. The Posen and Galicia of Shmuel – and the Silesia of Leib Blidin that Pevsner had referred to earlier – were part of Poland, not Russia, at the time when Pevsner was writing and part of Prussia at the time of the characters he was writing about. Elia Benjamin's son called himself Reb Gershen Tanchum Posnen not because this was a ridiculous name but because, at that time, Jews were being required to adopt surnames and some adopted the name Posnen because they lived in Posen (now Poznan). As for *The Dybbuk*, this was the title of Shloime Ansky's famous masterpiece of Yiddish drama, a story of mysticism and demonic possession in an Eastern European village.

After completing his family history, Pevsner added corrections and recommended that 'for this kind of Jewish life of small commerce and scholarship, you might care to look up the autobiography of Solomon Maimon, the rationalist philosopher (1753–1800), re-published by the E. & W. Library 1955'. He also supplied missing information about *The Dybbuk* (now correctly spelled), giving the dates of its first performance as 1920 and of its author as 1863–1920 but giving his name, oddly, as 'Solomon Rapaport (S. An-ski)'. These additions do not dispel the impression that Pevsner derived a certain satisfaction from being unaware of his subject, as if knowing too much about East European and Jewish history might be contaminating.

Pevsner's discomfort about his parents' Russian-Jewish origins seems to have been bound up in a fear about how they might reflect on him, starting with the surname he was born with. 'Pewsner', spelled with a 'w', went back to his grandfather, Shmuel Shmelkin Pewsner, and was a source of anxiety because it was not only East European and unGerman but inauthentic. Though his grandfather and father were Pewsners, his great uncle Vladimir[19] – his grandfather's brother – was called Posnjak (a Russified version of Posnen, his great-grandfather's name). On this he commented:

> The two brothers had different surnames. Posnjak is, *I am afraid*, the right one, derived from the preceding Posnen and *no doubt connected distantly* with Posen, where my story started.[20] Pevsner is a Jewish name in Russia which is not very rare and was adopted by my grandfather (in arrangement with someone really called Pevsner) for the reason that of two sons one had to serve in the army. The false name was intended to free the bearer from military service – a dubious manoeuvre, you might say . . . Anyway . . . that is how we are Pevsner and how . . . that mysterious character Antoine Pevsner, the abstract sculptor in Paris, and brother of Naum Gabo who have, as far as I know, nothing to do with us[21] . . . as well as the stranger in the London telephone book can also be Pevsner. [Author's italics.]

Elsewhere, Pevsner described his father simply as 'a Russian Jew' and recorded his given name as Gilel, apparently unaware that this was simply the Russian version of Hillel and that his father had therefore been named after one of the most famous rabbis in Jewish history.[22]

Hillel Benjamin – later 'Hugo' – was the only son of four children born to Shmuel Shmelkin Pewsner and his wife. Two of his sisters stayed in Russia. The youngest lived for a while in Switzerland, spoke very fast in a Russian accent and looked to Pevsner like 'an anarchist with black hair brushed straight back, a parting in the middle, and of course a bun. She married a Zionist sculptor . . . who became head of the Jerusalem Art School . . . and there were two children . . .; both became artists. They have both had exhibitions, the boy of abstract art,

I think, and the idea always embarrasses me that I might run into them.' The mother went on to write a book on general aesthetics. After keeping up a cursory correspondence, Pevsner lost her address.

Pevsner knew his father had been born on 18 January 1869 in Shklov, near Smolensk, in Byelorussia, now Belarus, where he believed his grandfather had settled. He apparently didn't know, however, when Hillel, or Gilel, had moved to Leipzig or how he'd come to change his first name to the German 'Hugo'. He'd been 'told' – his word – that his father worked for a company called Emil Barban, named after its senior partner, and that it was located at Brühl 69. This was 'the fur-trade street of Leipzig which always smelt of furs and their preservative against moths and was full of trading, gossiping and arguing Jewish businessmen.' The house was old and the staircase humble, he added.[23]

Pevsner seems not to have thought much of his father. Of his mother's marriage choice, he wrote: 'It seems curious that she married so unsophisticated a man as my father, though at that time, with his little moustache twisted up at the ends, he must have had some fascination for her.' Elsewhere he wrote: 'I don't think my mother thought he was a great success at business.' He noted that his father was once cheated out of a large sum of money by his senior clerk, but added that in spite of that, 'he earned enough, and more than enough, and we lived extremely comfortably'.

Hugo was, in Pevsner's words, 'wholly and active[ly] Jewish'. If that's the case, he would have wanted his two sons to be Jewish as well. For this reason, around the time when Nikolai was ten, Hugo paid a teacher to teach him Hebrew. It wasn't a success:

> I . . . had Hebrew lessons for a time from [a] Dr Kohn. He had a black beard and sometimes fell asleep a little during lessons. They were just lessons in reading Hebrew – without actually understanding a word. But reading was necessary for the Jewish first Communion (Barmizvo) [sic]. In the end, I never took it, and now I don't remember the letters any more. The lessons must have been about 1912–1914.[24]

Historically, Jewish boys were taught to read and write Hebrew (by their father) before being taught to read and write the language of their country of birth. With assimilation, the learning of Hebrew often became secondary; sometimes it was ignored altogether. It was required, however, for the Bar Mitzvah ceremony, the religious initiation process by which Jewish boys, around their thirteenth birthday, mark the start of what Judaism regards as adulthood by singing, in Hebrew, at least three verses from the weekly synagogue recitation of part of the first five books of the Old Testament.

Preparation for the Bar Mitzvah could begin at any time but was often left until after a boy's twelfth birthday. It involved learning a system of musical phrases and memorizing how to apply them to a Hebrew text. It required practice but wasn't normally a problem unless Jewish observance in the home had already

broken down. Even if, by the age of twelve, a child felt that Judaism was intellectually unsustainable or simply boring, this wouldn't usually express itself in
a refusal to go through with the ceremony, because that would be an act of
defiance against the parents' wishes.

For many émigré Russian-Jewish families, however, Jewish observance in
the home had indeed broken down. It was common for families who'd left
self-contained Jewish settlements in Eastern Europe and beyond to feel released
from centuries of cultural confinement and to give up their association with
Jewish practice and belief, deliberately and by conviction or casually, through
indifference.

In Germany, there were two other factors that encouraged Jews to question
their religious loyalties. One was the Enlightenment, which had given rise to a
specifically German-Jewish movement called *Haskalah* (the Hebrew word for
enlightenment). In the early nineteenth century, Napoleon had transformed
attitudes to Judaism throughout and beyond the French Empire – which briefly
included parts of Germany – by determining that Jews constituted no threat
to the body politic and should no longer be barred from participating fully in
public life. One consequence of this was that many German Jews either gave up
being Jewish, in the light of their potential integration, or, inspired by the Jewish
philosopher Moses Mendelssohn, devised a new type of Judaism with Germany
at its centre. Unlike Jewish communities in Eastern Europe who'd remained
untouched by Napoleon and therefore had no incentive to assimilate or modernize, German Jews would no longer wait for God to ordain the rebuilding
of the Jerusalem Temple that the Romans had destroyed in AD 70 and without
which their religion had spent nearly two thousand years in limbo; instead,
'Reform Judaism' would make a public commitment to what it regarded as the
most cultivated nation on Earth and the most favoured by God. Each German
town would have its own 'temples' (no longer 'synagogues') and services would
become more formal and church-like, with organs, professional choristers, mixed
seating and uncovered heads. In particular, German would replace Hebrew for
much or all of the liturgy. Even among Germany's Jewish faithful, there was
therefore a presumption against traditional Jewish practice.

In the country at large, there was an even stronger presumption against Jewish
practice, in the form of institutionalized anti-Semitism. In England, Protestantism
had helped to dismantle some layers of prejudice against Jews, especially during Cromwell's Commonwealth; in Germany, Martin Luther's attack on the
Papacy 125 years earlier had reinforced it, legitimizing the scapegoating of Jews,
individually and collectively, for whatever ills Germans felt strongly about at
any moment. Anti-Semitism in Germany was reignited in the early nineteenth
century, when it was conflated into a concern about nationhood. Before 1806,
Central Europe had consisted of over 300 separate political entities. The Congress
of Vienna in 1815 reduced this to thirty-nine but liberal Germans wanted further reductions so Germany could emerge as an identifiable, independent state.

Initially such thinking was benign and embracing; later in the century it became openly xenophobic. Although Judaism had existed on German soil at least as long as Christianity, even sophisticated circles came to see Jews as an alien element whose presence defeated the promise of a clear-cut national identity.

The anti-Semitism of Germany's rising nationalist movement was summed up by the historian Heinrich von Treitschke in his notorious remark of 1879, that 'Die Juden sind unser Unglück' ('The Jews are our misfortune').[25] In the elections to the Reichstag in 1907, a self-styled Anti-Semitic Party won sixteen seats and formed part of the chancellor's[26] ruling bloc. Jews continued to be barred or considerably restricted from taking up state employment, including teaching and the law. Their only remedy, encouraged by Bismarck and institutionalized until the collapse of the Weimar Government, was to renounce their religion. There was therefore every reason for a young Jew in Germany to regard Judaism as a relic of the past and an impediment to the future. The most telling indicator of this is that in the first two decades of the twentieth century, half of all German Jews married a non-Jewish partner – traditionally seen as a revocation of Jewish identity or an irreversible step towards it.

Pevsner was born on 30 January 1902. In the Jewish calendar, this coincided with the twenty-second day of the Hebrew month of Shevat. Had he gone ahead with it, he'd have delivered his Bar Mitzvah recitation in one of Leipzig's thirteen synagogues and temples on 6 February 1915. His refusal to do so can almost certainly be put down to the fact that from the summer of 1914, his father was absent.

Hugo – known to other family members as Hügchen – seems to have been most notable to Nika for his absences. Twice a year, he was in the habit of travelling to trade fairs in Russia: in the summer to Nishni Novgorod and in the winter to Irbit in the Urals. On his return he'd tell Nika stories of his adventures and about how, when he was young, he'd travel across Russia on a sledge, how he was once pursued by wolves, how a driver had upset a sledge and then run away, and how on the Siberian railway the trains would stop long enough at each station for 'ample' meals, pre-booked by telegraph, to be consumed before setting off again. As an adult, Pevsner seems to have found these stories of his father more vivid than any personal memories he had of him.

Although Annie had accompanied Hugo on one of his Russian trips to Nishni, and had once visited Paris and London with him, Hugo invariably travelled alone. Pevsner remembered what he called 'family holidays' – including trips to Ostend in the summers of 1913 and 1914 – being taken with his parents' closest friends, Arthur and Mitja Nikisch,[27] but usually without Hugo joining them. In the same way, when Annie visited Forel in Switzerland, Hugo had bought a house for her there but hadn't joined her on her first trip or any of her return visits.[28]

Hugo's visit to Russia in the summer of 1914, when Nika was twelve, had lasted longer than in other years because his business was failing and he'd needed to sort out problems of supply. Usually he was able to travel freely, but with Germany and Russia now at war, movement was restricted. Unable to get back to Germany directly, he'd eventually headed for Sweden, which had declared itself neutral in the war (though initially slightly biased towards Germany), and was allowed into the country in December. He obviously liked it there because instead of returning to Germany, he moved into a hotel in Stockholm – the Hotel Continental in the heart of the city, opposite the Central Station – and remained there for the whole of the war. During that time, he worked for an established Scandinavian fur products company, the Skandinaviska Pelsvarufabriken, with premises just a few streets away and contacts overseas.

By the time of Nikolai's planned Bar Mitzvah in February 1915, Hugo had been away from home for more than seven months, during just that period when Nikolai would have been making religious preparations and when a little fatherly intervention might have been needed. But with Hugo in Sweden, Annie was in charge of the home and although she could be strict with other members of the family, she may have been too preoccupied by her own concerns, and too indulgent with Nika, to have insisted on his doing something he didn't want to do.

But perhaps she did insist. In his family history, some twelve years after her death, Pevsner included a confession in which he wrote:

> My own development was in the years of adolescence actively in opposition to her and her values. I was unjust and cruel to her in those years and even later.

In the key episode in that conflict between mother and son, Annie had a nervous collapse four days before Nikolai's ill-fated Bar Mitzvah, checked herself into a clinic and stayed there for eleven days, leaving her two boys in the care of her housekeeper. It's hard not to attribute the causes to Nikolai's attitude to Judaism, his unwillingness to go through with his Bar Mitzvah ceremony, the disappointed expectations of friends and family, and the wasted cost of the unrealized celebration. Annie may not have been actively interested in Jewish practice but for Nikolai to have taken Hebrew lessons for two years, even with a teacher who sometimes fell asleep, seven months of which were outside his father's control, suggests at least a measure of maternal support, and further evidence of that will be seen later. Given his capacity for language, learning and achievement, Nikolai must also have felt a considerable aversion to what he was being taught to have been willing to give it up with nothing to show for his efforts. He may have argued with his mother as his Bar Mitzvah approached or he may simply have suffered from a performance anxiety that turned into a hostility towards what he'd failed to accomplish. It's not surprising, therefore, that when given the opportunity to study Hebrew at school, he said no.

3

Friends

Throughout the war, Nikolai had to survive without a father. To what extent his father even kept in touch with him during that period is hard to know. The Pevsner archive at the Getty Research Institute in Los Angeles contains some seven folders of material related to Annie, including more than a hundred letters from the years 1938–1942, but almost nothing from Hugo. Did Hugo not write or did Nikolai not keep what he wrote? The difference is stark.

While Hugo was absent, Heinz became more extrovert. Nikolai, by contrast, turned inwards – 'a typical stick-indoors', remembered his sister-in-law, Marianne Kockel,[1] 'always reading'. In addition to his schoolbooks he read Goethe and Schiller, Shakespeare, the great Russian novels (in particular Dostoyevsky), and books on art, which his mother encouraged. Inspired by her, he even read English books, in spite of having not opted to study English at school. Among the books on his bookshelf in Schwägrichenstraße that started to supplant such children's books as Ernest Thompson's[2] *Bingo und andere Tiergeschichten* (*Bingo and other Animal Stories*) were Samuel Bensusan's *The Charm of Rossetti* and *The Masterworks of Constable*.

One aspect of Pevsner's inwardness lay in an exceptional desire for documentation and order. As an adolescent trying to make sense of the world, Nikolai converted every experience into a diary entry: dreams, gifts, writings, readings, quotations, even the diaries in which he did his documenting. He tracked changing moods for months in coloured graphs, counted chapter by chapter the number of pages he'd read in books, wrote definitive lists of great literature and pithy quotations, and detailed his journeys and his meetings. By the spring of 1919, aged seventeen, he'd made a catalogue of everything that he'd catalogued in the previous year:

Pevsner's journals	Volumes	Days	Pages
Preferences, observations and letters	5	311	166
Pevsner volumes	7	131	256
The catastrophe	1	3	35
Pevsner books	6	124	264
Experiences	16	234	580
Notes: Group 1	5	100	150
Notes: Group 2	7	283	217
Total up to 5 June 1919	**47**		**1,668**

This would never be the raw material of a communicable art but it was at least as extreme as his brother's more conventional excesses: girls, money and drink. Nikolai had made list-making into a private language, transcribed in a small, neat, regular handwriting and in a form of shorthand based on Gabelsberger, Germany's equivalent of Pitman, created in the 1820s by Franz Gabelsberger but superseded in 1924 by Einheitskurzschrift and now almost impossible to read. It's hard not to see Nikolai's cataloguing as a form of self-protection. Faced with his mother's command of the artistic world and Heinrich's command of the social, Nikolai responded by constructing a world of quantity and detail of which he alone was master.

Another aspect of Pevsner's inwardness lay in his sense of being unloved. His unappealing father was abroad. He was smothered by his bi-polar mother but also found her aloof and sometimes distracted and wrote that he was 'floating in Muo's circle'.[3] The only security in his life came from his parents' housekeeper, Anna Krause, to whom he turned for all his domestic needs.

And then, according to Pevsner family legend, something decisive happened. Shortly before his fifteenth birthday, he decided to take stock of himself. He felt he needed to take up a sport.[4] 'It was the winter of 1916–1917,' recalled Marianne Kockel – née Kurlbaum.

> It was half-way through the war and very cold. There was a coal shortage in Germany and the schools had what they called 'coal holidays' because they couldn't be heated. And so he took up skating. Everyone in Leipzig who could skate met on the Johanna Park pond. And on the other side of the park, not directly on the park but in the next parallel street, there we lived, right next to the secondary girls' school and the Thomasschule, at Sebastian-Bach-Straße 7. And on the other side of the park, about the same distance away, lived the Pewsners. So everyone met on the ice. My brother Dieter went to the same school as Nikolaus. He was in the form below but they were friendly. And through him, Nikolaus got to know my sister Lola, skating on the Johanna Park pond. That was in January 1917 when he was almost fifteen and she was still fourteen. And I believe he immediately decided to marry her.[5]

According to the family's version of events, Nikolai fell in love with Lola Kurlbaum – real name Carola – at first sight and the two were devoted to one another ever after. Pevsner's memory, nearly forty years later was different. In his rough notes for his family history, he wrote that he was introduced to Lola 'by fluke on 10 May 1917', that he found her 'steady but moody', that his friendship with her lasted only for a few weeks, that they didn't meet again until 1919 and that he didn't fall in love with her until 1920. But that account wasn't quite right either.

The notes he made at the time show that Nika did indeed meet Lola in January 1917, while skating, but that he'd first become aware of her some nine months earlier through his best friend, Helmut Meyer von Bremen, the son of his parents' friend Alexander von Bremen. The von Bremens and the Pewsners lived close to one another and Helmut and Nikolai walked to school together 'every single day'[6] for nine years. Some time around Lola's fourteenth birthday in April 1916, when Nikolai himself was only fourteen and three months, Helmut seems to have boasted that a girl called Lola was in love with him and Nika had made a note of this. A month later, Nikolai observed that Helmut's friendship with Lola had ended in 'mistrust and separation'. He eventually came across her on the Johanna Pond, spinning like a top on the ice, in January 1917. It was a meeting that would draw all three of them – Nika, Lola and Helmut – into a teenage love-battle involving promises, denials, threats and violence.

The adolescent love-pangs of a fledgling German art historian may seem a little beyond this present study but what makes them notable is Nikolai's behaviour. Until then, his horizons had been defined by the question of how he slotted into a home that was dominated by his mother and her occasional house guests, into a school dominated by his brother and his more *echt deutsch* class-mates, and into a country dominated by racial and religious barriers. His interests were similarly polarized between self-absorption and bookish speculations on politics and aesthetics. The advent of Lola transformed this world of problems into a world of possibilities. She was different, not part of Leipzig's aspirant Jewish culture, not male, not fiercely intellectual and not only not immediately available to him, as his caring housekeeper was, but in demand elsewhere. He was unsettled and fascinated by her.

A week or so after meeting Lola, around his fifteenth birthday, Nikolai wrote in his diary that he was secretly in love with her. Helmut's retreat the previous year had given him a clear run and if, a few days later, Helmut didn't exactly confirm he was no longer interested in Lola, Nikolai inferred this and concluded also that any liaison he began with her wouldn't harm Helmut's friendship with him. Satisfied that the way was clear, Nikolai met Lola again and by 26 February felt confident enough to write that love was growing between them. On the second Sunday in March, he received his first introduction to Lola's home in Sebastian-Bach-Straße. Ten days later on a Wednesday, perhaps on a day when his mother was not at home, Lola visited his parents' apartment. On 3 April, they met at von Bremen's home and later in the month Lola visited Nikolai's home again, again on a Wednesday.

The thought of Lola took Nikolai over. A month after meeting her, he started to dream about her: on the night of 24–25 February 1917 she was in a hotel corridor, on the night of 19–20 March in a wide open field, on 5–6 April in a large hall, on 20–21 April in a meadow, a week later in the music room of his home, and again in the music room three days later. Nikolai was so intrigued by Lola and by his own reactions to her that he threw himself into a frenzy of chronicling. He charted the occasions on which Lola wore a blue skirt, a cream-coloured skirt, a blouse with flower patterns, a blue silk blouse with flower patterns, a steel-blue blouse, a tartan silk blouse, a green silk blouse. He listed her 'peculiarities': her love of children, of red carnations, of white narcissi, of bitter chocolate, of red cabbage, of yeast-balls, of potato pancakes, of punctuality and of mandarins, and of her dislike of beer and beards and fish. He kept a book to record the presents she gave him. And having only started writing diaries a year earlier, three weeks after his fourteenth birthday, he now filled his diaries with observations about her. In the first, he took twenty-eight pages to cover just four days: seven pages per day; in the second he wrote almost two-thirds of a page each day. We know this because he catalogued his journals, calculating statistics on his output as he went.

All seemed to be going well enough for Nikolai to confess to Helmut early in May 1917 that he was in love with Lola. The claim was premature. On 20 May the friendship ended. This may be what Pevsner recalled coolly years later, but at the age of fifteen and three months it was high drama. Nikolai labelled the next two days 'Catastrophe' in his diary, though they also added materially to his yield. Meeting Lola had already expanded his writing to two, and then three, diary pages a day between February and May 1917. Losing her sent it up to nearly nine pages a day,[7] before settling back to its previous rate for the rest of the year. In his third diary of the year, begun in mid-April 1916, he wrote a page a day; his fourth and fifth took him to Christmas at a rate of just under half a page a day. Stress, uncertainty, conflict, emotion: Nikolai not only worked out his demons on the page but also kept a watching eye on how well he was doing in recording them.

Nikolai wrote extensively about what he thought of Lola and what she meant to him. Those papers are now either lost or not in the public realm but his notes survive. They give the impression that for all his passionate self-scrutiny, there was also something impersonal about his recording. His annotating of his dreams, for example, had to do with places rather than people and indicated how a scene was set rather than what took place, revealing a visual and architectural mind rather than a well-developed human instinct. His one hint of Lola's impact on him occurred in his family history of 1954 where he spoke admiringly of her family compared with his own, suggesting that it was her significance as much as her individuality that struck him.

Genealogists have two principal ways of describing lineage. The more common takes the form of a tree – an upside-down tree – with larger branches, smaller branches and twigs. The family tree increases in complexity as it proceeds in time and each structure is unique to each family. There is, however, a different way of describing families called the Ahnentafel (ancestor table), a structure introduced into Germany in 1896 by Stephan Kekulé von Stradonitz, a German genealogist born in Belgium.[8] Stradonitz's Ahnentafel is a list, not a graphic representation, that focuses on a given individual and goes backwards in time. Each person in the Ahnentafel has a number. The individual at the starting point is 1. The individual's father is 2; the mother is 3. The father's parents are 4 and 5. The mother's parents are 6 and 7. The father's paternal grandparents are 8 and 9, and so on, with men always appearing as even numbers and women always as odd. Relationships can therefore be calculated arithmetically. An individual x has $2x$ for a father and $2x+1$ for a mother. The method also delineates generations. Number 1 represents one generation, numbers 2 and 3 are the previous generation, numbers 4 to 7 are the generation before that, and numbers 8 to 15 are the one before that, so that any generation n is identifable by the number 2^n and each subsequent number up to $2^{(n+1)}-1$. This wonderfully mechanical arrangement honours direct ancestors and ignores everyone else – brothers, sisters, aunts, uncles, cousins – or acknowledges them only as annotations. The effect is that, unlike the graphic tree, the form of every family's Ahnentafel is identical. This makes it possible to pinpoint any direct ancestor. A maternal grandmother's grandmothers are always 29 (paternal) and 31 (maternal). Number 31's maternal grandmother is 107. Anyone between 64 and 107 must have lived six generations before the individual at number 1, and five generations before numbers 2 and 3. For any generation n, the bearers of number 1's surname (the line of fathers' fathers) is always represented by the number $2^{(n-1)}$.

One side of Lola's family had been included in a tabulation like this. Eduard Kurlbaum, born 1862 and a cousin of Lola's father, had produced an arithmetical lineage going back eighteen generations to the year 1247. 'It is a formidable document,' wrote Pevsner, and it was amplified, through marriage, by other individuals who provided a little extra colour. Tradition even claimed Charlemagne as an ancestor, although, as Pevsner wrote, 'Charlemagne as an ancestor seems . . . legendary according to the genealogical tables. Still the Kurlbaums are quite ready to keep him available for conversations with other family-proud people.' Other delights were equally piquant, such as 'the princes of Schaumburg-Lippe, one of the smallest principalities surviving in Germany to the revolution of 1918. They do indeed come into the family tree, but only via the wife of No. 16 who was called von Kotzenburg.' Lola's direct family, the Kurlbaums, went back eight generations 'to Johann Christoph Philips,[9] called Currelbaum, who about 1652–1671 owned a farm, Kurlbaum, near Dissen in the Teutoburger Forest, where Arminius had defeated the Romans in AD 9 . . . Mutti's [Lola's] family stories go not as far back as that . . .'

When Pevsner set out his family history in 1954, he used the main divisions of the Ahnentafel to structure his narrative, working methodically through each division and subdivision of his and Lola's families. He started with his father's side, then his mother's, then turned to Lola's father's family and ended with her mother's. This imposed some order on the tangles of family lore without sacrificing opportunities for commentary but it also separated branches of the family that were in fact connected. It meant, for example, that when his mother nursed his father through 'a tubercular infection, I think about 1904 or 1905', he ran up against a categorization problem: should he treat the story as an example of his father's impairment or his mother's devotion? He opted for the former.

The divisions also raised the question of where to locate himself. As author, he ought to have been number 1 in his own genealogy but he gave this position – unusually – to his brother and reserved for himself the role of moderator. As for his own appearance in the story, his level of participation was different with each parent. In the case of his father, his presence was fleeting. He told his children: 'On my and my father's side I have been able to trace your family back nine generations (including my own).' He then vanished from the scene. By contrast he popped up repeatedly in the second quarter of the narrative when dealing with his mother and her family: a telling indication of his varying loyalties.

A question of tone also separated his writing. He told his children:

> The fundamental fact you must keep in mind when you start reading now of what we know of your ancestors, is that you are, to put it in the Nazi way, 75 per cent Jewish, Jewish completely on my side, and Jewish also on your mother's mother's side. Your mother's father's side is genealogically very different from the three others, as you will see.

Whether or not this was meant ironically, it shows that more than twenty years after leaving Germany, the memory of racial labelling still hit a nerve. For this reason, and because Lola's father's history went back further than his parents' or her mother's, his history inadvertently highlighted his sense of being at a genealogical disadvantage. That the Kurlbaums could trace themselves back ten generations more than the Pewsners, and eighteen in terms of an unbroken German line, was a sign of their superiority. Having written about his own family, Pevsner started on Lola's family with an audible sense of relief and awe: 'With the Kurlbaums we are moving into a very different atmosphere.'

'Here,' he wrote, 'is a family of merchants and then civil servants, especially in the legal fields, with a documented family history right back into the seventeenth century, "eine feine familie", as Mutti [Lola] sometimes used to say.' Karl Friedrich Kurlbaum (1716–1766) was a merchant and senator or alderman. His son, Dietrich Adolf (1751–1816) became Stadtdirektor – 'presumably town clerk' – of Bielefeld. 'His wife was a Topp (1765–1822) of Lemgo. The Topps were an old Lemgo family . . . That the best of the gabled stone houses of Lemgo, the Hexenbürgermeisterhaus of 1581, belonged to the Topps is fairly embedded in the Kurlbaum traditions . . . but to connect [them] with . . . Kurlbaum is utterly arbitrary.' In the nineteenth century, Kurlbaums took a high place among Prussia's lawyers and administrators of justice. Lola's great-grandfather, who died young in 1833, had been a Regierungsrat.[10] His oldest son, Friedrich, born 1826, was a Geheimer Oberjustizrat[11] and Vortragender Rat[12] in the Ministry of Justice in Berlin, and married a Sezekorn, a family of high civil servants in Kassel. Friedrich's brother Karl, Lola's paternal grandfather, was born in 1830. Both he and Friedrich took part in the 1848 Revolution and both later joined the Commission that drafted the constitution for the newly united Germany of Bismarck. Karl also wrote the code of conduct for Germany's lawyers. In old age, when Lola knew him, he was President of the Oberlandesgericht[13] at Stettin, wirklicher Geheimer Rat[14] and Exzellenz.[15] A 'fine family' indeed.

Exzellenz Kurlbaum had four children. The eldest, Ferdinand, became a professor at Berlin University, married a Siemens, had a shooting estate and lived in a sumptuous house in Dahlem, next door to his brother-in-law Wiegend, who became a leading archaeologist and whose villa later housed the university's Institute for Art History. Of Ferdinand's two sisters, one married a future Geheimer Ministerialrat[16] in Berlin, the other a former Referendar[17] of her father's who became a Regierungsrat. The fourth child was Lola's father, Alfred Adolf Kurlbaum.

Pevsner adored Alfred. In his notes, he wrote of him as a 'genius – wide education – immediate reaction' and described him in his family history as 'the other central character' alongside Annie. Speaking for himself and Lola, Pevsner wrote that Alfred was

> greatly admired by both of us, and indeed a very remarkable and a very lovable character, warm, wise, wide of interests in all directions, endowed with an exceptional memory, lively, *charmeur*, and distinctly impetuous . . . What added so much to his charm was a naïveté which he never lost, that is, an ability to look at things and people for himself, and to make comments regardless of what might be expected of him. He was not handsome but had an impressive carriage . . . That he was full of stories and repeated the funny ones at intervals I know from my own experience, and his children teased him about it. Mutti adored him and misses him to this day.

Befriending Lola gained Nikolai something he craved and that his own parents couldn't provide: firm roots in German society and a respectable pedigree. He got the same reward from his friendship with Helmut, whose family was deeply involved in German theology,[18] and his satisfaction was probably compounded by the thought that in winning Lola, he was getting what Helmut had wanted. If this takes away from Lola's personal qualities and reduces her to a trophy, it's only because Pevsner left behind little evidence of the former and ample evidence of the latter. Ulrich Michel also attested to what was at stake in Nikolai's liaison with Lola Kurlbaum. Lola, wrote Michel, was 'the daughter of a lawyer who was permitted to plead at the Reichsgericht, in other words a lawyer at the top of his profession whose earnings were very high and who was without question one of the leaders of Leipzig society . . .'[19] For Nikolai to associate with Alfred Kurlbaum's daughter, said Michel, 'meant, so to speak, a jump of two steps in Society':[20] one step because Kurlbaum was a professional while Hugo Pewsner was merely in trade; two steps because Kurlbaum was a very high-ranking professional. He might have added a third step: the fact that Kurlbaum was Lutheran and not Jewish.[21]

One other factor separated the Kurlbaums from the Pewsners that was fundamental to German life in the early 1900s: their involvement in the army.

The war that broke out in 1914 followed more than half a century of Prussian militarism. In 1864, Prussia had fought alongside Austria, its main partner in the German union created in 1815, to acquire Schleswig-Holstein from Denmark, but Prussia turned on Austria two years later and defeated it as the supreme Central European power. Prussia then declared war on France, its western rival, and in January 1871, while besieging Paris, certified a reluctant King Wilhelm I of Prussia as Emperor of all Germany. Bismarck, who orchestrated Wilhelm's elevation, now set out to challenge Britain, acquiring territory in East and West Africa and the South Pacific and building up German naval power, to immense popular support, so that when Wilhelm's young grandson became Kaiser Wilhelm II in 1888, militarism was already an established part of German politics. For many, war now became not only a legitimate tool of foreign policy but the determining feature of German culture. ('Man shall be trained for war and woman for the procreation of the warrior. All else is folly', wrote Nietzsche, influentially. 'The strong men, the masters, regain the pure conscience of a beast of prey.')

When the First World War began – 'the war to end all wars' – Alfred Kurlbaum dutifully took up arms. 'He served for one or two years, first as a lieutenant, aged well over forty, in a prisoner-of-war camp, then as a captain in charge of a telegraph office,' Pevsner wrote. By contrast, Hugo Pewsner was away in Stockholm and Annie was all pacifism and anglophilia. There's every reason to think that Nikolai must have felt humiliated by his family's apparently unpatriotic behaviour, not least because there was nationwide pressure on Jews to prove their loyalty. In 1916 Germany was so convinced that Jews, especially Russian and East European Jews, were disloyal to the war effort that at the start of November the German military High Command conducted a Jewish census (Judenzählung) to establish the facts. The results showed that, by contrast, Jews were overwhelmingly supportive. Since this wasn't what the army had wanted to find out, the results were buried so that Jews could continue to be blamed by the country for failures suffered during the campaign.

In spite of the many differences in their background, Nikolai and Lola both had Jewish mothers. Alfred Kurlbaum, born in Magdeburg in 1868, went to school at the Joachimsthaler Gymnasium in Berlin, travelling by horse-drawn tram from his parents' home in Hohenzollernstraße. Many of his school friends were Jewish, including his best friend, Max Neisser, who went on to become a leading bacteriologist in Frankfurt, and Alfred was reputed to be so attracted to Jews that his family called him, not very charmingly, 'der Jude': 'the Jew'. Pevsner wrote that this teasing was meant in fun but that wasn't entirely true, because he also recorded that Alfred's elder brother Ferdinand – the Berlin professor with the shooting estate – lost touch with Alfred, apparently because Ferdinand and his family disapproved of Alfred's marrying a Jewish wife: Max Neisser's sister, Paula.

Paula was in fact Kurlbaum's second wife. He'd previously married Augusta

Koslowska, who died after a year of marriage, while pregnant, in the middle of a conversation. He married Paula Neisser, then twenty-four, in 1901, and Lola was born the following year. Although not brought up as such, Lola was therefore Jewish according to Jewish religious law, which takes the mother's religion as the determining factor.

Lola – losing her, winning her, keeping her – now became the focus of Nikolai's adolescent drama, a drama that went on for more than two years. In the summer of 1917, while on holiday with his mother in St Blasien, in the south of the Black Forest, he wrote that he'd been 'unfaithful'. Then, after school resumed in September, he found that Helmut was trying to win Lola back and this led to a new round of sexual rivalry. During October, Nikolai and Helmut kept squaring up for a battle and backing down. On 12 October Nikolai wrote that both were ready for a fight; forty-eight hours later, they finally got one. The next day, Nikolai recorded that he'd regained Lola; two days later he said she wanted nothing more to do with him and that any idea of a friendship was invention on his part. Towards the end of October, Helmut seemed sure of having secured Lola's love and was readying for another fight; by mid-November, he was giving his word of honour that Lola had never loved him and that his friendship with Nikolai was safe. Not for long. On 5 December the two boys had another fight (the only time in his notes that Nikolai referred to himself in the first person); six weeks later, Helmut was asking Nikolai to excuse him from his word of honour. And so they went on through 1917 and 1918, their hostilities mirroring the trench warfare of advance, retreat and stalemate 400 miles away on the Franco-Belgian border.

The situation was neither resolved not halted when tragedy struck. On 16 June 1918 Lola's mother died from cancer, aged forty-one, after an illness that had lasted a year.[22] Curiously, no record of her illness appeared in any of Nikolai's notes. He also seems to have been oblivious of the impact of this death on Lola, concentrating solely on the details of his triangular love match. Just two days before Paula's death, he wrote that Helmut had again given his word of honour that there was no love between himself and Lola; and two weeks after the death, the two of them were fighting again. Now Nikolai recorded that Lola wanted nothing more to do with either of them, but without any apparent insight into her psychological state.

Nikolai may have put Lola's mother out of his mind, however, because of her lack of welcome for him. According to Lola's sister, Marianne, Paula Kurlbaum did not approve of his relationship with her daughter, not only because the two of them were still very young but because Paula had other plans. Pevsner wrote about her later:

> I remember what she looked like but not much else, and Mutti [Lola] does not talk much about her. She was a practical and able woman who liked to run things herself, and she was certainly not lacking in resolution. Once in a concert when someone behind her made

noises with the programme she turned round without hesitation to rebuke him. Mutti was rather frightened of her: for although she was extremely devoted to her children, she was also ambitious for them.

He added, perhaps waspishly, that Paula had fallen in love with Alfred before Alfred had fallen in love with her.

4

Death

After the death of Friedrich Nietzsche in 1900, the new big voice to emerge in German literature was that of Thomas Mann. Mann wrote novels, short stories and essays; he also interpreted Nietzsche to the German public, likening him to the fashionable Russian novelist Dostoyevsky, a favourite of Heinz Pewsner's, in respect of their writings about the ordinary and the extraordinary, the hollowness of common morality and the freedoms available to those who choose their own destiny.

Nikolai was very taken with Mann, largely because Mann represented the idea that one could be exceptional without having to be wild or intemperate, and without conforming to the convention of the alienated nonconformist, but simply by applying a searching intelligence. Mann's intelligence − his close observation of detail, his wide knowledge (among other things he'd studied art history), his articulacy and his sober objectivity, his 'Sachlichkeit' − corresponded to how Nikolai saw himself. Nikolai also liked Mann's conservatism and the way that Mann explored the status quo, in contrast to Nietzsche and Dostoyevsky and their protagonists, whose depth of feeling challenged it to the point of destruction. And Mann, though great, was not remote: he lived next door to the rector of Munich University, who happened to be Lola's uncle. That added to Lola's charisma as well.

As a teenager, Pevsner drafted several short stories in which he tried to pay homage to Mann. Most proved too hard to sustain and ended abruptly. One, based on himself and Heinz, was called 'The Two Brothers' and referred to what he labelled his 'Dostoyevsky ethic'. Another, 'Spa Music' ('Kurmusik') was about a character not unlike Hans Castorp in Mann's novel *The Magic Mountain* (published in 1924 but already being drafted as a novella in 1912) who's entranced by a beautiful woman whom he sees in a sanatorium but can't win. A third, called 'The Last Hour' ('Die letzte Stunde'),[1] was actually dedicated to Mann and sent to him for his approval, under the pseudonym Nikolai Allo. What Mann thought of this offering isn't known, but a few years later, while studying in Frankfurt am Main in the winter of 1922−1923, Pevsner managed to get invited to Lola's uncle's house on an occasion when Mann was dining there. Over supper, the conversation turned to plans for the following year's holidays and Mann said he didn't enjoy swimming when he was on holiday. 'But you did swim at Aalsgaard,'[2] Nikolai cut in. 'You mentioned it in *Tonio Kröger*' and Mann was impressed at his recall.[3]

Where Pevsner disagreed with Mann was over his attitude to the war, a political conflict Mann construed in Nietzschean and mystical terms, at variance with his normal moderation. In an article entitled 'Gedanken im Kriege' ('War Thoughts'), published in the *Neue Rundschau* newspaper in November 1914, Mann wrote about the war as a millennial struggle for the survival of Germany's soul. The Teutonic primitiveness of Germany was under attack, he argued; the battle to save it was holy and cleansing. He repeated himself in the last weeks of the war in his *Reflections of an Unpolitical Man* (*Betrachtungen eines Unpolitischen*), which called on Germany to make one last stand against Western modernity.

Mann's main thought in the *Betrachtungen* was that under the seductive influence of France, pre-war Germany had become too civilized. Germany was best when it was at war; in peacetime one could forget how beautiful it was. The soldier in the artist's soul should therefore praise God for the collapse of a peaceful world because peace was boring.[4] He also argued that character was more admirable than virtue and had to be protected. All nations aspired to 'civilization', which the French had foisted on them, at the expense of their own identities; far more precious was national culture because it was unique and irreplaceable. Should Germany lose the war, all that was essential to it would become polite and insipid: its poetry and music would be replaced by prose, its Protestantism by universalism, its national feeling by humanitarianism, its daily life by society, its aristocracy by democracy, its ethics by politics, its irony by radicalism, and its pessimism by progressivism. Mann's one consolation was that if Germany were defeated and had to start again, a broader system of public education might bring about a Nietzschean aristocracy of merit – an idea that Annie Pewsner's teacher Ernst Bergmann would promote when the war ended.

The *Betrachtungen* appeared in October 1918, a month before the end of the war. Nikolai, aged sixteen-and-a-half, read it at once and was disappointed by its emotionalism and what he saw as its betrayal of intellect. He therefore wrote to Mann, observing that some of its ideas were outdated (the belief, for example, that Sachlichkeit – objectivity – in German ideas and politics was unGerman) and arguing for greater balance and moderation. In particular, he urged Mann to write a new piece for the papers, recanting his views and adopting a middle way between German reverence and Western enlightenment. On 16 October Mann wrote back, thanking him politely for his thoughts but rejecting 'with horror' the idea of writing another *Betrachtungen* and insisting there was nothing 'antiquated or out of date' about insisting that 'it was impossible to link intellect and politics in the land of Luther and Goethe.' (Mann did step back from these remarks during the 1920s, however, explaining that during the war, he'd feared that the triumph of Western democracy would not only destroy Germany but his own function within it as a German writer. As it was, his career survived and in 1929 he won the Nobel Prize for Literature.)

Nikolai's correspondence with Mann illustrates what he wanted from Germany during his adolescence: not the extremism of Nietzsche but something more measured – intelligent political management accompanied by a respect for the past. In view of the heroic status he'd later achieve as an interpreter of Englishness, how did this correspond to his adolescent view of England, Germany's wartime enemy? England didn't dominate European culture as France did – it had little reputation in art or music – but it had leapt ahead of Germany in its democratic development, its legal and constitutional structures, its industry and economy and its social development, and many liberal-minded Germans had looked to it as a model for more than a century. Considerable attention had also been paid to the informality of its late nineteenth-century architecture by Hermann Muthesius, who'd spent eight years as cultural attaché at the German Embassy in London from 1896 to 1904 and had published an influential three-volume study called *Das englische Haus* (*The English House*).

By the time the war broke out, however, anti-British hysteria had touched almost everyone in Germany, including the most reasonable and educated people. Ninety-three academics had signed an *Intellectuals' Manifesto* in 1914, defending Germany against foreign complaints of bellicosity and responsibility for the fighting. It was also generally agreed in Germany that the new Reich had legitimate claims to be treated like an empire but was being held back by a conspiracy involving France, Russia and Britain acting in concert (a view that would be repeated after the war and developed further by the Nazis). This was the political rather than the mystical case for war and it was felt by the Kaiser, the military and the country as a whole.

In spite of his letter to Mann, there's no reason to think Nikolai would have felt any differently from the majority of the population or that he wouldn't have been intensely supportive of Germany and the war effort. Evidence against this would have to show he was drawn to the pacifist movement his mother had connections with, or to the workers' movement, but no such evidence exists. It's also fair to assume that his adolescent conflicts with his mother extended to their political views. There's therefore no reason to assume Pevsner had a natural affinity for England in his youth, as English writers have always suggested, and every reason to assume he didn't (which may explain why he chose not to study English at school). As a conventional boy, he'd have shared his country's suspicions of Britain, France and Russia, agreed with the wish to reverse France's political and cultural dominance of Europe and approved the general principle that England's global arrogance, expansionism and economic power needed to be checked. He'd also have shared the frustration that built up as the war dragged into its fourth year.

By the spring of 1918 it was obvious to most Germans that the fighting wasn't going to end well. Nothing about the Imperial Emperor's military strategy had gone as planned. Germany's build-up of arms and belligerence had been intended to bluff Europe into submission. Instead, it drew Austria-Hungary, Serbia, Russia, Germany, France, Belgium, Britain and Italy and many other nations including, in 1917, the USA, into the bloodiest confrontation the world had ever seen. From the summer of 1914 to the autumn of 1918 some seventy million men were put into uniform, twenty-one million soldiers and civilians wounded, and fifteen million killed. From wanting to be a more dominant player on the world's stage, Germany had become a pariah.

For Germans this was doubly damaging because they'd remained uninvaded and their military had performed well tactically but were facing an ever greater chance of Allied victory without having actually lost. This gave rise to bitterness at the government from all sides: from the left for waging a war that mostly hurt the working class; from the centre for choosing to fight on and bringing the country to its knees when a more advantageous peace could have been negotiated; and from the right for the army's failure to capitalize on what seemed like a position of strength on the Western front. This latter failure was blamed not on the military but on supply problems that in turn were blamed on Communists and Jews, both of whom were accused of disloyalty and of having fomented strikes to paralyse the war effort – the popular Dolchstoß ('stab in the back') legend that was widely adopted and that provided the main platform for the rise of National-Socialism.

In July 1918 a French and American counter-offensive took place. It was followed by decisive British, French and Belgian advances in August and the routing of Germany's Austrian, Bulgarian and Turkish allies in Serbia in September.

A huge change now took place in Central Europe. October saw the effective end of the Austro-Hungarian and Turkish empires and their reduction to insignificance. In November, the German Emperor abdicated and fled to Holland. Countries that had been invisible for years now reappeared (Poland, Estonia, Latvia, Lithuania, Albania and Hungary itself) and new countries were created (Czechoslovakia from Bohemia, Moravia, Ruthenia and Slovakia; and Yugoslavia from Serbia and Montenegro). Germany itself was stripped of its colonies and forced to give up to its neighbours – France, Belgium, Poland and Lithuania – territory that had been disputed for centuries.

Instead of bringing a return to normality, the armistice signed on 11 November threw Germany into chaos. There were strikes in the larger towns and ports, all ruling monarchs were forced to step down, and leaderless gangs of demobilized soldiers wandered round the country, creating mayhem. In the absence of a workable constitution, and with the possibility that Germany might follow Russia's lead and become a soviet republic, nationalists and Communists now saw opportunities to pursue their separate goals. In this way a process began in which Germans were forced to take sides for and against increasingly extreme political alternatives.

Just as the war was ending, Hugo made a return visit to Leipzig, using a passport he'd obtained from the German consul in Sweden on 5 October 1918.[5] It wasn't his first visit. A year earlier, between November 1917 and January 1918, he'd represented his firm on two consecutive business trips that took him to Breslau (now Wrocław) and then Copenhagen to attend emergency meetings

called by the firm's bank. At the time he'd not needed a passport and was able
to rely on entry and re-entry visas to get him where he wanted to go[6] and he'd
taken advantage of those trips to visit his family. The appearance he put in on
that occasion wasn't just social, though. While Hugo was working for his Swedish
firm, he was continuing to run Emil Barban, the Leipzig fur haulier he'd bought
into as a co-partner in January 1895, but he needed help. He therefore used the
opportunity of his visit home in late 1917 to beg Heinz, his elder son, not to go
to university when his school career ended the following summer but to join
the family firm instead and run it in his (Hugo's) absence.

A year later, at the start of October, Hugo had to travel abroad again, this time
to sort out problems with his fur suppliers in Russia. With the collapse in trade
caused by the war, the suppliers were complaining about not being paid and
Hugo was sent to meet their representatives in St Petersburg to try and extend his
company's credit terms. Having met them, he paid another visit to his family.

Whatever arrangement he'd tried to set up in St Peterburg must have come
undone because by the end of the month the principal owner of the company
in Sweden was telegraphing Stockholm's Aliens Department asking for Hugo
to be allowed back to Sweden urgently. On 2 November Hugo applied to re-
enter Sweden and was refused, possibly because he was no longer financially
secure. In a panic he telegraphed the Swedish Embassy in Berlin, explaining
that his firm was going into liquidation, that he had to get back fast and that
he'd been living in Stockholm for four years and paid his taxes there. He
then hurried to Berlin to put in another application for re-entry and was
refused again. It took a third application before the Swedish authorities agreed,
on 10 November. It was the same day the Allies handed Germany their terms for
an armistice.

What Hugo's brief and stressed reappearances in 1917 and 1918 had meant
for Annie is hard to say, though it's notable that in two of her communications
to him in this period she seems much more loving towards him than one would
have imagined from Pevsner's later remarks about her. Pevsner failed to mention his father's visits in his family history, giving the impression he was more
comfortable when Hugo was away. It's not hard to say what Hugo's reappearances meant for Heinz, however. Heinz loved his father dearly; and Hugo, in his
own way, loved and admired Heinz, perhaps even favouring him over the more
bookish Nika. And when Hugo asked Heinz to run Emil Barban for him at the
end of 1917, Heinz had agreed to do so, partly because it was a way of holding
onto his father in his absence. In the end, however, Heinz couldn't carry out
his father's wish because just as he was leaving school, in August 1918, he was
drafted into the army.[7]

Why Heinz would even have thought of sacrificing his career for his father
seems to have been lost on Nikolai. Heinz was so bright that the Thomasschule
had let him jump a year in 1914–1915 and by the time he'd graduated he'd
already published a paper in a mathematics journal and had Leipzig professors

asking his advice.[8] Pevsner described him as 'over-intelligent, thin, Jewish [and] sensuous' in the rough draft of his family history but deleted three of these adjectives in the finished text. He wrote instead that Heinz was 'very intelligent, very precocious, and had wanted to study economics and history'.[9] What he didn't write was that his brother missed his father in a way Nikolai didn't.

With the war virtually at an end, Hugo was allowed to return to Sweden but Heinz was still away on basic training. At first, wrote Pevsner later, Heinz seemed to be one of the lucky ones because there wasn't time for him to get to the front, but 'in the mood of the defeat after the war, and the return of young officers, he got into what well may be called bad company. His friends had more money than he; the girls about the circle were not very desirable. There were night clubs, drinking and promiscuity.'[10] Two months earlier, in September 1918, Nikolai had written him a birthday poem, marvelling at his rakishness. Loosely translated, it reads:

Dir widme ich hier dies Gedichtchen	To you I dedicate this verselet
als Wiegenfest-Geschenk von mir.	As a birthday gift from me.
Es kommt nichts vor als die Geschichtchen,	It's nothing much but little tales
Die Du mit neunzehn hinter Dir.	Of you, with nineteen years gone by.
Ich Dichter für 'Familienfeste'	A poet of family celebrations
'ne Rolle auch, die mir nicht steht,	May not be my choicest role,
Probiere ich trotzdem aufs beste,	But nonetheless I'll try my best,
Vielleicht gelang dies Alphabeth.	Perhaps this alphabet will work.

———   ———

Andrea wollt' nicht von Dir lassen,	Andrea didn't want to leave you,
Obwohl sie bald Dir war zu viel.	Though she soon got just too much.
Hat Armand Blum im Bridge 'drei Asse',	Armand Blum, with three Bridge aces,
Gewinnt er glänzend jedes Spiel.	Wins each game quite brilliantly.
Der Carli Flinsch, zwar sehr begehrlich,	Carli Flinsch, although most handsome,
Er störte Deine Kreise nie	Never put your clique at risk
Der Deli wurde Dir gefährlich.	There, though, Deli posed you dangers.
Du siegtest und besassest sie.	Then you won and conquered her.
Die Ella, von semit'scher Rasse,	Ella, of semitic background,
In einen Harem passt sie gut.	In a Harem would do well.
Die Finny, Mannequin prima Klasse,	Finny, first class mannequin,
Doch stark verdorben bis aufs Blut.	Corrupted to her very blood.
Die Groos sinkt sicher zu Lorette.	Miss Groos falls flat before Lorette.
Die naechste fesselt Dich viel mehr:	The next one captivates you more:
S'ist Hansi, die zwar Operette,	It's Hansi, one-woman Operetta,
Doch wahr und kitschig liebs' Dich sehr.	True and kitschy, but loves you so.
Die Ilse amusierst [sic] Du weidlich	Ilse is a mild amusement

– Dich Hysterie bleibt eine Qual! –
Die Kitty chic, an Schönheit leidlich,
Ist Dein Amouren-Ideal.
Der Lucie, erstes Abenteuer
Auch Carli Flinsch ihr eigen nennt.
Maruschka, lasterhaft, voll Feuer
Sie liebte einst den Captain Kent.
Der Nora Feuer Stars nur schaffen,
Du hast sie nur mit Pausen gern.
Die Otto liebt den Domizlaffen.
Sie ehelichte Morgenstern.
Frau Pevsner weiss von Deinen Sünden
Ist sie entsetzt? Ist sie gerührt?
Für Q. ist einfach nichts zu finden,
Ehe Du die Ilse Quaas verführt.
Die Refardt hatt' 'ne lange Aera.
(Genau so lange wie sie hier!)
Schmidt-Lorenz aber, der aus Gera,
Der lag besoffen neben Dir
Den Thieme führ'tst Du an der Nase
Und nahmst ihm seine Hansi weg.
Das Unikum der Lampestrasse
Hat einen sehr geheimen Zweck.

II

Was würde wohl der Vati denken,
Kennt' er Dein folgenreiches Tun?
Der Walli meint', er könnt' durchs
                Schenken
An Hansis schönen Busen ruhn.
Die X, die liebst Du augenblicklich.
Vielleicht ist 's auch die Y.
Wird Deine Zukunft weiter glücklich?
Ich weiss natürlich nichts davon.

———

Die Feder aus der Hand nun lass' ich
Und wünsche Dir für alle Zeit:
Erfolge: viel. Moneten: massig
Und immer Glück und Heiterkeit.
Und ausserdem noch selbstverständlich
Nie wieder Schulden-Schweinerei
Und damit schliesse ich nun endlich
Dein treuer Bruder
                    Nikolai

– But hysteria's such a pain! –
Kitty, chic, a tolerable beauty,
She must be your ideal love.
Lucy, your first real adventure,
Claims that Carli Flinsch is hers.
Depraved Maruschka, full of fire
She once loved her Captain Kent.
Nora's fire gave only sparks,
You just like her now and then.
Miss Otto loves her Domizlaffen,
But then she married Morgenstern.
Mother Pevsner knows your sinning.
Is she shocked? Or tolerant?
Couldn't find a name for Q,
'Til you seduced young Ilse Quaas.
Refardt had a decent innings
(At least while she was close at hand!)
Schmidt-Lorenz, the chap from Gera,
Lay down drunk right next to you.
You led Thieme by the nose
And took his Hansi girl away.
The uniqueness of the Lampestrasse
Has a very secret role.

II

What indeed would Father think
If he fathomed all you've done?
Walli guesses that through gifts, he'll

Rest on Hansi's lovely breast.
One brief moment, you love X.
Perhaps that's also true of Y.
Will you be happy in the future?
That is something I don't know.

———

So I must now put down my pen
And wish you this for ever more:
Success: a lot. Money: masses
And always luck and merriment.
Apart from that, I need not say it,
Never again those filthy debts:
And thus I'll draw this to an end
Your devoted brother
                    Nikolai[11]

This ingenious alphabetic poem shows Nikolai making light of a personality very different from his own. Once Hugo had gone back to Sweden, however, Heinz started to go off the rails and Nikolai felt there was increasingly little to make light of. Years later, in a book on the photography of Helmut Gernsheim, Pevsner would describe the head of Edward II's effigy at Gloucester Cathedral as 'tragic, dissipated, Dostoievskian';[12] in his youth he'd described Heinz the same way. Part of him saw in Heinz the romantic, excessive, self-destructive qualities he'd read about in Dostoyevsky and that Rilke had glorified in portrayals of the artistic anguish and of young heroes acting selfishly or antisocially to prove they'd achieved a level of existential insight too sublime for others to share. But Nikolai also knew his brother's behaviour wasn't the product of adolescent nihilism, or the pain of love, or anguish at the unfairness of the world, as literature presented it, but more tangible factors: debt, drink, depression, his father's absence and his unfulfilled obligation.

Heinz's intemperance grew bad enough for Hugo to visit Leipzig again in February 1919 but without bringing any lasting comfort. On one occasion when Annie was out of town, Heinz had got involved in a fracas in a club involving women who were apparently paid to keep quiet about him.[13] On another occasion he tried to commit suicide. In an attempt to divert him, Nika wrote a little play that the two of them acted out one night in the Johanna Park near their apartment. In a letter to his brother the next day (24 June 1919), Nika spoke about waking up and feeling he'd metaphorically 'leapt over the fire' – a reference to a game of dare played by children at Lent – the previous night, and of hoping to be able to do so again without burning his toes.

Nikolai's attempts to engage his brother were in vain; on 30 June 1919, a week after their night-time adventure, Heinz drowned himself in the Johanna Park lake. (Friends and family were told it was a boating accident.)[14] Pevsner wrote later of his brother: 'He talked to nobody about his troubles – a curse in our family – but I should have guessed enough to prevent his suicide, especially as he had made one attempt to drown himself shortly before. But I was blind or too young, and it happened.' (In other notes, written in the present tense, Pevsner noted that his brother was 'drawn into a duel-of-love craze' and that 'I do not save him.')

Rather than being interred in a Jewish cemetery, Heinz was cremated – against orthodox Jewish law – and buried in Leipzig's main municipal cemetery, the beautiful Südfriedhof park that houses the Völkerschlachtdenkmal, the vast, brooding centenary memorial to the defeat of Napoleon at the Battle of Leipzig in 1813.

Heinz's death brought Hugo home for a third time. Annie had telegraphed him in Sweden the day after the suicide: 'HEINZ SUDDENLY FALLEN ILL IN BAD CONDITION WOULD BE GRATEFUL IF YOU WOULD COME IMMEDIATELY KISSES.'[15] Hugo had gone straight to the passport office in Stockholm and had asked for a visa that would let him attend the funeral in Leipzig and return to Sweden six weeks later.

The journey meant he'd have to miss a meeting being held in Stockholm the very next day to register a new company in which he'd have a quarter share: the Swedish Fur Trading Company,[16] given an English name because the majority of its business was going to be channelled through London rather than Leipzig and other European fur-trading centres.

Without access to Pevsner's private papers, it's once again impossible to say how Hugo was greeted on his return but emotions must have been mixed. He'd not been on hand to prevent Heinz's spiralling out of control; presumably he felt some measure of guilt. Annie, meanwhile, according to Ellen Dreessen, tried poisoning herself.[17] As for Pevsner, he later said that Heinz's death was a 'terrible blow' to his parents – but of his own feelings, he said nothing. His future sister-in-law, Marianne Kockel, commented: 'Old Mrs Pevsner suffered a lot from the death of her son and reproached herself for not having understood him properly, and every year, as the anniversary of his death approached, she got very ill emotionally, but . . . how my brother-in-law reacted, he never said. I mean, we talked about many things but never about this.'[18]

Nikolai was seventeen-and-a-half when Heinz died and blamed his father at least in part for the death. This is evident in his family history, where he wrote that Heinz, three months short of twenty, 'knew no longer . . . where to turn and killed himself' because (implicitly) their father 'lived still in Sweden at the time'. Heinz died, Nika felt, because he was conflicted about the duty he'd be taking on as the elder son. Nika couldn't forgive his father for that; but he wasn't ready to forgive him in any case. For a quarter of his life, his father had been a stranger to him and he'd welcomed that distancing. Heinz had needed his father more; Nika had needed him less and he'd matured without any counter-influence to his culturally ambitious mother and his socially ambitious school. Everything he later said about Hugo suggests a snobbish aversion. He now saw him, in his own words, simply as 'ein kleiner Russe' (a little Russian), one of those 'gossiping and arguing Jewish businessmen' he'd seen on the Brühl. Nikolai hadn't just lost a brother; he'd lost a parent too.

A month later Annie was still in a delicate state and Hugo applied to the Swedish authorities for visas that would allow her and Nikolai to join him for four-to-six weeks in Sweden. He explained to the authorities that he couldn't stay away from Sweden any more and was able to take care of them. They'd return in mid-September so Nikolai could start school again.

As always, Nikolai dealt with his feelings not by talking about them but by putting them down on paper. In an essay the next summer, on the thirtieth anniversary of the death of Vincent van Gogh (29 July 1920), he directly addressed the question of suicide. Although Cézanne may have been a more talented artist, he wrote, van Gogh was the more significant, not only as an Expressionist artist in his own right but as the prototype of what an Expressionist should be. That was because in addition to embracing all the characteristic qualities of Expressionism, van Gogh was also an remarkable individual – a vital feature of art at the moment of its transition from Impressionism to Expressionism, when the sort of person you were started to mean more than the sort of pictures you painted.

> To be a great artist today, one has to be an outstanding human being. And that's what van Gogh to a great extent was. There was hardly another personality among painters who was as significant in this way, beyond his art. For van Gogh, painting was just a means of expressing, in public, those feelings and thoughts that poured out of him in whatever shape or form.
>
> Imagine someone with iron energy, a burning temperament and an enthusiastic and idealistic longing for universal happiness held back by an extremely weak constitution and an unexpectedly sharp ruling intelligence and you've got the precondition for van Gogh's life and art.

Van Gogh had started out wanting to be a teacher, then a preacher, Nika wrote. He then discovered he could devote himself to his ideas through art and so he learnt to paint. He developed his skills in The Hague, Antwerp and Paris. That left him just four years in which to prove himself.

> It was in that short period of time that he created his masterpieces: those landscapes, still lives and portraits that one can find either uplifting or awful. They're not representations of nature, they're the battle of a man filled with raging emotions, struggling for something unprecedented: the subjugation of the subject by the artist's emotions. It was a tragic struggle and ultimately an unsuccessful one, for it required a massive effort not to be destroyed by it, and van Gogh was already weakened by over-exertion, so that it could only end in insanity – nature's revenge for the never-ending expenditure of energy that van Gogh put himself through. That's how he created Expressionism, from inside himself, over two years.
>
> But beyond van Gogh's art, his intellect deserves even more attention because there's an intelligence that was working and watching while his temperament and passions were raging underneath. It's something that can never be completely admired, the way that – even during his lunacy in Arles – this intelligence kept going, observing but detached. If you read van Gogh's letters . . . you can see a quietness and clarity in his psyche that doesn't seem to match his explosive pictures. And it's this supremacy, this relentless self-discipline, that enables him to paint such artworks.
>
> It was self-discipline that constrained his fantasies when he copied Millet and Delacroix; self-discipline, when he voluntarily went into the asylum in Arles in 1888; and it was the ultimate self-discipline that led to his suicide in 1890. Had he been undisciplined or stupid, he would have gone on recklessly until the end. Instead, van Gogh chose his end, and we have to admire that death more than anything else about him.
>
> He watched his decline in utter quietness and clarity, and he must have realized there were only two possibilities . . . He had either to try and live healthily, which meant giving up his exhausting art, or keep on working and find that after a few years he was no longer able to. Both options, van Gogh must have realized, meant losing life's battle: one

physically, the other mentally. So he chose a third way, the only way, in which he came out the winner: he ended his life, deliberately bringing his work to a halt when he was at his creative climax, because nature wasn't kind enough to let him go on.

Even though we have to mourn his early death, van Gogh's suicide can only elevate him in our eyes. Nothing can be more misleading than to blame it on mental derangement. It's the very opposite: van Gogh never saw more clearly than in the moment before he shot himself. He knew he'd fulfilled himself intellectually and didn't have the strength to do what he'd done again. So he quietly took the only available path and shot himself. For us today, there's only sorrow about the necessity of his death and the enrichment of his spirit and his art that made him the first and most important Expressionist.

This meditation, characteristic of its time in its idealization of morbidity, is a revealing example of Pevsner's intellectual flexibility. By nature, he wasn't an Expressionist: his response to Thomas Mann showed that. He believed in art but hated emotional excess – and suicide was the ultimate expression of emotional excess. On the other hand, he couldn't allow his brilliant brother to have failed. He therefore took the model of van Gogh to show that suicide could be a rational choice and that it took exceptional character to pull it off. This meant having to honour a type of art – Expressionism – that wasn't natural to him. It's an essay where the ends – the salvation of Heinz's memory and the desire for consolation – justified the means.

By the time Pevsner wrote his essay on van Gogh, the political situation in Germany had been transformed. In the power vacuum that followed the Kaiser's flight, the country had been declared a republic and networks of locally elected soviet-style workers' councils had been set up all over the country. In Leipzig, the city was taken over by a collective of workers and soldiers: Germany's transformation into a Communist state now seemed a real possibility. Then in January 1919, the majority Social Democratic Party (Sozialdemokratische Partei Deutschlands – SPD) that led the pro-tem administration held elections and won a reasonable victory. It went on to head a centrist coalition supported by two smaller parties, the mainly Catholic Centre Party and the party that Pevsner's mother got involved with, the newly formed German Democratic Party (Deutsche Demokratische Partei – DDP).

The DDP – slogan: 'Against Dictatorship' – had come third in the January elections, with just over eighteen per cent of the popular vote, compared with the Social Democrats' thirty-eight per cent and the Centre Party's twenty per cent. In just ten days it had helped frame a new constitution.

For some, the Democratic Party had a moral duty to succeed. It was 'rich in distinguished bourgeois intellectuals and progressive industrialists . . . abundant in talent, decent in campaign methods, rational in its programme'.[19] It was also the inheritor, between 1919 and 1933, of German attempts to live by good intentions. The highpoint of this aim was the meeting, in February 1919, of delegates elected the previous month. In attempting a new start, they chose to gather not in the imperial capital of Berlin or Potsdam but in Weimar, the home of Goethe and thus the symbolic home of German humanism. For this reason, the republic and its fourteen-year existence would be referred to later as the Weimar Republic or simply Weimar, a name that now conjures up an attitude of mind as well as a political reality: poetic freedom, moral courage and cultural experimentation in the face of the failure of the old order that Thomas Mann had spoken out for.

Annie Pewsner tried to put the loss of Heinz out of her mind by throwing herself into the new political climate. She revelled in a sense of liberation and spent Hugo's money impulsively. 'Immediately after the war,' Pevsner wrote, 'she became interested in Expressionist art and poetry, bought many and good minor things (Archipenko and so on) and had readings of poets at our house. I remember Theodore Däubler especially vividly. He once stayed for several weeks, if not months, rather to our despair.'

That Nikolai was more unsettled than his mother during this period is evident from his writings. Unlike her, he had nothing to cheer about in the new political climate. Following Paula Kurlbaum's death in the summer of 1918, he'd also had to suffer Lola's withdrawal of affection. The frenzy in his diary entries now cooled down significantly. For the next fourteen months there were no more references to Lola or Helmut and his entries slowed to half a page a day. Apart from the dubious pleasure of seeing his father, there continued to be little emotional stability in his life.

Annie embraced Germany's collapse as a fresh opportunity. She also set to work to lead her son towards a career that would restore his faith in himself, taking him on visits to look at architecture and sculpture. Consequently, Pevsner wrote, 'it was certainly she who fostered my early decision to become a Kunsthistoriker [art historian]', even though art history, a newly fashionable subject, was regarded by many Germans as 'brotlose Kunst' ('unprofitable work' – literally, 'breadless art'). It was, wrote Pevsner later, 'a type of profession which my father cannot have fully approved of. However . . . he was much too good to interfere.'[20]

Hugo may not just have been 'too good' to interfere; he may also have been nervous about alienating his second son after the loss of his first, especially in the face of his determined wife. If so, Nikolai dug his heels in and Hugo was forced to put his hopes into the possibility that Nikolai's cousin Heinrich Pollack – five years old in 1919 – would eventually come into the business and take it over instead. There was a lot of moral pressure on him to do so. Hugo, while in Sweden, had been giving financial help to Heinrich's mother, Annie's sister Ida, who lived in Berlin and couldn't cope financially after the unexpected death of her husband Walter Pollack in 1914 and the arrival of her own mother, Jeannette, now widowed, back from England, after the end of the war. Later, Hugo courted Heinrich by giving him his late son's signet ring – a gift from Arthur Nikisch – on the grounds that their initials were the same. When Heinrich told Nikolai what Hugo had in mind for him, Nikolai took sides with him against his father and came up with a plan to help him avoid Hugo's clutches, possibly acting as he felt he should have done when Hugo had ensnared, as he saw it, his brother. Heinz Pewsner's ring now belongs to Heinrich Pollack's grandson, who added the name Heinz to his own in order to inherit it.[21]

5

History

Pevsner was still a schoolboy during the chaos that followed the First World War. Although no one in his own family had been killed on active service, he suffered the death of his brother Heinz as an indirect consequence of the war and saw many other families having to adjust to life without fathers and sons or with shell-shocked veterans. War had reduced Leipzig's population by some four per cent, the Thomasschule was having to survive with fewer teachers, disabled soldiers were reduced to begging on the streets and women were having to seek work in factories and offices because the main breadwinner in the family was dead or no longer able to earn.

In March 1920 Pevsner made a note in his diary about the Kapp Putsch. Under the Versailles Treaty, signed in June 1919, Germany had been required to reduce its armed forces from 350,000 men to a maximum of 100,000. That left a quarter of a million decommissioned and demoralized soldiers who didn't know what to do. Many had joined autonomous right-wing paramilitaries known as Freikorps and now refused to demobilize. One group, led by General Dr Wolfgang Kapp, showed its strength by taking over Berlin. The new Weimar Government, unable to persuade the army to suppress the putsch, decamped to Dresden and called on left-wing workers to defend the new constitution by striking. Ulrich Michel recalled that during this crisis the Thomasschule 'was temporarily occupied and used as a barracks by one of the Freecorps' and that there was little support for the government from the staff because 'none of the teachers was very much pro-Weimar; like all the mass of the bourgeois Germans they regarded the state without an emperor or king at its head as something rather suspect.'[1]

Against this unsettled background, great efforts were made to make life bearable, though some efforts only heightened the strangeness of the times. Between 1919 and 1920, for example, the Quakers in Birmingham, who received funding from the chocolate-making Cadbury family, gave gifts of chocolate soup to Pevsner and other schoolboys in an attempt to restore morale and these were received with some amusement.

Domestically, Hugo began to make regular visits to Leipzig and to stay for longer periods. Between November 1919 and May 1920 he made three visits home, the last of which lasted the whole of the summer, during which he took Annie and Nikolai on holiday to a spa to take the waters and relax together. He then stayed on in Leipzig for most of the autumn, returning to Sweden at the start of the following year to wind up his new company. He resettled in

Germany in the spring of 1921 and the Swedish Fur Trading Company was finally dissolved three years later.

Life now seemed a lot happier in the Pewsner home. Whatever difficulties there may have been in the past, cousin Heinrich wasn't aware of them and enjoyed the company of his reunited aunt and uncle, in spite of having to run the gauntlet of the staff at the railway station.

> Uncle Hugo (called 'Hügchen') and Aunt Annie lived in Leipzig, which was then the centre of the European fur trade ... Leipzig, at the confluence of the Pleisse and Elster rivers, was also the centre of the German book trade and was known for its music, choirs and concerts. The great trade fair in Leipzig drew a public from all over the world ... and it had the biggest railway station of Europe [one half for Saxon trains, the other for Prussian]. It was said that people weren't treated that politely at the so-called Prussian station. Prussians weren't liked, especially when they came from Berlin. For my mother that wasn't a problem: she was born in Leipzig and kept her Saxon dialect all her life. For me it was better not to open my mouth that much.
>
> My uncle was modest and kind. He spent most of the time at work. When he got home in the evening, tired from the day, he still had time for me and we'd play 'Lion Hunting', a board game. In his early life, Uncle Hugo had survived an attack of tuberculosis but an asthmatic cough stayed with him all his life, worst in the mornings.
>
> Nika was always a good friend to me, just like an older brother. I enjoyed his companionship and the way he treated me, being younger. Early on, this meant playing with me; later it meant sharing thoughts with me about art, books, politics and many other things. I learned a lot from him.
>
> When I was young he gave me two hand puppets, both apes. He called one of them 'Ape Nedolf' and the other 'Ape Adolf'. I took care of them carefully and gave them back to him a couple of years later, because he said he wanted to give them to his children when he was older. I thought it was fantastic that he was already planning for this: at the time, having children seemed a long way away. I was also allowed to play with his big model train set. The set came with little model figures, passengers who were dressed in old-fashioned, pre-war clothing. There was also a destination board that said 'St Petersburg'.[2]

Pevsner was now getting to the end of his school career and was starting to think about university. The Thomasschule had an arrangement with Leipzig University that allowed boys in their last year to audit university courses of their choice. Pevsner took advantage of this, planning an ambitious regime of study that would enable him to work as fast as possible and get as much experience as he could so he could graduate with a doctorate by the time he was twenty-two and marry Lola, whom he'd by now got to know again and was desperate not to lose a second time. The subject he chose was art history.

Art history in Germany, a century ago, was not an easy option. Art of the ancient world was far more important than it is today and served as a continuing source of inspiration. A large part of the art-history syllabus at Leipzig was therefore devoted to Classical and Etruscan archaeology. Pevsner took the need to understand this art very seriously but also thought that European history had to be studied intensively if the context in which European art was produced was to be understood. He therefore decided that for a large part of his studies, he'd immerse himself in general history, which he saw as also explaining German history and the turmoil of recent years. This combination – general history and art history – was crucial to the shaping of his later work.

The teaching of general history in the early 1900s concentrated on the evolution of nation states and their interrelationships. The days before the emergence of nation states were regarded as benighted – the 'Dark Ages'[3] – and that darkness referred not just to historians' lack of knowledge of the people of the times but to their view of them. By contrast, the period before that in which Rome had ruled Europe was seen as a period of light, partly because it was better documented: an important consideration for a historian. Rome had brought Europe a common law, a common language and a common currency, but these gifts were too sophisticated for the primitives of Europe to value them. In spite of enjoying Roman civil infrastructure, Roman military protection and a Roman international trading zone, Europeans preferred to complain about their loss of freedom and self-determination. Eventually they harried the Romans into returning home, undid all the good that had been done and went back to sordid lives of gloom and conflict.

The idea of Rome's superiority and of Europe's inability to appreciate it lies at the heart of what historians used to call – with more confidence than today – 'Western civilization'.[4] For hundreds of years, it was understood that there had once been a Golden Age, an apex of enlightenment, and that it had been followed by a decline. Until the rise of historical studies in the late Middle Ages, that Golden Age was biblical but as history began to challenge theology, it was relocated into what was called the Classical age. It was therefore not unusual that observers should look back romantically to the Roman Empire as an instance of an alien but superior culture taking up residence in Europe, only to be rejected because of the people's refusal to recognize its excellence, an idea rooted in the rejection of Jesus only a few centuries earlier.

In Britain, the popular children's encyclopaedia that Enid Blyton was famously employed on in the early 1930s showed how this loss was conveyed to young British readers before the war. The Romans in Britain, it said, 'although stern masters, were wise and just' and their departure after nearly 400 years 'was a heavy misfortune, and brought about much unhappiness'.[5] In Germany, the departure of the Romans was more ambiguous because Germany itself had withstood invasion. Anyone studying history, philosophy or politics would therefore have learnt that although less affected by Rome, and thus less civilized, Germans had proved the equal of Rome and had thereby inherited the rights to the Roman succession right down to the present day.

The main inspiration for this narrative was the great nineteenth-century

German historian Leopold von Ranke. Ranke was a liberal rationalist who in the preface to his *History of the Latin and Teutonic Nations* (1824) maintained that history had no instructive or moral purpose and deserved to be studied for its own sake. His writing didn't aspire to history's traditional task 'of judging the past and instructing the present for the benefit of the future ages', he said; 'it seeks only to show what actually happened' ('wie es eigentlich gewesen'). In spite of those caveats, he predetermined the outcome of his *History* by stating 'I regard the Latin and Germanic peoples as a unit' and ended by allowing for the possibility that the union of those peoples was so blessed that his deciphering of its history might reveal the 'hand of God'. Pevsner regarded Ranke's word as definitive.

How that history was explained by German historians is illuminating. First, the tribes that had brought down the Roman Empire had to be shown as not supplanting Rome but as attempting to become Rome. Second, they had to be shown to be Germanic. That meant disposing of the eastern or Greek part of the Roman Empire (Byzantium) and concentrating instead on the western part. The problem was that the Western Empire now lay in the territory of the Franconians, who'd given their name to what we now call France ('Frankreich' in German): the realm of the Franks. German historians therefore had to stress that in spite of their name, the Franks weren't the same as the French: they were Visigoths, Burgundians and numerous other Germanic tribes, as well as the descendants of Romans. Post-Roman European history then turned into a story of preferred racial groups, starting with the Merovingians, coalescing through war into political unity and evolving towards statehood.[6]

Pepin the Elder served the Merovingian dynasty in the years around 600 as a mayor. His descendants gained power, enabling Pepin the Short to displace the Merovingian line and become the first Carolingian king in 751 (the name 'Carolingian' deriving from the name of his father, Carolus – or Charles, or Karl, or Karol – Martel). After his death in 768, this Pepin was succeeded jointly by his sons Carloman and Charles as kings of his inner and outer lands, but Carloman quickly abdicated and Charles became sole ruler in 771. Charles (or Karl or Karol or Carolus) expanded his kingdom to include what's now France, Germany, Austria, the Low Countries, Switzerland and northern Italy. He also established a new capital beside the Rhine at Aachen, an old Roman fort on what is now the French–German border. Here he built a Roman-style palace and other buildings that he decorated with imported Roman statuary. He also renamed himself Charles the Great or Karolus Magnus (hence 'Charle-magne', in the French-Latin of the day; 'Karl der Große' to the Germans).

Charlemagne is the central figure in this narrative. He was ambitious and visionary but oppressed, German historians argued, by the memory of a greater past: that of Rome. He therefore started to build a political culture that borrowed from Roman models. Its key was standardization, centralization and order, and through the agency of a civil service he sent inspectors to ensure that these virtues were kept up in the exercise of the law, the minting of currency and the administration of weights and measures. Charlemagne empowered local rulers in a way that increased regional dependence on the centre and initiated regular military campaigns that expanded his borders and developed the art of warfare. He also reformed education, broadening the range of teaching offered by his palace school.

By the year 800 Charlemagne was sufficiently pleased with his efforts that on Christmas Day, he went to Rome to have his authority sealed by the Pope, who rebranded him Charles Augustus. Thus Charlemagne became the first ruler of a revived Roman Empire of the West that, with a few convolutions, would turn into what later became known as the Holy Roman Empire and that survived until 1806. By a neat sleight of hand, Charlemagne also became the model for Prussia's King Wilhelm I, whom Bismarck rebranded as emperor of all Germany in the Hall of Mirrors at Versailles on 18 January 1871.

One problem with this idealization, for Germans, was that its exclusive German character was always being threatened by outsiders. Charlemagne's dynastic grip was brief. After his death in 814, his son Louis I (also known as Clovis[7] or Ludwig or Lewis) failed to pass the empire on intact and had to partition it among the three surviving children of his two marriages. Following a civil war, the Treaty of Verdun in 843 saw the creation of what would become a French kingdom to the west and a German kingdom to the east, with a short-lived third kingdom in between called Lotharingia (later Lorraine in French; Lothringen in German), a region rich in deposits of iron ore that its French and German neighbours would battle over for centuries after. This polarization of northern Europe into a French zone and a German zone either side of a third disputed zone became a permanent condition of the Continent, affecting the struggle not just for territory and resources but also for values, culture and identity. Thus Germany always had France alongside it, ruining the dream of its own hegemony.[8]

Another problem was that a millennial empire that Germans liked to think of as essentially German became cumbersome and ineffective. When Charlemagne's line expired in 911, the dukes of the East Frankish kingdom decided to elect a German – Conrad I, Duke of Franconia – as successor, and Conrad was followed by his son, Henry I, Duke of Saxony, and grandson, Otto I (Otto the Great). Otto marks the start of a crumbling of Germanic power. In 962 he went to Rome, as Charlemagne had done, to be crowned king of Rome by the Pope, but the sanctioning of him as Europe's ruler had the effect of diverting his attention, and that of his successors, away from domestic issues. German-Roman rulers now spent more time in Italy than at home, leaving Germany to be run by a council of nobles. Refusing to accept the principle of hereditary succession, the council insisted on retaining the right to elect monarchs of its own choosing through the mechanism of an electoral college[9] until the fifteenth century, when the Habsburg family became virtually dynastic rulers (though the electoral college remained in place). Thus an empire that was born in France and called itself Roman was ruled over by Germans who lacked the autonomy to manage it. In terms of effectiveness, that made German leadership of Europe a hollow inheritance and gave Germans a very different sense of their own history from the English, who could look back on a thousand years of increasing power, prosperity and competence.

Of particular concern to German historians was the fact that although the Holy Roman Empire lasted almost a millennium,[10] they saw its latter end as one of hopeless confusion and its passing as ignominious in being dissolved by a Frenchman: Napoleon. At best, they thought its loose consensual structure may have kept the peace among the hundreds of little states that it fractured into but only, if at all, because it was clunking and ineffective. What it hadn't done, they thought, was exercise efficient, centralized control. In addition, although the Holy Roman Empire was historically a German entity, many Germans felt betrayed by its complexity and multiple loyalties, especially in its continuing subservience to a Catholic emperor in the face of the rise of Lutheranism and Calvinism.[11] The Heiliges Römisches Reich, it seemed, had allowed other nations such as France and England (but also Holland and Denmark and Sweden) to overtake it. And so when Prussia and then Germany emerged in the nineteenth century as less complicated – and more Protestant – entities, there were great expectations among many educated Germans of at last participating in a simple, dynamic political programme that would reverse centuries of frustration and under-achievement.

The job of the history profession in late-nineteenth- and early-twentieth-century Germany was therefore a complicated one. In theory, German historians promoted history not as a servant of the state but as an autonomous science that weighed up evidence impartially and only fortuitously supported the political status quo. In practice, they took from Ranke a model that made sense of and supported Bismarck's Reich, reinterpreting that model in its most positive light and remedying its deficiencies.

By the time Pevsner started preparing to study history in his last year at school, German history had long established its principal methods and goals: mainly, the consideration of official documents and the elaboration of the story of the state. He was therefore not moving into a field that was either novel or innovatory. On the contrary, having made great strides in the mid-nineteenth century (and having profoundly influenced the teaching of history in other countries, notably England), German history by the 1920s had become institutionalized and conservative. Even where historians promoted the liberal values of constitutionality and freedom of speech, they usually also promoted the interests of Prussia's and Germany's ruling elite, even after the arrival of the social democratic movement in the 1860s had led some historians towards greater openness and independence. So united, in fact, was the history profession in its conservatism that in 1898, a Prussian law[12] banned Social Democrats from obtaining university posts and a lecturer at Freiburg in 1916 was pressed by his colleagues into giving up his teaching permit because of his opposition to right-wing elements while working for the Foreign Office in Berlin. That conservatism in the history profession would continue right through the Weimar years, the Nazi years and even into the 1960s.

This is the history Pevsner launched himself into and evidence of it can be found throughout his reading notes, made while preparing for university in his last year of school. That reading was extensive. He spent the autumn of 1920 working through various volumes of Bruno Gebhardt's[13] *Handbook of German History* (1901) – one of the great workhorses of German history and a book he'd make frequent use of in later life. In October he continued with Karl Hampe's[14] *German Imperial History in the Time of the Salian and Hohenstaufen Emperors* (1909). By the start of November he'd read excerpts from Bernhard Heil's *German Towns and Citizens in the Middle Ages*[15] and around the end of 1920 he was completing Volumes 2–4 of Karl Lamprecht's[16] *German History* (1891–1893), which dealt with the years 800–1500. That meant that before his university education had even begun, Pevsner was already steeped in questions relating to Germany and in particular to German mediaevalism, the period historians were starting to see as defining Germany's essential 'Geist'. (The fact that he read all these works in alphabetical order of author suggests he was working through a reading list supplied by Leipzig University.) As for Ranke, he'd already read him as part of the school syllabus.

Pevsner's study of art history was motivated by different factors. The fact that his parents' Schwägrichenstraße apartment was adorned with the latest books and magazines on art, as well as the paintings, small sculptures, ceramics and good furniture that his mother bought and that his father paid for, meant that an interest in art already felt like a natural counterpart to a cultured life. Art history was also, as Nikolai had shown in his essay about van Gogh, a way to understand and be associated with what at the time was seen as the 'romance' of an artistic temperament without actually taking on the risk of being an artist. But more than this, art history was an exciting and still relatively new academic subject in which German and German-speaking scholars were leading the world in documenting and interpreting the evolution of artistic activity and in developing appropriate modes of analysis. To study art history in the Germanic world at the time was therefore to belong to the winning team in a great international race to colonize and make sense of the past.

Art history particularly appealed to Pevsner because it brought professionalism and discipline to a field he felt was otherwise mired by dilettanteism and speculation. In a BBC radio talk he gave in October 1952,[17] he said that amateur scholars might write with more elegance and vitality than specialists because they had more practical experience of life and literature but were likely 'to venture on wild theories in the absence of sufficient information of what has already been ascertained by others' – a judgement that may reflect how he'd regarded his mother's interest in Guyau. Art historians could bring authority to the discussion of individual works but, more importantly, they provided a system for defining the structural relationship of all works, and it was that that made art history an academic subject.

The formation of art history as a discipline was something Pevsner credited in his radio talk to the Swiss art historian Jacob Burckhardt, who'd studied general history under Ranke in Berlin and who'd first promoted the rules of art history in his *History of the Renaissance* (1867) – 'to this day the best textbook we possess, a record surely of durability'.[18] Burckhardt had established the classification of art on stylistic grounds as the basis of all art history, Pevsner said,[19] and explained that this was fortified in the 1890s by three other art historians, all working on roughly the same approach. The first of these was Burckhardt's student and successor Heinrich Wölfflin in Basel. Pevsner later wrote of him: 'Wölfflin was a matter of course. I read him while still at school. The conception that the history of art is the history of what and how the eye sees was easily absorbed and had something very tempting.'[20] Wölfflin, he said, argued that different epochs saw and therefore represented objects differently – Ancient Greece seeing things in isolation, for example, and the Baroque age seeing things in ensemble. To find a common language for these many variations, Wölfflin therefore limited the art historian's job to identifying the characteristics that important works of the same period shared, and used this method to define the differences between Renaissance and Baroque art. Burckhardt's other principal followers, Pevsner continued, were August Schmarsow in Leipzig and Alois Riegl in Vienna and both used essentially the same method as Wölfflin but applied it to different subjects: Riegl concentrating on Late Antiquity and Early Christianity, and Schmarsow on the analysis of historical architecture.[21]

The point of Pevsner's radio talk in 1952 was to persuade British universities to teach art history at a time when it still wasn't on the syllabus, and he presented the subject in terms of its own evolution as a discipline on a par with science. He showed that art history had developed different theoretical approaches but also argued that it could function as a background and parallel to general history, which is what it had always meant to him. What he didn't do was suggest that art history could make the pulse race – presumably because he didn't feel the case for teaching should depend on emotion. But this is how it had originally affected him, and he'd said as much in an early draft of his talk. While criticizing art-historical research that produced results no one could see the point of, he'd written:

> It can be fascinating to read, say, how different epochs represented death or justice but we may in the end still have only a cataloguing of species and subspecies *instead of something stirring and illuminating*. [Author's italics.]

When he came to give the talk, however, the words 'something stirring and illuminating' were deleted. In spite of this, those words reflected what the subject meant to him when he first contemplated his future career.[22] That's because it had been brought to life for him not on the printed page but in the lecture hall, in a university course he'd attended while still at school. That course was given by a man whose name has been written out of mainstream art history and whom Pevsner failed to mention in his BBC talk but whom he later praised as the person who'd 'impressed me most'[23] of anyone he'd ever come across in the field – perhaps the most charismatic art historian of his age in Germany.

6

University

The university course Pevsner audited in his last year of school was given by Wilhelm Pinder, who'd just spent his first summer as Leipzig's newly appointed chair of art history. How Pinder was chosen for this post and how he fitted into the tradition of teaching at Leipzig is something we'll come back to in a later chapter. At this point, we need to see what impact he had on Pevsner while Pevsner was still at school and in the following year, before Pevsner came directly under his wing at Leipzig.

Pevsner heard Pinder lecture in the winter of 1920–1921, around the time of his nineteenth birthday. The subject was 'Attitudes to Art in Different Periods'[1] and Pevsner took extensive notes – on Masaccio, van Eyck, the character of German art and other topics. He was so excited by the course and so grateful for being allowed to attend it that at Christmas he sent Pinder a bunch of flowers. They probably then met, with Annie as chaperone, to plan Pevsner's academic path. At that meeting Pinder would have advised the young man to spend a semester each under three of art history's greats – Heinrich Wölfflin at Munich, Adolph Goldschmidt at Berlin, and Rudolf Kautzsch at Frankfurt am Main – before returning to Leipzig to begin doctoral work that he himself would supervise. He probably also advised Pevsner to attend a colloquium he'd be holding on mediaeval architecture at Berlin the following winter.

Pinder had arrived in Leipzig from Breslau (Wrocław) University in the spring of 1920, shortly before his forty-second birthday. He was a specialist in German mediaeval sculpture, a still novel branch of art-historical study at the time, and had a reputation for being able to enthral academic and lay audiences. A sense of his magnetism can be reconstructed from notes made by Annie the following year. On Pinder's advice, Pevsner had moved to Munich for his first university semester and in June, while still there, asked his mother to attend a Pinder lecture for him in Leipzig that he couldn't get to. She went and took notes, writing on sheets of waste headed paper from the Swedish Fur Trading Company, the company Pevsner's father was in the process of winding up.

The lecture was not about art history as such but about Oswald Spengler's view of art history. Spengler had caused a sensation three years earlier with the publication of a vast prognosis of doom for Western civilization, *Der Untergang des Abendlandes* (*The Decline of the West*). Spengler's writing was characteristic of the Expressionist mentality of its time: brilliant but deranged. Rooted in the millennial view that coupled Germany to Ancient Rome, he'd argued that cultures were living organisms that went through phases of childhood, adulthood and old age, the most successful of them overtaking other civilizations before lapsing into decay and being overtaken themselves. This had happened before – 'Classical civilization rose like a giant in the Imperial age, with all the trappings of youth and strength and fullness' – and was now going to be repeated in 'another decline ... that will take place during the first centuries of the next millennium but that can already be seen and sensed all round us today: the decline of the West.'[2]

Spengler's vast vision of successive epochs all struggling to find their own voice and style made him a favourite commentator in the intense debate about destiny that transfixed Germany after the First World War. In a single sentence he could speak of the 'majestic wave-cycles' of 'Aryans, Mongols, Germans, Celts, Parthians, Franks, Carthaginians, Berbers and Bantus', link 'the head of Amenemhet III (the so-called Hyksos Sphinx of Tanis) with the domes of Hagia Sophia and the paintings of Titian' and invoke the Babylonians, Indians, Chinese and Mexicans in a way that made the Eurocentrism of Western politics and scholarship look petty. On the other hand he was obsessed by the minutiae of Germany's past and future and spoke unpredictably – sometimes rationally, sometimes mystically – about the inability of his fellow Germans to see things as he saw them. But how sound was he? Pevsner and his mother were both intrigued to discover Pinder's opinion, not least because both of them already knew Pinder and respected his views.

'My darling honey!' Annie wrote to her son on 26 June 1921. 'Today, Sunday, your excellent letter arrived. It appeared as ever and as ever it was very enjoyable. The scarlet fever business is over with, then: that's good news.' She went on:

> The reply to your Pinder query is somewhat delayed because the lecture took place only yesterday evening. Mrs Bergmann [Ernst Bergmann's wife] and I had drifted to the Women's High School and from there to the University and found the assembled Fichte Society community in Lecture Hall No. 36. Otherwise, we would have wandered to the Volkshall in the hope of finding salvation somewhere else. Nobody would give me any information. Just then, our friend Pinder entered, youthful and in good spirits. He talked like a movie, exceedingly quickly and in incredible haste, hardly leaving himself time to breathe: you know, that breathlessness that right away condemns the pencil to powerlessness. No thought of note-taking at the overwhelming profusion of words and examples. I must thus content myself to fill these sheets, which should have served as a verbatim record for you, from memory, with the help of just a few poor notes.

The theme of the talk was 'The Fine Arts as Cultural Symbol' and Annie summarized it by quoting or alluding to what Pinder had said and then adding her own comments.

> Spengler's work is scientific poetry but doesn't stand up to scientific criticism. That's not a criticism but an appreciation. I couldn't have written it. Anybody who's read him

absolutely launches into a debate . . . The pessimism is a bit like Schopenhauer's. The result is that no one person can judge the complete works; one can only judge one's own field and extrapolate from there to other works.

From the field of art history, there's no doubt that Spengler regards the barriers between cultures as insurmountable, but not so the barriers between epochs . . . In Spengler's opinion, a Westerner should comprehend and feel each epoch of his own culture but not necessarily those of any other.[3] Our friend Pinder knows archaeologists who . . . know . . . every tiny corner of the Parthenon frieze but reject and misunderstand the German Baroque.

[As for Spengler's reading of art history], he only seems to know Riegl[4] [the Viennese art historian credited with formulating the idea that ages and nations have an internal dynamic – a 'Kunstwollen' – that expresses itself in its own artistic style, and that it was the job of the art historian to articulate]. Of other [art historians] he has no idea. With great aplomb he advances notions that experts have long taken for granted. He pushes open doors that are already arrogantly open: that the Germans of the twelfth century couldn't achieve anything, for instance – and here, quickly, a small aside about Kunstwollen and a swipe at horrible Gothic people! To us modern Germans, man in the art of the thirteenth century is of course beautiful but [Spengler] finds Egyptian and Negro art [more] magnificent. Watteau would have been incomprehensible to the Greeks, says Spengler; but so would Rembrandt have been to the artists of the Naumburg sculptures.

Annie continued by noting a string of Pinder's criticisms: of Spengler's distinction between the Apollonian's three-dimensionality and disdain for history and the Faustian's more complex sense of space and respect for history ('Quite wrong: the Baroque demolished [mediaeval] churches and replaced them with Baroque churches . . . [and] Michelangelo demolished perfect frescoes to make room for his own works'); of Spengler's conviction that Carolingian culture is really a mixture of Arabic and magic ('the Cathedral of Aachen is a mosque'); of his belief in the superiority of Greek over Romanesque architecture in its mastery of space ('Obviously Spengler has never seen a work of Romanesque architecture, otherwise he would have to have felt its strong corporality'); of his assertion that the representation of nudes ceased in the Renaissance ('Quite wrong: Michelangelo's works and ceilings are full of nudes'); that the art of Rubens is green-blue because it's Catholic and that Protestant art is brown ('Quite wrong: Rubens is red'); that distant scenes are always given a blue tinge but never those close up ('Quite wrong: see Grünewald and Turner with red and yellow tinges in the wide distance and the grey of the antique right in front'); that Michelangelo is for Spengler the awakening of the antique ('Quite wrong'). Then she finished:

So, my honey, these are my notes. He still quoted hundreds of examples that I couldn't write down in the immense speed and because I unfortunately neglected to read the requisite Spengler chapter beforehand I know nothing about the subject and besides I'd spent the whole day in Frohburg and came to the lecture just in time, dead tired and terribly annoyed about disagreeable things going on in Frohburg.

About all these tomorrow or the next day. Also the reply to your letter. For today only this report, which I hope will give you some idea of the content of the lecture.

Now the Michels are coming!

Kisses from Dad and your Muo

It's clear from this fizzy letter that Pinder was a captivating speaker – and that Annie was an attentive listener. She took education seriously and had strong feelings about her son's likes and dislikes. Although he'd excelled at school and had ended up as the best student of the year, she'd protested strongly at the valetudinarian address he'd given at his graduation ceremony a few months earlier in March 1921. On that occasion, shortly after his nineteenth birthday, he'd talked about his admiration for Thomas Mann, and Annie, who'd attended the talk, had been upset, because she felt Mann's conservatism made him an unsuitable mentor. Pinder, three years younger and 'our friend', was livelier, fresher and much more disarming.

Pevsner didn't attend Pinder's Spengler lecture in June 1921 because he was in Munich. During that first semester of his university career, he attended a history colloquium by Steinberger on the relationship between individual states and the totality of Germany in German history;[5] a course by Paul Wolters, Munich's professor of classical archaeology, on the representation of the gods in Greek art; at least three art-history courses: two by Max Hauttmann, a generalist, on the history of craft production and a related series of stylistic-criticism exercises for beginners; and a course by Wölfflin, Munich's chair of art history, on the art of the Italian Renaissance. (He may also have heard lectures by Hans Rose, later persecuted by the Nazis for his homosexuality, and on nineteenth- and twentieth-century art by Hugo Kehrer, Munich's professor of mediaeval and later art history and a specialist in Spanish art.)

Munich and Wölfflin didn't provide Pevsner with the encouraging start his discovery of Pinder had promised, however. Wölfflin, who was Swiss, had become uncomfortable teaching in Germany. He'd resigned his chair in Berlin before the war because he'd found the climate under the Kaiser inhospitable to modern and foreign ideas, and now, after the war, was becoming even more oppressed by the country's growing chauvinism.[6] Although his lectures had been popular in Berlin, in Munich he'd started delegating his teaching to assistants, and at least one student who'd enrolled there to hear him – Rudolf Wittkower – went away again because he found Wölfflin stiff and remote.[7]

But where Wittkower felt disappointed, Pevsner felt inadequate. Wölfflin would stress to his students that art history required practical and not just academic skills. 'The work of art history begins with seeing and ends in describing', another former student said of Wölfflin's legacy. 'Seeing is the necessary step towards describing, just as describing is the test of seeing. Both of these operations, at once extremely simple and extremely complex, are preliminary steps in any serious "explanation" of a work of art.'[8] Wölfflin's groundedness seems to have defeated Pevsner at first. In July 1921, as the semester drew to a close, he confided in his diary:

> It's really sad. Pevsner lacks a feel for spatial qualities and thereby any sense of the particular values of buildings. It's something I don't believe he could learn. What's more, he's got an underdeveloped memory for form and colour, and he can't remember anything, so he's quite unable to draw comparisons.

Pevsner's semester in Munich unsettled him in other ways too. Munich was his first experience of living on his own and he was having to put up with conditions far more primitive than he'd been used to in Leipzig. His rooms, at Augustenstraße 3/III, were bare and poorly furnished. He didn't have a reading lamp at his desk and he couldn't concentrate easily on his work because the summer heat meant he needed to keep the windows open, which made the room noisy. Trams rattled by night and day. A neighbour on one side, a woman, whistled all the time and a neighbour on the other side, a man, practised singing exercises. Food was still rationed and the bread he hoarded and lived off quickly went stale. And then he caught the scarlet fever that was going round the district.

For relief, he'd visit friends of his parents and go on bicycle tours. Sometimes he'd look at places connected with Thomas Mann, on other occasions he'd put his bicycle on the train and go to look at church sculpture elsewhere – in Regensburg and Augsburg, for example. He'd dress in green warm-weather knickerbockers for these trips and make piles of sandwiches for himself filled with lard (not something his father would have approved of), which made his wrist ache when he tried to spread it.

Pevsner's discomfort in Munich was not only domestic. His semester coincided with the visible collapse of Germany's economy, the start of hyperinflation and worsening political unrest. Four days before the end of the war, Social Democrats had declared Bavaria a free state and toppled the Wittelsbach monarchy; five months later, the Bavarian Soviet Republic was proclaimed. That in turn was brought down a month later, at a cost of 700 lives, by right-wing army loyalists and two divisions of Freikorps. In this polarized political climate, several extremist parties were created. One, based in Munich, was called the German Workers' Party (Deutsche Arbeiterpartei or DAP), a grouping that under the influence of one of its members – an army spy called Adolf Hitler – changed its name in 1920 to the National Socialist German Workers' Party (Nationalsozialistische Deutsche Arbeiterpartei or NSDAP), or Nazi Party for short. By 1921, during Pevsner's first university semester, that army spy was becoming one of the Party's most effective rabble rousers, building membership from fifty-five when he'd first joined in 1919 to over 3,000 two years later. Pevsner couldn't have been unaware of the Nazis during his time in Munich, or of the hysterical tone of their public rallies, any of which he may have watched or read about in the papers.

After returning to Leipzig for the summer, Pevsner moved to Berlin in the autumn, to study under Adolph Goldschmidt. In preparation, he read *Religious Architecture of the West*[9] by Georg Dehio and Gustav von Bezold but refused to read Émile Mâle's[10] *Religious Art*[11] (about art in France up to the end of the Middle Ages), because it was only available in French. Pevsner had studied French at school but wouldn't use it, in protest at France's treatment of Germany following the war. He regarded the French and the French language as detestable. He therefore got his mother to read the book instead and make notes for him in German.

Pevsner arrived in Berlin on 18 October and, anxious perhaps about his performance in Munich the previous term, launched himself into a colossal programme of study. Over the next few months, he took four archaeology courses (three by Hans Dragendorff on general background and a fourth by Ferdinand Noack on Greek art since Alexander the Great). He also took two philosophy courses (by Alois Riehl on the history of philosophy and Wilhelm Spranger on Kant) and no fewer than eight courses in art history. These included two by Oskar Wulff, Berlin's professor of East European art history, focusing on the evolution of the fine arts, two by Werner Weisbach on Italian Baroque painting and the representation of interior space between 1400 and 1700, and three by Adolph Goldschmidt, Berlin's chair of art history, on representations of the birth of Christ, Dutch painting of the fifteenth and sixteenth centuries, and Albrecht Dürer. In addition he attended Pinder's colloquium on mediaeval architecture, heard other single lectures, including Goldschmidt on Naumburg Cathedral, and read Goldschmidt's 1910 book *The Gospels in Goslar Town Hall*.[12]

During his time in Berlin, Pevsner visited his aunt, Ida Pollack, and her son Heinrich, and would have seen his grandmother Jeannette, who now lived with Ida, though he said nothing about her in his later writings. Heinrich remembers him being a surprisingly entertaining older cousin.

At home we had a wall clock that chimed a bit of the Big Ben tune each quarter of an hour and completed the full tune on the hour. The clock came from my [late] father. My mother didn't like it much: the melody bothered her and luckily we were able to turn it off. But when Nika came to visit us we'd turn it on. He made up a game for me that made use of it. When the clock chimed we had to make faces as if we'd been bewitched and then keep the face until the quarter of an hour was over. Of course, he had to show he could do what he challenged me to do and so he became a victim of his own invention. My mother and I enjoyed his visits to Berlin. We liked listening to him when he played the piano, even though he didn't think he was any good. We also went on walks with him through the parks and castles of Potsdam. Historical places that normally wouldn't have got much attention from us were brought alive by his knowledge and the way he explained them.

While entertaining and instructing his young cousin, Pevsner discovered from his aunt that opposition to Jews emanated not just from the extreme right but from the liberal-minded quarters of his own university. Her late husband Walter, who'd died unexpectedly in 1914, had been a law lecturer who should have been able to get a teaching position at Berlin but was barred because of the quota system that the university operated against Jews.[13] Heinrich, aged only six, had already taken steps to protect himself from this apartheid:

> There were terrible restrictions on Jews before Hitler. This is one of the reasons I became a Christian. My father was asked by the government to be baptized – all the Jews were asked to become baptized and to take the state church under the emperor. The emperor wanted Jews to be baptized and our culture is a Christian culture and if you want all the rights and no restrictions, you had to be a Christian. My father never took baptism but he felt that life might be easier for me if I did. This decision was made very early: he died before I was two years old. I heard about Jesus when I was five years old and when I was six I had to attend school and got permission to attend Christian education: my mother had nothing against it, because of what my father had said. And then came a time when class notes were given out to everyone and I had none. I asked why and they said 'You're still registered as a Jew.' So I had to convert. There were many who became Christian for this reason. Heine said conversion was 'the ticket of admission to our culture'.[14]

It's not surprising, in this context, that what Pevsner had seen in Munich and what he now learnt from his aunt in Berlin exacerbated his worries about his own identity as the son of Russian-Jewish parents – 'little Russians' ('kleine Russen'), as he called them. He therefore took steps to divest himself of his parents' religion by going to a cleric in Potsdam – the historic and religious centre of the state of Brandenburg, which Berlin had grown out of – from whom he took instruction, got baptized and became officially registered as a member of the Lutheran (Evangelisch) Church, the mainstream faith of northern Germany. Shortly afterwards, he took steps to change his name to Nikolaus. His years as a Jew were over.

Pevsner wrote later that he'd taken the conversion 'seriously enough'[15] at the time, but since there's no evidence of his having been interested in religion before that date, it's fair to assume that his conversion was driven more by practicalities than by theology. Fear must have been a major factor, in view of the rate at which anti-Semitism was starting to colour German politics; so too was the fact that everyone else seemed to be converting. But a third factor was negative reaction to the greater visibility of Jews in the new Germany. After a century in which they'd carefully tailored their identities to suit German tastes, German Jews were now becoming more evident in public life – in art, music, journalism, film-making and business – and more confident. At the same time, impoverished Jewish immigrants, dispossessed by post-war instability in the newly emerging countries of Eastern Europe and the newly created Soviet Union, were now arriving in Germany in droves. These immigrants were very obviously alien – alien in appearance, alien in clothing and speech, very often living from hand to mouth, and reliant on soup kitchens and charity – and their presence undid the efforts at assimilation that Germany's Jewish community had been committed to for the previous century. Jewish Germans disliked the newcomers as much as non-Jewish Germans did and although legislation brought in by the Weimar Government meant that Jews no longer needed to give up their religion, in practice thousands continued to do so, in order to prove their Germanness and separateness from people they regarded as Slavic Jewish peasants.[16]

The individual who urged Pevsner most passionately to take on the protection of Christianity was probably Carola Kurlbaum. 'After my sister passed her Abitur in 1921,' recalled Lola's sister, Marianne Kockel, 'she was sent for a year to Kassel, to a school for household studies, as was proper – a boarding school, a Zimmersche foundation.'[17] That school was the first of several such institutions created in Germany by a theologian, Karl Friedrich Zimmer, who also founded the Evangelical Diakonia Association (which still exists). The school opened in 1894 with the mission of awakening a sense of social consciousness in its boarders and giving them the tools for their future duties as married or unmarried Protestant women. Its curriculum included courses on Samaritanism, charity and civic education.[18]

Two years after the death of Lola's mother and Lola's distancing of herself, she and Nikolaus had resumed their friendship, apparently without their parents knowing. That friendship became increasingly important to both of them during Lola's year away. While in Kassel, according to her sister,

> she conducted a secret correspondence with Nika, and he also visited her secretly. They were both nineteen. And they got engaged secretly. When she was twelve, my sister had got a small golden ring from my father with some greenish precious stone on it, and she always wore it. And she made it a present for Nika and he always carried it in his wallet – because he couldn't put it on, after all – and that was their secret engagement.[19]

Lola's year in Kassel overlapped with Nikolaus's year in Munich and Berlin, and since he became a Lutheran while she was at her missionary boarding school, it's likely that it was as a result of what she was taught that she came to see it as her duty to try and save his soul for Jesus, just as her soul – Jewish on her mother's side – had had to be saved.

On Lola's return to Leipzig in the spring of 1922, she and Nikolaus revealed their secret friendship and became officially engaged. They then enrolled, on 28 April, as students at Leipzig University, she as Student No. 1,015 and he as Student No. 1,016, which means that when they attended the university registry together, he gallantly stood to one side while she handed in her application first. Thanks to his conversion he was now able to complete the personal file the university kept on him in a way that made him appear to have always been a Christian. 'On 30 January 1902 was I, Nikolai Bernhard Leon Pevsner, of the Evangelical-Lutheran faith, born in Leipzig', he testified, ensuring that this future historian's origins didn't appear on the record. It was a disguise he kept up throughout his life. In a BBC radio programme in November 1954, he said of himself 'My origins are in a part of Germany which is Protestant and in this country I would certainly be called very low church indeed', much as the brother of the French specialist Victor Klemperer, whose Nazi-era diaries were published posthumously in 1995, prefaced his doctoral thesis with the note 'I was born the son of a country cleric' when his father was in fact the Rabbi of Landsberg.[20]

Pevsner may very well have converted, in addition, to please Wilhelm Pinder but though Pinder may have smiled, he would have been unimpressed by such externals. What Pinder was interested in was race, not religion, which was fast emerging in Germany as the key to the most pressing scholarly questions in the humanities. Pinder thought race was so important that it coloured the way his own subject was taught and understood. Twelve years later, Ernst Kitzinger, who studied under Pinder at Munich in 1934, remembered him making gibes about Erwin Panofsky, who was Jewish, and saying of him: 'Whoever doesn't see this hasn't got it in his blood',[21] but Pinder was already talking about these ideas in the early 1920s and went on to include them in one of his most important books in 1927.[22] There he argued that cultural development was predetermined by underlying biological forces, again stressing race. Religion, precisely because it was capable of being acquired, was therefore a triviality for him. Pevsner, for all his wish to become more acceptable, as he saw it, within Germany, was therefore no better off.

Herman Gundersheimer, who became professor of art history at the American University in Washington and who'd studied under Pinder at Leipzig, was struck by the impact Pinder's thinking had had on Pevsner, who was one year ahead of him:

> In Leipzig . . . Pevsner was still remembered as very close to Pinder. It was known that he had very close professional and personal connections with him. It was said that [Pevsner] stressed that he wasn't Jewish, which seemed very strange to those who knew him as the son of a Jewish family . . . I only met him on one occasion but I remember distinctly that my fellow students told me not to be surprised about his detached attitude, which they ascribed to his reserve towards Jews.[23]

'My mother had, I think, nothing against it, but it must have hurt my father', Pevsner said later of his conversion. 'However, as I have said before, he was much too good to object or indeed say anything.' His mother must also have been too good to say anything, otherwise Pevsner would have been able to say definitively how she felt. To her niece Ellen Dreessen, the daughter of one of her three brothers, she said in the late 1930s 'You're the last member of the Perlmann family not baptized: promise you won't be.'[24]

7

Leipzig

Pevsner spent four semesters under Pinder at Leipzig University. The first was in the summer of 1922, something he'd been anticipating keenly for a year and a half. Naturally, he attended all three courses that Pinder was offering: a beginners' course that was one of only two that Lola signed up for, an advanced course, and a third on artistic representation in the Middle Ages. He also took three courses on Hellenistic art and other topics by Leipzig's professor of classical archaeology, Franz Studniczka, two courses on aesthetics and on art and artistic creativity by the philosopher Johannes Volkelt, and a series by the modern historian Erich Brandenburg on general history between the Congress of Vienna in 1815 and the unification of Germany in 1871.

The following semester, winter 1922–1923, Lola took only one course at Leipzig. Pevsner, by contrast, was busy at Frankfurt am Main, taking two classes on the history of portraiture and on German Baroque sculpture with Leo Bruhns (who'd take over Leipzig's chair of art history from Pinder in 1927 and edit Pinder's *Collected Writings* in 1938), two more with the archaeologist Hans Schrader, one with Max Sauerlandt on the art of the goldsmith, and two with Frankfurt's chair of art history, Rudolf Kautzsch, on German Baroque architecture and on markings in art.

Back in Leipzig for the summer semester of 1923, Pevsner took ten courses while Lola took two – the last she'd ever take. He then took another six courses in the winter of 1923–1924 and three in the summer of 1924, while finishing his dissertation. Of all the twenty-eight lecture courses and seminars that Pevsner attended at Leipzig, a third – nine – were given by Pinder.

In addition to his art-history major, Pevsner took an ambitious number of history classes. In the three semesters he spent at Leipzig after returning from Frankfurt, he studied Saxon seventeenth- and eighteenth-century history with Rudolf Kötzschke and took a course on the theme of political diplomacy and its motives with Fritz Rörig, who'd been doing work on the Baltic city of Lübeck to illustrate the impact of the Hanseatic League on Germany's late-mediaeval economy. These courses were followed during the winter by a lecture series given by Siegmund Hellmann, Leipzig's professor of mediaeval history, on general mediaeval history from the dissolution of the Carolingian Empire to the end of the Crusades, as well as exercises on Gregory of Tours and French history in the sixth century. In his last semester, he took three more courses, including another by Hellmann on German history up to the end of the Middle Ages. It was an exceptional commitment to learning.

To look at how the history and art history that Pevsner studied at Leipzig affected his development, it's worth looking first at how these subjects themselves developed at Leipzig. Leipzig University, founded in 1409, was slow in introducing history as an academic discipline, partly because of the way that academic and political aspirations clashed. In 1830 the state of Saxony had granted the university autonomy and this had led to an immediate expansion in its scientific and medical departments, in competition with Prussia, where Education Minister Wilhelm von Humboldt had twenty years earlier set national standards for educational reform when founding the University of Berlin. Some twenty years later, after the failure of the Liberal Revolution in 1848, Saxony clawed back much of this autonomy,[1] leaving the university caught between a wish to modernise and a wish to conserve, both of which worked against the interests of the humanities. It wasn't until 1877 that Saxony thought it worth appointing a chair of history at Leipzig.

By contrast, Berlin – committed to academic autonomy and methodological discipline from the start – had offered Leopold von Ranke a professorship in history in 1825 and a chair in 1840 so he could expand Humboldt's vision. At Berlin, Ranke had established the basic procedures for the 'scientific' study of history: dependence on reliable and testable source material and the use of rigorously objective and transparent ways of interpreting them – albeit coloured, as we've seen, by nineteenth-century Prussian biases. Ranke encouraged historians to focus on small, manageable topics, trace causative relations between events, avoid the luxury of generalization and speculation, and hold back from trying to second-guess history's meaning, since if a meaning existed, it should be self-revealing and not imposed. These ideas, and his seminar method of teaching, influenced the entire Germany university system.

Ranke developed his methodology as a corrective to the equally influential Georg Hegel, who died in 1831. Hegel, a philosopher-mystic who'd studied theology, constructed a philosophical system that explicitly supported Prussian patriotism. Unlike Ranke, he believed in the legitimacy of abstractions and generalizations, of parcelling up periods of time and groups of people, and of identifying inherent qualities. He thought a universal argument was working its way through history and revealing itself in the ideas and expressions of young cultures as they gained supremacy over older ones.

This process of alternating thesis and antithesis, Hegel believed, would eventually lead to a perfect synthesis: the ideal society – an idea that attracted Prussian militarists as it treated the idea of German supremacy as an inevitablity and one that justified all means, making war and those who waged it the virtuous tools of cultural progress. Ranke, also a patriot, regarded Hegel's thinking as an intellectual abuse. As far as inherency and inevitability were concerned, he insisted that all events were individual to themselves: 'All epochs are immediate to God', he said, meaning there was no obvious progress or evolution through time.

The history institute that Leipzig's first chair of history, Carl von Noorden, set up in the late 1870s was constructed along the lines of Ranke's, but what gave it its special identity and distinguished it from Berlin was the established pre-eminence of Leipzig's scientific work, particularly in the field of psychology. Pioneering experimental research in physiology and psychology had begun at Leipzig under Ernst Heinrich Weber, who lectured on 'psychophysics' from 1857, and that work was carried forward by Wilhelm Wundt, who taught courses on consciousness from October 1875.

Like Forel, Wundt dominated his field in his time but is now largely forgotten except by specialist historians. His reputation might have survived longer had he pushed for experimental psychology to become more independent and focused, as it became in the USA; instead, he remained a philosopher all his life (and stayed within the faculty of philosophy), attempting to produce a unified field theory that was implausibly grand and all-embracing, and insisting that mental activity was unrelated to physical processes in the brain, which meant his most important observations weren't truly testable or capable of prediction.[2]

Wundt was nonetheless of exceptional interest, especially because of the laboratory work and demonstrations he carried out in the Institute for Experimental Psychology that he established in Leipzig in 1878 – the world's first. Some 17,000 students and others are said to have attended his afternoon lectures, partly to see the strange new instruments he designed for measuring flows of consciousness.[3] One of those students was Karl Lamprecht.

Lamprecht attended Wundt's lectures on philosophy while taking his doctorate in 1877–1878 and became involved with him again when he returned to Leipzig to teach in 1891. By then, Lamprecht had devised a broad, contextual theory of history writings that saw generalization and interpretation, both of which Ranke had warned against, as necessary and appropriate. Although accused of sloppy thinking, Lamprecht felt history was too complicated to be broken down into discrete events and gave more emphasis to cultural expression, which he saw as a shorthand for historical truth. This provoked a debate in historical circles that left Lamprecht somewhat isolated as a controversialist.

Lamprecht formulated his approach at Leipzig through the creation in 1909 of an Institute for Cultural and Universal History.[4] Where Ranke and his followers were, at most, interested in the motivation of individual leaders, Lamprecht looked at the psychology of population groups: Massenpsychologie. This ought to have resonated with the ideas of Wilhelm Dilthey, the philosopher who in 1883 had challenged historians to go beyond the narrow focus of political history and look at the social context of ideas: Kulturwissenschaft or Geisteswissenschaft – the science of culture or the science of the spirit. Instead, Lamprecht was criticized by historians who regarded his emphasis on social history as provincial and unworthy. In 1916, the year after Lamprecht's death, the conservative mediaevalist Georg von Below expressed the hope that 'the monster of a major science of sociology will never be born', adding later that sociology was something historians could do without. Such was Lamprecht's impact at

Leipzig, however, that when Wilhelm Wundt gave his final lecture in 1917 at the age of 85, he chose to speak not about personality or behaviour or the science of the mind but about national or racial psychology: Völkerpsychologie. Through Wundt, Lamprecht had turned the study of racial behaviour and thought into an approved academic subject.

With the exception of Rörig, the historians Pevsner came into contact with at Leipzig were men who were thirty to forty years older than he was and whose ideas had been shaped – for and against – by the presence of Wundt and Lamprecht. Kötzschke, a Protestant, had taken his doctorate under Lamprecht, who then installed him to look after the Seminar für Landesgeschichte und Siedlungskunde. Since he was Lamprecht's protégé and Lamprecht was disliked by the faculty, Kötzschke didn't receive a full professorship until 1930 but he did carry out formative work in the relatively new field of economic history, especially as it applied to rural life in Saxony in the Middle Ages and to Saxony in the eighteenth and nineteenth centuries. Controversial at first, his work, with Lamprecht's, laid the groundwork for 'scientific' claims by Germany to territory beyond its eastern borders, on the basis of genealogy, art, architectural styles and other newly fashionable data.[5]

Erich Brandenburg, also Protestant, had arrived in Leipzig at the same time as Kötzschke, in 1894, and had already been installed for twenty years when Pevsner arrived. Unlike Kötzschke, Brandenberg was interested in big historical personalities and milestones, and in parallels between Germany's fortunes during the Reformation and under Bismarck.

The much younger Rörig, a Catholic, only taught at Leipzig from 1918–1923, but instructed Pevsner in the workings of the state and the proper use and interpretation of archive material.

Of all the history staff at Leipzig, it was probably Hellmann whom Pevsner had the greatest investment in, if only because Hellmann taught from his own textbook (*The Middle Ages to the End of the Crusades*),[6] which Pevsner read three times in quick succession between 20 April and 28 May 1924, in preparation for the oral examination Hellmann would give him and that would partly gain him his doctorate. According to Hermann Heimpel, a student and later junior colleague of Hellmann's at Leipzig, Hellmann had been an exemplary educationalist in his previous university post in Munich. His textbook was part of the world history series edited by Ludo Moritz Hartmann, an Austrian who'd studied under the historian Theodor Mommsen at Berlin and who was central to efforts to make Austria into a democracy by modernizing its education system, as Mommsen had done in Germany.[7] Hellmann was a committed nationalist but was also on the political left. Because of this, when Saxony – having become a Socialist republic after the war – gave him his professorship at Leipzig in 1923, its history faculty protested and he was received 'frostily'.[8]

Like Gebhardt's *Handbook of German History*, Hellmann's textbook was a substantial work and far beyond what was available to English students at the time in its scope, professionalism and presentation. It was set out in a way that emphasized its scientific character. It declared its sources in advance, assessed their meaning and significance in a four-page introduction, listed other writings on the subject and added a statement of intention. Chapters began with a list of sources and commentaries, and four general bibliographies were included that recommended French books for French history and English books for English history in addition to listing German publications, an indication that proficiency in other European languages was assumed – a notion still foreign to English scholarship a century ago. This transparency was meant to demonstrate the openness of Hellmann's method and the grandeur of history as a modern and democratic science – a 'Wissenschaft'.

In spite of that, *The Middle Ages to the End of the Crusades* contained features that were not wholly scientific, not least in its attempt to synthesise Ranke and Hegel. In his analysis of the Middle Ages, for example, Hellmann focused on the emergence in the West of nationality, nationhood and nationalism. He depicted nationhood not as a haphazard and unplanned development, or the work of individuals, but the product of 'ein *Versuch*' – an effort – by the entire populace of the time, as if they sensed where the future was heading and acted in harmony to try and achieve it.

Hellmann also wrote about the legitimacy of Germany's succession from Rome and its imperial mission. In his speeded-up vision of European history, cultural development swept across the continent from east to west and then turned back on itself like a parabola when it got to mediaeval France. It was on what is now French soil, he said, that all the great cultural innovations of the Middle Ages were fashioned and from where a centralized Romano-Germanic culture started to expand. He saw the Crusades as that culture's most brilliant attempt to export its values, albeit unsuccessfully, and praised its annexation of its northern neighbours – today's Scandinavians, Slavs and Hungarians – as a more fruitful, if less dramatic, achievement, resulting in a pool of shared values from which Russia and Turkey were long excluded.

Hellmann was influential in the way he used language. He talked about the evolution of mediaeval Europe as a 'battle' between old conditions and new, and of 'energies' and 'flows' in 'overlapping processes'. Nationality, nationhood and nationalism, he said, sprang from a conflict between the remnants of the Roman Empire and a new age, from which grew three new social forces: monarchy, aristocracy and the various estates of peasant farmers, merchants, craftsmen and soldiers – a division of society he may have borrowed from Max Weber, whose works he co-edited. Mediaeval monarchy he saw as a centripetal, centralizing force; aristocracy as the opposite – a centrifugal force; and four phases of struggle between these forces had given rise to various types of kingdoms in different places. Alongside these phases (from absolutism through feudal aristocracy to clerical bureaucracy), he observed a second process in which the emerging state and the church, its intellectual superior, went from separate coexistence to rivalry and thence to a joint authority unique to the Middle Ages.

Hellmann's begging of questions, his appeal to abstract forces, his circularity and his lack of true historicity seem not to have been troubling at the time he was writing. In addition, he cast a thousand years of German history in a positive light, redeeming Germans from what Prussian propagandists – including the young Goethe – had described as centuries of cultural humiliation by the French. (These paradigms didn't save him. Although he converted from Judaism to Protestantism, the Nazis threw him out of his job at Leipzig when they came to power in 1933 and replaced him with Heimpel. Three years later, at the age of sixty-four, he was persuaded to go to England to find a new position but returned to Germany empty-handed, and found little else to do but play the piano and read the Classics. In 1942 he was transported to the Theresienstadt concentration camp and died there a few months later.)[9]

Neither in his subsequent writings nor in his bibliographies did Pevsner name Hellmann or give him credit, yet his copy of Hellmann's book shows signs of having been heavily used and seems to have been the main source, or a principal source, for many of the ideas and mental structures we now think of as Pevsner's. Talking about nineteenth-century art in *Pioneers of the Modern Movement*, for example, Pevsner saw a parabola of artistic influence sweeping in from the east (Italy) to the west (England) and then back to Germany. He also thought in terms of neatly defined ages, of efforts to unify disorder, of the overthrow of dominant cultures by more enlightened movements with their own heroes and group will, and of Germany and England as partner nations at the summit of cultural achievement (Germany first, then England). Parallel ideas can be found in his later *An Outline of European Architecture*, where he talked about energies and flows in the evolution of culture and in the character of individual buildings.

Although art history might seem like a small branch of general history, it was always a quite different subject, and different again at Leipzig. In 1873, Leipzig's philosophy faculty applied to the state of Saxony for permission to create a chair of mediaeval and later art history. The original idea was to affiliate with the new chair of the theology faculty 'to give those studying [theology] the chance of deepening their study in the area of church art'.[10] This initiative was taken up by art historians who wanted to see not just church art but the whole of mediaeval and later art represented, and by general historians who simply wanted to expand the range of historical study. The application succeeded and within the year, Leipzig fell in with efforts throughout Germany to raise art history to an academic discipline with its own agenda, curriculum, function and methodologies.

The first head of Leipzig's new Institute of Art History was Anton Springer. Springer had been born in Prague in 1825 when Bohemia/Teschen was still part of the Austro-Hungarian Empire. During the 1840s he'd supported the opposition Czech nationalist movement, as well as the activities of German radicals, in the belief – widely shared by liberal intellectuals – that revolution in Central Europe was necessary and inevitable. When it failed to materialize, Springer thought it prudent to leave Prague, rather as Mommsen had thought it prudent to leave Leipzig after being arrested and then dismissed as a liberal agitator. Although Springer's subject was contemporary politics, he got a job as an art historian at Bonn University and remained there from 1852 to 1872. During that time he rose from Privatdozent to professor but lived under constant suspicion and was persecuted and spied on because of his earlier political associations, even though he'd become a German nationalist.

In May 1872, Springer was made rector at the University of Strasbourg, which Bismarck had just won back from the French. He set out his principles for reconstituting the university as a German institution in his inaugural lecture, declaring that academic freedom was paramount.

> As its first and sacred right, German scholarship asserts the independence and freedom of investigation. No one shall prescribe its role. No one shall determine in advance which way its involved road will go ... For how can it reach the truth if it does not have the right to test everything, to spare nothing, to dare all, to leave nothing aside out of fearful aversion?[11]

This message of intellectual openness, delivered a couple of months before his forty-seventh birthday, impressed Leipzig sufficiently for Springer's name to be added to the shortlist for its first chair of art history. (Also on the shortlist were the distinguished Hegelian historian Karl Schnaase, as well as other lesser-known figures: Von Bettburg, Lübke, Lützow, Messner, Julius Meyer and Otte.) Leipzig liked the fact that Springer was both a historian and an art historian and that he'd written authoritatively and extensively in both fields. As late as 1944 Springer's *History of Austria* was being praised as 'to this day perhaps the best comprehensive work on the Austrian revolution of 1848',[12] but in the course of just six years he'd also brought out his *Compendium of the Architecture of the Christian Middle Ages* in 1854, his *Handbook of Art History* in 1855, his *History of Pictorial Art in the Fourteenth Century* in 1858 and his *Iconographical Studies* in 1860, among other works.

Springer was committed to a line of inquiry that sought to reconcile the history of aesthetics with practical observations and interpretations of national character. In 1855, three years after gaining his teaching licence in Bonn, he'd written in his *Handbook*:

> Art history should represent the appearance of beauty in its progress through time; describe the inner essentials of artistic ideals; provide historical accounts of particular types of art; but at the same time sketch a graphic picture of the creative imagination of various nations and show the connection between that and the rest of what history deals with.

He'd also written positively about the enlargement of the German Reich, about the case for reabsorbing territory from Austria, and against the ideas of Hegel.[13] In his inaugural lecture at Leipzig in 1873 (on 'Legitimacy in the Development of Pictorial Art') he determined that art history was to be rigorous and not literary. He said: 'The nature and rules of art-historical activity are only established through historical research' and went on to warn against artistic mystification. The job of art history, he added, was to explain the relationship between the artist, the work and the times.

Springer's successor at Leipzig was August Schmarsow. In his radio talk of 1952 Pevsner ranked Schmarsow as one of the three leaders of the modern generation of art historians, along with Wölfflin and Riegl,[14] and felt he'd been especially important in putting architecture at the centre of art-historical studies. The operative idea that lay behind Schmarsow's first and decisive books in the mid-1890s, said Pevsner in an autobiographical essay in 1969, was 'Einfühlung', our sense of empathy with geometrical forces, 'the vertical raising us, the horizontal widening us'. This interest in the psychological experience of art came directly from Wundt, though Pevsner preferred to give it a more artistic-philosophical provenance, sourcing it instead to the father-and-son writers on aesthetics, Friedrich Theodor Vischer and Robert Vischer, in the 1860s and 1870s.

Although Schmarsow had just retired from Leipzig's Institute of Art History by the time Pevsner got there, Pevsner felt later that his own 'peculiar Leipzig initiation' had depended far more on Schmarsow than he'd recognized at the time[15] and regretted that Schmarsow was 'still far too little known in Anglo-American circles'. To make up for that deficit, Pevsner incorporated aspects of Schmarsow's spatial preoccupations into his *An Outline of European Architecture*, giving numerous examples of how architecture is felt and sensed. Writing about Gothic architecture, he talked about the smooth spatial rhythm at Notre Dame Cathedral in Paris, the speed of the eastward drive at Chartres and the sense of being pressed forwards in the naves of Rheims, Amiens and Beauvais. Writing about Baroque architecture over four centuries later, he talked about Borromini's San Carlo alle Quatro Fontane as a 'full-blooded organism' with 'intertwined' elements that produced 'a rolling, rocking effect' that communicates itself to us in a luscious wave of empathy in which 'we can stand nowhere without taking part in the swaying rhythm'.[16]

Not everyone was as enthusiastic about Schmarsow as Pevsner. Where Pevsner was able to salvage Schmarsow's ideas by treating them as sensual and organic, others found him irredeemably mechanical. Franz Wickhoff, the founder of the Vienna School of Art History, felt that Schmarsow lacked a 'grasp of history and the basic questions it poses' and regarded his presence in Leipzig as 'a blight on the profession' of art history, especially in view of the strength of mainstream history teaching at Leipzig.[17] Werner Weisbach, a pupil of Schmarsow's in the early 1900s and a contemporary of Pinder's, found him fussy and pedantic and criticized his first lectures for using mathematical formulae, leaving him with the sense that Schmarsow's 'feeling for art was shallow'.[18] Even enthusiasts recognized that Schmarsow was an acquired taste, as Oskar Wulff recalled in 1933:

> I can still remember the stir that Schmarsow's first class created among an audience mostly untrained in philosophy and ignorant of the recent psychological trends in aesthetics. People were completely dumbfounded. Likewise, his inaugural lecture, 'Das Wesen der architektonischen Schöpfung',[19] was baffling in its novelty, and set off an almost universal opposition to his barely disguised disapproval of all theoretical instruction.

If Schmarsow was not to everyone's liking, he did at least work hard. On his arrival at Leipzig in the winter of 1900–1901, he gave two lecture courses (on eighteenth-century art history and on architecture as art) and held critical exercises on Rubens and Rembrandt in his research seminar. The following summer he held courses on Renaissance architecture and on the paintings of Raphael, and took his advanced students on study tours of Saxony and Thuringia to look at mediaeval paintings. He also complemented his Renaissance lectures with special research exercises on the work of Burckhardt. Almost twenty years later, following his decision to retire at the age of sixty-six, he was still working at the same rate and held two one-hour open seminars each week on the aesthetics of painting and four one-hour seminars on Old Dutch paintings from Hubert van Eyck to Quentin Massys.[20] He also held a higher-level course at Leipzig's Institute of Art History on issues connected with van Eyck's early history. During his final term in the winter of 1919–1920, he gave a weekly one-hour course on the special characteristics of Gothic and early Renaissance architecture in Italy and four one-hour classes on paintings and painting culture in Italy in the fifteenth century, the Quattrocento.

Throughout his career at Leipzig, Schmarsow's seminars made up almost half the art-historical teaching then on offer in Leipzig (courses on archaeology being a separate requirement of the curriculum for art historians) and conveyed a mass of information and methodological guidance that stood apart from his more polemical ideas. When Pevsner spoke of having been influenced by Schmarsow, that legacy was made up not just of Schmarsow's ideas but of the idea of teaching as a massive personal obligation and of the distinction between data and interpretation.

Although Schmarsow taught at Leipzig until February 1920, he'd decided to retire in the summer of 1919. On 28 October the philosophy faculty met to discuss his replacement. Schmarsow attended the meeting, held in the office of Berthe, the dean, along with other faculty members: Studniczka, Volkelt, Walter Goetz, a historian and sociologist, and Heinze, an art historian. Together they drew up a list of twelve possible successors, none of them internal: Wiese, Kautzsch, Knapp, Hildebrandt, Pinda [sic], Worringer, Brinckmann, Rintelen, Tietze, Grisebach, Vitzthum, and Hagen, Vitzthum's assistant.

One other name was excluded right from the start: Max Dvořák, Pevsner's second favourite art historian.[21] Dvořák wasn't widely admired in Leipzig at the time and Studniczka, whose father was Czech, warned his colleagues that unlike Springer, Dvořák was an unreformed Czech nationalist. He may only have been pointing out that Dvořák's candidature might be obstructed by Saxony's Ministry of Culture and Public Education, the body that ratified all university appointments, but his intervention ensured that Dvořák's name didn't come up again. The committee did agree, however, that Schmarsow's replacement must be the top man for the job and asked Studniczka to carry out more research.

A month later, on 20 November, the committee met again, this time without Schmarsow and Goetz but with Georg Steindorff, the director of Leipzig's Egyptology Institute. After a long discussion during which the name of Ernst Wiese was considered, the committee decided on its preferred candidates. In second place was Vitzthum, the chair of art history at Göttingen; in third place was Kautzsch, from Frankfurt. The dean recorded this in the minutes, adding that the committee would have placed Kautzsch in first place were it not for the fact that he too could be politically 'difficult' for Leipzig. Studniczka was asked to produce formal reports on the committee's finding to send to the Ministry. He duly wrote to the state government on 24 November that all three candidates had previous links with Leipzig, and went on to describe them.

Rudolf Kautzsch, born in Leipzig and the oldest at fifty-one, had taken his doctorate at Leipzig and been first director of Leipzig's newly created Book Trade (Buchgewerbe) Museum from 1898, having worked as a Privatdozent at Halle in the two years before.[22] His early doctoral and postdoctoral work had been on mediaeval German book illustration and he'd published various studies on this subject between 1894 and 1904. In 1903 he'd become professor of art history at the Technical University of Darmstadt, then occupied the same post at Breslau from 1911 and at the University of Frankfurt from its founding in 1914. During this time he'd worked on architectural and sculptural monuments and in 1917 had challenged Wölfflin's formalism on the grounds that it was one-sided. The committee liked Kautzsch's versatility and intelligence and the popularity of his lectures but on purely practical grounds it thought Kautzsch was probably too old to want to start building up a department at Leipzig, where art history was still of less interest to students than it seemed to be at Frankfurt. 'In any case, we won't win him without considerable sacrifice', it concluded.

Georg Vitzthum – Count Vitzthum von Eckstädt – had studied jurisprudence and art history at Berlin and Munich, finally gaining his doctorate at Leipzig in 1903 for work inspired by Schmarsow on the thirteenth-century Italian painter Bernardo Daddi. This led to pioneering work in untangling aspects of English, Dutch and Rhineland art, the results of which appeared in his study of mediaeval Paris miniature painting from Saint Louis up to Philip de Valois (1907). On the strength of this, Vitzthum became Schmarsow's teaching assistant at Leipzig[23] and was given an associate professorship in 1910 after he'd agreed to turn down the directorship of the painting collection at Dresden. Two years later he moved to Kiel, where at least three other universities – Graz, Freiburg and Göttingen – started courting him. Without being a captivating lecturer, he had warmth of personality and a good reputation for guiding students through their discipline. The committee noted that he hadn't published much recently because he'd spent the whole of the war in uniform, but that volumes by him on painting and sculpture in the Middle Ages were now appearing. In spite of this, it regarded him as well qualified in problems of mediaeval 'Geistesgeschichte' – the almost untranslatable word in German art history for the relationship between art and the underlying forces that shape culture, philosophy, politics, religion and science – and competent enough in Renaissance and post-Renaissance studies.

8

Pinder

Georg Maximilian Wilhelm Pinder was Leipzig's first-choice candidate to succeed August Schmarsow. He was forty-one years old, said Studniczka, and the third generation of a family of well-known art scholars. Born in Kassel, his university career had begun at Göttingen (1896–1897), where, like Vitzthum, he'd first studied law. He then tried archaeology at Berlin and Munich (1897–1899), before turning to the more unusual subject of art history at Leipzig (1900–1903). His doctoral thesis dealt with the Wundtian-Schmarsowian idea of rhythm in Romanesque interiors in Normandy. He'd gone on to write two architecture books for Langewiesche's *Blue Book* series – on German mediaeval cathedrals (1909) and on German Baroque architects of the eighteenth century (1913) – and although they'd been meant for a popular audience, they'd attracted acclaim for their range, their passionate treatment of art and national identity, and their power of expression. His study of the little-known mediaeval sculpture of Würzburg (1911) had given that city a European dimension it hadn't known before and won him a commission from the *Handbuch der Kunstwissenschaft* encyclopaedia to write its volume on German sculpture from the end of the Middle Ages to the end of the Renaissance.

Pinder's teaching career had begun in Würzburg, where he'd obtained his doctorate in 1905. In 1911 he'd taken over Kautzsch's professorship at Darmstadt, replacing him again in 1915 when Kautzsch moved from Breslau. He'd served briefly in the war before being invalided out, and had taken a position at Strasbourg until caught up in a general expulsion of German teachers by the French in 1919, as a result of which he was called back to Breslau.

In its research, the committee had been repeatedly struck by talk of Pinder and of his growing reputation not just as an important writer on art but as a thrilling lecturer and winning personality. It concluded that Pinder was the most suitable man for the job. What it doubted was whether Pinder had enough time or experience to train research students. For this reason, with all the usual principled resolve of a university body, it bottled out and decided in favour of the more experienced and more versatile Kautzsch, without mentioning the 'difficulty' of his political beliefs. It added, however, that if the Ministry preferred Pinder, it should move fast because he was heavily in demand and had been offered the chair at Göttingen five times in the previous nine years.

The committee sent its proposals to the Ministry three days later. It convened again on 9 December, probably following a request for further information caused by a split between supporters of Pinder and Kautzsch. Not wanting to take sides, Studniczka dissented, proposed Vitzthum as a compromise candidate and called for a further report. This must have forced the issue because on 20 December, a letter arrived from Pinder accepting the committee's invitation. On the last day of the year, the government of Saxony (its letterhead showing the word 'Royal' newly deleted) ratified his appointment and named him to take over Schmarsow's chair from the beginning of April 1920.

At Leipzig, students of art history also studied archaeology and each subject had its own institute operating out of the same building. Archaeology was the senior subject. It had developed out of the Classical syllabus (Latin, Greek, ancient philosophy and Classical law) and, as noted earlier, was almost exclusively limited to the Greeks, Etruscans and Romans. When Schmarsow was appointed, he'd been outnumbered three to one by archaeology lecturers, all heavily engaged in teaching. By the time of his retirement, the balance had shifted two to one the other way, with Studniczka bearing the archaeological load on his own, giving two or three series of lectures each semester and a separate course on ancient art history.

Pinder arrived in Leipzig for the summer semester of 1920. In that first term, Studniczka's lecturing included courses on Old Italian and Roman art history up to the end of the Antique, an introduction to consecration reliefs, an exploration of Greek consecration reliefs, problems in completing and dating the work of Greek sculptors, the art of Caesar's time, and representations of divine character in antique art, as well as an advanced course on issues to do with antique pictorial art. Students could also attend related lectures in other departments. (In 1919, for example, they were referred to Kötzschke in the history department for lectures on the development of cultural identity and artistic life in Saxony and could take courses on Christian art in the theology department.)

Under Pinder, the variety of teaching at Leipzig increased dramatically. Various short-term Privatdozenten were brought in – Voss in 1920, Suter in 1922 and Beenken in 1923 – and Steindorff, the Egyptologist, started to lecture more frequently as well. Pinder's own first lecture schedule consisted of four weekly one-hour sessions on definitions of different periods in mediaeval and later art history, and a weekly two-hour tutorial on stylistic criticism, with field trips to see original works. In his second semester, in the winter of 1920–1921, his weekly teaching commitments included a special one-hour course, by appointment only, on German painting around 1500, four lectures on German sculpture in the fifteenth and sixteenth centuries, and tutorial exercises on northern European art in the same period for advanced students.

Studniczka had reported to the Culture Ministry about the originality of Pinder's teaching style but hadn't gone into detail about his background or his academic record. One feature of Pinder's character was his musicality and sociability. It was a shared love of music, for example, that had brought him into August Schmarsow's circle at Leipzig while he was a student. Professor and pupil played music together – Pinder was a pianist, Schmarsow a violinist – and through this they became friends. Pinder also chose as his doctoral subject the idea of rhythm in architecture. At his first doctoral examination (Prüfung) in February 1903, however, neither Studniczka nor the great Wundt was wholly convinced of Pinder's performance and each awarded him only a second-class grade; Schmarsow alone treated him more kindly with a first. Later in the year, Pinder's finished dissertation was graded not by Studniczka or Wundt but by Kautzsch and this time both he and Schmarsow gave Pinder top marks.

The problem with Pinder was that he wasn't obviously academic. He was bored by ideas and theories per se, especially other people's, unless they had the power to excite; what mattered to him was impact, the emotional effect that ideas might have, and the drama of communication. This filtering out of the dull, he believed, gave him a clarity that set him apart from his colleagues, many of whom seemed to enjoy wordiness for its own sake: often the more impenetrable the better. In a letter to Pevsner in the late 1920s, he spoke of an event that gave him 'the immodest impression of seeing more accurately than the experts'.[1] Years later, in a filmed interview, he said:

> If anyone ever asks me what my method is, what's your school, what's your direction, I start to get embarrassed. Thankfully, however, I remember one of many lovely conversations I had in my unforgettably short time in Strasbourg with Georg Dehio. Dehio said to me one day: 'School? I have no school. Direction? I have no direction!' I, too, also cannot say that I actually consciously followed any definite model . . . I have no special educational aims . . . and I'm happy that way . . . What, then, have I tried to teach? One comprehensive principle: always try to see everything as if for the first time.[2]

Outside the lecture room Pinder got involved in pranks and theatricals, played the piano in public (in spite of having lost a finger in the war) and designed masks for Fastnacht, the students' Shrove Tuesday carnival.[3] Becoming one of the 'Pinder-Kinder', as his students were known, meant entering into a rebellious pact against convention that contributed further to the charisma Studniczka had reported on and brought a vast and, for many, refreshing change.

While other art historians wanted their subject to be purer and more Rankean, Pinder followed Lamprecht in looking at how art, politics and society overlapped. He also stressed the physicality of art: the idea of direct contact with source materials – looking, touching, feeling – rather than concentrating on archival study. Both approaches brought accusations of populism, superficiality and imprecision, which meant that Pinder-Kinder could be regarded with suspicion if they didn't reinforce their academic credentials elsewhere. 'As a student of Pinder, I realized he was very one-sided', said Kitzinger about Pinder in Munich in 1934. 'I [had intended to go] to Hamburg to study with Panofsky. I was attracted to the Warburg and would have got from Panofsky the tools of the trade to deal with non-visual sources.' Instead, Kitzinger studied under Pinder, happily but warily, and with the focus mostly on the visual. 'Everything was to do with *looking* and with the work of art itself.'[4]

Pinder liked to be adored. In 1921 a contemporary and fellow student of Pevsner's, Wolfgang Hermann, moved to Leipzig, in spite of what he regarded as its 'hateful provincialism', solely on the strength of reports that Pinder was more exciting and more progressive in his willingness to take on marginal subjects. What Hermann found was a head of department who was more relaxed about where the boundaries of art lay than Wölfflin, under whom he'd been studying at Munich,[5] and more interested in an artist's life and times. He also found Pinder to be a lively and amusing lecturer, and kind and helpful to his seminar students.[6]

As a student at Göttingen University in 1896, Pinder had joined the local chapter of the 'Allemania' Burschenschaft (student association), a patriotic and at the time relatively inoffensive fraternity. His association with Allemania qualified him, when he moved on to Leipzig, to become a member of its old Burschenschaftlers' Union, 'Die Vereinigungen der alten Burschenschaftler zu Leipzig'. This clubbable band of lawyers, doctors and other professionals had a stated mission: 'the revival and practice of the Burschenschaft spirit among old Burschenshaftlers, and caring for the initiation of young Burschenschaftlers and supporting them in their efforts'. Its goal was 'to foster excellence in our young scholars and train men of strong character for whom a love for the German people and fatherland remains at all times the rule of conduct for all behaviour'. Posters of the time show that the association was also meant to transcend politics: 'Party differences and politics are not allowed in union conversation. (Meetings on the third Monday of every month at 8 pm in the little room at the Kitzing and Helbing Inn, Schloßgasse 22.)'

Pinder capitalized on his sociability to became the darling of German art history – though one whom post-war historians, especially outside Germany, have subsequently accused of contributing nothing of lasting value to his subject, in common with most other art historians who remained in Germany during the war. He played no part in the continuity of Wölfflin's grand conception of an 'art history of anonymity' that Schmarsow was engaged in and that Theodor Hetzer restored when he took over Pinder's chair in Leipzig in 1934; on the contrary, it was his personality rather than his thought that seems to have been most persuasive. He was noted for unearthing new and startling facts but could be cavalier in the way he used them.[7] Above all he was a performer and a charmer, 'ein eleganter Mann', a mixture of courtesy and flirtatiousness. At the end of his lectures he'd take the red rose he wore in his buttonhole or kept in a long-stemmed vase on his desk and present it to one of his female students.[8] He also fell in love with and married one of his students, divorcing his first wife Ernestina, the mother of his three children.[9]

No student of Pinder's interviewed for this book spoke badly of him. 'I must confess that I really worshipped him, just like my fellow students,' said Bernhard

Degenhardt, who took his doctorate under Pinder in the early 1930s. 'His style seemed to me to be clear and great. Like the rest of his generation, he was, so to speak, an "Expressionist" but that only increased his effect.'[10] Kitzinger also found Pinder a vivid lecturer:

> He opened our eyes and we learnt to see things and to verbalize. This was where his real genius came out: in his great visual sensitivity and his use of language to characterize visual style and aesthetic qualities. [He] was a very exciting teacher for beginners. He was very allusive: it comes out precisely in his writing. He wrote just as he spoke . . . He'd say: 'In Mannerism, if you wanted to assassinate someone you sent him a poisoned glove; in Baroque, you used a dagger.' You never forgot it.[11]

'History of art was a very small world then', recalled Elisabeth Paatz, who in 1927 took her doctorate under Vitzthum at Göttingen, where her father was the registrar. 'We all knew each other. There was no single way [of teaching or studying art]. We each went our own way. Leipzig had become the top university [for art history] by then. Our model was Vitzthum but Pinder at Leipzig had a different approach. Sometimes we felt him to be more old-fashioned but he was also more expansive. He had presence. He was also more famous. He was a great formulator and inspiring. He could fly over facts in his inspiration. Facts were not so important to him.'[12]

Florence Mütherich remembers Pinder's distrust of books and his stress on the need for first-hand experience. 'Pinder gave us immediate contact with works of art. Other [lecturers] were theoretical. Pinder didn't theorize . . . He'd take all his students – not just the wealthier ones – on end-of-term excursions. We'd go to Rome or somewhere local. Sometimes a trip related to his lectures: for example, to Magdeburg. The trips were very carefully prepared. They involved assistants and the help of local people.'[13] Only when visits were impossible would he lecture. 'He'd introduce us to how to look at a work of art . . . He taught us how to describe and look.'[14] But he disliked using slides as teaching aids. 'He'd warn against the use of photographs', recalls Elizabeth 'Lucy' Holt, who studied under Pinder in Germany after being taught by Oskar Hagen at Wisconsin University. 'He felt the highlighting and shadow in a photograph could make a sculpture look too romantic. His most important work was his two volumes on sculpture. He was constantly defending sculpture and constantly worried when photographs introduced painterly qualities to sculpture.'[15]

Pevsner came under Pinder's influence at a turning point in Pinder's career. Pinder's early work had built on Schmarsow, who in turn had built on Wundt. In Wundt's experimental work on mental processes, for example, he'd built several laboratory instruments for testing human response, one of which was a 'rhythm machine' or 'beat apparatus'. This consisted of a rotating drum with adjustable pins that banged out set rhythms, and Wundt was demonstrating it – to large audiences – in 1903, at just the time when Pinder was working on his art history dissertation and writing about the sensation of rhythm in architecture as caused by other sorts of pins: rows of architectural columns.

After graduating from Würzburg in 1905, Pinder turned his attention to German mediaeval architecture and sculpture, and the promotion of Teutonic primitivism as an alternative to the dominant culture of French refinement. In the 1920s, as Pevsner's student career was beginning, Pinder became interested in 'bad' Italian art of the mid-to-late sixteenth century and the excesses of the seventeenth- and early-eighteenth-century Baroque period. Then in the 1930s he went back to German mediaevalism again.

'In his preface to [his volume on mediaeval German sculpture in] the *Handbuch* [*der Kunstwissenschaft*], he said his view of sculpture was always concerned with European themes', recalled Kitzinger.

> But by the 1930s, he was looking at Germanism. When I got to Pinder in 1933, he was so obsessed with German art that I almost never heard anything about Raphael except in seminars on Michaelangelo. He hardly mentioned the Renaissance: he wasn't interested. He was completely caught up in the definition of Germanism. He'd undergone a strange conversion . . . In fact, the germs of Pinder's approach already exist in Wölfflin. Wölfflin also played off nationalities in his book *Italy and the German Sense of Form*. Pinder gave a [similar] course of lectures called 'German and French art', involving a comparison of the sculpture of France and, say, Bamberg. The object was visual confrontation, to show that the two were quite distinct, and to derive the German essence.[16]

The roots of Pinder's obsession with Germany were apparent at least fifteen years before Kitzinger encountered him. Pinder's arrival at Leipzig in 1920 coincided with the seventieth birthday of the historian Georg Dehio, whom he'd known in his couple of years at the German University in Strasbourg – the university that Springer had germanized in his year as rector. Dehio was more of an archaeologist than a theoretician, uninterested in questions of epistemology and methodology and careful to avoid getting caught up in the art-historical battles that were going on around him – even refusing until 1876 to identify himself as an art historian. Concentrating on his own work, however, he carried out some of the most important documentation of German art ever undertaken. Of particular note are the two-volume surveys of religious architecture in France and Germany he undertook with Gustav von Bezold over the course of eighteen years, and his five-volume *Handbuch der deutschen Kunstdenkmäler*, which appeared between 1905 and 1912 and itemized Germany's most important artistic landmarks.

Dehio was also a conservationist and campaigned for the protection of art and architecture as a national resource. He'd begun his *Geschichte der deutschen Kunst* by stating that for him and for the book he was writing, art was just one means – and a very effective one – of defining the essence of Germanness (Deutschtum).

Pinder marked Dehio's seventieth birthday with a Festschrift essay that was at least as revealing of himself as it was of Dehio. In it, he charted Dehio's career and achievements, starting with Dehio's education at Dorpat and then Göttingen under George Waitz, and his thesis on Hartwich von Stade, the archbishop of Bremen. He referred to Dehio's first journey to Italy in 1876, which launched him into what Pinder called his ten-year 'Italian phase', and the two-volume history of the archbishopric of Hamburg-Bremen that he submitted to Munich University in 1877 for his teaching diploma. He then detailed Dehio's many scholarly writings including his research into the emergence of brick as a building material, his travels to France with von Bezold (his 'French phase'), his appointments as professor at Konigsberg in 1884 and at Strasbourg in 1892, and his conservation work, most notably over the survival of Heidelberg Castle, under the slogan 'Konservieren, nicht restaurieren!' ('Conserve, don't restore!').

None of this was unusual. What was unusual was Pinder's tone and appproach. Instead of attempting a coherent summary of Dehio's place as a historian, he offered random comments, heady but synthetic, that conveyed little real grasp of the man as an individual and less interest in him. (He wrote in the same way in the Festschrift for Wölfflin's seventieth birthday fourteen years later.) Part of this can be put down to style: Pinder's enjoyment of language often compromised what he wanted to say.[17] But he also found Dehio more interesting as a symbol than as a real person. Dehio had been born in Tallinn[18] in Estonia when Estonia was still a German province, and Pinder chose to praise him as an archetypal German colonial, emphasizing the attributes that provincials brought to the Reich and the idea that Germany's annexed territories were the depository of tendencies that Germany itself had lost through cosmopolitanism:

> He who has given us so much is a Balt, a very conscious and passionate Balt, and that has always meant a very conscious and passionate German.

Pinder imagined Dehio as having imbibed the spirit of Goethe's Weimar, 'a naturally conscious gentility and exclusivity' that the Estonian soil had absorbed and given its own flavour to, but wrote also of Dehio's 'inner loneliness that always characterizes strong artistic natures . . . [and] for whom, through the land of their birth, a high and enduring connection is more natural than it is to the son of the north'. He then itemized qualities of Dehio's that he depicted as innate virtues of 'a Baltic literato': his clarity of thought and expression, his Goethean 'feeling of responsibility for language', 'the urge for lucid causative relationships, the resistance to impurity or muddy sentiment, against glibness (Zungunreden), the ability to think as an artist.'

Pinder emphasized ethnic identity again when he wrote an eightieth birthday tribute to Richard Graul, the director of Leipzig's Grassi Museum, who in 1911 had supported a manifesto, a *Protest by German Artists*, by Carl Vinnen, criticizing the ill effects of foreign art on German art. ('He's a German and he's always been aware of his Germanness . . . He possesses a Germanness of Viennese colouring, which is more easily understandable to our western neighbours.') That, however, was in 1942, three years into the Second World War; twenty-two years earlier, Pinder was writing in the aftermath of the First World War. As a result of that war, Germany had lost Baltic Estonia and France had reoccupied Strasbourg, where Dehio had been installed for the previous quarter century (and where Pinder had taught until expelled by the French). This is how Pinder wrote about that loss in his Dehio essay:

> We have had to abandon [Dehio's] tribe, perhaps for ever. For twenty-six years he worked in Strasbourg where he created an institute with ideal working conditions. Strasbourg too is abandoned, perhaps for ever. In 1918 the French, as they were wont to do at the time, told the creator of that institute to cross the Rhine bridge, lonely, suitcase in hand, to the abuse and beatings of a paid mob and the spittle of whores carted along specially for the occasion. Dehio had to leave, of course, and his fine institute will remain screwed down in a coffin as long as the French go on preventing any serious examination of anything ever connected with Germany. Also perhaps for ever.

To this angry and self-pitying eulogy ('we Germans aren't hurt by the thought of this as the scenario for our future'), Pinder added his thoughts on how Dehio would be affected by Germany's enforced isolation. Dehio's seventieth birthday, he wrote:

> should be an opportunity for the whole of the art-history community to celebrate. Misguided European sentiments, however, will limit the number of public figures who'll join in this thanksgiving to German scholars of historical subjects, but all real intellectuals of our people have reason to participate.

At the same time, Pinder regarded intellectuality and Europeanism – as it was starting to be dictated by non-Germans – as a kind of treachery, and he contrasted Dehio to

> that kind of rootless intellectual employee without tribe, people and history, who some of our people today look to as an ideal. For the intellectual, 'it's all the same whether he was born in Krotoschin [a half-German, half-Polish town noted for its Jewish population] or Paris', says the intellectual.

This ardent nationalism is consistent with the fury felt by Germans after 1918, the popular allegation that the war had been lost because of Germany's Dolchstoß (the 'stab in the back') by intellectuals and Jews, and the hardships and humiliation caused by the level of reparations insisted on by the French. It was intensified by outrage at the destruction of monuments – mediaeval churches, sculptures, altar pieces, town halls and civic collections, especially on the Western Front –

that German art historians, inspired by Dehio, blamed not on Prussian military adventurism but on Allied villainy.

Typical of this intemperate, accusatory, self-excusing attitude was a German report drawn up by the Leipzig- and Strasbourg-educated art historian Paul Clemen in 1919 on the condition of architectural remains in the different theatres of war, and the measures that Germany and Austria had taken for their preservation. In addition to listing the damage done to 'whole stretches of that France and Belgium that we loved and whose monumental art creations we admired as one of the highest expressions of Northern art tendencies', the report went on to contrast Germany's responsible approach to war and its obligations to art history with the savagery and unwarranted destruction carried out by France and England:

> When the French . . . used one of their important art cities, such as Reims . . . as one of the headquarters . . . as a sally port for the great spring campaign in 1917 in the Champagne, they thus *compelled* us to bombard this town and expel the enemy from it, just as was done in the northern section of the front in the case of Ypres, which was held by the English. On the other side, however, the English and French artillery, with complete cold-bloodedness and fully conscious of what they were doing, seemed to have no misgivings, under the similar pressure of military necessity, about bombarding and eventually totally crushing and ruining St. Quentin, into which not a single shell of ours had fallen.[19]

Behind Clemen's complaint lay an older one:

> We quietly confess, even today, that we have admired and honoured, and still admire as artists, Maeterlinck[20] and still more Verhaeren,[21] although they have uttered about us the most bitter and hateful words which have ever been poured out upon any nation; with a shake of the head, with indignation or a smile, we have noticed amongst our violent accusers, men whom up till then we had regarded as representatives of the great international community of intellectual workers, such as the aged Anatole France and Henri Bergson. If the first protests from Germany, even the full-toned declaration of the German Intellectuals, were not always happily conceived, even so, on the other side, the first representatives of French intellect signed a document which is full of exaggerations and errors. What is now necessary is impartial justice.

And behind this complaint lay an even older one:

> Modern European history only records two periods of deliberate and, to a certain extent, programmatical destruction of works of art, and these do not emanate from Germany. The first is the iconoclasm in the Netherlands between 1566 and 1568, which nearly blotted out an almost unparalleled rich art period; the other is the great French Revolution, for which at that time the word . . . 'vandalisme Jacobin', has been coined. The Thirty Years' War caused nowhere in Germany, in any one single district, such thorough destruction as

the Palatinate suffered in the third annexation war of Louis XIV (1678), in which Mélac, who had already ravaged Holland terribly, systematically laid waste this prosperous land. Still worse than the fate of the Belgian towns in the sixteenth century was the misfortune which befell Brussels in 1695: the French, under Villeroy, proclaimed on this occasion the bombardment of the innocent town, which destroyed the whole mediaeval city, with the exception of Ste. Gudule and the Town Hall.

It was in this context, with German art historians stepping up to defend their country's reputation against the historic brutality of the French, that Pinder found his voice. Where in the 1910s he'd wanted to show that Germany's artistic heritage was equal to the artistic standards of other European countries, by 1920 he was arguing that it was Europe that had failed when measured by Germany's standards. He therefore enlisted Dehio as his ally, quoting Dehio's famous remark 'My true hero is the German people' and demonstrating, at the core of his essay, Dehio's discovery of his Germanness and his acceptance of the exclusive demands this made on his mission as a historian, after his flirtations with Italy and France ('Now [from 1907] it is Germany and only Germany to which all work is devoted.').

Pinder went on to illustrate the implications of this for Dehio's outlook. Compared with the mythical intellectual from Krotoschin or Paris, he wrote,

Dehio says the exact opposite: 'No clear strong individuals can be created without the enhancement and purification of the type and talents of their tribe.'[22]

We can't know if Dehio was comfortable with Pinder's appropriation of him or whether Pevsner found Pinder's use of Dehio in any way objectionable. But the art historian Trude Bondi, who worked as a researcher and co-writer for Pevsner in London, reported simply many years later: 'Pevsner had been Pinder's best student and he absorbed Pinder.'[23]

Pinder's interest in Dehio was not one-dimensional, however. There was much that appealed to him about Dehio, not least the relative informality of his writing. In his Festschrift essay, Pinder quoted what Waitz, Dehio's doctoral professor at Göttingen, had said about Dehio's Habilitationsschrift – 'but it reads like a novel' – and Dehio's response: 'I have written this book with the wish that it should be read. It wants to be complete in its way and of immediate effect, not just an assemblage of material for my successors to draw on.' That was a wish that Waitz's circle apparently found odd but that Pinder relished and that Pevsner would take to heart.

9

Dissertation

Young Nikolaus studied hard so he and Lola could marry as soon as he graduated. When he wasn't reading or writing or attending lectures, he was looking
at the art he'd been reading or writing or being lectured about, sometimes with
Lola, sometimes alone. On one occasion he went round Halle with a soldier
who'd been demobilized and whom he met on a train. They spent the day
looking at church architecture and sculpture until a churchwarden got upset
and told them to go away: probably the first time Pevsner was ever evicted from
a building.

While Nikolaus did as much studying as he could, Lola did as little, and then
gave up altogether. What brought her studies to an end was their unexpectedly
sudden decision to get married on 23 July 1923. It was not a propitious time for
a wedding. Apart from Nikolaus's being completely committed to his studies,
the country was in turmoil. After the war the Great Powers had imposed peace
terms so harsh that Germany could only meet them by printing money, with
the effect that the currency collapsed, wrecking the country's economic and
political stability. Before the war, the German mark had stood at twenty to the
British pound; by the end of the war it had more than halved to forty-three and
then continued to plunge further. In the summer of 1922 Ernest Hemingway,
working for the *Toronto Daily Star*, reported changing ten French francs – worth
about ninety Canadian cents – for 670 marks and that with the mark at 800 to
the dollar, foreigners could obtain a five-course meal in the best hotels for as little
as fifteen Canadian cents – a sum that few Germans could by then afford.[1]

Throughout the country, workers were striking for better pay to keep up with
rising costs and banks were printing more money to meet the demand for cash.
This drove inflation higher, created panic, worsened social disorder and produced
a climate of accusation in which factory owners, stock market investors, anyone
with foreign funds, and Jews, were singled out for blame by newspapers, rioting
mobs, discharged soldiers, the unemployed and political extremists.

By the following summer, things were worse. The country was now printing
banknotes with a face value of up to 100 million million marks. In Kaliningrad,
then known as Königsberg, on the Baltic, the editor of the local newspaper
described conditions in working-class areas as worse than the slums of Egypt and
said that nearly 50,000 petits-bourgeois were having to exhaust their savings to
survive. In Saxony, with foreign trade at a near standstill and factories reduced to
short-time working and enforced unemployment, Communism was growing and
groups of Socialist enforcers, said to be backed by Soviet agents – the self-styled

Red Centuries (Rote Hundertschaften) – now outnumbered the police three to one.[2] Wolfgang Hermann, Pevsner's fellow student at Leipzig, remembered that 'at the height of the inflation, rates of exchange were announced at midday. Lectures stopped and we streamed out of class at 11.45 am so we could do our shopping before the prices went up.'[3]

It was in that climate that Nikolai and Lola married. By all accounts it was a strange ceremony. In addition to his parents, it was attended by her father, Alfred Kurlbaum, and her new step-mother, Margarete Siebert,[4] whom Kurlbaum had married in 1919, a year after the death of Lola's mother. Pevsner described Margarete later as 'a rather masculine, intellectual, strong-boned and badly-dressed woman, who had a reputation as a writer of historical and other novels'.[5] It was felt by the Kurlbaum sisters that Margarete was glad to get Lola out of the house. 'She wasn't a wicked woman or cruel step-mother,' recalled Marianne Kockel, 'but she had, let's say, very little understanding of children. She was a decided intellectual, had taken her degree in 1908[6], improbably early, so [our father] gained a lot from her superior education ... but in company she was cool and was certainly glad that my sister left home early.'

Marianne, Lola and Nika clearly didn't like Margarete and didn't make much effort to help her fit into the Kurlbaum household as Alfred's third wife. Although her doctorate, from Munich, was in art history, Pevsner also didn't credit her for influencing his decision to follow suit, or for his choosing Munich as his first port of call on his university tour, or for introducing him to her Munich friend Ricarda Huch, who entertained him during his first university semester in the summer of 1921,[7] or for advising him, around the time of his baptism in 1921, to change his name from the Russian Nikolai to the more German Nikolaus, the idea of which Marianne Kockel attributed to her. He did credit Margarete with persuading Kurlbaum to let Lola marry quickly but said she'd only done so because Lola had become the mistress of the house after her mother's death, and that Margarete found this 'rather a problem'. Reading between the lines, Lola was bossy, the others unwelcoming and the new wife miserable – and no one knew how to make things better. For Pevsner, years later, Kurlbaum's choice of partner was simply an 'error'.[8]

Wolfgang Hermann, who attended the wedding ceremony, found the atmosphere tense. Although he was enrolled in Pinder's seminar, he wasn't close to Pevsner and was surprised not just to be invited but to be asked to act as a witness. A more obvious candidate, he said, was Ernst Michalski, who was a real friend of Pevsner's, but Hermann thought Michalski had refused to witness the ceremony because he was 'more Jewish' than Hermann and disapproved of Pevsner's marrying outside the religion he was born into. Although Hermann was from a Jewish family, he'd been baptized and remained convinced he'd only been asked to help out because he 'fitted in' with the Pevsners and 'suited their needs'. Michalski, he thought, was 'a little shocked' that Hermann had agreed to be 'made use of' in this way.[9]

Members of the Pevsner family believe other issues colour this story and
that Hermann was dyspeptic and suffered from a lifelong jealousy of Nikolaus.
Whether true or not, the memory of Pevsner's wedding always troubled him.
'We weren't friends before or after. Were there no Leipzig friends he could have
asked? Either he didn't know anyone else or he didn't want them at the wedding.
[The thing was,] his father and mother were extremely Jewish. His father still
spoke in broken German. I imagine he didn't want to present his parents to his
friends: he was embarrassed by his own family. I thought it was very disrespect-
ful . . . I discovered later [in Berlin and London] that he was very unpompous
– very fluent and very unconventional. He must have stimulated many people.
But in Leipzig, he gave the impression of being dry, exact, ambitious, diligent,
unimaginative. We just weren't each other's cup of tea.'[10]

A credible reason for the unusual atmosphere Hermann sensed at the wedding,
and the co-opting of his assistance rather than that of a friend, is that Lola was
being rushed into marriage because she was pregnant. If so, she would have found
out only a week or so earlier. Pevsner told his children later that 'it may well have
been connected with [Margarete's] pleadings' that he and Lola were allowed to
marry while both were still students, and this was consistent with Marianne's
line that Margarete wanted Lola out of the house to make the Kurlbaum home
a happier place for herself. But if Lola was pregnant, it was probably Margarete
who made both families realize that a quick solution was needed.

Among the reasons for speculating that Lola was pregnant is the fact that her
first child was born unusually early, thirty-five weeks to the day after the wedding – not definitive evidence of having been conceived five weeks before the
wedding but a good possibility. In addition, the idea of getting married while
both were still students was not at all what she and Nika had imagined. Nikolaus
was a meticulous planner and had celebrated the New Year by sending Lola a
poem that made it quite clear their wedding wouldn't take place until after he'd
graduated in 1924:

> 1922 is here
> Our love must stay a secret, dear.
> But when it turns to '23
> I'll choose you for the world to see,
> And when we get to '24
> We'll stay together for ever more.[11]

It's possible, of course, that Nika and Lola may have decided they couldn't remain
apart any longer, but this doesn't sound like Pevsner, who was usually cautious
rather than impulsive. In addition, the wedding took place on a Monday, in a
Leipzig register office, and was a very small affair, which was odd in view of
Kurlbaum's eminence. He had a wide network as a leading barrister at Germany's
Imperial Court of Appeal, he'd become the President of the Society of German

Lawyers in 1920 and a wedding was a perfect opportunity for a grand reception. And yet very few people seem to have been invited. Heinrich Pollack remembers that neither he nor his mother, Annie's sister Ida, attended, in spite of their closeness to the Pevsners. Nor do Pevsner's children seem to know any details of the wedding except that it took place.

If there had been a sudden need to change their plans, it wasn't entirely surprising. Lola and Nikolaus had been physically close, as his secret diary of dreams and meetings showed. While he was a student in Berlin, in the winter of 1921–1922, Lola would stay with her widowed grandmother, Julie Neisser, in Genthiner Straße, so he could visit her. The grandmother's bachelor brother Heinrich Sabersky lived there too and it was in his book-lined library that the two spent 'a quick courting hour after lunches', forcing Uncle Heinrich, 'courteous and embarrassed', to knock at his own door before entering.[12] Around this time, Lola's father, the admirable and highly esteemed Ober Reichsanwalt Alfred Kurlbaum, was also starting an affair – under the noses of his wife and children – with a young woman whom Margarete Siebert had brought with her to the Kurlbaum home and whom she cared for as an adopted daughter.[13] (As a result, he and Margarete separated in 1924.) Sex, in newly liberated Weimar Germany, was everywhere.

The Pevsners' honeymoon lasted four weeks. 'They started off in Munich, staying overnight in the student digs of a friend', recalls Marianne Kockel.

During the night the police knocked on the door because someone had reported them for 'cohabiting'. It was very strict in those days but they were able to show their freshly baked marriage certificate. They then went to Hinterstein, near Obersdorf [in the very south of Germany, on the northern edge of the Austrian Alps].[14]

Although Pevsner later came to enjoy long walks in the mountains, Hinterstein was not his natural territory.

My sister complained that [Nika] was so little of an athlete. We were brought up much more in the fresh air and we also had the family vineyard in Blutengrund outside Naumburg, where we went every week and helped out in the garden. We were so much more agile and supple and [Lola] annoyed him by pointing out that he wasn't that physical.[15]

Something else made him uneasy on his first night in Hinterstein and when Lola asked what was troubling him, he admitted he couldn't face the prospect of four weeks' holiday without working. He then revealed a suitcase of books he'd brought with him and that had to be read. Only when he'd established his need to work for at least part of every day, and she'd agreed, did he feel able to relax.

The outside view of the young couple was that they were insulated from economic and domestic hardships by their parents. According to Hermann, Pevsner and Lola had both had the advantage of living at home and Ulrich Michel believed that 'owing to the [trading] connections of his father with [other] countries, the Pevsners were able to weather the storms better than salaried people.' Pevsner also thought that Alfred Kurlbaum was making more money than ever – perhaps because of the quantity of litigation that inflation had given rise to. In fact, Hugo's income didn't ever return to its pre-war level after he got back from Sweden because the centre of the fur trade had migrated from Leipzig to London; and Marianne Kockel insisted that 'when [the Pevsners] went on their honeymoon, it was during the inflation and one had no money at all; my father certainly didn't'. Nonetheless, when Nika and Lola got married, they felt able to take on the extra expense of moving into their own flat. They chose an apartment on Dittrichring, in the very centre of Leipzig, right next to the Thomaskirche. 'It was a small upstairs flat with a living room, a study and a dining room, and a staircase that led up to a bedroom in the roof and a kitchen, which wasn't very convenient.'[16]

Lola now kept house while Nika studied. Marianne remembered that with a child on the way and lots of running up and down the stairs, her sister got tired easily. Nikolaus didn't help. One of the first things to happen after they moved in was that Lola asked him to knock some nails into the walls so they could put up pictures and he smashed one of his fingers with the hammer, drawing blood. According to family lore, he did this deliberately, to prove he was impractical and shouldn't be asked to do household chores again.[17] Nor was he. His sister-in-law added: '[Lola] acknowledged his superior intellect and of course his vast knowledge and above all that his work had first priority. And so she did everything – and it was a very firm bond.'[18]

With the support of his wife and parents and parents-in-law and sister-in-law Marianne, who assisted Lola during and after her pregnancy, Pevsner concentrated on his studies and the writing of the dissertation he hoped would earn him his doctorate and launch him on his career as an academic. He opted to write about the buildings of Leipzig two centuries earlier. It was an unusual choice. The safest topic for an art historian at the time was Italian art between 1500 and 1520 – the highpoint of the Renaissance. If one strayed, it might be to earlier Italian art, later Italian art, Renaissance art in other countries, earlier and later art in other countries, etc., but the Renaissance was the core, and a core value was that the art under consideration should be religious, which meant Christian, which meant Catholic. In choosing to study the architecture of Leipzig, Pevsner was therefore straying by several degrees: although his survey would include churches, his topic was secular, not sacred; it was about bourgeois and not aristocratic art; it was about buildings and not painting or sculpture; it was two centuries late; and it was about Germany and not Italy. It was also of little public interest: in short, a perfect Pinder cocktail.

None of the historians Pevsner named as art history's founding fathers on the radio years later had ventured as far as this and nor had his teachers. Wölfflin at Munich hadn't done so, in spite of his important 1888 book *Renaissance and Baroque*, nor had Wölfflin's student Max Hauttmann, whose 1920 dissertation dealt with the (mostly Catholic) religious architecture of Bavaria, Franconia and Swabia between 1550 and 1780. Kautzsch at Frankfurt hadn't done so and nor had Goldschmidt at Berlin. Bruhns, whose lectures Pevsner heard, had completed his doctoral thesis in 1920 on the early Baroque, but this dealt with sculpture at Würzburg and was an extension of what Pinder, Bruhns's superviser, had been doing before the war. The person who'd come closest to Pevsner's subject was Hans Rose, Wölfflin's student at Munich, in a dissertation he completed in 1921 on late Baroque secular architecture from 1660 to 1760, but Pevsner's focus would be far narrower than that: one town and a lot of town-houses.

The choice was even odder in view of the fact that there were far more exotic buildings of the same period only sixty-five miles away in Saxony's capital, Dresden. The most notable of these was the Zwinger, by Pöppelmann, an outrageous Baroque folly made up of six ridiculously ornamental pavilions built over a former dungeon, of which Pevsner would later say:

What an exultation in these rocking curves, and yet what a grace. It is joyful, but never vulgar; vigorous, boisterous perhaps, but never crude. It is of an inexhaustible creative power, with ever new combinations and variations of Italian baroque forms placed against each other and piled above each other, up to the electoral crown pirouetting on top of the bulging cupola. The forward and backward motion never stops.[19]

To turn instead to Leipzig seemed perverse. Even the photographs Pevsner collected in the 1920s showed that mainstream architecture in his home town had little to commend it. The buildings he'd be concentrating on doubled as commercial premises, built in the 1700s for merchants who'd originally lived above the shop. They were big – typically seven storeys high: considerably larger than housing in England of the period – and shapeless. They were also shabby, their plasterwork tired, their window heads sagging, their woodwork rotting. For all their swags and keystones, they seemed past their prime and it wasn't immediately obvious that they'd ever been more distinguished. They didn't compete with the great palaces of the nobility of the same period – or even, for Leipzigers in general, with the showy new buildings that had been going up in their town in the past thirty years.[20] Did Pevsner even like these buildings?

Did he like any buildings? In all his writings as a schoolboy, alongside his reverence for Mann and Nietzsche and Dostoyevsky, Pevsner had made not one mention of architecture: not new, not old. What he had displayed, however, was an aptitude for documentation and the working out of problems; and it was there that Leipzig offered opportunities.

The architecture of the eighteenth century had been as much a problem for art historians in the nineteenth century as nineteenth-century architecture would be for historians in the twentieth. It was unfashionable and unpopular and no one thought of it as having any artistic value. How then could one categorize it in art-historical terms? German builders of the period were far from sophisticated, wrote Pevsner later. 'The majority of the German eighteenth-century architects . . . were not really architects in the renaissance or modern sense. They were brought up in villages to know something about building, and that was enough. No big ideas about professional status entered their heads. In fact the sociological position of architects in Germany before the nineteenth century was still medieval.'[21] None of the names Pevsner would mention in his dissertation was even big enough to be included in the history of European architecture that would become his masterwork. In addition, by the art-historical standards of the day, Leipzig as a town didn't count.

Pevsner's solution was to associate Leipzig's town-houses with the newly fashionable label of Baroque. 'Baroque had originally signified odd, especially of odd shape,' Pevsner explained in his *Outline*, years later. 'It was therefore adopted to describe an architectural style which to the Classicist appeared to revel in odd, extravagant shapes, that is, the style of Italy during the seventeenth century. Then, chiefly in the [1880s] and chiefly in Germany, it lost its derogatory flavour and became a neutral term to designate works of art of that century in general,'[22] although as late as 1946, in England, Pevsner's pupil Reyner Banham remembered A. E. Richardson, the professor of architecture at University College, London, saying 'Baroque? Baroque? It's just a corruption of the Portugese word *barocco*, which means a black pearl. It's nothing to do with architecture.'[23]

Pevsner had the more neutral definition of Baroque in mind when carrying out his doctoral work. Later, his use of the term became more portentous. In his *Dictionary of Architecture* (1966), he defined Baroque as 'characterized by exuberant decoration, expansive curvaceous forms, a sense of mass, a delight in large-scale and sweeping vistas, and a preference for spatially complex compositions'.[24] Elsewhere he wrote of the ingenious three-dimensional compositions of Baroque architecture coming together to create drama and surprise and 'spatial sensations' in ways that parallel Baroque opera. The town-houses of Leipzig have none of that, and Pevsner indicated as much in the cautious title he gave his thesis – *The Architecture of the Baroque Period in Leipzig*[25] – acknowledging that his subject was Baroque by virtue of its age rather than its aesthetic qualities.

Even then, it was still provocative in the early 1920s to suggest that Leipzig's town-houses had merit of any kind, and Pevsner's case for studying them rested partly on existential grounds rather than artistic: the claim – not authenticated in the thesis – that Leipzig had 'a larger number' of Baroque-period houses than other German cities, that they'd apparently been thought highly of in their day (by Goethe, for example) and that they'd survived.[26] This argument was bolstered by the fortunate discovery that Leipzig's city archive possessed a large collection of documents relating to these buildings that had never before been examined.

It was the assessment and ordering of material in the city archive that formed the backbone of Pevsner's achievement and he quickly publicized what he'd done by hurrying his source list of documents into the *New Archive for Saxon History and Archaeology* (1924) and submitting a paper on 'Leipzig Baroque Housing' for inclusion in the *Reports of the State Association of Saxony for Homeland Conservation* (1925). This contained, among other things, Pevsner's tabulation of what bricklayers, stonemasons, carpenters and locksmiths were paid in 1724–1727, presented in a format almost identical to the entries in his schoolboy diaries and to tables on population in the introductions to his later *Buildings of England* books.

The thesis itself synthesized his data into a piece of writing as dramatic and entertaining as any of his later works. Much of the material was organized around the 'unknown' builders he'd allude to but not name in his *Outline* in 1942 – Johann Gregor Fuchs (1650–1715), David Schatz (1668–1750), Christian Döring (1677–1750) and George Werner (1682–1758) – and the architectural theorist Leonhard Christoph Sturm (1669–1719). The Pinderian frisson came from breaking new ground and turning base metal into gold.

Pevsner wrote not just to elucidate Leipzig's Baroque buildings but to elevate them, giving them a status as works of art they hadn't even had in their own day. He did this by emphasizing the uniqueness of their origins not as the product of church or royal patronage but of Leipzig's Kaufmannschaft – its commerce – and, more specifically, its Messen (trade fairs). 'Leipzig,' Pevsner said, 'was not the residence of an absolute ruler and enjoyed none of the advantages that were connected with one. Rather, the fate of the town rested exclusively in the hands of the merchants, whose most respectable representatives formed the Town Council.'[27] By their solidarity these merchants had made Leipzig's fairs larger and more important than any others in Germany, a situation they did all they could to protect.[28] On two occasions they'd stopped Saxony's ruler from building a castle in their city and forced him to rent a town-house while the fairs were on, like everyone else. Out of this shrewdness emerged the urban phenomenon Pevsner was intrigued by: new workers' housing built by textile manufacturers alongside new pleasure gardens beyond the town ditch, and deep courtyard houses with narrow frontages in the centre of Leipzig where merchants would make, store, show and sell their goods.

Pevsner's manner of writing showed diligence and imagination, using a variety of art-historical techniques to bring their work to life. It was alternately descriptive (of plans, elevations, builders' careers and contruction processes), romantic (showing the emotional impact a building might have on the viewer or the biological energy it seemed to contain, in the manner of Schmarsow), formal (looking at what a particular feature might say about Baroque as an evolving style, in the manner of Wölfflin), and sociological (though Pevsner regretted later it wasn't more so[29]). This variety demonstrated an eclectic, even Victorian, facility as an art historian. It also demonstrated an instinct for what would be productive. Cornelius Gurlitt and Gustav Wustmann had published an earlier and 'fundamental'[30] inventory of noteworthy monuments in 1895–1896 but Pevsner had come across so much more material than Gurlitt had been aware of that he was eventually only able to incorporate an eighth of it.

One technical weakness in the study lay in its wish to present Leipzig as exceptional without providing comparative evidence that measured how much it differed from other towns. The reader was therefore left at a disadvantage when Pevsner observed that 'Without a doubt, no other German town had such a wealth of great artists and scholars associated with it [during the Baroque period]' or when he asked, rhetorically, 'Where in the fifth decade of the eighteenth century could one possibly come across a list of names all gathered together to equal those of Bach, Lessing, Klopstock, Gottsched and Gellert?'[31] He also quoted Goethe's memory of being overawed by Leipzig as a student, without acknowledging that Goethe had a habit of being overawed by whatever he gazed on. In this way his dissertation blurred the line between scholarship and advocacy. It co-opted famous names to make Leipzig look glamorous but made no effort to prove they were all attracted to Leipzig for the same reason or that they had a measurable impact on the city once they were there.

This weakness in the dissertation may be bound up in the fact that Pevsner had a personal interest in Leipzig: it was his home town and it pleased him no more than it pleased Ulrich Michel. For centuries it had been overshadowed by royal Dresden. It didn't have the architecture, the artistic resources or the social caché to compete. Even with its phenomenal population growth between 1850 and 1900 (from 63,000 to around 600,000), putting it on course to outflank Dresden in numbers and economic activity in the twentieth century,[32] it was still Saxony's second city and its virtues were those of a second city: more democratic, more equal, more bourgeois. Trade had made Leipzig powerful and allowed it to acquire the academic and musical prowess normally monopolized by the aristocracy and the Church, but trade had also kept it mercantile. It was Birmingham to Dresden's London, Chicago to Dresden's New York.

Choosing Leipzig was practical, however, because it meant that, in his first year of research at least, he could live cheaply with his parents and be near Lola. For this reason, instead of looking for somewhere more ennobling, he ennobled Leipzig. His choice was in sharp contrast to those English art historians who rounded on him just before and after his death: the people whom Reyner Banham called the 'National Trust Navy'[33] and whose interest in English architectural history seemed interwoven with a wish not just to study the upper classes but to become them. Pevsner was doing the opposite. He felt the disability of being associated with Leipzig but he embraced it. This meant embracing the one subject his disappointingly unintellectual and socially embarrassing father was at the centre of: the architecture of Leipzig's fur-trading streets, with their smells of furs and mothballs and their gossiping, arguing Jewish businessmen.

A German publisher, with no irony intended, described Leipzig as Pevsner's 'Vaterstadt' – literally his father-town or home town – and Pevsner must have felt this strongly in his two years of research. His father was a Kaufmann (business-man), with premises at the heart of the district Nikolaus had become interested in. In fact, apart from Katharinen Straße, no street in Leipzig provided him with more material for his dissertation than his father's street: Brühl. What did that mean to him? Was the study of Leipzig's fur district a way of understanding his father's world from an academic perspective or did it only make his father seem more alien by comparison? Did he think it offered a way of reaching out to his father or did it only emphasize their differences? Was it that by giving dignity to the Brühl he was giving dignity to his father and, by extension, to himself, or was he – Nikolaus – the only intended beneficiary? If he could show that Leipzig's run-down, unloved commercial centre had a respectable historic and artistic pedigree, that enhanced pedigree must surely reflect better on him.

10

Mannerism

And then he moved to Dresden. And not just to Dresden but to an internship at what until six years earlier had been the Royal Picture Gallery, the Königliche Gemäldegalerie,[1] where he hoped to devote his time to the study of sacred art in the late Renaissance. So much for architecture! So much for secularism! So much for Leipzig! So much for straying from the norm! In a review he'd written of one of Dehio's guides to German architecture, Pevsner had commended Dehio for restoring a belief in the importance of German art to the German nation and challenging Germany's misguided sense of inferiority to Italian culture. Yet here he was, defying Dehio's nationalism and going from the periphery of art-historical research to its Italian centre – with some relief, one has to suppose.

More than that, his internship put him at the administrative centre of one of the world's most important and on the face of it most conventional art institutions, an institution made up largely of works assembled in the first half of the eighteenth century by two successive rulers of Saxony who happened also to be kings of Poland, and rhapsodized over by Goethe in his memoirs more extravagantly than anything he'd rhapsodized about in Leipzig, as Pevsner must well have known. Pevsner was now just a desk away from the director, Dr Hans Posse, who'd joined the gallery in 1910, been appointed its director in 1913 and had just brought out a new guide to its masterworks. The internship might be an unpaid position – that was how prospective academics built up their standing and experience in Germany – but it offered privileged access to some of the leading figures in Germany's art-history network and to the works in their care.

Was that what Pevsner wanted? In view of his research topic at Leipzig and his later reputation as a promoter of modern architecture, it's not immediately easy to connect Pevsner to the world of old masters or see why after leaving Leipzig he would have headed first for a position in German museology. That's because the public image of Pevsner is of the figure he became in later life when, as an expert adviser in planning disputes, he tended to favour new buildings in any dispute between new and old. In the 1920s in Germany he was far more conservative. He found the modern world disappointing and offensive and had as yet no special commitment to the architecture of his own day. The new skyline that had risen up around him in Leipzig was full of what he regarded as Jugendstil vulgarity, with sculptures of nymphs and animals, swags of flowers and musical instruments, strange lettering, colourful mosaics, exotic tiling, exaggerated gables, inflated cornices, busy window surrounds, fussy oriels, gargantuan keystones, chunky stone quoins, patterned balconies, overpowering portals, illustrative reliefs and oversized doorknobs, all in unexpected varieties of historical styles. One of the biggest construction sites in his childhood was the previously mentioned Neues Rathaus, the New Town Hall, which he would have seen on his way from Ferdinand-Rhode-Straße to the Brühl.[2] Pevsner thought it all deplorable. In his dissertation, he condemned recent urban planning out of hand for ruining Leipzig's historic record.

Dresden, by contrast, was sumptuous. Historically, it had been the main residence of the dukes of Saxony and was strengthened against a Turkish invasion in the sixteenth century. It became a stronghold of Protestantism after the Reformation but reintroduced Roman Catholicism when its ruler, Elector of the Holy Roman Empire Frederick Augustus I, converted to Catholicism to become King of Poland in 1694. Polish wealth and Catholic exuberance turned Dresden into an architectural wonderland. From the early eighteenth century its rulers built a spectacular new royal palace (the Residenzschloss), transformed various churches (the Frauenkirche, the Hofkirche and the later Kreuzkirche) and created the Zwinger. Even more impressively, the director of its picture gallery got to live on site in one of the pavilions in the Großer Garten.[3]

Pevsner's unexpected attraction to Dresden argues compellingly that his doctoral work was not just a piece of scholarship but an escape into history. Having completed it, and having thereby paid off his debts to Leipzig, to his father, and to Schmarsow's belief in architecture's supremacy over the other arts, he was now free to retreat even further. And so, instead of developing his research by exploring Baroque architecture in other German cities, or in other types of buildings, or in pre-Baroque or post-Baroque Leipzig if his main interest had been Leipzig rather than the Baroque, he ran to Dresden to throw himself into the sixteenth-century religious paintings of Catholic Italy.

In fact, Dresden was only a half-way house in his ambitions. He was now a father – a daughter, Uta, had been born on 24 March 1924 at the Leipzig Women's Clinic, while he was working to complete his doctorate – and he needed to start earning a living, but he really wanted nothing else than to be doing postdoctoral work at the epicentre of art history, in the heartland of the Renaissance, in Florence. His target was Germany's Art History Institute, the Kunsthistorisches Institut that Schmarsow had lobbied for in the 1880s and that was formally inaugurated in 1897 after the art historian Heinrich Brockhaus gave up part of his apartment in Viale Principessa Margherita to make space for it. There's no evidence that Pevsner had had any previous connection with the institute,[4] but after finishing his dissertation he'd written to its new director, Heinrich Bodmer, about the possibility of a fellowship. Bodmer seems to have replied that there were currently no vacancies for 'Stipendien' in Florence but that if Pevsner wanted to wait for one to come up, he'd put in a good word with Posse (whose work on the Roman high-Baroque painter Andrea Sacchi[5] the institute was about to publish) about employing him in Dresden for the summer as a volunteer. Pevsner consequently wrote to Posse on 3 July, quoting Bodmer's support. He added that he'd also been recommended to apply by Professor Richard Graul, the director of Leipzig's Grassi Museum (which his father was a patron of) and respected editor of one of Germany's leading journals of art history, the *Zeitschrift für bildende Kunst*.

That Pevsner was perfectly qualified for an internship was not in any doubt. He'd submitted his completed dissertation on 10 May 1924. Pinder had finished reading it on 24 May, Studniczka on 28 May, and both had given it the highest possible rating – 'ausgezeichnet!' ('outstanding!'). Each had then given him an oral examination: Pinder on art history and Studniczka on archaeology, with Hellmann testing him on general history. All found him exceptional and he was 'promoted' – recommended for a doctorate – by Pinder on 4 June. He did, however, have a strange foreign name, which may explain why his letter to Posse was both over-eager and patrician in tone. Having taken his oral examinations, Pevsner said, he 'wanted to turn to a museum career' and was standing by 'each day and each hour' to discuss this with Posse in person. He was, however, at the moment relaxing at his father-in-law's country estate in Naumburg, where the post was fairly unreliable, and so he asked Posse to be good enough to give him a few days' notice. He named Bodmer as a referee, along with Pinder and Studniczska.

Having already been tipped off by Bodmer, Posse responded warmly to Pevsner's approach – though in writing back it took him three attempts to spell Pevsner's name correctly: 'Herrn Dr Nik. Peosner, Peusner, Pevsner'. Because of Naumburg's 'rotten' post (Pevsner used the schoolboyish word 'miesig' to describe it), Pevsner didn't get the letter for another six days but was so keen to start that he suggested meeting Posse at the picture gallery two days later, quoting the time of his train – one originating from Amsterdam – and apologizing in advance if it ran late. (The Amsterdam train was itself liable to be held up by late postal deliveries.) The two met on Friday, 11 July 1924 and got on so well that Pevsner wrote a formal letter of application the same day, following it up a week later with testimonials from Studniczska and from Pinder, who spoke of Pevsner as having been part of his closest circle of students and as having rare ability, talent and diligence.

On 19 July Pevsner was signed off by Leipzig University and received his doctoral certificate on 26 July. Meanwhile, Posse contacted Saxony's Ministry of Education to ratify the arrangement and on 28 July received confirmation. Posse had been told by Bodmer that Pevsner was only looking for a few months' work, but as a result of their meeting, Pevsner had asked, or agreed, to stay for a year. The Ministry approved this, but on the express understanding that payment was out of the question, that the position could be revoked at any moment, and that Pevsner shouldn't imagine it gave him any right to be considered for a salaried job if one should become available. He would start work on 15 August 1924, aged twenty-two-and-a-half.

Dresden's Old Masters Picture Gallery – the Gemäldegalerie – contained numerous masterpieces. Among its principal works were paintings by Raphael,

Giorgione, Titian and other Italian Renaissance painters as well as late Renaissance (Mannerist) and Baroque work. Dutch and Flemish art of the seventeenth century was represented by Rembrandt and his followers and by Vermeer, Ruysdael, Rubens, Jordaens and Van Dyck. There were important Old German and Old Dutch paintings by Jan van Eyck, Dürer, Cranach and Holbein, and a number of seventeenth-century French and Spanish works by Poussin and Lorrain, and by Ribera and Murillo. It was also the repository for work by notable artists from Saxony and Dresden itself.

Pevsner was assigned, at his own request, to the Italian department, where, in addition to general office work, he may have supported Posse in locating potential new acquisitions for the gallery, researching their provenance, and cataloguing and installing them once they'd been acquired. This is speculative because detailed records of the period haven't survived, but during Pevsner's time over fifty works came into the Gemäldegalerie's possession that overlapped with his field of interest, including two Tiepolos, one of which he wrote about.[6]

It's a matter of record, however, that Pevsner conducted tours of individual departments of the gallery, especially for the Workers' Education Committee of the ruling Social Democrat administration, on Sundays before opening hours.[7] He was joined in this work by two other volunteers. One was Karl Jähnig, already at the gallery when Pevsner arrived. The other was Ernst Michalski, his closest friend at Leipzig University and another member of Pinder's inner circle, who'd become an assistant six weeks after Pevsner, possibly on Pevsner's recommendation.

Pevsner was surrounded at the Gemäldegalerie by a small peer group of recently graduated scholars, a majority of whom had been supervised by Pinder and all of whom were now specializing in aspects of Italian and German art from the early Renaissance to the late Baroque. In addition to Jähnig and Michalski there was Erna von Watzdorf, who joined in January 1925 and who'd go on to become one of Dresden's most important curators and specialize in the work of the leading goldsmith of the German Baroque and in the history of Saxony during Roman times. When Watzdorf left in February 1926 she was replaced by Hildegard Marchand, who was also a fellow-student of Pevsner's under Pinder and who'd written her doctorate on the fifteenth-century sculpture of Halberstadt Cathedral before working as a volunteer for Graul in Leipzig for fourteen months.

Taken together, their work helped to develop their own and Dresden's reputation. Pevsner assisted Dresden further by publicizing Posse's work in leading journals. In 1925, for example, he wrote about the Gemäldegalerie's new acquisitions of Italian art[8] and about the reorganization of its collections.[9] In 1926, having been kept on for a further year, he reviewed Posse's book on Sacchi that the institute in Florence had now published.[10]

Pevsner's efforts in the gallery were backed up by a seemingly inexhaustible appetite for new literature. In addition to reading widely and incessantly in German, he read in Italian and English, occasionally in Dutch, Swedish and Finnish, and just sometimes, and very grudgingly, in French. He'd perfected his Italian and English with the help of Heinrich Sabersky, Lola's great uncle, in Berlin. Sabersky, whom Pevsner remembered for his 'white bipartite beard',[11] was a bookseller[12] and philologist who'd written language manuals for the publishing firm of Langenscheidt, including its Italian and English volumes.[13] 'Langenscheidt had developed a system for learning languages,' Wolfgang Hermann remembered.

> It gave you a simple sentence in three lines: the first line was the sentence in the foreign language, the second was the translation and the third was the pronunciation. You read line one, covering lines two and three with a screen, and translated it. Then you checked line two to see if you'd done it right – and then you had to decline each noun and conjugate each verb. Then you checked your pronunciation. I tried using it to learn Russian. I gave up after two or three chapters because it drove you mad – but you certainly learned. And this is how Pevsner learnt Italian. It was unbelievably difficult but he persevered. That's revealing.[14]

Nikolaus used Sabersky's manuals to improve his Italian and English, but according to Marianne Kockel, Sabersky had tutored Nika personally in Italian while Nika was studying in Berlin,[15] and a receipt exists, written in English, dated 3 December 1922, showing that Pevsner had received six English lessons in the previous month. These efforts helped Pevsner develop not only the specialist vocabulary of art and architecture that had been used 400 years earlier but also everyday language skills. This made him remarkably efficient in carrying out his own primary research and in absorbing up-to-the-minute information that other historians were producing. (Oddly, though, when a young art historian asked his advice many years later about producing a synoptic dictionary of architectural terms in the main European languages, he advised against on the grounds that it was too difficult.)[16]

Some scholars have suggested that Pevsner's education had had a 'specific' focus on the Renaissance and Baroque or that he'd had an 'intense' interest in sixteenth-century Italian art while at university. Both claims are premature since, as we've already seen, his education had been exceptionally broad and he'd applied himself intensely to all of it. It's true, however, that he now immersed himself in this area. In addition to writing about the Gemäldegalerie he started contributing articles on sixteenth-century artists to scholarly journals. Towards the end of 1924 he also set out to write his first book and approached the publishers of two rival art encyclopaedias – Athenaion in Potsdam and Propyläen in Berlin – with the idea of bringing out a volume on Italian painting from the end of the Renaissance through to Rococo.

Athenaion's *Handbuch der Kunstwissenschaft*[17] was the more respected and longer established of the two. It had been founded by Fritz Burger with Alfred

Brinckmann in 1912 and Brinckmann had taken over the editing when Burger was killed at Verdun.[18] It was consciously interested in bringing on younger historians and new ideas and it was for this series that Pinder had written the volume on mediaeval German sculpture. Propyläen had begun printing its rival *Kunstgeschichte* in 1923.[19] Both brought out part works and then bound them into finished volumes.

It was Propyläen that got back to Pevsner first. Early in 1925 it made him an offer he felt very pleased with himself for getting. Marianne Kockel remembered him saying how he'd gone into Posse's office very proudly to show him Propyläen's letter and been disappointed that Posse wasn't impressed. Posse thought Propyläen's illustrations were pretty but its texts second-rate. 'And Posse, who had a very Saxon accent that's not easy to understand, warned him: "Da gännen Se sich Ihren Ruhm kleich an der Wurzel apkrapen"[20] – meaning "Do that, and you might dig your reputation up by its roots."' So Pevsner turned Propyläen down and pursued Athenaion instead – successfully.

Pevsner needed to find the right publisher because his goal, in his proposed volume, was to write the definitive map of post-Renaissance art up until the start of Romanticism – a project that would make his name. He would take works and artists that were well known and others that had never been noticed before and subject them to an intensive analysis, relating the appearance and compositional style of particular pictures to other pictures by the same and other artists, and then to ever larger criteria such as where they were produced, the date when they were produced and finally the undercurrents of the prevailing culture.[21] He would then compress all this information in order to define once and for all the characteristics of eight different periods of art – a project equivalent, in Pevsner's view, to defining the properties of a molecule.

The work would be neither pure art history nor general history but a fusion of the two, Pevsner said later, linking 'the most important facts of Italian sixteenth-century painting and sculpture with the spiritual situation of the same decades' – from about 1520 to 1590 or 1600.[22] This inclusive approach reflected a pooling of Pevsner's admiration for Pinder, the tradition of teaching at Leipzig, and the decision that had governed the whole of his education: the importance of studying general history as well as art history. It contrasted diametrically with work also being done in Dresden by his friend Michalski who, in his studies of the Rococo, was insisting that there was no necessary relationship between art and religion and politics, and that Geistesgeschichte was an unnecessary encumbrance and should be sidelined.[23]

What propelled Pevsner's work was the conviction that art was starting to become comprehensible in a way it had never been before and that what he was doing was new and essential. Great strides had already been made in unravelling the Renaissance and in showing that what had been thought of as the decline of the Renaissance in the seventeenth century was in fact an altogether different phenomenon – the Baroque – with its own perfectly respectable characteristics and rules. (In 1875 Burckhardt had written from Rome: 'My respect for the Barocco increases every hour'.) Satisfied that this had been dealt with, Pevsner now chose to show how the Baroque period needed clarification, especially the muddle about how it started and ended.

Of special interest here were paintings that fell into the gap between the Renaissance and the Baroque, a gap that hadn't yet been looked at carefully and appeared to have no merit. This meant dealing with three generations of artists who'd lived in the shadow of Leonardo and Raphael and whose work had none of the same qualities of perfection and balance seen in the great masters. To a modern eye, their work seemed awkward and badly composed and Pevsner's task was to explain why this was. He did this by defining the dominant mood in mid-sixteenth-century Italy as mystical piety, Jesuitry and the suppression of the individual, and then showing that contrivance in paintings from Bronzino to El Greco, for example, was neither unintentional and deficient nor deliberate and skilful but simply the very thing you'd expect to see from artists working in that place at that time, and therefore historically legitimate. This was Geistesgeschichte at work.

The label for this new category of art was 'Mannerist' and Pevsner claimed, in 1964, 'I carry some of the responsibility for Mannerism having become a term defining a certain style in art, a style with positive qualities like the Renaissance and the Baroque', adding that 'the recognition of Mannerism as a style in its own right is due to Max Dvořák in Vienna in 1917, the publication of his views in 1921[24] and after, and to Wilhelm Pinder (who taught me the history of art) and his lectures of 1923 and 1924'.[25] Recognition of Mannerism made it possible for Pevsner to classify the early material in his *Handbuch* not as a preliminary form of Baroque but as something different. (Work that followed the early, high and late stages of Baroque he classified as proto-Romantic and then Rococo, though insisting later, and rather confusingly, that Rococo was 'not a separate style. It is part of the Baroque, as Decorated is part of the Gothic style.'[26])

Whatever else motivated Pevsner, his interest in Mannerism was also a continuation of his argument with the much-disliked Margarete Siebert Kurlbaum, Lola's step-mother. Although Pevsner credited himself with being one of the originators of the idea of Mannerism in the mid-1920s, Siebert had used the word some twenty years earlier. In her monograph on *The Representation of the Madonna in Old Dutch Art from Jan van Eyck to the Mannerists*,[27] she'd touched on the phenomenon of Mannerism in Holland. Of Quentin Massys (c. 1465–1530), she'd complained about phoniness of representation in his attempts to be modern and of constructional problems only a van Eyck could solve; and she'd regarded Jan Mabuse (c. 1478–1532) as 'even weaker than Massys' and 'even more defeated by the new manner'. This was a different subject from Pevsner's Italian Mannerists because she was talking about old northerners who couldn't manage the transition from Gothic to Renaissance, whereas Pevsner was dealing with young southerners for whom the Renaissance was already history. Siebert also used the word 'Mannerist' pejoratively, whereas Pevsner talked about it in terms of what it meant for artists who employed mannered techniques. Her view was critical; his was historical, but he gave no credit in his writings to the fact that she'd already been applying the Mannerist label.

The scholarly activity that Pevsner, Michalski and their colleagues were involved in at Dresden at the start of 1925 was as formidable as any that might have been encountered at a university faculty, though in the absence of any clear documentation, it's hard to tell where the balance lay between research Pevsner was doing for Posse and research he was doing for himself. Pevsner's volume of the *Handbuch* was scheduled to appear in instalments from late 1925.[28] By February of that year he was already in close correspondence with museums, galleries, churches, palaces, villas, local authorities and private collectors all across Italy and elsewhere in Europe, asking questions about their sixteenth- and seventeenth-century holdings and requesting photographs. In March he was reading background material on Ignatius Loyola and urban life in the time of the Counter-Reformation by the German cultural and economic historian Eberhard Gothein. He was also seeking guidance from other historians.

Of particular interest to Pevsner was Giovanni Battista Crespi (1573–1632), otherwise known as Cerano. Pevsner regarded Cerano as the most important artist in Milan and one of the best of the whole period,[29] and wrote about him in the 1925 *Yearbook of the Prussian Art Galleries*.[30] Cerano specialized in scenes of religious intensity: Jesus appearing to the Apostles, for example, or the *Messe des heiligen Gregor*, and like many other painters of the Counter-Reformation, his pictures were designed to carry an explicit Catholic message. What did that mean for Pevsner as a recent convert to Protestantism?

It's arguable that no one who professed Judaism could feel completely at home interpreting Christian iconography because the images, coming on top of centuries of Christian anti-Semitism, were too loaded. Even though the study of art history was no longer tied to Christianity, religious imagery didn't stop being religious just because it was now being studied outside the context of the church, and historians from Jewish backgrounds who worked on religious iconography in this period had overwhelmingly either already converted to Christianity or came from families that had converted. (An exception was Goldschmidt at Berlin, whose lectures on the representation in art of the birth of Christ Pevsner heard in his semester there.) Even today, Christian iconography is still not an obvious subject for a Jewish scholar, any more than it's an obvious source of imagery for a Jewish artist, a topic explored by Chaim Potok in his novel *My Name is Asher Lev*.

The question of whether he might be accused of trespassing on territory that wasn't native to him was something Pevsner was sensitive to and he touched on it nearly thirty years later in a radio talk[31] about Basil Spence's new design for Coventry Cathedral: the propriety of engaging with a religion one doesn't profess.

I gather that Mr Spence doesn't go to church every Sunday and I am what you would call chapel and not church – certainly not C. of E. Can he therefore[32] design a cathedral and should I keep my mouth shut about his design? Well – I don't know ... [Some] would deny Mr Spence the right to design Coventry and me to think aloud about his design because we are not as close to the spiritual content of the Church of England as say Sir Ninian Comper or Mr Betjeman. Well, once again, I don't know.

The answer, Pevsner said at the time, was to treat one's task 'with respect and humility', but it's clear that in spite of feeling he needed to become Christian in 1921, he didn't think – unlike Pinder – that 'racial' or 'tribal' or religious or family or personal background compromised intellectual competence, and certainly not his own. Religious content in art wasn't what Pevsner cared about, even in Mannerism's most extravagantly religious paintings. What he was interested in was how a work fitted into an artistic-cultural schema, irrespective of the ostensible subject of the painting. His combination of art history and general history offered him a way of approaching paintings that might have had no other existence than as religious icons for four centuries and giving them a new purpose.

What made Cerano important to Pevsner, for example, wasn't what made him important as a religious propagandist for his church patrons in Milan. It was 'his exceptionally well-developed sense for abstract form and cool, clear colour', making him 'one of the last big preachers' not of the Gospel but 'of the Mannerist ideal'.[33] This revisionism, which made religious art illustrative of everything in its surrounding except the praise of God, was very much in line with what Athenaion's *Handbuch* was set up to explore. Its limitation, Pevsner admitted some years later, recalling an outing with Michalski, 'I can tell you from experience, is that two ardent students of the history of art could go to a museum and debate wildly over, say, a mediaeval relief and only on the way home realize that neither of them remembered what it actually represented.'[34]

Although Pevsner was an art historian, he believed the harnessing of general history and art history qualified him to talk about the roots of everything. His art-historical labels, such as Mannerism and Baroque, were therefore definitions not just of periods in art but of the entire psyche of Western civilization at a particular moment. His certainties on this subject brought him into collision with Werner Weisbach, two of whose lecture courses he'd taken in Berlin and who'd criticized Schmarsow for lacking feeling. In 1921 Weisbach had published *Baroque as the Art of the Counter-Reformation*.[35] The book seems to have gone unnoticed at the time, but four years later, in 1925, Pevsner, in what looks like an academic grudge fight, brought it to prominence in a review that attacked Weisbach and promoted his own alternative view that the natural style of the Counter-Reformation was not Baroque but Mannerism.[36]

The review – 'Gegenreformation und Manierismus' – may have pushed Pevsner to go further than he was really comfortable with but it served as a test case for his foregrounding of history. His main complaint with Weisbach was that Weisbach's history was sloppy. 'Today more than ever,' Pevsner stated, aged 23,

> art historians tend to neglect the basic historical framework in favour of the study of formal development, and this easily leads to misconceptions as to the conditions under which works of art have been produced, and consequently to errors of interpretation. This is why I think it necessary to establish a historical framework for the study of the development of Italian Mannerism.[37]

Discomforting Weisbach was easily done, Pevsner believed, simply by showing that Weisbach had allowed the Counter-Reformation to last from 1520 until 1750 instead of ending it in 1620. By letting it overrun for 130 years, he'd overlapped into the Baroque period and then back-dated Baroque characteristics onto the previous century. Pevsner argued that because the Counter-Reformation didn't exist in the eighteenth century, this back-dating was meaningless. He then corrected Weisbach by explaining exactly what was going on during the Counter-Reformation and what its artistic parallels were. The Counter-Reformation, he said, involved an escalation of religious feeling by the Catholic Church that led away from the harmony and balance of the Renaissance towards the ever-increasing harshness, intolerance and authoritarianism of the Roman Inquisition. The function of art in this period was the propagation of piety. In consequence, figures in paintings became mere symbols whose individuality was suppressed in favour of anonymous crowds, overcomplicated draperies, unnatural shape-making and sexual suggestiveness – and that was Mannerist art.

Pevsner's analysis of Mannerism in this essay was itself harsh and intolerant and has every indication of having been soured by his view of Weisbach. It's hard to imagine that when he first began his work on Mannerism, he was as scathing of it as he became in his attack on Weisbach and there are enough examples of his writings where he wrote warmly of individual artists and their work. And yet in 'Gegenreformation und Manierismus', no one emerged well because art had to comform to a view of Mannerism so partial that it had every appearance of being a witch-hunt of exactly the kind he accused the Counter-Reformation papacy of conducting.

Whether this aggressive finger-pointing was itself a reflection of the times is to follow Pevsner down his own path of cultural commentary, but, just seven years after the end of Europe's most devastating war, he may have been recognizing parallels between the modern age and the devastation caused to Germany by Catholicism, in his view, during the Thirty Years War (1618–1648). In any case, his approach was quintessentially a north-German Protestant view and depended on his unquestioning acceptance of the historical work done by Ranke, especially in his *History of the Popes*, by Gothein on Ignatius Loyola, and by the Catholic historian Ludwig Pastor, an Austrian whose own *History of the Popes* was an attempt to defend the Papacy contextually and correct Ranke's errors but which Pevsner turned on its head to support Ranke.[38] Unsurprisingly, a closing footnote acknowledged: 'I owe some of the ideas that appear above to lines of thought that [Wilhelm] Pinder will hopefully soon be developing [in an article of his own] in this publication, and to their formation in lectures and seminar exercises that I took part in [with him]'.

This is not to minimize the 'reign of terror' that was perpetrated by the Papacy under the influence of various sects from the Sodality of Divine Love, founded in 1518, to the brothers of the Misericord and the Jesuits in 1540, and Pevsner was justified in talking about the necessity of reading 'the grisly details of interrogation and torture (in Soldan's *History of Witchcraft*) before one can picture, as an art historian must, the true nature of the age', and of the 'quasi-mediaeval religiosity' that prevailed under Gregory XIII, 'a time of banditry and gang warfare in Rome, but also of the processions of flagellants described by Montaigne', even if he relished doing so. Nor is it proper to insist that because every artist didn't display every characteristic that Pevsner identified, his thesis was invalid. But it's true that in his wish to make Mannerism stand as the grim face of fanatical, politicized Catholicism, he engaged in what he later called 'lusty generalizations'[39] from which he had to keep retreating (such as the prevalence of suggestive eroticism in Mannerist art, in spite of its 'total absence', which he acknowledged, 'in the most important Mannerists, Tintoretto, Bassano, El Greco, Barocci, Cerano, Zuccaro and Calvaert') and that he yoked together unconnected historic figures in order to suggest a common character to the age.

Pevsner's defence was that he was quoting impeccable historical sources. 'To protect myself from the objection that I have forced historical facts into a parallelism with facts in art, I shall make a point of quoting verbally, as often as possible, the standard historical studies of the Counter-Reformation', he said in his introductory remarks. 'Without exception, these reveal that the facts are agreed, and that only my conclusions are new.' It was a loose defence that excused him from doing any original historical research himself, but since he'd gone further than any other art historian had done, it was a defence that served his purpose for several years and he was well received.

In 1925 Bodmer at the Kunsthistorisches Institut responded to Pevsner's work on Cerano in a letter that said: 'I can't do otherwise than agree with all your remarks' and invited him to discuss matters of mutual interest when he was next in Florence. Walter Friedländer, who'd already been working on Mannerism, was also complimentary, commenting that although he had arguments on specific points, in general 'I'm delighted that we agree on the basic ideas about the perception of that particular period, 1520–1580 (or later), and that my old chestnut about the autonomy of the Mannerist style, for which I've been fighting for so long, is now finally accepted.' In 1926 Pevsner's former lecturer in Frankfurt, Leo Bruhns, now at Rostock University, replied warmly about his work and also invited him to meet him for further discussions on the subject.

The issues that now seem problematic in Pevsner's work didn't seem problematic at the time because he was doing work that seemed far more 'scientific' than what had previously been available. In addition, his writing, like Ranke's, was persuasive and it read well – as it still does. For that reason, by the time the various instalments of his *Handbuch* had been brought together for publication in 1928, Pevsner – in spite of his own cultural prejudices and his susceptibility to the demagoguery of Pinder – was starting to be a figure to be reckoned with.

As Pevsner became more sure of himself, he took on important and sometimes controversial new tasks. In 1928 he carried out an important redating[40] of the life of Caravaggio, whose wish to shock in the early 1600s had brought renewed interest in him in the 1920s.[41]. This drew a compliment from the Finnish historian Tancred Borenius, with whom Pesvner had been in touch in London, congratulating him 'on such a valuable and, indeed, on certain points revolutionary contribution to the knowledge of the great artist'. It also drew a complaint from a historian who objected that Pevsner's redating had relied on the wrong pictures to make its case and had made too much use of the complainant's own research, which hadn't been sufficiently credited.

Finding the art world could be unforgiving, Pevsner himself became combative and was scornful of anyone who fell short of his standards, including older figures whose reputations were already established. In a 1926 review of a book by the artist Ludwig Lang that attempted to explain the Baroque, he remarked, cuttingly:

> That such a job can be done, Pinder's *German Baroque* has shown; that it can only be done by an eminent figure with as much wealth of thought as power of diction, this book sadly proves.[42]

Weisbach, almost thirty years older, was certainly wounded by what the art world had called 'the Pevsner Polemic' in 1925 and in the same year Pevsner upset Herman Voss, curator of painting at the Kaiser-Friedrich Museum in Berlin (and later, Posse's successor at Dresden), in his review of Voss's *Baroque Painting in Rome*.[43] 'Someone called Pevsner' had claimed that the book contained information on every insignificant Roman Baroque painter, Voss complained, when in fact, on the very first page of the foreword, Voss had specifically stated he'd been selective about whom to include. It was also wrong for Pevsner to say he'd held back from dealing with problems of stylistic analysis and composition and wrong to say his introduction kept up a polemic he'd been trotting out for years. Pevsner responded at once:

> Your reply . . . absolutely astonished me. The deliberately offensive tone, which you find fitting, was a complete surprise for I was aware only of friendly encouragement from you for my Cerano work, which I certainly paid my respects for in the proper way. You must

therefore have extracted from the short review a maliciousness that it in no way contains and I wonder in vain how you could have assumed it.

Art historians can apparently be touchy. But what we see during Pevsner's Dresden years is a growing assurance and certainty of touch as he started to make a name for himself in post-Renaissance studies. His young cousin Heinrich Pollack was most impressed. He'd been taken to Dresden by his mother while suffering 'the most terrible cold I've ever had, but I wanted to see Raphael's *Sistine Madonna* under the expert tutelage of my cousin, and I didn't regret it'.[44]

11

Dresden

When Pevsner began his internship at the Gemäldegalerie, he, Lola and their new baby had had to move out of their small flat in Leipzig and find lodgings in Dresden. 'There was a housing shortage at the time,' remembered Marianne Kockel, 'and so to begin with they lived in a house of friends of my parents, which they rented furnished, fairly near to the Großer Garten, the big Baroque park like the Englische Garten in Munich. The following summer, Nika went to Italy for research, Lola moved to my father's vineyard to save money on rent and the people let to someone else. [When he got back,] they moved to new accommodation.'

This became their pattern. In the autumn they'd rent somewhere to live for the year, in the summer they'd move out, Pevsner would go to Italy to do research and his wife would go back to her parents' country home in Naumburg. In the autumn of 1925 'they moved into an apartment in the same neighbour-hood.[1] The next year they moved again, this time not so close to the Großer Garten, into a two-family house where a young married architect couple lived, a little older than them, and [Nika and Lola] lived upstairs. They had a children's room and a bedroom, and a study for him, and a kitchen and bath.'

Pevsner must have found himself over-stretched at Dresden, given the demands of his work for the picture gallery and of his own research. But in March 1925 he took on a new activity that would extend him in an entirely different direction. He came in contact with Friedrich Kummer, a theatre critic who edited the arts section of the *Dresdner Anzeiger*, one of Dresden's two daily newspapers,[2] and became the paper's art reporter, taking over from Richard Stiller and contributing articles on a freelance basis once or twice a week. A normal article would be about a new exhibition, either at one of Dresden's public galleries or at a private salon (most commonly the Galerie Arnold and the Emil Richter Gallery, but also the Fides, the Kühl and the gallery started by the photographer Hugo Erfurth). He wrote initially as Dr N. P. but from July 1925 under his surname or as 'Dr Nik. Pevsner' and very occasionally as 'Dr Nikolaus Pevsner, Gemäldegalerie, Dresden', and in his first year produced over forty reviews between 20 March and 14 December.

Writing for the *Anzeiger* was Pevsner's first professional exposure to modern art. It gave him a small income and the self-respect that came from earning it. It also provided him with a new status in Dresden as a local opinion former. Whether talking about new German masters – Kolbe, Kirchner, Holder, Beckmann – or provincial exhibitions by, for example, the Saxon Art Association,

Pevsner brought the same encyclopaedic quality of appraisal he brought to the sixteenth century. In his first four months with the paper, he only wrote about Dresden but gave a vivid account of the town's apparent vitality as the leading centre of modern art in East Germany, in competition with Berlin to the north and Munich to the south. From the summer his reports occasionally included accounts of art he'd seen elsewhere: a new exhibition of old master paintings at the Berlin Academy of Arts, an arts and crafts fair at the Grassi Museum in August, and statues of Greek goddesses in the Berlin Museum – material that makes it possible to track the timing of some of his movements around the country. Mostly, however, he was writing about modern art and the reception it was getting – his first sign of any interest in the art of his own time and an indicator of his remarkable ability to absorb and process new information.[3]

In addition to what he said about art, Pevsner's *Anzeiger* articles give an insight into what art said about him, particularly in his role as a conservative counterweight to the influential local critic Will Grohmann, who'd been involved in the Dresden Secession Group of 1919 and had links with the radical new art school, the Staatliches Bauhaus in Weimar.

Particularly revealing was Pevsner's coverage of a dispute within the Dresden Artists' Union (the Künstlervereinigung), a loose association of Dresden artists that included members of the Secession. In July 1925 he'd written about the opening of the union's annual exhibition on Lennéstraße. In the course of that piece, he'd called on it to explain the 'strange change' in its board of directors and its expulsion of some of Dresden's most prominent artists. Not receiving a reply he wrote two more pieces in August, attacking the new guard. The union had always been scrupulous about ensuring its shows were of the highest quality, he said, and had encouraged young artists with all its heart. 'It was all the more astonishing, then,' he continued,

> that the same young Expressionists who'd only got onto the board with the support of the older generation should now seize the running of the organization, repay their sponsors with ingratitude and force them out of office, without any personal restraint. We're not so cut off that we can't recognize youth's capacity for self-renewal in associations such as this. Today's public figures were also radicals and aggressives once. But the situation here was always that the unfailing sensitivity of the older generation smoothed the path for those of the new generation. No one could ever complain of being neglected, and so they don't now have any right to quote the last generation's struggle for existence, because that struggle never struck a political wrong note, in spite of strong opposition from old people at that time ... It's a given that men like Tessenow and Albiker, Sterl and Ludwig von Hofmann, Rösler and Gußmann, to name only a few from their generation, stand on a far higher level than, let's say, Schubert and Bockstiegel in theirs.[4]

Pevsner discounted the fact that contemporary art in Dresden had always been troubled and treated modern radicalism as a discourtesy to a better past. His view of the Secessionists – who were in fact making their last bid for survival before disintegrating – was evidently that they were simply unruly, both in their character and in their art. In a follow-up article, he typified young artists starting out in 1913 as so driven by absolutism that they felt they had to overturn and violate nature with garish colours and cubist forms, while their counterparts in 1925, especially in Germany, only returned to nature so they could maliciously or demoniacally exaggerate it, in the manner of Dix and Gross.

It seems not to have occurred to Pevsner that there was a similarity between the distortions in modern art and the very work he was concentrating on in Italian Mannerism.[5] The turmoil he commented on in the Dresden Artists' Union also matched the turmoil going on in the country as a whole and in particular within Pevsner's mother's party, the DDP. The DDP had entered government with great moral ambitions but was let down by its lack of political intelligence and its organizational incompetence. Its founders included academics and professionals who lacked experience of political power and were unable to pool their differences for the common good. Their approach to politics was more theoretical than practical. While idealizing democracy, they found democratic procedures unfamiliar, failed to explain themselves adequately to the electorate, failed to support their Socialist coalition partners on core issues and wasted their efforts in petty squabbles. Their enemies branded them 'the Jewish Party', but as they declined in popularity, that label became more and more inappropriate. Their more liberal leaders resigned and those who remained floated off to the right until their key beliefs – anti-Semitism, anti-republicanism, nationalism and racism – were barely different from the most right-wing parties. Eventually they renamed themselves the Staatspartei.[6]

What's most surprising about Pevsner's writing on Dresden is that although he was only an intern at the Gemäldegalerie, he considered himself free to take a stand on positions that were complex and polarized, and to identify individuals for praise or condemnation, even though by doing so he might be compromising his ability to work with them in the future or embarrassing his employers and the state. How the Gemäldegalerie responded to these writings, or how they may have looked to the public, is unknown. It's most likely, however, that what Pevsner felt about the Secessionists coincided with what he knew Posse would approve, since the names he reserved for praise were all involved in the running of a vast international exhibition Posse was organizing for the following year and that Pevsner had been brought in to work on just a month after he'd started writing for the *Anzeiger*.[7]

The history of international art exhibitions in Dresden went back nearly thirty years. The first, conceived and directed by Karl Schmidt, a local master carpenter and entrepreneur, was held in 1897 and was notable for incorporating not just paintings but applied art: domestic goods and handicrafts from all over Germany, Tiffany glass from America, and furniture by the influential Belgian architect Henri van de Velde.[8] The exhibition promoted various messages – some moral, some practical, some work-related and some cultural. The moral message was that artists, architects and craftsmen (designers as such didn't then exist) could play a role in making life better. The practical message was that furniture didn't need to be fussy and ornamental or keep reworking French Rococo. The artisanal message was that artist-craftsmen deserved to be paid better and receive due credit for their work. The cultural message was that Germany needed to modernize if it was to compete better in the new world. These various ideas came together in a general assertion that simpler, sturdier, more reliable domestic goods by no-longer-anonymous makers would improve the standard of living, bring society up to date, make life more democratic and raise Germany's profile.[9]

By whatever criteria the 1897 exhibition was judged, it was subsequently seen as a success. Architects took from it the idealistic notion that they in particular could reform society through design; the city authorities came away convinced that big exhibitions were good for the local economy and for Dresden's reputation. Further exhibitions followed, some international and some national. Six were held between 1897 and 1904, putting the town on the map decisively enough to persuade the National Organization of German Applied Arts Associations to move its Third German Applied Arts Exhibition to Dresden from Munich, where the two previous exhibitions had been held in 1876 and 1888. This move was seen as a coup for Dresden and the state of Saxony and was pushed for by the art historian to whom Pevsner's Leipzig dissertation owed so much: Cornelius Gurlitt, who was then involved with the Technical University of Dresden.

The financial gains that could be made from promoting good design sparked considerable new thinking: at a civic level about the attraction of providing showcases for new art, within industry about how production methods could be simplified and made cheaper, and at a union level about whether people who designed and made furniture should receive fees and royalties in addition to salaries or piecemeal pay, and about how much public exposure and name recognition they should get. These various considerations were invariably sublimated, in public at least, into more elevated talk about the need for aesthetic unity and artistic brotherhood.

Dresden had been unable to mount big exhibitions during the war but the town was keen to start them again once hostilities were over. In addition to various smaller and shorter-lived exhibitions, it staged four grand Annual Shows, all intended as trade showcases, in the summers of 1922–1925 and all focusing on the applied arts.[10] During 1925 it was decided that the 1926 Annual Show would be the turn of painting – and this Annual Show would double as Germany's first international art exhibition since the start of the war.

Since life in Germany was not yet back to normal, the organizers accepted it would be hard to emulate pre-war standards; international participation would therefore have to be smaller than they'd have liked. But after a long gap in

Germany's cultural relations with the rest of the world, there was a strong wish to show as much as possible of what was going on abroad, while always avoiding art that had been designed to make money. The exhibition would therefore include work by whatever important names it could attract, as well as including local representation, but it wouldn't try to advance a view about where art was heading.[11]

For anyone who only knows Dresden as a tourist destination, the idea that it was also a centre of one of the most progressive art movements in Germany may seem incongruous. But Dresden had always attracted artists and craftsmen and with the rise of Socialism in the nineteenth century, workers in the arts came to the city to join associations that protected and advanced their interests, adopting various political affiliations as they did so – some to the left, some to the right. Dresden was the home of Die Brücke, a quarrelsome group of artists that came together in 1905 to try to bridge the gap between traditional German painting and the new Expressionism. It was also where Hellerau was built – Germany's first garden suburb, founded in 1909 by the same man who'd devised the city's 1897 International Exhibition, Karl Schmidt,[12] and an immediate magnet for progressives and utopians. It was not inconsistent, then, that where the international exhibitions in Munich in 1876 and 1888 had concentrated on the art of the past – the Renaissance and Baroque and 'the work of our forefathers' ('Unserer Väter Werke') – the Dresden International Exhibition of 1926 would be decisively new.

Planning for the exhibition began in 1924 under the leadership of Robert Sterl, a local painter and the headmaster of the Academy of Fine Arts of Dresden. Sterl became ill, however,[13] or else objected to the recent activities of the Secessionists. In early spring 1925 he resigned and his duties were taken on by Hans Posse, because of the Gemäldegalerie's responsibility for painting. It was then that Posse asked Pevsner to help him.

How Pevsner contributed to the exhibition cannot be said with certainty. Posse reported to his board of trustees that he himself had travelled to France, Belgium and other European countries (but not to the USA, England or the USSR) to select works for the exhibition[14] and Pevsner confirmed, in the first of his newspaper reports about the exhibition the following year, that Posse had spent a year travelling at home and abroad in preparation for the exhibition. There are no public records to show whether Pevsner accompanied Posse on any of these visits but Pevsner had certainly gone to Paris in October 1925, during the last month of the celebrated Paris Exhibition, and may have travelled with Posse or acted as Posse's ambassador.[15]

For most of the time, however, Pevsner would have remained in the gallery during Posse's absences and a letter from Posse still exists, advising a transport firm that Dr Pevsner would take receipt of its delivery of a work of art.[16] It's noteworthy, however, that in Posse's foreword to the catalogue of the exhibition, Pevsner alone of the Dresden staff was singled out for a mention – as 'an industrious and untiring helper'.[17] It's hard to conceive how he had the time to be the hardest-working member of Posse's team when there was so much else he was busy with. It presages the familiar remark in later years that there must have been several Pevsners because time was too short for there to have been only one.

The International Exhibition of 1926 provided Pevsner with a chance to become familiar with not just the leading contemporary artists in the world but the entire infrastructure that lay behind them: owners, agents, galleries, dealers, insurers and shippers (his father's field of expertise). In the one-year run-up to the show and its five-month duration from May to October, he dealt with galleries throughout Germany; with public galleries in Amsterdam, the Hague, Basel, Berne, Zurich, Brussels, Budapest, Helsinki, London, Prague, Stettin and Vienna; with private galleries in those cities and in Paris, New York, Lucerne, Geneva, Lausanne and Stockholm; and with some 140 private collections. He came in contact with members of various honorary committees – one for senior political representatives, one for less senior figures and for local trustees – and with the executive committees for administration, finance, building and press relations. He came across Heinrich Tessenow, one of the architects of Hellerau garden city, along with Herman Muthesius and Richard Riemerschmid, who was called in to rebuild the inner structure of Dresden's Exhibition Palace and add a new courtyard to it especially for the international show. He also did considerable library research on how international exhibitions in other countries had been staged and visited the great Paris International Exhibition of 1925 to get some perspective of his own.

Pevsner's visit to the Paris Exhibition in the late autumn of 1925 proved to be a milestone in his research. That exhibition, delayed since 1914, ran for five months during the summer of 1925 and was intended to reassert France's supremacy over the arts, now that the war was over. It was the exhibition that introduced Art Deco to the world and established it as the new style – an audacious gesture at a time when other countries were concentrating only on their own artistic identities. Where cubes and planes in German art meant Teutonic fracture, for example, in Art Deco they meant cosmopolitan elegance and chic; where German zigzags spoke of angst, in Art Deco they echoed exciting African rhythms. Where art from the rest of the world was self-referencing and nationalistic, France's contribution, and indeed the whole concept behind the exhibition, was universal, confident and positive – an invitation to a new post-war stylistic harmony.

The Exposition Internationale des Arts Décoratifs et Industriels Modernes, as the French exhibition was called, was also a slap in the face for Germany. Germany alone of the major powers was not invited to participate[18] and was humiliated further by France's provocatively devoting three pavilions to Alsace, the long fought-over region that Germany had annexed from France in 1871 and that France had regained in 1918. The Paris Exhibition was war by other means.

Pevsner understood this clearly and took a stand against everything Paris represented. Twelve years later he wrote:

> It was the ominous Paris Exhibition of 1925 which must be held responsible for the introduction of bad 'Modernism' . . . Jazz fittings, that is, fittings with pseudo-cubistic, angular glass panels, became the fashion. Similar spiky forms had had a great vogue in Germany about 1922–1923 in connection with the style which dominated in 'Expressionist' painting during these most restless years of postwar change. In Germany, however, a reaction against the vulgar commercial caricatures of this type set in immediately.

Germany was chastened, Pevsner went on, by the introduction of simple, unadorned designs from 1923 that he claimed 'steadily gained ground'. Not so in France, where the 1925 Paris Exhibition became 'an inexhaustible source of sham splendour'.[19]

The two exceptions to the overwhelmingly decorative thrust of Paris were the Soviet pavilion by Konstantin Melnikov and the Pavillon de l'Esprit Nouveau by Le Corbusier. For Pevsner, the Melnikov building could be dismissed on the grounds that the USSR wasn't part of Europe and therefore fell outside the European Geistesgeschichte that it was his role to elucidate. The Le Corbusier building was different. It was intrinsically a denial of everything that the Paris Exhibition stood for. Instead of applying the decorative gimmicks of Art Deco, it offered a simple disposition of spaces and surfaces that so offended the organizers that they tried to hide it away behind a high fence. The fence was removed on the orders of the French government, but when the exposition's international jury threatened to award Le Corbusier's work first prize in spite of this, the Académie Française moved to veto the international jury's vote.[20]

One might have thought that Pevsner would have embraced Le Corbusier as a fellow critic of Art Deco. He couldn't do that, however, because Le Corbusier, though born in Switzerland, was too francophile to be an ally. Instead he tried to find a way in which he could help Germany to fight back on his own – against Art Deco, against the insult of the Paris Exhibition and against Le Corbusier, whom the world had hailed.

A trip to Dessau the following month could have told him whether there was anything in what the Bauhaus was doing that might salvage Germany's glory. From 1570 Dessau had been the capital of Anhalt, one of the smaller states of the Holy Roman Empire, and developed in the eighteenth century as an attractive Baroque town. In the nineteenth century, however, it became an industrial centre,[21] produced cars and engines on an assembly line from 1912, and during the First World War saw the Junkers Company divert from making radiators to making aircraft.

In 1919 the architect Walter Gropius had established his new art school, the State ('Staatliches') Bauhaus, in Weimar, the capital of the Grand Duchy of Saxe-Weimar some seventy miles away, effectively replacing the Grand-Duchy School of the Applied Arts that Henri van de Velde had created in 1906. Within five years of its founding, however, political and practical opposition to the Bauhaus had become acute. From the start the school had been seen by outsiders as a hotbed of left-wing radicalism, and although Gropius had meant it to earn revenue from designing for industry, it was badly in debt. For these two reasons, Weimar's right-wing authorities, having already cut its funding, threatened it with closure. To pre-empt this, Gropius decided on 26 December 1924 to dissolve the school himself and look for a better location.

Recognizing the Bauhaus's need to be close to industry and potential clients, it occurred to the art historian Ludwig Grote that Dessau would be a good alternative home and he persuaded its mayor, Fritz Hesse, that the town would gain from the Bauhaus's presence. On 24 March 1925 Dessau's municipal council voted in favour of giving the Bauhaus a new site. After further negotiation, Gropius won agreement that the Bauhaus should also absorb the existing Dessau School of Arts and Crafts and Trade School instead of the other way round.

It was obvious to Gropius that the Dessau School was too small to house both institutions. He therefore persuaded the mayor to fund a new building that Gropius would design, to include workshops, studios, a technical school, an auditorium with a stage, and a dining hall. The new building would be connected by a bridge to a second block, originally intended for the Dessau School but that the Bauhaus took over once it was complete. Gropius also got approval for four houses – one for himself and three semi-detached houses for his senior staff: one that paired László Moholy-Nagy and Lyonel Feininger, one for Georg Muche and Oskar Schlemmer, and one for Wassily Kandinsky and Paul Klee.

Gropius's designs were ready by mid-summer and contracts were let, but strikes delayed the start of building work until September. In the interim, teaching for the winter semester, which started on 14 October 1925, was held in an old textile mill and an old rope factory. A topping-out ceremony for the main building wasn't held until 21 March 1926 but construction of the masters' houses proceeded much more quickly and a topping-out ceremony was held for them on 15 November 1925,[22] with a formal opening party a few weeks later on Saturday, 4 December.

Pevsner could easily have attended the topping-out ceremony of Gropius's masters' houses, either in his own right as a reporter for the *Dresden Anzeiger* or as Posse's proxy. He'd just been to Berlin to visit galleries in connection with his own research and since there was now a fast new rail link from Berlin to Dresden that skirted Dessau, he could have fitted a visit in on the way back. He could even have sounded out Bauhaus artists about their possible participation in the Dresden exhibition. Several of the most important artists did go on to show there: Dix (who two years later would be appointed Professor of the Dresden Academy of Art), Schlemmer, Muche, Moholy-Nagy, Klee and Kandinsky, though as Annegret Karge, who has been working in this field,[23] points out, the actual recommendations about whom to invite from the Bauhaus would probably have been made through Will Grohmann, the art critic who lived and taught in Dresden, because Grohmann had connections with the school, which Pevsner didn't, and was a member of the honorary committee (Ehrenpräsidium) of the exhibition, which brought him in frequent contact with Posse.[24]

Pevsner seems to have chosen not to visit the opening ceremony, though.[25] For one thing, at this stage in his life, he was no keener on the Bauhaus than he was on the Secessionists. That year's Annual Show in Dresden had featured model housing, for example, and in a series of three articles he'd written about the show in July, Pevsner hadn't mentioned the Bauhaus once, although it was starting to be spoken of elsewhere as the litmus test of modern ideas (even if it didn't yet have an architecture department), nor had he mentioned Gropius, in spite of every opportunity to do so.[26] Instead he commended Tessenow, Ernst May, Oscar Niemeyer and Bruno Paul[27] (whose liking for flat roofs Pevsner thought inappropriate in Germany's climate)[28] and complimented the designer of the show, Paul Wolf.

It wasn't because Gropius wasn't involved in the Annual Show that Pevsner didn't mention him: Bruno Taut was also not involved but still got named. Pevsner didn't mention Gropius because he didn't think highly of him at the time. Gropius was running a school with a reputation as Germany's 'cathedral of socialism'[29] and Pevsner no more wished to champion Socialism than did the authorities in Weimar.

Had Pevsner attended the topping-out ceremony, he'd have seen in any case that Gropius's latest work had taken a Corbusian turn. Although more rooted to the ground than the Pavillon in Paris, Gropius's masters' houses at Dessau were also made up of intersecting asymmetric cubist boxes with cantilevered balconies and upper floors. They had none of the lightness of Le Corbusier but they were significantly more French than Gropius's more eclectic and heavier-looking work of the previous ten years, and they had big windows – unlike all but one of Gropius's earlier buildings, the windows of which were tiny. They also had flat roofs, in contrast with Gropius's model factory in 1914.

The Bauhaus buildings at Dessau could therefore not have provided ammunition for the assault Pevsner wished to mount on Le Corbusier and France. Le Corbusier, he wrote later, was a man 'who – we all know – is always so anxious to prove that he has been there before or that he told you so'.[30] But in this case Le Corbusier was right. In October 1923 Gropius and his new wife Ilse Frank had visited Paris at Le Corbusier's invitation for an exchange of ideas. Gropius had given Le Corbusier copies of the photographs of American grain silos that Le Corbusier went on to publish in his *Vers une Architecture* as if they were his own; in return, Le Corbusier had given Gropius inspiration. He'd shown him round two new houses he'd designed: one for his painting collaborator Amédée Ozenfant, completed the year before; the other, just finished, a double house for Raoul La Roche and Albert Jeanneret. Gropius was overwhelmed and wrote that their 'unprecedented freshness ... greatly excited me'. Since precedence was one of the key things that art historians look for, and since the Bauhaus buildings were only just coming to completion, it was clear that Pevsner wouldn't have been able to credit them as an original conception, whether he liked them or not. And since he must have seen photographs of the new buildings subsequently, it can't be insignificant that in all the articles he went on to write for the *Dresdner Anzeiger*, he continued to say nothing about the Bauhaus, apart from one passing reference, almost as if he was making a virtue of not doing so.[31]

The following month, on 8 December, Lola was admitted to the Women's Clinic in Leipzig again, where she possibly had a miscarriage or a stillbirth. She remained there for a week. Whether she was at full term or at an earlier stage of pregnancy is unknown. The impact on Pevsner is also unknown.

During the first half of 1926 Pevsner's work for the Gemäldegalerie was taken up almost wholly with work on the International Exhibition. When the exhibition opened, on 12 June, it contained about a thousand works of art from nineteen countries,[32] over 460 artists[33] and a smattering of older moderns.[34] Only Delacroix represented anything earlier than the mid-nineteenth century.

The USA didn't yet have a reputation except in popular culture and its showing in the 1926 exhibition left nothing in the memory, Pevsner wrote in one of his subsequent newspaper articles.[35] England's performance consisted of Vanessa Bell, Roger Fry, Duncan Grant, Augustus John, William Roberts, Walter Sickert, Stanley Spencer and Wilson Steer — artists of national but not international importance. France's presence was not huge but more robust. But all the guest countries were overwhelmed, inevitably, by the number of artists from the host nation, including Beckmann, Dix, Schlemmer, all the members of Die Brücke[36] except Bleyl (who'd stopped exhibiting by then), half the members of the Neue Künstlervereinigung München,[37] and more than half of Der Blaue Reiter.[38]

The Pevsner and Kurlbaum families flocked to Dresden to see what Nika had been up to. 'The museum was exhibiting modern painters,' recalled Marianne Kockel, 'and that's where I first confronted Nolde, Klee, Slevogt and so forth. I was then nineteen — I'd just passed my Abitur.' Pevsner took away two mementoes of the exhibition: a couple of declaration forms signed by the artist Max Liebermann for a painting by Manet he'd sent to the show: *The Bunch of Asparagus*, valued at 100,000 goldmarks. (This painting, sold by Liebermann's granddaughter to the Wallraf-Richartz-Museum in Cologne in 1968, was originally bought from Manet in 1880 by the collector Charles Ephrussi, who paid 200 francs more than Manet was asking for it. Manet rewarded Ephrussi's over-payment by painting him another picture — of a single stick of asparagus. Liebermann acquired *The Bunch of Asparagus* from the Berlin art dealer Paul Cassirer in 1907.)

For the public at large and for the organizers, the 1926 International Exhibition represented Germany's triumphant return to the world's stage, attracting over three million visitors in four months, even though it broke no new ground and relied mainly on painters who'd already made their reputations before the war. It had a room for Constructivist art, designed by El Lissitzky, but it failed to recognize the wartime and post-war anti-nationalist, anarchic phenomena of either Dada[39] or Surrealism. In spite of that, and in the belligerent climate of the time, some regarded it as a provocation. Members of the German Art Society (Deutsche Kunstgesellschaft) objected that the exhibition's choice of German artists favoured Expressionist deviationists whose love of the unusual and unnatural in art undermined the ordered structure of German society. In particular, the society's members anathematized Max Liebermann, the hugely popular German Impressionist who'd been given a small retrospective in the exhibition, on the grounds that he was Jewish and therefore 'unGerman'; it also disliked Lovis Corinth, who'd died the previous summer and who'd also been given a small exhibition, because his painting *Ecco Homo* made Jesus look 'too semitic'.[40] In later years the society's leader[41] recalled that members had been infuriated by the way the press had segregated 'older' and 'younger' painters on the basis not of their ages but their style of painting[42] and had concentrated on German 'moderns', whose work they saw as international rather than German, at the expense of völkisch favourites such as Thoma and Trübner.[43]

It would have been Grohmann's writings that the Society was unhappy with; Pevsner's approach to the exhibition was more explanatory than critical. After taking a one-month holiday during the show's first month, he'd returned to Dresden in June and written fifteen articles about the exhibition in the *Dresdner Anzeiger* over the summer: an introductory article on 10 June, a double-page spread on the opening ceremony three days later and eight further pieces on the various national sections up to the end of July. Finally, during August, he'd assessed Germany's own contribution, dealing first with its traditional artists and then, in two articles, its 'moderns', leaving local Dresden painters until last, also in two articles.

Pevsner's aim in these articles was to cover everything and to do so in as constructive a light as possible. He was enthusiastic about the artists of Die Brücke, the majority of whom, as he pointed out, were from Saxony and therefore local. He complimented Nolde on 'the deep glow of his colour' and other Brücke painters on their greater assurance, even if some like Kirchner and Schmidt-Rottluff had lost their 'youthful energy'. But he was also quite comfortable with the 'older' German Impressionists, with Thoma, whose *Bathing Boys* he complimented, and with Trübner, whose *Girl with Folded Hands* he described as 'masterful'. It was works such as these that allowed him to conclude that 'besides France, it is Germany that leads in art today' and to speculate on 'whether one could argue not only whether Germany hasn't produced more profound Expressionists than France but whether the Impressionists of our country aren't worthy of attention on a par with the French classics, while still maintaining their own German character'. His reports presumably went down well as an endorsement of the International Exhibition but it was odd, nonetheless, to see a volunteer at the

Gemäldegalerie passing judgement in public on the work of his boss.

Pevsner's term as a volunteer at the picture gallery was due to finish at the end of September, just ten days before the closure of the International Exhibition and around the same time as his second child was due. Although Pevsner still longed to move to Florence, this was not the best time for a change and so, in the first week of August, he asked Posse if he could stay on for another six months. Posse duly wrote to the Education Ministry of Saxony:

> Dr Pevsner has proposed to be allowed to work from October 1926 for a further half-year as a volunteer. Pevsner has proved himself outstanding in his work for the Gallery and for the International Art Exhibition; and since no other application exists at the moment, the management gives its warmest support for this request, particularly as Dr Pevsner can provide help on the printing of the big catalogue that's now beginning.

Two weeks later, the Ministry wrote back, granting its approval for an extension until the end of March 1927. During those six months, Pevsner became involved in the production of the gallery's catalogue, a useful volume of nearly 350 pages and over fifty illustrations that came out the following year and gave a detailed provenance for every work. He was also assigned to help prepare an exhibition of graphic art by the German Artists' Federation, the Deutscher Künstlerbund, that was due to open in June 1927. This exhibition, far more modest than the international show of the previous year, was hosted by the engravings department of the picture gallery, the head of which was the Dutch specialist, Zoege van Manteuffel. Among the artists it showed were Hermann Glöckner and August Dressler.

In spite of Pevsner's commitments, the temptation to try for Florence became too great to resist when he heard, in February 1927, aged twenty-five, that the Saxon Ministry of Education might be advertising a grant for an art historian to work at a foreign institute. On 24 February he wrote to the Ministry, pointing out that he'd assisted the Italian department of the Gemäldegalerie and that it would be of the greatest importance for him to be able to work on Italian art in Italy itself and make use of the Art History Institute's resources. Four days later Posse wrote again in support of Pevsner's application, repeating how much Pevsner had proved himself at the gallery and how greatly a stipend would benefit his career. A month later the Ministry wrote back to Posse to say it was in favour of a grant in principle but that any decision would have to wait until the regional parliament had ratified its budget and that Pevsner would have to be patient for the moment. While waiting for the Ministry's approval, Pevsner came in contact with visiting scholars, among whom was the archaeologist Ludwig Curtius, director of the German Archaeological Institute in Rome, who'd recently been doing work on the Pompeian Villa dei Misteri – the Villa of the Mysteries – with its strange frescoes that show either bridal or Dionysian initiation rites.

In the end, the Ministry didn't support Pevsner's application and he left the picture gallery on 31 March, though he seems to have gone on helping with the German Artists' Federation's graphic art exhibition on an informal basis for the next couple of months. He also wrote a brief article about it in *Der Sammler – The Collector* – in mid-June, as well as writing a seventieth-birthday appreciation of van Manteuffel's predecessor at Dresden's engravings department, Max Lehrs, who'd retired in 1923–1924. He then went to Italy to do research while Lola went back to stay with her father in Naumburg, taking Uta, now three, and Thomas, who'd been born on 2 October of the previous year.

Around this time, Alfred Kurlbaum decided to change his living arrangements and commissioned Arnulf ('Arno') Schelcher, the architect whom Nika and Lola had been living with in Dresden, to build him a new house in Mainzer Straße, a quiet road just two streets away from where he'd been living in Sebastian-Bach-Straße. The commission was made possible, Pevsner told his family later, by his father-in-law's growing prosperity during a particularly successful period in his life. During the mid-1920s 'he ... received [an] honorary degree, ... travelled much, gave us money most generously, took Mutti[44] (and also once me) in the summer to Sils Maria [the Swiss mountain resort where Nietzsche spent his summers between 1881 and 1888], bought books lavishly, had his bust modelled by Bleeker,[45] and so on'. By 1930 Kurlbaum would earn more than 80,000 reichsmarks, equivalent today to £750,000, in just three months.

During 1927–1928 building work proceeded on Kurlbaum's house, which Pevsner wrote of as one of the first private houses in Leipzig 'in the twentieth-century style', if not the first.[46] Marianne, Lola's sister, went on to live there with her father until her marriage in 1931. 'It was in the Gropius style', she said, adding with some satisfaction: 'the whole of Leipzig was scandalized' – though the building was little more than a white house with a flat roof. (Pevsner's opinions on flat roofs don't seem to have carried as much weight with his father-in-law as those of Schelcher, the architect, but Schelcher also went on to design a much more völkisch house for Otto Dix on the shores of Lake Constance.)

While working on the last instalments of his Italian art book, Pevsner looked for a publisher to bring out his doctoral thesis. Thanks to his time at the Gemäldegalerie, he found one – not in Leipzig, which would have seemed the more likely place in view of its topic, but in Dresden. Wolfgang Jess had started out as a publisher in 1920 by absorbing the publishing house of Gerhard Kühtmann and concentrating mainly on art books. In 1922 he'd brought out two architecture books on Saxony and one on Venice, in 1924 a book on old Dresden and in 1926 a study of Rome in the Middle Ages. A book on Baroque architecture in Leipzig seemed to fit well with his list and he agreed to publish the work, which meant that Pevsner had to spend the second half of 1927 rewriting and expanding his text and getting better pictures taken. It's not impossible that Hugo funded the publication.

Pevsner knew of Jess – who eight years later would publish the Festschrift for Wölfflin's seventieth birthday – because in 1926, he'd brought out the catalogue of a watercolours exhibition held in parallel with the International Exhibition, from May until the end of September. 'It was at that exhibition, in the gardens of the picture gallery, on the Brühl Terrace, that my father bought two Nolde water-colours,' Marianne, Lola's sister, recalled: '200 marks each, and I've still got one of them. Very beautiful, very beautiful. And Lola got the other one. Originally they were bought to hang in my father's dining room to the left and right of the door: one above the table and one above a small chest of drawers . . . Lola's had flowers; mine is really much less conventional. I also have a picture by Slevogt and by Barlach, though I can't remember if they came from that exhibition or the later one [on graphic art] that Nika was involved with.'

12

Göttingen

At Christmas 1927 Pevsner contacted Wilhelm Pinder for advice on his future career. Pinder had just moved from Leipzig to take up the chair of art history at Munich where he was immediately elected to the Bavarian Academy of Sciences. Pevsner hoped there might be a teaching position for him in Munich's Institute of Art History. Pinder suggested he try instead for a position at Göttingen, the university Pinder himself had repeatedly turned down offers from in the past.

Göttingen was a modest university, with just over 4,000 students and 300 teaching staff. Its mathematics department was one of the intellectual powerhouses of the world, but its art-history institute – its Kunsthistorisches Seminar – was small and sleepy. As at other German universities, the institute was a branch of the philosophy faculty and had its own painting and graphic art collections but its teaching staff consisted of just two people: Count (Graf) Georg Vitzthum von Eckstädt, one of the front-runners for the chair of art history at Leipzig that Pinder had got in 1919, and a Privatdozent, though as a result of a departmental reorganization in 1925, it had taken on three archaeology lecturers who'd previously been coupled with Classical philology.

Göttingen had nothing like the reputation for art history that Berlin, Munich and Frankfurt enjoyed: the universities Pevsner attended as a student. It was weak administratively and unambitious in its teaching, and on both counts the root cause was Vitzthum. 'Shortly after taking over his duties in Göttingen [in 1920], he suffered a nervous collapse which resulted in a drastic reduction of his working capacities and his literary output', recalled one of his staff.[1] But Vitzthum was a friend of Pinder's and Pinder thought highly of him. 'Vitzthum was academic and serious, a good scholar, but limited in what he could do because of a lung condition he'd picked up while serving in the trenches during the war,' remembered Edeltrud König, a student at Göttingen in the early 1930s. 'He wasn't able to breathe easily, had attacks of asthma and looked pale. He and Pinder had got to know each other by chance during the war when they were marching into the Champagne region of France. They'd received orders to attack Reims Cathedral but, being art historians, they'd agreed to take a stand and warned their men that the cathedral was sacred and shouldn't be damaged. Both of them told the story independently in later life.'[2]

Elisabeth Paatz,[3] another former student, also remembered that 'Vitzthum had suffered in the war. It affected his nerves. He had attacks of depression. For two or three months every four or five years, he'd have to go to a sanatorium. But it didn't affect his lectures: he was always clear and concise and I always went away with lots of notes because he was broad and knowledgeable. Compared with Pinder, he was more concentrated. Vitzthum could be inspiring but simpler. Wölfflin also – an inspiring lecturer but slower in his delivery because he was Swiss and ceremonious. You couldn't learn as much from him as you could from Vitzthum.'[4]

Probably on Pinder's recommendation, Vitzthum invited Pevsner to meet him in Göttingen. According to Vitzthum's daughter, Agnes Schmidt-Jüngst, 'Vitzthum was very demanding and was looking for a strong personality. Pevsner must already have been rather famous because my father made him apply for the post. It wasn't something Pevsner had applied for himself.'[5] Vitzthum and Pevsner met in March and Pevsner then sent testimonials from Pinder and Studniczka (but not Posse), both praising his academic skills and personal qualities. But Pevsner was evidently unimpressed by Göttingen and continued to look for other positions, including a professorship at the Technical University in Dresden.

In the meantime, Wolfgang Jess published Pevsner's rewritten thesis and Athenaion brought out the collected partworks of his writings on Italian art in a volume called *Baroque Painting in South-Western Europe*[6] that included a monograph by Otto Grautoff on Baroque painting in France and Spain, a subject Pevsner must have turned down. Pevsner sent complimentary copies to everyone he thought might advance his career. From at least one person whose opinion mattered to him, he didn't get the reception he must have wanted. On 10 October Pinder wrote him a hurried note to say he hadn't had time to read the book but that on quick inspection it looked as good as he'd anticipated – adding, with the insensitivity of the showman, that he'd written an aria he thought was rather good and was hoping to meet the celebrity who'd sing it at the German Academy the following day.

This disappointing reply came on top of problems Pevsner was experiencing with Athenaion, which was now threatening to charge him for submitting his manuscript late and for sending more material than he'd originally agreed. Pevsner reacted by taking soundings from other academics who'd also written volumes in the series – Pinder in Munich, August Mayer, also in Munich, Paul Frankl in Halle, and Curtius, the archaeologist he'd met at the engravings collection in Dresden – and found out that they'd all had overruns on time and words without the publisher's making a fuss.

He also wrote to August Schmarsow with a copy of his book, and got an ironic letter back in which Schmarsow complained about his own problems with publishers, who in 1897 had failed to sell his book about the Baroque and Rococo after Wölfflin had trashed it, and hadn't even tried to salvage the remaindered copies. Pevsner's volume of the *Handbuch* had been forwarded to Schmarsow at the Pension S. Caterina in Siena and Schmarsow had to pay not just excess postage but a special customs tariff for bound books in foreign languages – a total of five lire and seventy centesimi. But he'd got over it, had settled down to read the book, and now spoke of Pevsner as the fourth member in the art-historical geneaology that descended from himself via Kautzsch and Pinder – a sensational honour. Armed with the replies of the other historians and bolstered by Schmarsow's words, Pevsner urged Athenaion to be more forgiving.

Pevsner met Vitzthum for a second time in October and agreed, perhaps reluctantly, to submit a formal application for a teaching post. As a result, Vitzthum was able to announce at the 9 November faculty meeting that he wanted Pevsner to join his teaching staff.

Vitzthum told the meeting he'd been impressed by Pevsner's writings and by reports he'd heard about him from students. He thought Pevsner and his existing Privatdozent, Wolfgang Stechow, would work well together, Stechow concentrating on northern European art and Pevsner on the art of Italy. Pevsner's speciality – Italian art of the sixteenth to the eighteenth century – was a field Vitzthum admitted he himself knew nothing about and couldn't hope to cover in his own teaching. Pevsner's interest in how art history related to general history was also something unfamiliar to Vitzthum (even though he'd been complimented on his grasp of this by Leipzig's selection committee in 1919) and it was something he hoped would 'introduce a new and not unwelcome note' to the university.

Vitzthum went on to describe Pevsner's doctoral work as precise and methodologically sound, and said it showed an interest in explaining artistic development in the context of the artists themselves, their racial background and their geography – an interest he said was no doubt inspired by Pinder but that Pevsner had taken further. As for Pevsner's *Handbuch der Kunstwissenschaft* volume, he thought it was an odd piece of work because it was more a summary of newly established data than a piece of original research in itself, but was valuable because no other summary was available for this period of Italian painting. Following the meeting, the book was circulated to seven members of the philosophy faculty.

At the start of the following year, Pevsner was invited to Göttingen again, examined orally on 13 February 1929 and invited to give a trial lecture. The lecture took place on 23 February and dealt with the way in which the Italian Renaissance had affected German art. According to Edeltrut König, Pevsner travelled to Göttingen from Dresden, forgot to take his notes and had to reconstruct the entire talk on the train. His performance didn't suffer and his licence to teach (on mediaeval and later art history) was given and sealed on the same date.

Nikolaus and Lola and the children immediately moved out of their lodgings in Dresden and into a friend's flat in Göttingen, registering the date of their arrival as 6 March 1929. Application was made for Pevsner to be installed as a Privatdozent – an unsalaried lecturer paid directly by his students – and he began to make preparations for teaching in the winter term, although he also seems to have taught informally during the summer.[7] At the start of May his level of fees was approved by the Prussian Ministry for Science, Art and Education. He was now twenty-seven.

Göttingen was a congenial town to live in. Three years later John Ratcliff, a young English student who was taking a course there under Pevsner, wrote home to his mother to say that 'The country from Kassel to Göttingen was simply lovely: there were some very fine views, pine woods – just the sort of country one reads of in Hans Anderson's fairy tales' (by which he of course meant the Brothers Grimm). The town was very well situated, he thought, with hills and 'interminable woods'. It was smaller than Dijon, where he'd studied the previous term, but with more open streets and better shops.[8]

Ratcliff had been to school at Shrewsbury, where his modern languages teacher had been a student of Hans Hecht, Göttingen's head of English. Because of that connection, Ratcliff stayed with the Hechts[9] while studying at Göttingen.

Already the spring flowers are up in the woods – Frau H[echt] and I went and gathered some yesterday afternoon, having some coffee and cake at a nearby farm. These woods are really lovely, and of course stretch for miles and miles – perhaps we should call them a forest in England: apparently we are about two hours' journey from the centre of the Harz mountains; the hills look lovely round, and remind one of north Wales. Then in the valleys are pretty little villages with half-timbered cottages and bright vermillion roofs, which give a delightful dash of colour to the scene. Everywhere one goes one always meets people walking, although naturally one can always escape them if one wants by going further into the depths of the woods ... Of course they are a little politer to strangers than we are, and in going into shops one has to take one's hat off. At the hairdressers, they use clippers worked very neatly by machine instead of by hand ...[10]

Obviously struck by German coiffure, he noted a month later that 'Men wear their hair very short.' As for the university,

Like so many Germany universities, [it] overwhelms the comparatively small town, and one sees nothing but masses of students everywhere. The average student, as students abroad, is poor, yet despite the fact, very hard-working and cheerful. The ones I have been introduced to are awfully nice, and took a great interest in me ... As regards the buildings of the university, they are scattered all over the town: the principal one is the Auditorium – an ugly affair but with quite good lecture halls. Then there is what they call the Seminargebäude, the building in which are all the seminaries or faculties of the university. As a building it is also very nice and they have made the utmost of what they had. It is simply but well decorated and clean. Each floor is occupied by two seminaries, which have their Hörsaal, or lecture room, their library, 'office' and 'Direktor' or head professor's room, so that each seminary is a compact whole ... This English seminary has, I am told, the second-best English library on the Continent – I must say it doesn't look very big but it contains a lot, including some very interesting books on art and architecture ... The archaeological seminary is on the ground floor and has a very efficient Hörsaal, with several lanterns, blinds which go up and down by machinery, and each desk has a separate shaded electric lamp, for most of the lectures are accompanied by slides.[11]

In a normal semester, Vitzthum and his assistant taught no more than two courses each, but in three out of ten semesters in the past five years, Vitzthum had done all the teaching himself – a brave effort, in view of his state of health. A man of habit, he'd typically lecture each Monday, Tuesday, Thursday and Friday morning from 11 to 12, with a two-hour practical class for advanced students each Tuesday afternoon or Saturday morning. His syllabus was pedestrian and unvarying: fifteenth-century German painting; sixteenth-century German painting; art of the High Renaissance in Rome and Florence; sixteenth-century Dutch painting; Raphael; Rembrandt.

'Unlike Pinder, Vitzthum didn't laugh or smile, but he took care of his students and would visit them if they were in trouble', said König. 'He was also a count and very conscious of his family background but modest at the same time: always wore the same clothes. We had the feeling that he was always judging us and expecting good manners. He'd invite us once to his house but that was all. He was very formal.'[12] Agnes Schmidt-Jüngst recalled, however, that although her father didn't enjoy socializing, he thought it important that his students did and therefore invited them to his home each Sunday for lunch.[13]

Pevsner's arrival gave Vitzthum a second Privatdozent, increasing the department's teaching capacity by fifty per cent. Stechow, the other Privatdozent, had been a schoolboy in Göttingen. He'd served in the army from the outbreak of war, been captured by the Russians in 1915 and been sent to a prisoner-of-war camp in Siberia for two-and-a-half years[14] before being released in 1918. Returning to Göttingen after the war, he'd taken his doctorate under Vitzthum and then volunteered at the Kaiser Friedrich Museum in Berlin, going back to Göttingen as a teaching assistant[15] in the winter semester of 1923–1924. He became a Privatdozent in the summer of 1926.

Before Pevsner's arrival, Vitzthum's department offered five courses each semester and about ten hours of teaching each week. In Pevsner's first official semester (winter 1929–1930), the number of courses went up to seven and the number of weekly teaching hours to fourteen. That gave art history at Göttingen more bulk; but what Pevsner brought, in addition, was a personableness and flair that set the department alight. That was new for Göttingen and new for Pevsner. Until now, he'd often appeared shy, serious and cool when on duty. His friends had been few because he'd had too little time to socialize. His commitments were first to his work and only then to his family and the outside world. But as a young married lecturer of twenty-seven, he suddenly flowered into an engaging and popular figure. Like Vitzthum, he held an open house every week for his students[16] and his students evidently enjoyed being entertained by him – testament to what he'd learnt from Pinder.

'People I knew who'd studied with Pinder in Munich said I should go to

Pevsner's lectures', recalled Edeltrut König, who enrolled at Göttingen six months after Pevsner had arrived. 'We had two-hour seminars from 8 to 10 pm each week in the seminar building in Nikolausbergerweg – now the archaeology school – and after each session we'd sit and drink and be very convivial. We'd sometimes go to the Rohns restaurant and dance outside in the summer. Sometimes Lola would come too but mostly she'd be at home with the children, so we'd sometimes end up at their home. Stechow couldn't invite us so often because he was more concerned with his orchestra. His seminars were on Thursdays: then he'd go to rehearse – the academic orchestra: mainly students. He also played the piano: he looked wonderful in tails! But Pevsner was very hospitable.'[17]

'Pevsner [had] a lively temperament but was quite strict in his methods', said Horst Gerson, who arrived half a year later again. 'Many students found him . . . more stimulating and exciting [than Stechow], in spite of his pedantic rules like seating us apart during exams like schoolboys, to prevent us cheating! I don't think Stechow felt any rivalry with young Pevsner. After all, a handful of students got along with them both in a friendly atmosphere, and excursions and Sunday outings contributed to that greatly.' Of the two, Pevsner's lectures were more enjoyable. Because he was musical, Stechow often used musical metaphors to make points about paintings ('C-major there, E-major there') but 'by comparison with Pevsner [Stechow was] less sharp in formulations and less explicit in theoretic summary . . . [and] his class lectures seemed to me lengthy rather than entertaining.'[18]

Carmen Gronau was in her fourth year at Göttingen and had just given up her doctoral work when she discovered Pevsner. 'He was wonderful with us students, a marvellous teacher and fun. We used to dare him to include one unusual word in his lectures each week and I remember 'Winnetou' [the Native American hero of Karl May's novels about the Apaches], which he incorporated quite logically. He held a very popular seminar that winter about Romanesque sculpture, looking at photographs that had to be dated and classified. Quite brilliant he was, and one remembered rather obscure connections all one's life – just as, years later, we drove through London suburban streets and I learnt to date terraced houses to within years.'

Adolf Isermeyer remembered Pevsner as an unconventional lecturer. 'During his lectures he would wander backwards and forwards and he would operate his own slide projector. He'd also invite us to his house after his seminar, and that was odd too. There were fifteen of us. He had a big record collection – he had the Toscanini version of the *Barber of Seville* but also another version. He played the other conductor first, then Toscanini, and demonstrated the differences in their interpretation. Sometimes we went for lunch or dinner. His wife was the daughter of the President of the Reichsgericht and his father was well off, so he enjoyed quite an expensive way of life.' He would also lead his students on architectural tours: a two-day visit to Gotha near Weimar, a trip to see the twelfth-century abbey church in Gandersheim, a trip to Hildesheim, a two-week trip to Venice.[19] 'It was very rare for parties of students to make trips in those days but Pevsner knew Venice very well indeed: he'd been there before when researching an essay on Tiepolo.[20] One of his favourite students was Dora Büchting – not especially intelligent or pretty but Pevsner paid for her on one visit because she didn't have enough money – and she wasn't even majoring in art history. But the rest of us paid for our own expenses.'

Not always. 'He'd invite us on sightseeing tours – three-day visits staying in youth hostels and travelling by train', added König. 'And we students were very poor. And we were invited to his house to eat – and it was all financed by his father. He never admitted it was his father. He'd say it was given by someone who didn't want to be known ("ein nicht genannt sein wollender Spender") but other friends knew and they told us, after he'd left Göttingen.'

Isermeyer recalled his fellow students making a Festschrift for fun on Pevsner's thirtieth birthday in 1932. 'A firm specializing in heating installations had a calendar showing a nude standing next to a chimney and as a joke, a student called Abrahamsohn did an interpretation of it as if it were a Rembrandt [whom Pevsner had taught a course on in 1930–1931]. The firm was called Hezold and it was in a town in Saxony called Kurtchenbroder. Saxons pronounce the letter K like a G and their Ps like Bs, so when Abrahamson noted the Latin signature on the painting, he quoted it as "Gurtchenbroder me binxit Hezoldus"[21] because Pevsner was a Saxon. There was also a station in Gandersheim that had been built in Romanesque style in 1860 and a student called Wersche interpreted it as if it was really twelfth-century. And someone called Schöne contributed something: about ten of us in all. It took three weeks to complete – we did it over Christmas – and it was completely private. There's only one typescript: I was the editor. On the day of his birthday he was giving a lecture and I made a little speech and presented it to him before his lecture began. He wrote each author a separate letter and each one was very funny. We didn't do this for Stechow: he still lived with his mother and we rarely went to his house. But Pevsner entertained us, gave us hospitality – juice but no alcohol – and we'd stay there till twelve or one in the morning.'

Pevsner's Göttingen years were probably the happiest in his life. He had a young family, he was the liveliest of a small academic staff and he was surrounded by admiring students who found him amusing and whose attention he captured in memorable ways. He was also becoming known in art-historical circles. Early in 1929 the editor of the Thieme-Becker artists' lexicon, Hans Vollmer, started asking Pevsner to write about subjects that other historians weren't available to complete. In February Vollmer offered him the entry on Magnasco because the acknowledged Magnasco specialist, Benno Geiger, was travelling in Italy and couldn't be located, and in May Vollmer offered him Lorenzo Lippi because Voss and 'Fräulein Dr Kurze'[22] had, in Vollmer's words, 'left me in the lurch'. In the meantime, Pevsner had asked Vollmer to let him write about Peter Parler, the

architect of Prague Cathedral and the Charles Bridge, and about other members
of the Parler family, all German sculptors and architects, and had become sufficiently haughty to pen a long and bad-tempered attack when he got the proofs
back, complaining about how Vollmer had edited him.

Vitzthum had hired Pevsner on the basis that his expertise in Italian art would
dictate much of what he taught, and in the late 1920s it was this subject that still
dominated Pevsner's interests. Pevsner divided his work on Italian art into two
categories: categorization and research. His interest in categorization lay in dis-
tinguishing Mannerism from Baroque, showing that one was the one true style
of Italy in the sixteenth century and the other the one true style of Italy in the
seventeenth century and subdividing both into their early, high and late stages.
Having dealt with Mannerism in the mid-1920s, he now turned his attention
to Baroque, publishing a paper in 1928 on the stylistic character of early and
high Baroque[23] and a sequel in 1932 on the crisis in Baroque of 1650. Quite
separate from this work, as Pevsner saw it, were his case studies of individual
artists: Cerano in 1925, Caravaggio in 1927 and 1928–1929 and Procaccini in
1929, and one of the first things he did when he arrived in Göttingen was to
publish a synopsis of his recent work on eighteenth-century Venetian painting in the *Göttingsche gelehrte Anzeigen*, the university's annual compendium of
scholarly essays.

The eminent church historian Hans von Campenhausen,[24] who lectured
in Göttingen from 1930 and had a special commission to study early church
archaeology, recalled that 'Pevsner and I often discussed art-historical topics. He
used to ask me for background material on religious tendencies in the eighteenth
century.'[25] In spite of this interest, Pevsner only gave three courses on Italian art
in the seven semesters that he spent at Göttingen: on Michelangelo, in his very
first term, on Mannerism in the summer of 1931 and on the characteristics of
fifteenth-century Italian paintings in the winter that followed, and stopped writing about it altogether after 1932. It was left to Vitzthum and Stechow, whose
interests overlapped each other's more closely than they did Pevsner's, to work
through the basic issues of Renaissance painting, while occasionally looking at
Rembrandt and Dutch art as well. Why?

A partial answer may be that Pevsner's change of direction was a response to
personal changes and changes in the national mood. Three projects he'd been
immersed in had come to an end: the publication of his thesis, the publication
of his Italian book and his work at the picture gallery. Painting itself, which
had seemed so vital when he first arrived at Dresden, now seemed less urgent
to him – as it did to the public. Their lack of interest (in Pevsner's view) had
brought about the closure of Dresden's four most important private galleries –
the Baumbach, Erfurth, Arnold and Fides – thereby putting its very future as
an art centre at risk, a subject he wrote about in two of his last articles for the
Dresdner Anzeiger in 1929.[26]

Having witnessed the collapse of the Dresden Secession and the Artists'

Union, both in 1925, Pevsner was also put off by what he'd seen of the politics that lay behind art and by some of the people involved in it,[27] and he may also have felt that in spite of its aspirations, what had attracted an audience of three million to the International Exhibition – but not to Dresden's failed galleries – was not its art but its commercial appeal as a spectacular, the same quality that had made a success of the four previous Annual Shows. In this he would have been sharing the growing distaste for the idea of art, and especially for art as the manufacturing of 'exhibition objects', with all its associated pretence, felt in certain progressive circles. That distaste was encapsulated by the architect Peter Behrens, whom Pevsner admired, in 1922 when he spoke of his 'dearest wish no longer to speak of art' and his desire that 'those of us who concern ourselves with the field [should] call ourselves craftsmen' instead.[28]

Pevsner's change of mood accompanied a sense that normality was returning to Germany. Unemployment was still high, the government was unpopular, the Reichstag was fragmented and inharmonious, and most political parties continued to operate their own private armies, but the currency had stabilized with the introduction of the Reichmark in 1924, new industry was booming, economic output was increasing and governments were holding together for longer than they'd managed in the early 1920s, in spite of the difficulty in forming coalitions. In addition, foreign tourists were visiting Germany again, the arts were thriving, and in the summer of 1928 Germany had done well at the Amsterdam Olympics after being excluded from the Paris Olympics of 1924. Enough national self-confidence seemed to be at large for Germans subsequently to speak of 'the Golden Twenties'.

The counterpart of this growing confidence in the future was a craze for the past and specifically for the mediaeval. Newspapers started using Gothic lettering instead of or alongside modern fonts – the *Dresdner Anzeiger* had only used Gothic – and mediaeval themes were a favourite of German film-makers, not just in what we now think of as 'art movies', like Fritz Lang's *Nibelungen* and F.W. Murnau's *Faust* and Expressionist cinema, but in popular cinema, where mediaeval settings gave silent films a dramatic or völkisch appeal. The idea of mediaeval communality and craftsmanship even appealed to the radicals at the Bauhaus, the very name of which was a reference to mediaeval building guilds.

Driving this mediaeval fad, especially after the Kaiser's failure to achieve his war aims and his desertion to Holland, was the belief that the war had changed everything, that the romantic delusions of the past were dead and that there now had to be a focus on fundamentals. Germany's emulation of France's Belle Époque had gone on too long, as Thomas Mann had said. The country had to get in touch with itself and the origins of that self resided somewhere in the Middle Ages, before its splintering.[29]

Pevsner was evidently attracted by the idea that the Middle Ages were simpler, healthier, blunter and more defiantly German, and by the consequence of that idea: that embracing mediaeval virtues in the past would foster mediaeval virtues in the present. He'd always valued moderation and straightforwardness and missed those qualities in his own work, which until now had been about artistic extremism and emotion. He started to be irked that in his dissertation on Leipzig 'no consideration was given at all to the peculiar, indeed unique, function of the high merchants' houses. They contained shops and flats and were regularly cleared of domestic tenants for the Leipzig fairs, in order to become exhibition premises to show and sell from samples of merchandise.'[30] He felt an over-regard for the artistic had distracted him from more obvious issues in his thesis and he was disappointed in himself.

It was around 1930, when he was twenty-eight, that the focus of Pevsner's professional interests began to change, he noted later. 'What had happened was that I had turned from Baroque architecture to Mannerist and Baroque painting ... and found it wanting in power of conviction. When my volume of the *Handbuch der Kunstwissenschaft* was finished in 1928 and I started teaching in Göttingen University, I began to feel the need for an art less rhetorical and more responsible.'[31] What he wanted to concentrate on now, he said, had less to do with imagery and shape *per se* than images and shapes created by 'function' – the new vogue word. He labelled this interest 'social history', though little social history ever entered his work.

Pevsner expressed this change of direction by giving over more of his teaching time at Göttingen to mediaeval studies than to any other subject (something he never referred to when talking about this period in later life), as if understanding the Middle Ages was the most important thing his students had to know. He gave three courses on German mediaeval sculpture, a fourth on mediaeval architecture, a fifth on pre-mediaeval architecture (the buildings of the Merovingians, Carolingians and Ottonians) and a sixth on German architecture in the time of Dürer.[32] He also took advantage of the expertise around him to attend Friedrich Neumann's lectures on German literature of the early, high and late Middle Ages that ran uninterruptedly between 1929 and 1932.

German mediaevalism embodied virtues Pevsner felt were important to the modern world. One of these, he wrote later, was that 'Gothic . . . is so essentially based on a cooperation between artist and engineer, and a synthesis of aesthetic and technical qualities'. Pevsner contrasted that happy state of cooperation and expertise, rather confusingly, with the fragmentation of the modern world. 'Today the patron is not an architect, the architect not a builder, the builder not a mason, let alone such distinctions as those between the heating engineer, the air-conditioning engineer, the electrical installation expert and the sanitation expert', he wrote, as if what he called 'splitting up our activities into smaller and smaller competencies' was undesirable. In fact, breaking architectural design into small specialities works very well, but Pevsner's experience of fracture in Weimar politics and the politics of art must have convinced him that fragmentation was the cause of complexity rather than the solution to it. The problem with architecture, he suggested, was that there were too many experts. How much happier a group project was in the Middle Ages when 'the names of these men, immortal as their work seemed, did not count. [Then] they were content to be workmen working for a cause greater than their fame.'[33]

13

Interlude

Pevsner's change of direction towards what he called 'an art less rhetorical and more responsible' was also the result of another department at Göttingen taking an interest in him. Shortly after Pevsner arrived at Göttingen, Hans Hecht at the department of philology – the languages department – had asked him if he'd like to teach a course for which he was largely unqualified. In an interview with Frank Herrmann, the historian of Sotheby's, in 1976 Pevsner said – in a very condensed summary of what actually happened – 'There was a great tradition of English studies at Göttingen. I was supposed to give every semester a one-hour-a-week lecture on some aspect of English art and architecture. I did that [in the winter of 1929–1930] but then found I couldn't really do it . . .'[1]

That 'great tradition of English studies at Göttingen' went back to a programme developed by the Prussian government[2] called Förderung der Auslandsstudien – Promotion of Foreign Study – under which universities and colleges were allocated a foreign country to learn about. The initiative had originally been introduced during the First World War, in the academic year 1916–1917, with the idea that a better understanding of foreign countries would lead to better relations and improve Germany's long-term political and economic prospects. Britain and the USA were assigned to Göttingen, which duly set up an Anglo-American Society – its Englisch-Amerikanischer Kulturkreis – which survives today as the university's Centre for American Studies (Zentrum für Amerikastudien – the Anglo having been dispensed with). The society aimed to develop links with English-speaking countries, set up a library and run a programme of lectures by university staff and guest speakers. (Among its highlights were such treasures as a talk on 'English Youth: where it stands and how it thinks' by a Mr Collingridge and a demonstration of English and Gaelic folksongs by a female Scottish choir.) As professor of English literature, Hecht chaired the society and organized its activities.

Göttingen wasn't given Britain by chance. The university had been founded in 1734 by England's King George II, who was also the Prince-Elector Georg August of Hanover, and its 'history, holdings and charter were not only influenced by British culture of the eighteenth century but . . . in turn influenced British culture',[3] in the view of some in the university. The university library, also founded in 1734, 'was part of a plan to establish permanent memorials in Germany to the Hanoverian dynasty in Britain'[4] and during the late eighteenth century it gathered one of the world's most important collections of scholarly works on Shakespeare. Outside the university, a century later, parts of the town were built like an English garden city, with villas in different styles and greenery and winding streets characteristically called 'Way' (Weg), such as Rohnsweg, where Pevsner would sometimes take his students to eat, and Friedländer Weg, which the Pevsner family moved to in June 1929, after a few months staying with their friend in Geistraße.

In his first course on English art and architecture, Pevsner relied on the resources of the philology department's English library, which, as John Ratcliff observed, was said to be the second-best English library on the Continent. That was helpful, but Pevsner was held back by his lack of background in the subject and his dislike for what he knew of it. In spite of his mother's anglophilia, there was little about England that pleased him. He'd found the country ugly, primitive and hard to comprehend on his visit as a boy. An early and apparently frightening experience had occurred when he was visiting his grandparents in London and what he thought was a room at Hampstead tube station trapped him inside its closing doors and then shot up into the air. It was the lift. How could he not regard England as Germany's mortal enemy, alongside France, in the First World War after that?

He was unimpressed by English art because it had contributed nothing to the main currents in Western civilization he'd been interested in defining and applying labels to. Of the almost 2,600 paintings in the collection of the Dresden Picture Gallery, only five were English and they were thought so little of that one of them – the only English picture from the nineteenth century: a painting by Thomas Brown in 1893 – had been thrown in with the gallery's small American collection.

Dresden's International Exhibition hadn't made him think differently. Writing about England's showing in the *Anzeiger* at the time, he'd observed that painting was low on England's cultural agenda. 'For England, the modus operandi seems to be one of decent eclecticism – nothing exciting, everything measured and conventional.' If one accepted that the best that England could do was conservatism, then the best example of conservatism was Wilson Steer. Stanley Spencer, though more 'modern', was still exhibiting pre-Raphaelite tendencies; William Roberts's one small contribution to the exhibition probably raised expectations too high. 'Apart from Duncan Grant, a younger painter of French influence, the rest were, by German and French standards, no more than middling fare', Pevsner wrote. The only thing that attracted him to the fine arts in England was the possibility that they could be used to delineate England's national character, just as Pinder had used German art to delineate German national character. Fortunately, that was exactly what Hecht wanted him to investigate, alongside his own courses on Englishness in English literature.

There was, however, one area of English art that Pevsner thought worthy of notice: its applied arts – its Kunstgewerbe – because there alone, English achievements had briefly contributed to Europe's cultural development, which is what he ultimately cared about. He explained his thinking in a lecture titled

'Community Ideals in Nineteenth-Century Art' in December 1929, in his first full semester at Göttingen. According to two surprisingly full accounts of this talk in two Dresden newspapers, Pevsner argued that parallel to the chain of pictorial art from Courbet to Max Liebermann, there was a moral chain – less apparent but more significant for the present day. This moral chain stretched from the German-speaking Nazarene painters of the early nineteenth century to the German Bauhaus – which Pevsner was now starting to place in a historical perspective – in the early twentieth, with England as a bridge between the two.

The Nazarenes had first come together in Vienna around 1808 and had tried to live by the principles of truth and friendship and the rejection of bravura and sham, he said. The English Pre-Raphaelites, from 1848, had taken these ideals further. They in turn had inspired William Morris, who'd founded a firm to produce anonymous and socially useful products that were neither mechanized nor high art but that failed because they were too expensive and over-refined. Henri van de Velde, around 1890, had turned to the machine and identified engineers as the architects of the future, as a corrective to the self-indulgence of the Jugendstil movement. And finally, the Bauhaus had tried to renew the idea of community craftworking within the supremacy of architecture.[5]

Pevsner told Frank Herrmann in 1976 that at Göttingen he was supposed to give a one-hour lecture each week on an aspect of English art and architecture, but then found he couldn't do it properly 'without knowing England'. That was because he couldn't relate what he liked about England to what he disliked. He'd also been criticized in one of the two newspaper reports on his lecture, on the grounds that in making out his moral chain argument, he'd selected his evidence and glossed over inconsistencies. Walter Holzhausen, Pevsner's replacement on the *Dresdner Anzeiger*, had quoted what he'd said respectfully and without comment, except to say – as Vitzthum had said of Pevsner's *Handbuch* volume – that the theme was odd but showed Pevsner had independence of vision. But 'G. P.' in the *Dresdner Neueste Nachrichten*, while agreeing that Pevsner had an 'unusually large number of ideas', thought that if Pevsner was going to observe lines of connection, he should observe lines of differentiation too. 'You can certainly find correlations . . . but just as many differences too,' he said, pointing out that the Nazarenes were Catholic while the Bauhaus was Communist, the Pre-Raphaelites were apolitical while Morris was Socialist, and that Gropius had been at odds with van de Velde in 1914 rather than his disciple.

Pevsner asked his father to send him copies of the reviews and would have been surprised that 'G. P.' didn't follow his thinking. The moral chain – artists working for the good of society rather than in their own self-interest – seemed to be a historically compelling argument. He would also have insisted, correctly, that there was no reason why the differences 'G. P.' had observed should obstruct a line of influence; Pevsner wasn't saying the members of his moral community were identical, only that their moral beliefs connected them.

There was, however, a separate element in his argument that was new and more contentious: the idea that art historians now had to be part of the moral chain if they were to say anything of value to the modern world. It was an issue Wilhelm Pinder had also come round to and that he would write about in a passionate essay called 'Architektur als Moral' in the Wölfflin Festschrift of 1935:

> What is the purpose of art history today, where life is calling out for action? What can looking do, what should it do, when action has become the most necessary thing? . . . The details of the [new] movement go back some time but only now has its deeper sense become clear. It lies not inside the aesthetic arena but in the moral . . . We German art historians have an obligation to show and interpret this.[6]

Pevsner therefore felt he needed to go to England for two reasons: he needed information to help him connect what he admired about the country's arts and crafts tradition with its longer history of art, so he could flesh out what Englishness meant in his lectures for Hecht; he also needed information to help him bolster his argument about England's function as the link, between 1848 and 1890, in Europe's moral chain – an argument that made perfect sense to him but seemed not to have been understood by others.[7]

'So I got a scholarship through the professor of English to go to England. That was in 1930,'[8] he told Frank Hermann. The 'scholarship', which Hecht got for him from the Prussian Ministry of Education, would allow Pevsner to make a research trip to England during the summer instead of going on his usual study tour of Italy. The request was processed and approved during the spring of 1930.

The fact that Englishness was indeed his primary interest – and his means of extracting state funding – is confirmed by a remark he made in a letter to Lola on his arrival in England. 'The reason for my trip and the focus of my present work is of course Englishness just as Saxonness was the focus during my work on Leipzig', he said. In fact, Saxonness was not obviously the focus of his Leipzig work. At the end of his dissertation he'd introduced remarks about the ambivalence of Saxon character, not as the culmination of a developing argument but as the start of a new observation: Saxony's position halfway between Eastern and Western Europe. It was in this sense that national character was 'of course' Pevsner's reason and focus: it transcended data.

What Vitzthum made of Pevsner's jaunt, or of the sidelining of his own plans for the department, isn't recorded. On the one hand he'd hired an Italian specialist who'd gravitated towards German mediaevalism and now intended to become an expert in English art for another department. On the other hand, Pevsner's research would reinforce an existing strength at Göttingen – English studies – and might, like his Mannerism studies, lead to the development of a new art-historical category for the period from 1810 to 1910: the 'moral' century. One visualizes Vitzthum shaking his head in disbelief and retreating to his bed.

In preparation for his exploration of the entirety of English art, Pevsner wrote to contacts in England, asking for suggestions. One reply came back to him at the end of May from James Byam-Shaw, a Renaissance Italy specialist, who was staying at a hotel in Coburg when Pevsner's letter caught up with him and who'd already met Pevsner socially some time earlier. Writing in German, Byam-Shaw said 'Concerning the private collections in the country, other than Chatsworth and Kingston Lacy, I must first check documents in London because I can't remember [but] I'd suggest you visit Longford Castle;[9] next to Chatsworth it must be the best collection in the country. We hope in the next few days to meet a friend of my wife's and we'll ask her. Greetings to you and your wife.'

Although the state of Saxony had provided some of the funding for his journey to England, Pevsner had also discussed the costs with his father at the start of the year and his father, who'd supported him on an informal basis until now, had decided to put him on a more secure footing. Emil Barban, the founder of Hugo's firm, had retired or resigned from the company in 1923 and installed his son Heinrich, a lawyer, in his place. Heinrich had remained with the company as a limited partner for six years; at the end of January 1930 he'd quit. Hugo now brought in Nikolaus, also as a limited partner. The cost of giving his art-historian son a partnership in his fur haulage firm was 15,000 reichsmarks – equivalent to about £140,000 today: no small sum. This bought Nikolaus a share in the company's earnings, while limiting his exposure to the cost of entry. For this, unlike Heinrich Barban, he had to do nothing, though it's not impossible that with a trip being arranged to England and with more of Hugo's business being channelled through London, Hugo may have asked him to make contacts for him or set up a banking or credit facility for him while he was there.

Pevsner's later writing suggests he had a natural affinity for England, but his letters to Lola on his visit in 1930 show the opposite. His overall tone was more critical of the country than admiring, though he also dramatized his bewilderment at the differences between England and Germany to amuse her. He found English Classicism undersized and feeble, for example, compared with the Classicism of Europe and said he was a little relieved that the Duke of Marlborough wasn't at home to receive him when he went visiting with his letter of introduction because he found Vanbrugh's Blenheim Palace pinched, compared with the scale and drama of Baroque palaces on the Continent, and 'not to my taste'. The city of Bath also fell short, because of its inconvenience and the poor quality and condition of its architecture, with stonework covered in sulphurous crusts that wouldn't be cleaned and repaired until fifty years later. 'It's all black and with the rheumaticky patients everywhere it was rather *triste*', he wrote home. 'The English don't seem able to build a comfortable spa.'

It wasn't just the architecture that disappointed: it was the meanness. Pevsner complained about his difficulty in finding clean towels and decent heating in hotels and bed-and-breakfasts, and about the terrible food. A hotel in Richmond, Yorkshire, only had candles in the bedrooms; another, in Exeter, smelt of beer.

He also felt assailed by incivility. 'Why are museum attendants kind and helpful and attendants in churches so rude?' he wrote to Lola. 'Some people were lean-ing against pillars while a service was going on – probably foreigners – perhaps because they were overawed and didn't know where to go, but that's not allowed – but the way they tell you! "Please sit down or go outside." I guess they have to protect God from social gaffes, but good gracious! Italian churches with bicycles in the nave are so much nicer.' One of the few things that impressed him was Durham Cathedral, one of the most important Romanesque complexes in Europe, with its Benedictine monastery still intact on the south side. 'It's the first thing that's made my heart race', he reported; 'I'm just knocked over by it.'

The reality of England seemed not to match its own ideals or imperial reputation. In Germany, hardships caused by the Great Inflation hadn't damaged the middle classes' feeling of cultural superiority – often for very good reasons: higher standards of living, higher cultural expectations in art and music, and a sensuousness that Pevsner felt England lacked. In England, there seemed to be pride without substance. On top of that, Pevsner still felt the emotions of the war, the sense of injustice and blame in the years that followed, and the influence of Pinder, always burnishing a feeling of national exclusivity and competitiveness among his students.

In some cases, rivalry with England left Pevsner feeling vexed. He discovered, for example, that English museum catalogues and displays were often better than those he was used to in Germany. England also made him self-conscious. At the Yorkshire hotel that had only had candles, he was stared at because no one had ever seen a foreigner. Even in the streets he attracted attention. 'Englishmen don't stand and stare but I keep getting startled glances for a split second', he wrote to Lola. 'What is it? The hat? The socks? The horn-rimmed glasses? I don't know. Men's clothes here are very strange yet people find *me* strange: I don't know how.' He wrote as if he hadn't grasped that anyone seen in a busy English street making notes about the fenestration of public buildings armed with a sketch book, a *Baedeker* and a pair of binoculars would have attracted notice, especially if he was also reduced to wearing knickerbockers and patent-leather pumps, as Pevsner had to at the end of his trip, because his other clothes had worn out.

All in all, Pevsner's visit to England didn't set him on fire in the way his summer trips to Italy had done. It did however equip him with a new set of practical skills he'd draw on later in life. Travelling widely from one side of the country to the other, from Hull in the north-east, where he stayed with cousins, to Stonehenge and Exeter in the south-west, he got into the habit of doing his looking and note-taking during the day and putting his thoughts together on paper in his hotel rooms at night after supper. 'Generalizations are a luxury for the evenings', he wrote to Lola. 'In the daytime, I have to gather all kinds of details, sort out the structure and elevations, a history of the building as a text.' That account is of interest because it shows it wasn't the kind of work he'd been doing each summer in Italy, otherwise he wouldn't have needed to explain it to Lola: she'd already have known. In Italy, he was looking at paintings, in museums and private collections; in England, especially as his trip went on, he was becoming more and more distracted by buildings as he came up against the need for a fuller understanding of the country's architectural record. That's partly because he was having to make sense of buildings for which no equivalent existed in Europe. It's also because *Baedeker*, the guidebook he assumed he'd be able to rely on, proved wanting. His view of its limitations is revealed by the extensive marginalia he scribbled in his copy, showing how much extra material he thought it needed.

During his visit to London, Pevsner visited an aunt – Paula (or Paulette) Perlmann, a daughter of Jeannette and Saveli Perlmann and a sister of his mother Annie. '[Paula] had started a millinery shop and for a time seems to have made a success of it', he told his children later. 'She was very lively and very amiable – my father was first in doubt whether he was more in love with my mother or with her – but not very industrious or consistent. Her shop was called Madame Pervier . . . and she had comfortable rooms in Kensington, in Manson Place, off Queen's Gate. There she gave up her shop and went into the hat department of Marshall and Snelgrove's. That is where she was in 1930, when I first visited England.'[10]

The person Pevsner relied on most heavily during his three-month trip was Tancred Borenius, the Finnish art historian whom he'd been in contact with over Caravaggio dates and attributions while he was in Dresden. Borenius, now forty-five, had come to London in 1909 after completing his doctoral dissertation on the painters of Vicenza and had quickly gained a foothold in the art world as a protégé and friend of the art critic Roger Fry, succeeding Fry in 1914 as lecturer in art history at the Slade School of Art and therefore also at University College, London, which houses the Slade. In 1922 Borenius was made a full professor[11] and shortly afterwards became the fine-art advisor to Sotheby's, the London auction house. ('Sotheby's was mostly furniture and silver in those days and not so much pictures', recalls Borenius's daughter, Ursula Tarkowski. 'After the [First World] War, running a big house was hard and people were selling off their family belongings because they wanted to reduce their costs and needed cash, and they didn't know what they had, and so Sotheby's became interested in the sale of pictures as well – and there were Americans with their amazing fortunes. Suddenly pictures grew from there.'[12])

Borenius, who'd just that year moved from a flat in De Vere Gardens to a house in Kensington Gate, treated Pevsner kindly. Through his network of contacts, he set up introductions to curators and historians as well as to members of the nobility whose houses and collections he thought Pevsner would enjoy seeing.[13] Thus Pevsner found himself on 30 September 1930 taking lunch with Lady Harcourt at Nuneham Park, a mid-eighteenth-century Palladian villa with wings, just west of Oxford. He wrote later that the simple meal – fried goose livers on toast – was interrupted by the butler announcing to her ladyship that F. E. Smith, Lord Birkenhead, had died and asking if a wreath should be ordered. When he wasn't dining with the nobility or looking at buildings around the country, Pevsner would spend his days in museums and art galleries in London, arriving as the doors opened in the morning, staying until they closed in the evening and taking lunch at a Lyons Corner House.

In his visits to great houses, Pevsner often had to suffer being ushered round by staff who didn't give him enough time to look at what he wanted, or by owners who told him about things he wasn't interested in, like their butterfly collections or the milk yields of their cows. Even when he was on his own, however, he could come away frustrated. 'I spent an hour and a quarter in the cathedral,' he wrote from Hereford, 'in a terrible hurry and my heart pounding away. I can't remember much of it, I'm afraid. I wish I'd left some places out and looked at others quietly and in detail.' England was an opportunity, however, to practise compiling and sorting out data while on the move: 'I hope that the thousands of little stones gradually knit together into a meaningful mosaic. At the moment there are still some awful gaps, but some small pointers in the history of art are taking shape.'

Those small pointers became the basis of a substantial repositioning of himself on his return to Göttingen in the late autumn. In the winter of 1930–1931 and during every subsequent semester, Pevsner taught at least two courses for Vitzthum, one of which – with only one exception – was always on an aspect of English art. He first gave a course on the overall history of English architecture, then on English painting from the Renaissance to the Romantic movement, then on mediaeval English painting and sculpture and, after looking at artists' education in the summer 1932, on English art from the Romantic period to present. In short, England accounted for a third of all his teaching at Göttingen after the summer of 1930. At the same time, the focus of his attention was still much more on art than architecture. Although the details of his lectures can't now be reconstructed because his notes were destroyed by a bomb in the war, three-quarters of his lectures on England and on Europe were about art, not architecture.[14] He also remained overwhelmingly interested in a long view of history going back to the Middle Ages and not just recent history. These features of his teaching are usually overlooked.

Also overlooked is that in addition to his scholarship, Pevsner was an exceptional collector of visual material, both photographs and drawings. This had become essential for art historians. Bruno Meyer, who taught at Karlsruhe in the early 1870s, and after him Hermann Grimm at Berlin, had both made the use of 'lanterns' or slide projectors in art-history lectures routine; and Wölfflin, who took over from Grimm in 1901, extended this to the use of two projectors, side by side. This meant that lectures had to be illustrated. While Pevsner was carrying out historical research in England, he was therefore also carrying out picture research. Back in Göttingen, the pictures he'd collected or that copyright holders had sent him were rephotographed on diapositive film for slides, and this was work he organized himself.

In return for the help he'd received in England, Pevsner arranged for Borenius to be invited to Göttingen the very next term to give a series of lectures on mediaeval painting. ('He came for no pay, no fee,' recalled Pevsner later, 'and he gave his lecture wearing his gown. It was a great sensation; no one at continental universities wears a gown.'[15]) One result of the visit was that Borenius and a group of English friends gave funds to the English department at Göttingen to buy books, images and other art-historical materials.

Hecht and Vitzthum were so impressed by these initiatives that on 24 June 1931 they wrote a joint application to the dean of the philosophy faculty, explaining what Pevsner had done, academically and entrepreneurially, and recommending him for a salaried post:

> For several semesters Dr Pevsner has undertaken, at the instigation of the chairman of the Anglo-American Society, the job of developing a historically based account of English art in lectures. The lectures were accompanied by rich illustrative material, based on Dr Pevsner's findings during a stay of several months in England, and should be seen as an unqualified enrichment and extension of the courses of the Anglo-American Society. By Dr Pevsner's intervention, Göttingen has probably become the only place in Prussia where English art history can be studied professionally and there's no question that further breakthroughs will follow and that Dr Pevsner will achieve important and attractive results in this rich field of effort.

They also talked about Pevsner's helpfulness to their departments, his mediation in bringing Borenius to Göttingen, the gifts that had come from that visit, and his management of the new slide library and projectors – resources that with further growth would make Göttingen's English department the boast of the state. They then roundly complimented him on his academic prowess:

> He is undoubtedly one of the most gifted and most energetic art historians of the new generation. His published writings are already considerable for his age and further work can be expected from him in the foreseeable future. His interests relate both to specific problems of style criticism and philological history and to general questions of the history of artistic style and of ideas and culture. They range from the early Middle Ages to the artistic movements of the present, making his first five semesters[16] of teaching multifac- eted and independent in his choice of material. To his listeners, and in particular to the participants in his exercises, he makes high demands but he also shows how method and execution can lead to original and conscientious work.

Hecht and Vitzthum knew that in Pevsner they had an exceptional member of staff and one whom they had to retain. Over the next two days, however, Vitzthum realized that their letter would cause ill feeling if Pevsner was given a salaried post ahead of Stechow, because Stechow was six years older and had been at Göttingen six years longer. He therefore wrote again to the dean, reminding him that he'd already applied for Stechow to get a salaried post, that Stechow had already earned the approval of the Prussian Minister in Berlin and that Stechow's application should therefore be processed first. As a result, Stechow was promoted to an associate professorship – an 'Extraordinarius' – later in 1931 while Pevsner was told he'd have to wait.

Pevsner waited. While he waited he went on teaching. He also continued to write, though no longer for the *Dresdner Anzeiger*, where his contributions had become less frequent in 1928 and ended completely at the start of 1929, once his move to Göttingen was imminent. He'd then had seven papers published in academic and art-historical journals: four book reviews and three essays – two based on visits he'd made to Venice and Turin, the third on work he'd been doing on Procaccini. His output dropped significantly during 1930, the year of his visit to England, but when it picked up again, it's notable that the books he reviewed included studies of England. In 1931 one of six reviews he published was about the art of Lower Saxony in England;[17] and one of four reviews he wrote in 1932 was of Martin Briggs's *The Architect in History* – a book so quixotically English that, while far from ill-informed, it went from the Renaissance to the nineteenth-century in just one jump, ignoring other countries after the 1700s and repeatedly challenging the convention of architectural history by insisting on what wasn't known rather than what was. (Ernst Gombrich's teacher, Julius Schlosser, read this review and wrote to Pevsner to compliment him on it.)

A more substantial piece of writing was Pevsner's analysis in 1932 of late Baroque Italian painting – the last he'd write on the subject.[18] The purpose of the essay, which developed one of the themes of his *Handbuch* volume, was to show that while there was a stylistic relationship between paintings of the early Baroque and high Baroque, paintings of the late Baroque were stylistically different and showed characteristics of Mannerist art in the Late Renaissance – with the notable difference that artists were now repeating Mannerist elements, whereas the Mannerists themselves had been doing something new. The heroes of the late Baroque were also artists from northern Italy, Pevsner noted, and were resisting the conservatism and Classicism that restrained the imaginations of artists closer to Rome – a sign of his belief that northern-European Protestant humanism was more advanced than southern-European Catholicism.

The essay ended awkwardly with Pevsner acknowledging that the Zeitgeist that governed Europe during this period was French, but then getting into an argument with Hans Rose about whether the character of the late Baroque could be shown using French examples alone (and without referencing ecclesiastical architecture). Pevsner thought Rose, the art historian he may have heard lecturing at Munich in 1921, made too many concessions to the French and failed to relate art to general history.

When he stayed away from confrontation, however, Pevsner's essay was a thrilling piece of writing, taking the reader back to the excitement of his lectures and demonstrating the brio of total knowledge, spiritedly deployed. Here was Pevsner in full command. He seemed to know everything about his artists, the personal details of their lives, the influence of older artists, the influence of contemporaries and associates, their artistic development, their changing work methods, the way they handled their brushes and loaded their paint, the quality of their colour, the structure of their compositions and the unexpected similarities between their works and others. He also knew that he was all-knowing and that certainty gave the essay an electrifying quality.

Pevsner's essay reveals what it was that made his lectures popular – and what had made Pinder's lectures popular. For both men, mastery of Italian art demonstrated an intellectual imperialism: Germans hadn't invented the Baroque but they'd understood it better than anyone else. At the other extreme, the use of slide projectors had turned lectures into film shows at a time when movies were the new rage, giving art history a novel quality that seemed to put it ahead of other subjects. (Today's equivalent would be media studies, a direct development from art history.)

Ambition and sensationalism came together in Pevsner's analysis of sexuality in sixteenth- and seventeenth-century paintings – something that art historians had closed their eyes to before, in public at least. Sometimes his observation of sexuality was overt – in the scrutiny he brought to the predominance in Baroque paintings of nude bodies, often very oddly expressed (especially, in ceiling paintings, seen from below, the *sotto in sù* viewpoint in which bottoms replace faces as the main focus of the gaze). Sometimes his observation of sexuality was more implicit. In his essay on the late Baroque, for example, he contrasted two pictures of St Philip Neri, one early Baroque by Reni, the other late Baroque by Maratti, and said of them: 'Reni uses heavy materials with few folds; Maratti indulges in a soft, fragmented, unsystematic flowing movement, linking the Virgin with the saint in unarticulated waves and subsiding in gentle ripples below.' He extrapolated from this that the late Baroque period was itself sexualized. It wasn't just marked by 'libertinism' and 'sensuality'; it had feminine – or what he regarded as feminine – characteristics (it was 'frivolous, rhetorical, unreal', with a 'desire for decorative effect'). But that feminineness was also a sort of demasculinization. In the late Baroque, he wrote, 'the human figure is robbed of all the self-sufficiency, strength and weight that the [implicitly masculine early and high] Baroque painters had restored to it' and 'compositional coherence is sacrificed to a general, soft, decoratively effective wavy motion'. This was a description not just of individual paintings but of the character of the whole period. Pevsner saw in the Baroque a sexual energy that built up in its early period, exploded in its high period, and subsided in its late period.

An interest in sexuality also coloured Pevsner's 1925 discussion of Mannerism[19] and his argument that because of Jesuitry and the Counter-Reformation, art in the Renaissance moved from physical idealism into suggestiveness and prurience.

Thus Florence, 'which in Bronzino's lifetime had been so lacking in piety that between 1531 and 1548 no sacraments were received in the cathedral at all, now had an extreme orthodox faction that referred to a work of the school of Michelangelo as "a filthiness by the master of all filth, Michelangelo"'. Pevsner's general point here was that various painterly features[20] 'combine to produce a sense of floating, a disembodied quality which shows Mannerist art to have an inner affinity with . . . the mysticism of the Counter-Reformation'. 'Bernini himself knew the Jesuit spiritual exercises; and the visions of St Teresa are themselves full of erotic imagery', but the age of Bernini and St Teresa would never have allowed spiritual intensity to be expressed in the language of sexual intensity: it would have seemed a profanity. Thus 'No Mannerist figure is observed with the detached relish of Bernini's St Teresa, and the spiritual surrender of El Greco's mystics never resembles the sexual surrender of those of Bernini.' 'The erotic explicitness of Bernini's St Teresa . . . would have been an impossibility in the context of the Counter-Reformation and goes far beyond the eroticism of the secular art of the school of Parma.'[21]

The foregoing passage isn't just an analysis of the sexual character of the age: it's also an example of sexualization in Pevsner's writing. The repetition of 'Bernini' and 'St Teresa' has a teasing, rhythmic quality to it that suggests that alongside his critique, Pevsner was identifying with and enjoying what he was writing about. The recognition of this adds a new slant to his comments on, for example, the Dresden Zwinger where 'the forward and backward motion never stops'. The observation of Schmarsowian energy wasn't just about the apprehension of space, physicality and movement by the psyche; it was also about even more basic sensations.

14

Modernity

However challenging Pevsner's 1930 visit to England may have been, the trip was productive and he came to value it. Looking back on it twenty-five years later, he talked about the advantage of seeing a country with fresh eyes. With his background in Saxon Baroque architecture and Italian Baroque painting, he said, 'the contrast was complete, and it was, against all expectations, agreeable too. Stimulated by this accidental demonstration of opposite national qualities in art, I began to collect material on the subject.'[1]

The visit reinforced for Pevsner a thought he'd taken with him and that was gaining currency in the new Germany: that England had briefly played a role in the development of Europe in the nineteenth century but had failed to capitalize on its potential. What he'd seen of England – poverty, poor housing, aesthetic stagnation – confirmed this thought, and a further one: that the potential England had wasted in the nineteenth century was being realized in a German ascendancy in the twentieth.

The idea wasn't his own. In a Bauhaus pamphlet from 1923[2], of which he had a copy and in which the school had set out its thinking, a key sentence read:

> During the second half of the nineteenth century a movement of protest began against the devastations wrought by academies. Ruskin and Morris in England, van de Velde in Belgium, Olbrich, Behrens and others in Germany, and finally the Werkbund searched for, and found, a way to reunite the world of work and that of creative artists.

In that sentence, the author of the pamphlet – Gropius (or possibly Feininger) – had spelled out an intellectual succession: the dispossession in particular of the French École des Beaux Arts, which had dominated questions of European style for a century, by artists whose answer to French aesthetics lay in the functionalism of craft. It was a tantalizing idea – subordinating form to function and aesthetics to purpose – suggestive of a new type of art and a new society. It also suggested that in the Werkbund, Germany had done what England was unable to do. Pevsner found the idea so powerful, he decided to expand it into a book.

An impediment was that the book didn't have an obvious hero. Gropius's predecessor in Weimar, Henri van de Velde, was Belgian, while Gropius himself was apparently a Corbusian Socialist. Nonetheless, Pevsner decided he must talk to Gropius and wrote to him, asking for a meeting. They met, not in Dessau, because Gropius had by now resigned from the Bauhaus,[3] but in Berlin, where he was running an architectural practice. Pevsner referred to that meeting in a radio talk in March 1949. Gropius, he said,

> seemed somewhat formidable to me then. Besides, he wore a fringe – which was slightly disconcerting. I talked of my work and plans, and in connection with a book I was then thinking of writing and which I have since written, I was anxious to have his views on William Morris. I showed him a photo – that splendid photo with the high broad forehead and the flowing hair and beard which Emery Walker took – every inch a Viking. 'So that's Morris', said Gropius. 'I've never seen a picture of him and yet I owe him so much.'[4]

Judging by Pevsner's susceptibility to charisma and the breathless way he'd always write about Gropius afterwards, the experience of seeing the great architect face to face must have been overwhelming. Pevsner didn't record directly what was said, but the meeting seems to have confirmed for him that he could extend the line from Morris to the Werkbund just a little further and make Gropius its finale. In this way, he said later, 'the history of artistic theory between 1890 and the First World War proves the assertion . . . that the phase between Morris and Gropius is an historical unit. Morris laid the foundation of the modern style; with Gropius its character was ultimately determined.' This was profound. For Pevsner, what the master mason of St Denis had done for Early Gothic before the middle of the twelfth century, 'was done for the world at the beginning of [the twentieth] century by Morris and his followers – Voysey, van de Velde, Mackintosh, Wright, Loos, Behrens, Gropius'.[5]

Pevsner would have come away from his meeting with Gropius with three very appealing concepts. The first was that it was possible to view the whole of the modern period in terms of art, even when the artists in question were what we would now call designers and architects. That was helpful because it kept the subject inside his field of study as an art historian. The second concept was that ideas once seen as hostile to notions of what art was – in particular, machinery and standardization on the one hand and handicrafts on the other – were now at its very centre.[6] The third concept was that what Gropius called the new style was 'the genuine and legitimate style of our century',[7] an idea that matched Pevsner's previous efforts in identifying styles with ages and his assertion, for example, that 'Mannerism is *the* style of the sixteenth century in Italy.'[8] He could therefore justifiably divert part of his scholarly attention to Modernism and its precursors in the certain knowledge that he was still involved in Geistesgeschichte, which was partly why Vitzthum had brought him to Göttingen.

But there were two barriers Pevsner had to overcome before he could embrace Gropius as the messiah of the moral age. One was Gropius's public reputation as a Socialist or Communist. That barrier would have come down the moment Gropius talked to him about his work, which could only have revealed what we now know: that Gropius was above all a visionary capitalist whose goals were entirely bound up with the idea of manufacturing as a profit-making activity. He'd been politically conservative before the war and even his post-war awakening to the need for a new start hadn't attracted him to the left. He'd had to tolerate Socialism at the Bauhaus but hadn't been part of it and had tried to steer clear of it – not just to avoid provoking the Bauhaus's enemies in Weimar but because he had a political position of his own: that capitalism is necessary and that the job of the artist is to enlighten the client.

Pevsner's other barrier was Gropius's Corbusianism. Here, Gropius would have shown him that his recent change of direction was a response not to Le Corbusier but to his contacts with Dutch artists: in particular to Theo van Doesburg and Piet Mondrian of the De Stijl group; and that De Stijl sourced its inspiration to a German architect: Gottfried Semper, whom Pevsner would come to regard as 'the most important German architect of the Early and High Victorian decades'[9] and who wrote the book from which De Stijl took its name, *Der Stil* (1861–1863).

What redeemed Gropius even further was that, like Pinder and Vitzthum, he'd actually fought the French – on French soil, rising in the first few months of the war from sergeant major to lieutenant, taking injuries and on several occasions cheating death.

So all was well. And armed with those assurances, Pevsner went back to Göttingen to draw up a plan for his book and make out a case for a new field of study: the moral or social art of the modern age. The book was eventually published in 1936 as *Pioneers of the Modern Movement* and would be misunderstood in England as showing how English ideas had flowered in the international architecture of the twentieth century rather than, as he'd originally intended, how German culture had triumphed by picking up the baton England had dropped in the nineteenth.

One important consequence of Pevsner's visit to England was the extent to which his change of scene had stimulated him. He was now bursting with new ideas for subjects needing his attention. In one source, he wrote that 'About 1930 I began to concentrate on nineteenth-century architecture';[10] in another he wrote about starting to teach nineteenth- and twentieth-century architecture.[11] Elsewhere, he wrote of having given thirty-six lectures at Göttingen in 1930 on different types of nineteenth-century architecture – government buildings, theatres, libraries, museums, hospitals, railway stations, etc. – with a new emphasis not on aesthetics as such but on how aesthetics was determined by function, especially plans.[12] He'd also talk about two different strands that emerged in his lecturing at Göttingen: a strand of social history and a strand of British (not English) art and architectural history he defined in a fifth document as falling into three categories: mediaeval art and architecture; art and architecture from 1500 to 1800; and art and architecture from 1800 to 1930.[13]

In addition to new areas of teaching, Pevsner was spurred into new areas of writing. Within two years of visiting England he'd published two papers that marked out his new direction: an expanded version of his 1929 essay on community ideals among nineteenth-century artists that gave more attention to

Morris and his follower C. R. Ashbee that came out in 1931;[14] and a history of the architectural profession that appeared in 1932.[15] By 1932 he'd also completed most of his preparatory work for what became his *Pioneers* book, written a detailed study of the history of art education that was ready for publication by 1933, and carried out preliminary research on a history of working-class housing that he didn't go on to complete.

In the face of these developments, one issue continued to rankle: the reputation of Le Corbusier. Pevsner at last confronted the problem in a review he wrote of the German-language edition of Le Corbusier's *Collected Works*[16] for the 1931 edition of the *Göttingsche gelehrte Anzeigen* which, after acknowledging Le Corbusier's mastery of the new architecture, challenged him on almost everything he'd said and done.

Pevsner introduced his attack in terms of wishing to protect the interests of modern architecture. Le Corbusier had claimed in his book that the roots of the new style lay in the work of a handful of earlier French architects, notably Auguste Perret, Tony Garnier and Frantz Jourdain, and that Central European, Dutch and German architects had merely followed France's lead after 1900. Pevsner objected that if this argument were allowed to stand, it could be used by 'political' opponents of the new style in Germany. He therefore broke down modern architecture into a number of basic features – the use of artificial materials (iron, ferro-concrete and glass), skeleton construction and free space, ribbon windows and simple cubes, flat roofs and plain windows and doors – and tried to determine the national origins of each.[17] He had to concede, however, that the most important of these achievements – the use of iron and ferro-concrete – was wholly French and had indeed been accomplished by 1900, and that the German architect who best represented German interests after 1900, Peter Behrens, designed buildings whose appearance was at best 'transitional'.

Having lost that battle and got bogged down in a stalemate over whether the no-man's-land from 1900 to 1914 was really German or really French,[18] Pevsner trudged through enemy lines to train his guns directly on Le Corbusier himself. His first bullet was just a tracer: Le Corbusier, he said, had failed to acknowledge his debt to Behrens, whose office he'd worked in for a few months in 1911–1912. Then, having pinned Le Corbusier down, he unloaded a fusillade, alleging that Walter Gropius made Le Corbusier's view of architectural history look like that of an interior decorator.

Pevsner went on to attack the style and purpose of Le Corbusier's work. Le Corbusier had proved a fraud when measured against the burning social questions the rest of Europe had been facing since the war, he said. He might be a master of new materials but he was also guilty of 'a creative drunkenness of technical romanticism', given the urgent question of how to house people at a time when no one had any money. His buildings were unrealistic, expensive to build and heat, hard to live in and impossible to find privacy in. He may have wanted to build poems, as Pevsner quoted him saying, but he did so irresponsibly.

If you compare his houses with the housing developments of a Gropius, May, Haesler, it's unmistakable that it's these that stand at the centre of residential construction in the twentieth century, while his derive from the damaging nineteenth-century tradition of the artist as a free-floating genius making works for a narrow circle of aesthetically hypersensitive art lovers.

Pevsner's review – a German manifesto for the 1930s – staked out unambiguously his belief in the continuing need to resist French assumptions of cultural supremacy. By depicting Le Corbusier as a stylist and then attacking style as a betrayal of modern needs, Pevsner was allowing France its artistic dominance but then using that dominance to disqualify it from the twentieth-century agenda. This counterposed two national conceptions of international Modernism: one French, one German. It made the French view the more chic but the more old-fashioned and the German view the more respectful of global realities and therefore the more immediate. In this way, in spite of the efforts of the Paris Exhibition of 1925, Pevsner was able to present German internationalism as having the better claim as the new standard.

Pevsner evidently saw his essay as a statement of pioneering importance. Although it was only ten pages long, he presented it five years later[19] not as a review of Le Corbusier's *Collected Works* but as 'a short preliminary account of the parts played by the most important architects in the development of the Modern Movement'. As with his volume of the *Handbuch*, he made sure it was widely circulated – and its point was not lost on another Renaissance art historian, Justus Bier, a specialist on the fifteenth-century German sculptor Tilman Riemenschneider. Bier had written a criticism of Mies van der Rohe in the journal of the Deutscher Werkbund, complaining, similarly, that the preciosity of Mies's Tugendhat House made personal life impossible and turned the building into more of a showroom than a home. In February 1932, Pevsner sent Bier a copy of his Le Corbusier review and got a letter back saying it was 'outstanding', that Pevsner should publish a version of it in the *Frankfurter Allgemeine Zeitung* 'perhaps titled "Corbusier or Gropius"', and that Bier would like to meet and talk about 'this problem' in Hannover, if Pevsner ever visited.

The nationalistic impact of the essay wasn't lost on Walter Gropius, to whom Pevsner also sent a copy. Replying on 23 September 1931 in a letter typed wholly in lower-case, Gropius wrote:

I'm frankly delighted that the roots of the new architecture – which all Germany is involved with, especially personalities like [the Swiss] Dr Giedion,[20] whose work I highly value, but who undervalues the German contribution – are getting their proper place, and in an academic context . . . Your work is highly important.

Gropius – who still didn't know Pevsner well enough at this point to get his name right (he misspelled it as 'Puesner') – went on to stress the importance of the Deutscher Werkbund in 'preparing the way for modern architecture' because, he said, 'from early on, [the Werkbund] had, in its intellectual strata, given rise to a movement on which ground the new architecture proliferated – something quite lacking in France'. He ended by asking Pevsner to send him ten or twelve copies of his essay and to enclose an invoice.

With his Le Corbusier review in 1931, Pevsner felt he'd decisively outflanked France and was now in possession of a new final chapter to the history he'd been trained in. If the arts of the twentieth century had a social agenda and were part of a vast new programme of civilization building, they were no longer like the arts of the past and could no longer be described using the same art-historical terms and ideas employed in the past. These socially responsible creations had to be part of a different phenomenon with a different world view and had to be explained using different sources. The articulation of this history – the defining of this new period of Geistegeschichte – would now be his central concern and one he'd try to make his own.

Pevsner's wish to treat Gropius as the indisputable torch-bearer of German architectural hopes meant he had to confront another problem: finding a building of Gropius's good enough to serve as exemplar of the new style but also pre-dating comparable buldings by Le Corbusier. When the Americans Henry-Russell Hitchcock and Philip Johnson had gone on a tour of new European architecture in the late 1920s, they dated the emergence of the revolutionary 'International Style' to 1922.[21] The difficulty for Pevsner was that Gropius's work of around this period had nothing like the clarity or beauty of Le Corbusier's. Gropius's Bauhaus buildings (1926) had been upstaged by the Pavillon de l'Esprit Nouveau of the previous year. His Chicago Tribune design of 1922 was just a drawing. His theatre in Jena (1921–1922) was a modish remodelling. His various buildings for Adolf Sommerfeld (1920–1921) showed clever ways of using wood supplied or salvaged by Sommerfeld's timber firm but had nothing to do with new conceptions of space and form. Going further back, the hospital he'd built with Adolf Meyer in Alfeld on the Leine (1912–1913) was unexceptional and so was the von Arnim house in Falkenhagen, Pomerania (1911–1912). He therefore had to fall back on Gropius's very first two buildings, neither of which did entirely what was required of them: the Deutscher Werkbund pavilion (1914) in Cologne and, before that, the Fagus factory (1911), also at Alfeld on the Leine.

Three factors made the buildings Pevsner chose to demonstrate Gropius's supremacy deficient. First, there were problems with the buildings themselves. Although both buildings were novel, the glass façade and flat roof of the Fagus factory didn't lift the soul, as Pevsner agreed great architecture should, while the Werkbund pavilion relied for its impact on two glass cylinders that looked as if they'd come from a different building. The second problem was that the buildings seemed to have been built in the wrong order. The Fagus factory looked the more advanced of the two but was built three years earlier than the Werkbund pavilion and had failed to inspire any of Gropius's later buildings, which called into question its force as a paradigm. The third problem was that neither building was a sufficient example of the new style. These inadequacies were self-evident to Hitchcock and Johnson, who in 1932 identified the Alfeld factory as a precursor of the new style, just as Pevsner had done with Behrens's turbine factory, but argued (having seen it up close and not just from photographs) that its monotony and compromises let it down: its brick sheathings appeared like 'the last fragments of the solid masonry wall of the past', its entrance was 'symmetrical and heavy' and its overall composition had a 'decorative emphasis'. As for the Werkbund pavilion, they gave it no mention at all.[22]

The consequence of choosing the Alfeld factory and the Werkbund pavilion for Pevsner was that instead of ending his new history with the emergence of the new style after the war, he ended it just before the war began, concluding ambiguously with buildings that were 'the fulfilment of the style of the century' and yet not a part of it. His view was that 'the essential style of the twentieth century' was not the International Style of 1922 that everyone else recognized – Le Corbusier's style, in effect – but something more diffuse: the cumulative efforts of Wright, Perret, Garnier, Loos, Hoffmann and Behrens in the early 1900s, culminating in Gropius's synthesis of them, with all the difficulties of the Fagus factory and the Werkbund pavilion conveniently blurred, Gropius's subsequent buildings ignored and the political complexities of the Bauhaus rendered irrelevant.[23]

The construction of modern history in this form gave Pevsner the satisfaction of being able to deliver a calculated riposte to France, returning the insult the Paris Exhibition had meted out to Germany, and excluding France and Le Corbusier from his own exposition of the greats. Writing in 1936 about the 'new aesthetic potentialities lying in store for the twentieth century', he commented that

> Le Corbusier scarcely belongs to a book dealing with pre-war matters; and, though he has tried in his writings to make himself appear one of the pioneers, he was not among the first comers . . . The historian must emphasize this point, because Le Corbusier, partly owing to his magnificent artistic imagination and partly to a certain showmanship, has been taken for one of the creators of the Modern Movement. It is surprising how [quickly] historical facts already tend to become dim and legends grow up.[24]

Could Pevsner not congratulate Le Corbusier on an inherent French logicality? 'I feel ready to forsake French logicality without a murmur of regret',[25] he said later. Wasn't Le Corbusier rigorous? No: around 1924 'Le Corbusier committed himself to cubist forms [but] handled them less rigidly than Gropius.'[26] Wasn't Le Corbusier an artist, in a way Gropius never was? Yes, said Pevsner: but it was an irresponsible, self-indulgent art that took no account of what society now needed from architecture.

The idea of art history coming to an end in 1914, before the war, and of everything afterwards being merely a footnote was so important to Pevsner that it provided the framework for all his subsequent thinking. With only the greatest difficulty was he ever able to consider alternative approaches in later years. In the case of architecture, his invariable view of those who challenged Gropius was that they were deviationists and attention-seekers who needed to be opposed because they were deranged or self-deceiving or in denial about what mattered. To that extent, Pevsner wasn't a pluralist but an elitist: only art that conformed to the highest standards of logic and good sense, as revealed by Germany's heroes of design, was acceptable. It's vital that the reader recognize, however, that in insisting on logicality and good sense, Pevsner wasn't thinking of the white Cubist paradigm of, say, the Weißenhofsiedlung (1927) but of an earlier and slightly looser architecture conceived in the last years of the Empire, when architecture still had sloping roofs.

Meanwhile at Göttingen, Pevsner continued to expand his reach by making contact with the history department. During the summer of 1931, while giving three courses on Italian Mannerism, English painting and old German sculpture for Vitzthum, he co-presented an introductory course with Alfred Hessel, associate professor of mediaeval and later history, on the reading, interpreting and understanding of mediaeval texts. These lectures went so well that Hessel and Pevsner arranged to give another joint series of lectures two years later on the subject of handwriting and illuminated manuscripts. Pevsner was now teaching for three of Göttingen's departments and using every effort to become indispensable. Then the Nazis came.

15

Hitler

Opportunities in Göttingen couldn't have seemed more abundant for Pevsner. He was a prominent member of the philosophy faculty and took part in academic activities outside his own department. He'd established a reputation for himself as a specialist in sixteenth- and seventeenth-century Italian art and was now starting to address mediaeval and contemporary issues. The only upset was the delay in his getting a salaried post.

Outside the academic world, however, Germany was becoming more polarized. In the elections of 1928, the year before Pevsner had arrived at Göttingen, the always unstable Weimar Republic had seemed to gain strength, with the ruling coalition of Democrats, Social Democrats and centre parties winning 153 seats, just short of an absolute majority. In the same election, nationalists and right-wing parties had seen their vote drop by twenty per cent. But in the elections of 1930 the Nazi Party, which had taken just twelve seats previously, unexpectedly won 107 seats, making it the second largest party in the Reichstag. Two years later, in the first of two elections in 1932 (the July election), it more than doubled its previous showing and overtook the SPD by 230 to 133 seats to become the largest parliamentary force in the country.

There was no inevitability it would continue growing. In spite of his coming second in the presidential elections of 1932, a considerable amount of manoeuvring was taking place to prevent the Nazi Party's leader, Adolf Hitler, from becoming president. It was also always possible that the left might prevail. Outside the USSR, Germany had the largest Communist party in the world – the KPD – and throughout the 1920s it had gradually increased its representation in the Reichstag, moving up from eighth-biggest party in the 1920 elections to fourth-biggest in 1928 and third in 1930. In the second (November) election of 1932, it gained eleven more seats than it had won four months earlier, taking it to 100, its largest showing ever, while the Nazis fell back by thirty-four seats. At the same time, the Nazi Party was embroiled in internal wrangles, with battles for supremacy between its factions in Berlin (led by Gregor Strasser) and Munich (led by Hitler) and all the uncertainties and incompetences of a novice political organization run by amateurs in chaotic times.

Away from the Reichstag and the fight for national power, however, Nazism was building itself into a popular movement, at a time when Germany was rife with such groups – particularly among young people who wanted the security of a communalized Germanness. In Göttingen, Nazi support was evident much earlier than in many other towns and by the late 1920s the party was already so well established[1] that party members in Göttingen took it upon themselves to go to other towns to give speeches and build support.[2] According to the official history of Göttingen University, 'the greater majority of [the university's] lecturers in the 1920s were national conservatives, which necessarily meant they were also anti-Semitic',[3] and this was mirrored in the student body, which became steadily more right-wing during the 1920s as students became more organized and political. 'Characterized by anti-rationalism, the myth of the front-line soldier, ideas of national community, anti-Semitism and opposition to the Weimar regime, there was a great ideological closeness to the National Socialistic German Student Society, which gained the majority in the student representation at the [university] in 1931.'[4] In the elections of 1930 the Nazis gained over thirty-seven per cent of the vote in Göttingen, making it the largest party in the region.

By the semester of 1932–1933, according to the university, four out five male students belonged to one of the many Burschenschaften, among them the Normannia (which Adolf Kurlbaum belonged to), Hannovera, Germania, Holzminda, Königsberger Gothia, Frisia, Brunsviga, and Allemania (which Pinder belonged to). In Göttingen, half of these Burschenschaften were duelling fraternities and all were becoming infected by Nazism.[5] As early as 1927 the local branch of the Deutsche Studentenschaft, a union of the student committees of all German-speaking universities, had to be banned in the state of Prussia because of an attempt to Aryanize it, but continued to operate covertly and saw its elections become more radical as a result. By 1931 the university's student parliament had been taken over by a Nazi majority.[6]

As a student, John Ratcliff found Göttingen's student bodies colourful and innocuous:

> On Monday evening I went to hear a speech on Bismarck in the marketplace, as the university [was] celebrating the centenary of his Immatrikulation [his entry to the university] the next day. If the speech itself was boring, the costumes of the various Burgenschaften[7] [sic] and Corps were very interesting and picturesque, and against the old walls of the Rathaus, or town hall, looked just right ... These Burgenschaften [sic] and Corps ... play an essential part in university life here. They are, as you will have guessed, different societies of students. Each has its separate hall and colours, which consist of a flag, jackets which they don for their Saturday evenings, when they drink beer in the halls, and their caps, which are always worn. The difference between Corps and Burschenschaft – namely that a Corps was an aristocratic affair and a Burschenschaft a bourgeois – no longer exists now but some Burschenschaften and Corps are more aristocratic than others. Among their various activities is duelling, which is forbidden, and has to be carried out outside the town in the country in secret and in the early hours of the morning. All proper students have great gashes and scars across their faces and heads.[8]

A few days earlier, Ratcliff had attended a mid-week rally of students in Mariaspring, just outside Göttingen, where 'hundreds of students assemble[d]

... with their coloured caps of the different "Bürgerschaften" [sic] to which they belong, and with their corresponding flags'. The bright colours made for a pretty sight, Ratcliff thought, although 'we had heavy rain ... and so the place was not nearly as full as it should have been. They danced out in the open air, which apparently they do a lot round here in the summer.'[9]

'It is really very fascinating,' Ratcliff had told his mother the previous week, 'to hear groups of students coming down the hill singing songs as they go home from their walking. True, they have not outstanding voices, but they get together awfully well. I have never heard so much outside singing as here.'[10] The singing was not always charming. The Sturmabteilung (Storm Troopers or SA, the Nazi Party's private army – also known as Brownshirts) used to walk around town chanting Nazi songs and looking for fights. A favourite song went

> Blood must flow, blood must flow!
> Blood must flow, thick as hail like cudgels!
> But let's smash it to pieces,
> But let's smash it to pieces!
> That goddamned Jewish republic!

Ratcliff recalled also that 'the SA used to march up to a woodland meadow just above the house where I was staying and no doubt were "indoctrinated" by speeches. (I kept away.)' They would sing the Horst Wessel Lied, the Nazi Party anthem, as they marched, as well as a song about the heroism of the SA that began

> You storm-troopers, both young and old,
> Take a weapon in your hand
> Because the Jew lives foully
> In the German Fatherland.

The song talks about a young storm trooper who leaves his wife and child to pursue his destiny to blow up Bolsheviks and go into battle as a front-line soldier for Hitler, sure of either triumph or death for the fatherland. On one occasion, Mausi, the young daughter of Hans Hecht (who was Jewish), heard the song being sung and screamed when it got to the fifth verse with its line 'Wenn das Judenblut vom Messer spritzt':

> When the storm trooper goes in to fight
> He's full of happy courage
> And when Jewish blood spurts from his knife
> Then everything's OK, then everything's OK.

'It made me shudder,' Ratcliff commented many years later. 'Although Hitler was not yet in power, the political atmosphere must have been pretty electric – no doubt mixed up with the usual student goings-on . . . I also attended a series of lectures on the Versailles Treaty ("The World War and its relation to the present world crisis"), which were vehemently put over by a colonel, and which no doubt added fuel to the fire.'[11]

Although Ratcliff saw the Burschenschaften as different in their appeal from the SA, the overlap was growing (though Hitler would eventually ban traditional student groups on the grounds that they challenged Nazism's monopoly of the young). The appeal of Nazism was further reinforced when, on 21 July 1932, ten days before the first parliamentary elections of that year, Hitler himself came to Göttingen to give an open-air speech in the Kaiser Wilhelm Park in the wooded hills above the town.

The event, advertised in the local press, was meticulously stage-managed. A generator was shipped in to power the loudspeakers and lighting system, and lapel badges were sold with the motto 'Hitler Rally, Göttingen'.[12] The podium was decked with swastikas and flags, and when the doors opened at 3 pm, the scene was already dramatic. Local SA members ushered the crowd of 15,000 to their seats and phalanxes of Hitler's personal guard, the SS,[13] took up position, supported by children from the Hitler Youth. At 8 pm, Hitler's plane flew over the crowd on its way to the local airport and as people in the audience saw it, they shouted 'Heil!' and waved their handkerchiefs.[14]

Wilhelm Frick began the proceedings by giving a warm-up speech. Frick was an original member of the Beer Hall Putsch in 1923 and the first Nazi to hold a senior government post. His address lasted nearly two hours. It then started to get dark and a light rain began. The crowd got restive but when Hitler suddenly emerged, lit by spotlights, there were tumultuous cries and applause. Ordering the umbrella over the stage to be removed so he could share the rain with his audience, he talked about the decisive vote in a week-and-a-half's time. Half quoting Thomas Mann, he said Germany was poised between two worlds – a world of internationalism and a world of pure Germanism – and between a fractured Germany and a unified one. He talked of the economic damage done by the Weimar Government, of the impoverishment of the state and of the millions of workers unemployed, and said the Nazi Party alone was committed to the German Volk, which was unrepresented without it. He left the stage to wild applause and the singing of the party anthem.[15]

Hitler's reception in Göttingen was not unusual. His speeches were always popular, among supporters of the party and the merely curious, and tickets would change hands quickly, and at huge mark-ups, generating big profits for the local branches of the Nazi Party and for Hitler himself, who took fifty per cent of the house. A measure of his appeal in Göttingen is that his speech was made to an audience equal in size to a third of the town, and four times the population of the university. It was also effective: in the ensuing election, the Nazis polled an absolute majority, with fifty-one per cent of the vote.

In spite of Hitler's impact at Göttingen, few of the people interviewed for this book volunteered any memories of the politics of the period. Adolf Isermeyer had nothing to say about it, even though he's since been quoted on how he got to know people in the SA and the 'riotous parties' they used to throw. Hans von Campenhausen, the theology historian with whom the Pevsners would socialize, readily recalled Pevsner as having a liking for 'Schlagermusik' – the latest hits of the day – and bringing out records when he and his wife went to visit but nothing beyond that. '[Pevsner] was a tall, thin man: very refined but humorous, not dry. If we met, we met for tea. We smoked and chatted. At that time, we were just happy-go-lucky. We never talked about politics, I'm sure.'[16]

Edeltrud König, uniquely, recalled that 'Pevsner would talk politics with us socially but never took National Socialism seriously. None of us was Nazi. None of us took the Nazis seriously. Only one student – Dr Wien, son of the professor of physics in Jena[17] – felt Nazi sympathies. Pevsner told us this once with amazement. He himself would read the most serious papers – the *Vossiche Zeitung*[18] and others – slightly to the left but certainly not Marxist.'

But Nazism was still not quite the same thing as Hitlerism. The Nazis were seen as rabid and violent thugs, and Pevsner had come across their violence in Munich; but Hitler, though their leader, could be seen as something different: a counter-intuitive figure, not a Bismarck but an ordinary modern man, instinctual and able to articulate the concerns of ordinary Germans, who, in his ordinariness, promised to be the unexpected saviour German writers had long spoken of. 'Pevsner felt sympathy for Hitler's national feelings', König said. 'He felt like a German, agreed that Hitler represented a political turning point in Germany's history and felt grateful for him after the humiliation of Versailles. Hitler traded on national sentiment and that's what Pevsner was in contact with too when talking about art and national characteristics.'

Although much of the political debate in Germany was starting to revolve around the demonising of Jews and the need for racial purity, Pevsner – happily ensconced in his home in Friedländer Weg – felt insulated from any threat. He'd been born Jewish but wasn't Jewish any more and was therefore safe. So was his half-Jewish wife. So was Stechow, whose parents had already converted. So were their students Hans Gronau and his wife Carmen. They were all simply Germans like everyone else. And so were the Pevsners' three children: Uta, named after Uta von Ballenstedt, one of the patron founders of Naumburg Cathedral, near Lola's father's country estate;[19] Thomas, named after Thomas Mann; and Dieter (registered as Dietrich), born on 2 August 1932, two days after the elections that brought the Nazis to power in Göttingen.[20] The Pevsners further protected their children by not telling them of their Jewish origins. As far as the children knew, they were as Christian as everybody else.[21]

The Pevsners lived comfortably, in spite of Nikolaus's not yet having a state income. Isermeyer remembered them having a maid and a nanny and a good library. König recalled their having a lot of Meissen in the house, including 'a wonderful porcelain crucifixion group three-foot high which stood on a dresser, a Nolde and some other even more modern paintings given to [them] by Lola's father' and some Bauhaus chairs in cherry-wood, that had been a wedding present. 'It was all in very good taste', she said: 'the best of the old and the best of the new'.

Pevsner's living conditions contributed to his self-assurance as a member of the teaching staff. 'Pevsner's lectures were well attended with rapt attention,' said Ratcliff, 'perhaps because the art-history theories he propounded were novel in those days. Pevsner's class was quite small, being a rather specialist subject, but no more so than any other lectures I attended. [They] were given in a well-appointed building with up-to-date projection facilities, motorized blackout, etc., so they were evidently highly regarded by the university, where the basic discipline was science.' Pevsner used to discuss mediaeval sculpture – 'der gotische Schwung' (the Gothic movement) – as Germany's highest artistic achievement and mounted an exhibition of photographs he'd compiled of Gothic details, photographed from inaccessible vantage points, high up. Ratcliff claimed to recall that at the opening of that exhibition, Pevsner explained that Germany's appreciation of the Gothic Schwung was comparatively new and said that

> if one were to ask any engaged German before the war the simplest thing about mediaeval sculpture, he wouldn't know. Actually, during the eighteenth and nineteenth centuries, Germany looked to Italy for inspiration for her art – all the greatest poets and painters have always gone to Italy – but now I think they have at last discovered the branch of art in which they excel themselves. (Their nineteenth-century classicism and Greek Revival is *not* outstanding.)[22]

Because of Pevsner's reputation, some of Germany's brightest students started enrolling at Göttingen, including the daughter of Max Sauerland, the director of the art gallery in Hamburg, the son of the director of the State Museum in Kassel, and Wolfgang Schöne who went on to become the chair of art history at Hamburg. Pevsner's students used to call him 'des Herrn Gottes Bleistift' – the Lord God's pencil – because he was tall and thin and all-knowing[23] and Hecht made up a rhyme of his own that went:

Den langen Pevsner sieht man lungern	Lanky Pevsner's on the street
Privatdozenten müssen hungern![24]	Tutors can't get much to eat!

Hecht had advised Ratcliff before term began to avoid boring lectures, of which there were evidently plenty,[25] and deciding who and what was boring was part of the playfulness that Pevsner colluded in with his students. 'He detested flowery language,' said Isermeyer, 'like Leo Bruhns's at Leipzig. Bruhns wrote a six-volume history of art that was flowery and poetic and sometimes kitschy. When Pinder went to Munich, Bruhns took over at Leipzig and in 1936 became the director of the Hertzian Library in Rome. He was a very good director but we sometimes read his books in seminar to amuse ourselves.'

The Pevsners' older children, Uta and Tom, had become school-friends of the daughters of Pallister Barkas, a Quaker from England whom Hecht had brought into the philology department because he thought it important to have an English lecturer on his staff. Uta was in the same class as Barkas's elder daughter Enid. 'One of my first memories is of Lola taking [the two girls] to school together', remembers Enid's younger sister, Rosalind Priestman. 'It was 1930 and they were both six and that's how I got to know the Pevsners. I thought they were an attractive family and that Lola was very young. We sometimes went to Naumburg with them, to Lola's father's country house. We'd flood the tennis courts there in winter and use them as skating rinks.'[26]

As an Englishman, Pallister Barkas was more relaxed than the Germans around him, in style as well as politics. 'My father would give garden parties quite a lot,' remembers Priestman. 'Pevsner was very formal. It was perfectly normal among the Germans to present visiting cards to people, which we thought was very funny. And my father would wear Harris Tweed, while everyone else wore dark suits. People would remark on our informality, but my mother and father thought parties were just a nice opportunity to meet people. They loved university life. My mother had a very intellectual circle of friends – wives of professors – and had tea parties. Lola wasn't a part of that: she was more a housewife, because of her small children.'[27]

It was at one of Barkas's parties that he and Pevsner had what Priestman describes as 'a heated argument about Hitler's intentions towards the Jews'. 'My father said to Pevsner "What do you think about the Nazis?" and Pevsner said "They're a good thing: we need a bit of self-confidence." And my father said "Have you actually read *Mein Kampf*?" and Pevsner said "It's just propaganda: it's not to be taken seriously." He couldn't believe there could be any terrible repercussions. He was very typical of Jewish intellectuals who thought themselves completely German. My father was amazed at his obstinacy and refusal to take the threat seriously.'[28]

Pevsner was not alone. Because of the Nazi Holocaust, the extent to which especially bourgeois Jews in Germany had come to think of themselves as German is still little understood. Most Jews and former Jews identified wholly with the German state and its people. As German patriotism went from being a more liberal to a more conservative ideology in the late nineteenth century, Jews with an established position in Germany had also become more conservative until a love of country and a fear of Communism drove some to support political ideologies that openly rejected them and sought their removal.

It took many years for this sensitive subject to be examined because it was always assumed in the West that because the regime that eventually decimated Jewry was right-wing, its victims must have been left-wing (as indeed many Jews became in the decades after the Second World War). In addition, of those Jews who'd managed to escape or survive the worst excesses, those who'd supported the right couldn't be open about their pre-war political allegiances for fear of looking complicit in their own demise.

In 1978 the historian Carl Rheins carried out a comprehensive study of this subject in a doctoral dissertation about four nationalist or conservative Jewish groups that came into being after the First World War. 'Eager to demonstrate that they were patriotic Germans,' Rheins explained in his abstract, 'these organizations were prepared from the outset to impress right-wing, at times downright anti-Semitic, circles in order to be accepted as equals within the German Volksgemeinschaft.'

The most extreme of these groups was the Verband nationaldeutscher Juden (the League of National German Jews), founded in 1921 by Dr Max Naumann, a former captain in the Bavarian army. The Verband explicitly adopted anti-Semitic policies on the grounds that German Jews had more in common with Germans than with other Jews, especially East European Jews, whom Naumann described as 'pitiful creatures . . . of a not quite human level'. These efforts not only failed to placate racial anti-Semites but weakened Jewish resistance to anti-Semitism, says Rheins.[29]

If some Jews felt able to identify with extreme German nationalism, identification was that much easier for those who no longer saw themselves as Jewish, especially if they disregarded nationalism's more hysterical and aggressive forms. Pevsner, for all his moderation and analytical caution, seems to have belonged in this latter category, unlike those Germans who'd renounced their Judaism and felt passionately nationalistic but found the prospect of Hitler repellent. Victor Klemperer, for example, who became chair of romance languages and literature at the Technical University of Dresden in 1920, insisted it was he who was 'forever German' and 'a German "nationalist"' and the Nazis who were 'unGerman'. In the early 1940s he wrote: 'I'm German and I'm waiting for the Germans to return. They have gone into hiding somewhere.'[30]

Klemperer – now known only for his wartime diaries and forgotten as an academic – was, like Pevsner, interested in Geistesgeschichte and the way that developing ideas found expression in cultural and political forms, but where Pevsner's focus was on German mediaevalism and the late Italian Renaissance, Klemperer's was on France and the French Enlightenment. With that vantage point, he was already likening the emergence of Hitler at the start of 1933 to 'the Terror' that followed the French Revolution; by contrast, in all Pevsner's very considerable correspondence in this period, there's nothing to suggest he was either fearful or critical of the new Germany, or that he likened Hitler to negative historical models in the way Klemperer did.

This difference in approach is partly generational. Klemperer was born in 1881 and identified with the values of an older, more liberal peer group. Although committed to Germany and issues of national identity, he taught that Germany could learn from Voltaire, Rousseau and Montesquieu – those heroes of French rationalism whom Annie Pewsner believed in but who'd become anathema in mainstream German academic circles. The Göttingen mathematician Richard Courant, born seven years after Klemperer, also found the Nazis frightening. Priestman remembers talking to his daughter, Gertrud Courant, in late 1932 or early 1933 when 'garish [election] posters began to appear all over the town and aeroplanes – a rarity in those days – were seen trailing banners with "Vote for Hitler"'. She asked Gertrud how she felt about the prospect of Hitler's being elected and Gertrud told her that her father was petrified.[31] Pevsner, by contrast, saw himself as part of a younger generation for which the extreme right was an untested experiment that deserved a trial – and implicitly, therefore, deserved the right to make mistakes in what its defenders saw as a just cause, much as Gropius defended the Bauhaus's right to make mistakes.[32] That doesn't mean Pevsner couldn't learn from liberalism. In his 1928 essay 'Early and High Baroque',[33] he paid tribute to Klemperer's writings on France, thanking him for 'having given me more insights than any other [literary historian]' and identifying him as the very first person to see the equation between passion and reason in the French Enlightenment as central to an understanding of the period' – an idea Pinder would condense in his remark 'Wissenschaft ist Leidenschaft': science is passion.[34] Klemperer was, however, an older man and Pevsner's debt to him was purely scholarly. There's also a humanity in Klemperer's writings, for which there's no parallel in Pevsner.

Generational difference doesn't explain everything, however. Oswald Spengler was one year older than Klemperer but was admired by Pevsner for his ideas and his political outlook. In the same essay in which he complimented Klemperer, Pevsner remarked that 'one of Oswald Spengler's most profound and fruitful insights was that which led him to place the discovery of infinity at the centre of his presentation of Western culture' and Pevsner credited Spengler with being 'the first to perceive the immensely illuminating parallel between ... scientific discoveries, which transformed man's view of the universe, and the artistic innovations of the seventeenth century'. But Pevsner was also repeating Spengler's core ideas about the new German age – about the need for 'barbaric Caesarism', ruthless power, the combining of Socialism and Prussianism, of a 'Sonderweg' (a special German way), about hardness, duty to the state, courage and scepticism – when he wrote a couple of years later about wanting to master the creative energy of the world, 'a world of science and technique, of speed and danger, of hard struggles and no personal security'.[35] As it happens, Spengler found Hitler small-minded when they met in 1933 and refused to give the Nazi Party the support it craved from him, but he was nonetheless a litmus test for the right and no one from anywhere on the left of the political spectrum could have referred to him without feeling contaminated, any more than anyone on the far right could have happily quoted Marx or Freud.

By 1932 the Weimar Republic was becoming ungovernable. The 1930 elections had brought fifteen political parties into the Reichstag. The resulting instability was stirred into chaos by Nazi members, orchestrated by Hermann Göring, who sought to disrupt parliamentary procedures in order to prove that Germany's new democratic constitution, also in its experimental stages, couldn't work. At the same time, Paul von Hindenburg, the one symbol of steadiness, was coming to the end of his seven-year term as Reichspräsident and, aged eighty-four, had no wish to remain in office. He agreed to stand for election again only to keep Hitler at bay but took two rounds to get voted back in, in April 1932, during which time Hitler gained greater public exposure and then tried to use his popularity to press Hindenburg into making him chancellor.

Hindenburg resisted Hitler's pressure but was defeated by the failure of alternative manoeuvres. An army man, General Kurt von Schleicher, persuaded Hindenburg to appoint his proxy – the little-known Franz von Papen – as chancellor and then tried to tame Hitler by offering him a cabinet post. Hitler refused to be fettered and demanded an election as the price of his support for Papen. It was in that election that the Nazis more than doubled their showing to 230 seats, prompting Hitler to demand the chancellorship again. When Hindenburg refused, Hitler broke with Papen and the Reichstag was dissolved for a second time that year. The electorate punished Hitler for his inflexibility in the November elections but a string of other disappointments, including the resignation of Papen, his replacement by Schleicher and then Schleicher's resignation,[36] persuaded Hindenburg, finally, to back down and give Hitler the chancellorship. The position was ratified on 30 January 1933, Pevsner's thirty-first birthday.

Hitler immediately persuaded Hindenburg to dissolve the Reichstag again and hand the state of Prussia, including Berlin, to Papen, whom he'd had to accept as his vice-chancellor. Papen, under pressure, now allowed Göring, as Prussia's new Minister of the Interior, to instruct the police that the SA and SS were to be given absolute freedom. On 27 February a special attachment of the SA and SS exploited that freedom and burnt down the Reichstag building. The following day Hindenburg let Hitler rule by emergency decree. Hitler now used a combination of emergency procedures and thuggery to force state officials out of office and replace them with Nazi commissars. He also opened the first concentration camp, in Dachau, outside Munich, to imprison opponents of the party. When elections on 5 March failed to give the Nazis the two-thirds majority they needed to amend the constitution, an enabling bill was put to a specially convened meeting of the newly elected Reichstag in Berlin's Kroll Opera House on 23 March that would bring democracy to an end and make Germany a dictatorship. The bill was passed on a vote of 441 to 84.

In the same session, Wilhelm Frick, now the Interior Minister, submitted a new law to the cabinet to exclude 'non-Aryans' from being employed by the government and by government-funded bodies such as universities. Two weeks later, on 7 April 1933, the 'non-Aryans' law – officially known as 'Law for the Restoration of the Professional Civil Service' or the 'Civil Servants' Law' for short[37] – was passed in its final form.

Pevsner felt safe: he was no longer Jewish and, as he'd said to Pallister Barkas, the Nazis' threat of racial violence was no more than propaganda. His older son Thomas, brought up by his parents to have no knowledge of his Jewish background, felt the same way. 'I never felt threatened by the Nazis,' he said. 'I remember on one occasion that there were police sirens and asking what they were and being told that they were going to a Lokal [bar] to beat up Jews. I was never aware that any of this affected us. It was never an issue.'[38]

16

Dismissal

Pevsner's attitude to the new Civil Servants' Law – his belief that he was untouched by the new legislation and that the regime that had introduced it was defensible, even if it had acted excessively in this particular case – was not unique. The Prussian civil servant Fritz Rathenau (a cousin of Walther Rathenau, assassinated by nationalist extremists while serving as Foreign Minister to the Weimar Government in 1922) said 'That I did not see the coming storm in time or appreciate its full gravity was a failure of intellect but not one of character. Nor was I alone.'[1] Later, when Rathenau warned Göttingen's brilliant but pompous chair of mathematics Edmund Landau that if the Nazis came to power they'd incarcerate Jews in concentration camps, Landau is said to have replied 'In that case I should immediately reserve for myself a room with a balcony and a southern exposure.'

The Göttingen historian Hans-Joachim Dahms seems nonetheless to have misjudged the mood in Göttingen when he wrote, in 1983, that since the only person to take a stand against the new law was Göttingen's Nobel prizewinner for physics James Franck, 'it would appear that other university teachers threatened by these new regulations didn't recognize the seriousness of the situation.'[2] On the contrary, by mid-April 1933, events were worsening so fast that many members of the 'non-Aryan' population were already cowed.

On 26 March Hitler had called for a national boycott of 'Jewish shops' to take place on Saturday, 1 April, supposedly in response to an anti-Nazi demonstration in New York and what Joseph Goebbels, the Nazi propaganda minister, called 'a malicious hate campaign' orchestrated against Germany by 'international Jewry'. The boycott saw SA men posted in front of Jewish-owned shops, with triangular placards reading 'Whoever buys from the Jew supports the foreign boycott and destroys the German economy.' In addition, the new Civil Servants' Law had resulted in the sacking of an eighth of the senior echelons of the Prussian Civil Service, on political or racial grounds.[3] Under the new legislation, what counted was race, not religion. Conversion to Christianity therefore meant nothing; having even one Jewish grandparent now meant victimization. It was this climate of intimidation that explains why none of the staff at Göttingen University dared publicly support the stand taken by Franck, who resigned his chair in protest at the new law on 12 April; on the contrary, some forty-two professors and lecturers – fourteen per cent of the university teaching staff – curried favour with the new regime by jointly demanding that Franck be tried for his 'act of sabotage' and calling on the government to speed up the anti-Jewish purge.

On 26 April the *Göttinger Tageblatt* ran a news story that Prussia's newly appointed education minister, Bernhard Rust, had, in a not very charming euphemism, 'granted leave'[4] to six faculty members at Göttingen while the law decided what to do with them. The six were the social psychologist and educationalist Curt Bondy, the criminal jurist Richard Honig, the quantum physicist Max Born (who would win a Nobel Prize after the war), and the mathematicians Felix Bernstein, Richard Courant and Amalie Emmy Noether. The paper noted that more suspensions would follow, gave the names of thirty-four lecturers who'd been suspended at five other universities (Frankfurt am Main, Marburg, Königsburg, Königsburg Commercial College and Kiel), and repeated that apart from the suspensions, the education Ministry would be carrying out transfers of tenure very soon to transform the universities and 'reestablish their native character', as ordered by the new law.

According to Elisabeth Paatz, daughter of the registrar of Göttingen university, her father, Justus Theodor Valentiner, 'had no connection to any party or religion and was simply sorry, as an administrator, to lose his staff'.[5] Valentiner evidently felt that any effort he might make to keep his staff would compromise his position, though when fourteen colleagues asked him during the summer to try to protect Noether, he opposed them by informing the Ministry that Noether had always been a Marxist and couldn't be expected to support the state. He did however instruct the leader of the students' body to call off its boycott of one particular member of staff, the mineralogist Viktor Goldschmidt.

Over the course of April, university staff tried to decide where they now stood. Some got out of the country as quickly as they could; others, like Courant, tried to secure their positions by making use of an exemption clause in the new law for those who'd served in the First World War. 'We knew lots of people in Göttingen who lost their jobs', remembers Rosalind Priestman. 'Professor Courant was my father's greatest friend. He lost his job on the first day of the new law. It should have been a warning to Pevsner.'[6] Instead, Pevsner's initial reaction was to stay put, if possible, and support the changes.

His behaviour was noted with some surprise by Priestman's aunt, Francesca Wilson, the sister of Pallister Barkas's wife Muriel. Wilson, also a Quaker, was a Birmingham activist and school teacher who spent her life involved in refugee work. Between April and May 1933 she made a tour of the new Germany to assess the help that Quakers could give to those whose lives were becoming intolerable. During that visit she stayed with her brother in Göttingen and was there for May Day, the traditional workers' holiday that the SPD had banned in 1929 but that Hitler had made a virtue of restoring, before banning trade unions and imprisoning their leaders the next day.[7] Like John Ratcliff, she felt that Göttingen could put on a good show and in an article she wrote for the *Birmingham Post* a week later, she said:

A German university town is as good a place as any for an onlooker to study the

Revolution and the emergence of the Third Empire. Hitler and his colleagues are master showmen, whatever else may be said of them. On May 1, the whole place was ablaze with decorations – the streets festooned with the new red, white and black flags and with swastikas.

Even a small town like [Göttingen][8] mustered a procession of many thousands for Hitler's Day of Labour. For an hour-and-a-half I watched them pass – the SAs and the SSs in their khaki shirts and breeches brown or black . . . railway and post officials in brilliant blue uniforms, black-coated tradesmen and newspapermen, and students wearing the gorgeous colours of their associations, proudly displaying their scars (for duelling is officially permitted now). Employers and heads of offices march cheek by jowl with the humblest employee: this was to represent the reconciliation of the classes, about which Hitler has so much to say, and which is indeed one of the best features of his movement. The only absentees were women. Hitler wants to revive the good old Germany, in which women stayed at home, rocking cradles and obeying husbands.[9]

On Thursday, 4 May, three days after the May Day parade, Barkas held a garden party at which he introduced his sister-in-law to Pevsner, whose name she couldn't quite catch. Priestman remembers that Francesca Wilson 'liked him immediately'.[10] That evening, she wrote in her diary: 'Long talk with Peeschner [sic] in the afternoon. Peschner [sic] a Kunsthistoricker [sic] – fair type, very refined and cultural. A Jew but feels himself entirely German. Very nationalist in sympathy. Absurd situation for him. Could not send Uta to a Jewish school in Frankfurt because not enough in common with Orthodox Jews. Has had a *dringende Bitte nicht zu lesen* – [urgent 'request' not to teach]. They warned him that his students would make a row if he did.'

Later that month, Wilson quoted Pevsner at length in her *Birmingham Post* article:

One of the most interesting conversations I have had (and people still speak their minds very frankly) was with a Privatdozent, who the day before had been asked not to lecture. He was tall and blonde – only a German with a sixth sense for a Jew would have known that he wasn't Aryan – dignified and refined, not only in appearance, but in cast of mind. 'I love Germany', he said. 'It is my country. I am a Nationalist, and in spite of the way I am treated, I want this movement to succeed. There is no alternative but chaos, and I cannot want my country to be plunged into civil war. There are things worse than Hitlerism; I think your press in England does not realize that. And there is much idealism in the movement. There are many things in it which I greet with enthusiasm and which I myself have preached in my writings. I consider compulsory labour which is to start next January an excellent thing. All young men will have six months' service for the state, and no matter what their rank in life they will all work together. Hitler is planning public works on a vast scale to cure the unemployment problem, and I believe that he has the courage and will to do what he says. Then there is much that is puritan and moral in the movement – a great drive is to be made against luxury, vice and corruption.

> For fifteen years we have been humiliated by the outside powers. No wonder that
> Hitler appeals to our youth when he tells them to believe in themselves again, that the
> future is theirs to mould, that if they are united Germany will no longer be the pariah
> of the world. If there had been no reparations, and no invasion of the Ruhr and the
> Rhineland, there would have been no Hitler.[11]

In the same article, Wilson repeated, apparently uncritically, the same provocative
excuse for the Nazi Party's hatred of Jews she'd heard from another Göttingen
academic – someone she'd found unpleasant on a previous trip but now found
fascinating. He'd told her, and she'd accepted as plausible, that virulent anti-
Semitism was rightly targeted at Polish Jews but wrongly displaced onto German
Jews. 'The anti-Semitic propaganda of the last twelve years was largely directed
against Polish Jews, who fled to Germany on the Russian advance', she wrote.
'There were many of them poor, uneducated, half-civilized people, who, with
their inborn skill as moneychangers, made their fortunes during the inflationary
period and earned their unpopularity by their noisy *nouveau riche* airs and still
more by being mixed up in all sorts of corruption scandals and swindles.' The
trouble, apparently, was that there weren't enough Polish Jews in the country to
feed the people's hunger for scapegoats. 'Many of them vanished when the mark
was stabilized and went off to reap the harvest of the falling franc or to America.
Men of this kind are now confused with Jews long established in this country,
with the highest traditions of loyalty and good citizenship. A large percentage
of people recognize this mistake, though they can only say so in private.' The
result was that 'Every day during the last few weeks has brought terrible news
of some professor "given leave", some Privatdozent "requested" not to lecture.
Germans may be untainted Aryans (this is the word in vogue now) and good
patriots, and still be attached to their professors, or at least anxious to complete
their studies in peace and retain their pride in the glory of their university. But
... headquarters looks through the forms which every state official has been
forced to fill in. One Jewish grandparent is enough to damn a professor. So
[Göttingen] loses many of its most brilliant men, and from being one of the
foremost universities in Germany is reduced to secondary importance. No longer
will it attract students from all over the world.' For the majority, however, none
of this applied. 'If one is to judge by the speeches, the songs, the flag-waving and
the swastikas on the coat-sleeves and house-tops, Germany is happy, Germany
is as united as she was in July 1914, when she plunged into war with the same
spirit of jubilation and triumph.'[12]

Marianne Kockell, Lola's younger sister, thought there was no secret about
where her brother-in-law stood politically but felt his politics was simply a
reflection of his personality: he was a man who liked order. 'I know he saw all the
positive sides of National Socialism, which were probably the economic ones,'
she said, 'but that was because he was the sort of person he was. He got annoyed
when students walked out of the room during his lectures. That annoyed him

and he always said "What I'd really like is to lock them in. Once they're inside, that's where they should stay."[13]

Among Pevsner's inner circle of family and friends years later in England, those who knew about his politics chose to deny it, or not speak about it, or write it off as naivety and to offer examples of his impracticality – his inability to boil an egg or hang up pictures or mend a pipe or drive a car – as if the two went together. That may have been a necessary ploy to protect Pevsner's reputation in the years after the Second World War, but it was a falsehood and speaks badly of those who knowingly perpetuated it. His student and long-time colleague Bridget Cherry, for example, who worked under him and then succeeded him as editor of the *Buildings of England*, remarked in 2002 that 'the main thing to remember is [that] Pevsner was not clued-up politically. He didn't understand politics and so did not have a political position.'[14] This view of him is built on the idea that there were, broadly speaking, three sorts of people in Germany: progressives and liberals who opposed Nazism; racists, conservatives and nationalists who embraced it; and the politically foolish who were duped into supporting it. It's a faulty view because it invalidates legitimate political choices that happen to favour parties we now find objectionable – and that's undemocratic and condescending. In hindsight, Pevsner was wrong but he wasn't naïve: he and others had a view of the political situation they found rational and reasonable at the time.[15]

Pevsner's thinking was sustained by his social contacts. He was exceptionally fond of his mentor Wilhelm Pinder and strongly influenced by their continuing relationship. In 1925, six months after Pevsner had graduated, Pinder had written to his 'dear, faithful' former student, welcoming him back to Leipzig to give a lecture, sharing intemperate thoughts with him about Erwin Panofsky, and making extravagant compliments about how Lola always made him feel like 'a favoured grandchild' and how he adored the Pevsner household and its ambience, 'made up of people where I feel at ease and find understanding'.

Similar exchanges continued. In August 1928 Pinder thanked Pevsner for offering – albeit two months late – to edit a fiftieth-birthday Festschrift for him, replying that although he couldn't agree to the proposal because of his violent aversion to Festschrifts (even though he contributed readily to several), he welcomed the idea of commemorating old friends, especially in view of the goodwill and kindness Pevsner had always afforded him.

In November 1928 Pinder sent news that an aria he'd written for Vitzthum was going to be performed. And in July 1930 he responded to an apology from Pevsner for not having written sooner about arrangements for his study tour of England by thanking him for keeping him supplied with his 'beautiful' instalments to the *Handbuch*, which he promised to read as soon as possible (though the finished book had now been in print for two years), and talking about two Italian driving trips he'd made at Easter and Whitsun and about the enjoyable time he'd spent at the 'Quattrocento College' where, as quoted above, 'I have the shameless impression that I see things more accurately than the specialists.' He'd be going on a five- or six-week trip to the south of France that autumn instead of lecturing in Hamburg and a dancer called Elfriede Schulze had flown in and was dancing with renewed vigour at the Munich summer festival.

Pevsner continued sending Pinder his writings and in October 1931 Pinder praised him for his Göttingen essay on Le Corbusier, saying he found it extraordinarily interesting – 'brave and correct!' – and was in full agreement with it. He also apologized for not having written sooner because he'd been devoting himself to his music, and sent his warm wishes to Pevsner and to Vitzthum, who he'd heard had been ill again.

The affinity between Pinder and Pevsner, though sometimes one-sided, kept Pevsner receptive to Pinder's ideas. It didn't however stop Pinder from supporting the policy now being imposed on Germany's universities of Gleichschaltung or 'coordination', which subordinated all teaching to Nazi ideology and race theory – something his own teaching had in any case been gravitating towards for many years. This meant rewriting curricula according to what the Führer decided should be taught or what professors thought he thought should be taught, and revising and even eradicating subjects he had decided were 'Jewish' (psychology) or 'too Jewish' (mathematics and physics[16]).

In November 1933 Pinder was one of over 700 signatories to a university and college lecturers' 'Profession of Faith' in Hitler and the Nazi state.[17] In addition, on the eve of the 12 November plebiscite that asked the electorate to support Germany's withdrawal from the League of Nations and the Disarmament Conference, Pinder appeared alongside Heidegger at a demonstration in Leipzig, calling on educated people all over the world to be more charitable to the Führer. Pinder could do all this in the knowledge that the support he was giving to the Nazi tyranny would be damaging to people like Pevsner for whom he claimed great affection. Hans von Campenhausen, who'd frequently hosted the Pevsners at his home and been entertained in theirs, also signed up to the November 1933 Profession of Faith without any evident concern for the impact it would have on friends and colleagues.

Pevsner seems not to have been offended by this polite hypocrisy. Klemperer's reaction, writing about the academic expulsions around the same time, was quite different: 'Today, the rectors of Frankfurt University, the Technical University of Brunswick, Kantorowicz, the director of the Bonn University Hospital [and] a Christian business editor of the *Frankfurter Zeitung* were arrested . . . Everything I considered unGerman – brutality, injustice, hypocrisy, mass suggestion to the point of intoxication – all of it flourishes here.'[18]

Pevsner maintained the illusion that normal life could carry on. In February, he'd contributed an article to one of the local newspapers, the *Göttinger Tageblatt*, about the Dresden architect and city planner Fritz Schumacher, who'd taught alongside Cornelius Gurlitt at the Technical University of Dresden and whose exhibition designs in Dresden had been influential for the Deutscher

Werkbund. In March he contributed to the sixtieth-birthday Festschrift for Walter Friedländer a short essay about an unknown early work of the school of Caravaggio. And the *Göttingische gelehrte Anzeigen* in its April–May edition carried a review he'd written of a monograph about the Austrian artist Rudolf Pühringer, who specialized in monumental topographic painting.

By April, Pevsner should have been starting his teaching for the summer: a course of open lectures on German Romantic art, a course for the history of art department on English mediaeval architecture, a series of seminars on mediaeval book illustration and a course on handwriting and book illustration for the history department, in tandem with the department's Alfred Hessel.[19] All those courses were now suspended. So were Stechow's. So were Hessel's. Hessel, Priestman remembers, was unmarried but 'lived with a Fräulein', which gave rise to a number of small-town scandals. 'He lost his job early and my parents suggested that I go to him regularly for lessons in art history. He gave me [private] lessons in Renaissance art, which was wonderful for me but a great come-down for him. Some time later he got a letter from his brother, who was a professor in Berlin, to say he was being sent to a concentration camp. Hessel had a heart attack at the breakfast table as he read it.'[20]

Vitzthum, a resolute anti-Nazi and a supporter of the German People's Party,[21] which Hitler had banned after coming to power, tried to rescue his tiny department. He held discussions with fellow members of the philosophy faculty and its head, and with Göttingen's dean and rector, trying to find a way to protect Stechow and Pevsner. Two-and-a-half weeks later, on 17 May 1933, he put a request in writing to Registrar Valentiner, the godfather to his youngest daughter:

> It's not possible to say briefly what I've gone through during these last weeks ... Both my Privatdozenten have had their lectures put on hold until their legal position is clear, that is, both of them, for the whole semester ... One [Pevsner] is a Jew – well! The other [Stechow] has a Jewish mother but fought in the war and should therefore be inviolable. But – as one of our rulers put it to me – a Jew or half-Jew can't interpret German art competently! That's new dogma and can't be argued with. Both are also incriminated because I've got a bad reputation politically, even if I'm allowed to stay on. But I've got two Jews next to me: 'Unbearable!' What have I not tried, talked, negotiated – all ignored ...[22]

With no prospect of his being employed in Germany under the new conditions, Nikolaus discussed with Lola what to do next. She thought he should go to England, where he'd got family and where he'd made useful contacts in 1930. She also thought he should ask Barkas for advice, but in view of their recent argument about politics, he felt uncomfortable about doing so. His preference, in any case, was to sit out the crisis by getting a teaching job in Italy until the anti-Jewish hysteria in Germany died down: England, he felt, was the place where members of his family went when they'd failed elsewhere and he didn't want to be tainted in that way. He therefore contacted Pinder for a reference and Pinder wrote back promptly, commending him for being involved in German scholarship at the deepest level while being equally open to big historical and contemporary issues. Armed with this unintended mockery of Nazi discrimination, Pevsner went, a little earlier than usual, on his habitual Italian summer break.

While in Italy, Pevsner carried out research in the records of the Florentine Academy of Art. He offered the results of his research to the Art History Institute in Florence, which published them in that summer's edition of its journal. He also met Bodmer again to ask about the possibility of a research fellowship at the institute but, as the institute was a German state institution, Bodmer offered nothing more than he'd offered in the past. Pevsner therefore had to look elsewhere for fellow academics who might value his presence.

Pevsner could have turned his attention to any of the old Italian universities; he turned instead to the newly formed Accademia d'Italia at Rome University, a specifically pro-fascist institution. It occurred to him that he might start a course in German art history and he canvassed support for this idea with a number of leading scholars, including Giuseppe Gabetti, an archaeologist and German specialist who'd written about Nietzsche and fascism in the *Italian Encyclopaedia*, and the director of the Academy, Giovanni Gentile, the philosopher whom Benedetto Croce said 'holds the honour of having been the most rigorous neo-Hegelian in the entire history of Western philosophy and the dishonour of having been the official philosopher of fascism in Italy'.[23] Gentile had been the chair of philosophy at Palermo University between 1907 and 1914 and was brought into Mussolini's government in 1923 to reform secondary education, which he did, with considerable and lasting success. In 1925 he wrote the *Manifesto of the Fascist Intellectuals* (which was signed by, among others, Luigi Pirandello) and went on to ghost-write Mussolini's *A Doctrine of Fascism*, which he published in 1932 in the *Italian Encyclopaedia*, which he was the editor of.[24] Pevsner came away from these conversations with the impression that right-wing senior academics in a country that didn't object to Jews as Germany did might welcome him. With that hope, he returned to Göttingen and waited for developments.

While Nikolaus had been away in Italy, Lola had 'poured her heart out' to Barkas's wife Muriel.[25] She now heard back from Barkas that a new institution had been set up in England called the Academic Assistance Council. The Council, a parallel organization to America's Emergency Committee, was a commendable humanitarian body. The idea for it came from the Hungarian physicist Leó Szilárd, the man who went on to invent the atom bomb and who'd left Berlin for Vienna shortly after the burning of the Reichstag. Szilárd was convinced there was no future for Jewish or left-wing academics in Central Europe while Hitler was in power. In Vienna he co-opted the help of the Austrian economist Ludwig von Mises, who, in spite of his laissez-faire policies on money, persuaded the director of the London School of Economics Sir William Beveridge,[26] while Beveridge was in Vienna, of the need for intervention. Beveridge took the idea to the LSE – still very much the home of Fabianism – where academic staff agreed to commit a percentage of their salaries to a fund operated by the Academic Assistance Council that would pay leading scholars to lecture in Britain or elsewhere in the empire. The Council, praised by Albert Einstein in a speech at the Royal Albert Hall later in the year, was launched in May 1933. Barkas recommended to Lola that Pevsner put together a set of testimonials and apply to it for a job.

On 5 July 1933 Pevsner grudgingly wrote a clumsily worded letter to the Council that he was probably too proud to let Barkas help him craft:

> I have been advised by Mr P. Barkas (MA Durham), the English Lektor in the University of Göttingen, to apply to you for advice as to the possibilities of finding some employment abroad.
>
> As I am a 'Privatdozent' for the history of art as above, and was too young to have taken part in the war, I must expect to loose [sic] my *venia legendi* under the new anti-Semitic laws.
>
> The work for which I am specially trained is history of art as above, and I would be willing to go to any part of Europe, America or the British Dominions in which I could find suitable employment. Besides I consider that I would be able to act as a German Lektor in any university in the world.

He enclosed the reference from Pinder he'd taken with him to Italy and listed five other potential referees. At the same time he wrote to Borenius, explaining what he was doing and asking for help.

Borenius immediately wrote to the Council, saying Pevsner was well known to him, that 'as a scholar he [was] in the first rank of present German art historians' and that his work was so distinguished that, largely through him, 'Göttingen was on the point of becoming one of the principal centres for the study of English civilization in Germany.' Borenius heard confirmation by return – just six days after Pevsner had written from Germany – that Pevsner's application had already been received and his name registered. The Council's secretary asked if Borenius could think of anyone who might employ Pevsner and suggested contacting Professor William George (W. G.) Constable, the director of the Courtauld Institute of Art, which had opened the previous year as part of London University. This was an imaginative idea because Constable, previously assistant director of the National Gallery, was known to have a respect for international scholarship that was rare for England and Borenius was in any case already one of the institute's external examiners.

The fact that art history was not an established university subject made it harder for a foreign art historian to find work in England than for an academic in almost any other field. Borenius himself was fortunate to have taken over Roger Fry's lectureship in art history at University College, London, and to have elevated it into the Durning-Lawrence Professorship in 1922, but other than that, there were only the Slade professorships that Felix Slade had endowed concurrently at Oxford, Cambridge and London in 1869 and the Watson Gordon Professorship of Fine Art that was endowed at Edinburgh in 1879. Where institutions taught art history informally, it was not in the context of separate degree or diploma programmes but as an adjunct to other studies. Art-history teaching therefore tended to reflect the whims of individual lecturers, and lecturers were often practising artists or architects whose learning, however impassioned and informative, was the product of enthusiasm rather than systematic historical scholarship: the very thing Pevsner would take exception to in his radio talk of October 1952. The literature on art history was also less extensive and less authoritative in England than in Germany, and because art history was sometimes taught at art schools and evening classes to give art students a context for their own practical work, there was opposition to the idea of it as a university subject among many academics.

Borenius's reply to the Council reflected this, suggesting that 'although [Pevsner] could admirably fill any university post involving the teaching of art history, I fear the provision of any such post for him in England is not a matter of practical politics'. He thought Pevsner would be better off trying to find a post teaching German language and literature, 'at any rate for the time being'. There, jobs did exist.

Pevsner continued to write while waiting for the results of his Italian and English overtures, but with Germany now a dictatorship, there was a complete change of emphasis in his writings from art as a historical topic to art as a live issue.[27] In response to the politicization of education policy the Nazis were introducing, he wrote two articles about art education in secondary schools: one on the teaching of German art, the other on the teaching of art history. He also wrote two articles that directly addressed the politics of art. One was a review of an exhibition he'd seen in Rome that summer: the Exhibition of the Fascist Revolution that Mussolini had opened in 1932 to celebrate his ten years in power and to act as a propaganda exercise for fascist ideas and design. The other was an attempt – astoundingly presumptuous under the circumstances – to mediate in the celebrated dispute between Goebbels and the conductor Wilhelm Furtwängler, who'd taken over from Nikisch as director of the Leipzig Gewandhaus Orchestra and the Berlin Philhamonic Orchestra.

These articles show Pevsner responding to a situation that seems to have fascinated more than worried him. Rather than reacting emotionally to risks to his prospects and the well-being of his family, he seems to have felt privileged to be on hand to observe and comment on a great moment in human history: a seismic shift in the Zeitgeist – the end of one great Hegelian phase and the start of another. Although events were moving against him and the Nazi state was delegitimizing anything it thought stood in its way, Pevsner evidently saw a role for himself as a pundit and mediator. As he wrote in a letter to one editor,

'Herewith, a manuscript I'd like to appear as a booklet. Please read it and decide if you'd be prepared to publish it . . . You know as well as I do that nothing intelligent is currently being published in the field of art and politics – at least, nothing that will last. You can imagine that, in these circumstances, I'd want to bring this out very quickly.'[28]

Who in the new Germany was prepared to publish an academic whose career was in jeopardy because of race laws? Pevsner had standing among art-history magazines, but to write about political questions meant approaching a different tier of publications he hadn't written for before and among whom he had neither reputation nor – by Nazi standards – acceptability. Overtly Nazi publications wouldn't want to take his work. There were, however, numerous radical-conservative and nationalist-Protestant publications and it was to them he now turned: to *Zeitwende*, edited by three religious writers including the dean of the Protestant Church in Munich; to the *Theologische Literaturzeitung*; to the *Tägliche Rundschau*, an 'independent newspaper for objective politics, Christian culture and German folklore' that had just been taken over by *Die Tat*, which itself was becoming a Nazi propaganda sheet; to *Der Türmer*, an anti-Weimar publication that wrote about Blut-und-Boden ('blood and soil') mysticism, Germanic Christianity and racial biology; and to *Deutsche Zukunft*, a publication with a largely academic readership, among others.

Four of the ten periodical articles Pevsner wrote in 1933 show a shift towards political issues, but with that shift came an idealism that left some readers unpersuaded. In early April he'd argued in *Das Unterhaltungsblatt*, the entertainment supplement published by the *Vossische Zeitung* in Berlin, that being forced to teach German art would be inspirational for teachers in all fields, improving the standard of their teaching and helping their pupils to understand better the nature of their Germanness. Responding to this article, with its echoes of Thomas Mann and the aristocracy of merit that public schooling should foster, a reader in Stettin (then the capital of Prussian Pomerania, now Szczecin in Poland) suggested to Pevsner that he was being unrealistic:

German teachers may have a better or worse education, may enjoy poetry and understand the theory but it doesn't mean they can make pupils understand poetry. Most teachers are cold, unmusical and uncharismatic. It's the same for art education. You say yourself that teachers can't do much. It wouldn't help if historians and teachers of Germanism were forced to attend lectures on German art, as you suggest . . . Even if they found the lectures stimulating, it doesn't mean they'd be able to do what you have in mind unless they already had an innate feeling for painting or architecture and knew how to communicate it. Even scholars are far from able to pass on their knowledge . . . It's very difficult. The lowest rank of teachers is lower middle class: they're not paid much; they have to rely on books. And schools don't have the equipment for teaching art . . .[29]

Perhaps the most remarkable of this set of writings is Pevsner's response to the

Furtwängler-Goebbels controversy. Furtwängler, whom Pevsner thought an unworthy successor to his parents' beloved Nikisch, originally welcomed the arrival of Hitler but used the occasion of the Civil Servants' Law to write to Goebbels complaining about one of its consequences: the ban on his employing Jewish musicians in his orchestras. Furtwängler insisted that, while supporting the need to eliminate 'musical degeneracy', the most important distinction in music was not between Jew and non-Jew but between good and bad music. Goebbels, always a brilliant opportunist, exploited Furtwängler by having the letter published in the main Nazi newspapers, together with a clever reply of his own in which he argued that good art was not enough: that art must also train the people to be strong – in contrast with the modern art of liberal democracy that poisoned the people's will and alienated them from each other.

Pevsner's commentary, in July 1933, treated Furtwängler as an example of an older and outdated artistic culture and Goebbels as a forerunner of a new one. The main issue, he argued, was Furtwängler's comitment to '*l'art pour l'art*', an art 'cleansed of all purposes other than the aesthetic'. 'Art for art's sake,' he said, was the idea of the French Impressionists and of Oscar Wilde, and he quoted as Furtwängler's inspiration Wilde's remark 'There is no such thing as a moral or an immoral book. Books are well written or badly written. That is all.' Such an art, by definition, contributes nothing to the world beyond itself, he explained:

> [Art for art's sake] rests its faith in the idea that art represents a higher ideal than that of the state – indeed, the highest, human ideal of all. That means that the layman . . . reveres the artist above all others. This faith and the theory behind it originated around 1800. Today it belongs to the past. By today's thinking, the state – or rather the people whose will has become organized in the form of the state – has become the higher ideal and art the subordinate, and so quite reasonably, the individualistic artist who attacks the state is robbed of all support by it, however artistically valuable his creation may be.[30]

Although apparently seeking a reconciliation between Furtwängler and Goebbels, Pevsner repeatedly granted Goebbels the advantage in this essay. He saw Goebbels as having a more ambitious view of art than Furtwängler, a view that wanted art to do more than simply be itself but serve a purpose. What that purpose might be seemed to matter less to him than the fact that it had a purpose: what he objected to most was that in having no purpose, art might be lazy. Pevsner then supported this idea – 'it sounds revolutionary and it is' – by listing historical precedents, so that 'whoever follows this notion can call on the best traditions'.

> The whole grand art of the Middle Ages was one of service, Catholic art of the Baroque age, French art of the Classical period: they all served. The German Nazarenes wanted to serve when they turned passionately against the loose 'liberal' painting of the Rococo in around 1810. Only in the nineteenth century have portraiture, scenery and still lives

taken centre stage in artistic teaching. The new mentality will probably revive history painting. If this means an initial aesthetic loss, art producers will at least regain a healthy connection to their consumers. And this revival was inevitable, for Goebbels' argument connects past centuries seemlessly to what is most alive in the art of the last decades. The battle against Impressionism of around 1890 and then around 1905–1910 was about a new assessment of the content and purpose of an artwork. Take fine art and it's enough to recall van Gogh's longing for a new religious art, or Klinger and Hodler, Munch and Ensor. And what about the so-called (and wrongly called) Neue Sachlichkeit, and trendy poems, and documentary novels, and political films, and the musical youth movement, and the Protestant-liturgical music movement, and socialist painting? Aren't they all various expressions of a common longing to be united with the driving forces of the time and the fight for them?[31]

Here, Pevsner argued, the state had to take a stand.

Again and again, we have to decide whether it's better to suppress a work of art even though it may be worthwhile or tolerate a work of art even though it's worthless. You can see how liberalism has decided such issues in the last few years by its incessant whining whenever the censor has intervened against immoral and damaging works by gifted artists. The way Goebbels decides reveals unambiguously . . . that today's artist must serve the driving forces of his time, and be responsible, in touch with the people, and combative.[32]

Pevsner's belief that all art should now be applied art was the logical outcome of what he saw as the extending of the boundaries of Geistegeschichte by Goebbels, whom he flatteringly described as an art historian even though Goebbels had actually studied history and literature. Geistesgeschichte was now not simply a matter of articulating the underlying currents that had occurred in the past but of defining the underlying currents that would make the world a better place in the future. If that was the new task of the art historian – and Pevsner thought it was – then that was very attractive to him because it gave him a role in the new politics. For the first time, Pevsner concluded, custodians of art would have the power to ensure the right things got suppressed and the right things got promoted. Censorship and state planning would work together and art historians would direct them.

Pevsner's accommodation of Gleichschaltung into his own ideas is singular and contrasts with the behaviour of other prominent figures of the time. The architect Mies van der Rohe, for example, initially acceded to Nazi demands and allowed his designs to be festooned with swastikas and other Nazi insignia, but it's clear from his writings that he did so unwillingly and then retreated because he felt that what the Nazis saw as the greatness of their enterprise was actually a paranoid small-mindedness he refused to be belittled by. Pevsner's reaction was different. He gave no sign of wanting to reject anything about the new politics, only of wanting to remove the obstacles to his becoming more involved with it.

As the summer of 1933 went on, and with no sign of any response from Italy, Pevsner asked Registrar Valentiner to lend some help. Valentiner agreed, after making sure he wouldn't be compromising himself, and Pevsner drew up a letter, in Italian, for Valentiner to put his name to. The letter, dated 18 August and addressed to Gentile, stated that Pevsner was already known in Italy for his writings and now wanted to move to Rome and start lecturing on German art, a topic he felt deserved greater recognition in Italy. The letter added that the proposal was supported by Gabetti and two other academics, one of whom was the art historian Pietro Toesca,[33] and that there were no political objections either from Göttingen or the education Ministry in Berlin. Nothing more was heard and, in fact, no Jewish scholar was ever appointed to the Accademia d'Italia.[34]

Three weeks later, on 9 September, Vitzthum finally heard from Berlin about the fate of his staff. Stechow, as a war veteran and with only one Jewish parent, was allowed to continue as an associate professor; Pevsner, with two Jewish parents and not a veteran, was not. The managers whom the Nazis had installed to oversee the Privatdozentenschaft had no contact with the faculties and made all their decisions on the basis of paperwork and party policy, Vitzthum complained. They saw no reason to make any exceptions. In view of the new legislation, Pevsner's authority to teach was therefore withdrawn. His career as an academic in Germany was now over.

17

England

From the point of view of his vocation, there was now every reason for Pevsner to get out of Germany. There was every reason from the point of view of his safety as well. Since Hitler had come to power, lurid posters had begun to appear, with slogans like 'Where two Jews meet, they betray the Fatherland', 'The Jew is the root of all evil', 'The Jews are in league with the Devil' and, most pointedly, 'Jews not wanted here'.

'Notices used to be pinned on houses where Jews lived,' recalls Pallister Barkas's daughter, Rosalind Priestman, 'or they'd put up big placards on shops and my sister Enid and I would tear them down and then pretend we couldn't speak any German. We felt very protected by our British passports. My father still had the *Manchester Guardian* sent to him every day, often heavily censored in heavy, black ink or sometimes not delivered at all, and every day several university friends would come to our house to read it. They knew we were British and therefore safe and that we knew what was going on. My mother would deliberately buy things in Jewish shops when they started going bankrupt, but Nikolaus and Lola were more careful. When we walked past these notices one day, Lola hurried us on quickly.'[1]

Another complication was that children were now being targeted by Nazi propaganda. 'At our school there was pressure on us to join the Verein für das Deutschtum im Ausland (Association for Germanness Abroad, or VDA),' says Priestman 'and the school used to press us into supporting people in Sudetenland [in what was then Czechoslovakia] by giving our pocket money. They were trying to develop a German consciousness, to show that it was a shame the Sudetendeutsch couldn't even send their children to German schools. Rassenkunde – race study – was also pushed. One had to draw up family trees and show where one's grandparents had lived and where they'd been baptized and buried. Being Quakers, we hadn't been baptized, which was therefore a problem, and so eventually we were taken away from the German school, but we had to "Heil Hitler" on Hitler's birthday and all the history was slanted.'[2]

Pevsner contacted Borenius again and asked for news. There was no spare capacity for teaching at University College but Borenius had contacted W. G. Constable at the Courtauld Institute of Art and Constable had suggested that Pevsner come to London quickly so something could be arranged. In the absence of any other offer, Pevsner cautiously accepted and set about making arrangements for a new visit to London, one that would be of unknown length.

'The trouble was that the Nazis would only let you take ten marks out of

Germany,' says Priestman, 'so the Quakers had to find sponsors in England who'd put down guarantees so those they rescued wouldn't be a drain on the British economy if they got destitute.'[3] The level of those guarantees was set at £200 for adults – equivalent to a moderate professional salary for a year – and £50 for children. But who in England would guarantee Pevsner? Barkas graciously offered to write to his sister-in-law Francesca Wilson in Birmingham. Through her connections in the Society of Friends, Pevsner's name was brought to the attention of the Quakers' newly started German Emergency Committee. Even though Pevsner was unknown in England, the committee found sponsors who were willing to advance funds on the basis that they'd be repaid once he'd established himself. It was probably also the committee, based in London, that found lodgings for him with the family of John Fletcher, a Friend who lived on the edge of what Pevsner regarded as one of the only redeeming parts of modern London: Hampstead Garden Suburb.[4]

'When Nikolaus knew he was going to leave,' Priestman recalls, 'he'd set himself a target for learning vocabulary every day and he'd get us to repeat words for him to copy. I was called into his room in their flat in Friedländer Weg and asked to say words so he could hear how they were pronounced. He also asked me about how English table manners differed from German – but I didn't know. And that was after he'd got back from his summer trip to Italy.'

Pevsner's daughter Uta Hodgson says 'I don't really remember anything about his leaving. He was rather a distant father anyway. He'd work. He took an interest in us but he'd go off to Italy for months at a time and we'd stay at home.' But Tom Pevsner, the older of Uta's two younger brothers, does remember their father's parting. 'He was going to the station and we all said our elaborate goodbyes and he was gone. Then we were taken out onto the balcony of the house and, as a lovely surprise, there he was again! It was a staged surprise.'

Pevsner arrived at the port of Dover on 28 October 1933 and was given a visa that allowed him to stay in England for just five months, until the end of March 1934. He was met by Fletcher, some eighteen years older, who paid for his train ticket and took him to London. Fletcher was a committed pacifist and social activist, rather in the same mould as Pevsner's mother. In 1912 he'd worked his passage to Australia, where he'd assisted Quakers in their fight against compulsory conscription, and he'd continued to encourage conscientious objectors in New Zealand after the start of the First World War. For that he was imprisoned, and he was imprisoned again in England after the war, for two years, for further anti-war activities. On his release in 1920 he became involved in Friends' relief work, first in Germany until 1923, then in the USA until 1925. In 1927 he married Dorothy Ballard, settled in a newly built house in Hampstead Garden Suburb and then spent many years at Friends House in London developing international contacts and working for colonial freedom and civil liberties in southern and central Africa. In 1934, when Albert Schweitzer came to England, it was Fletcher who organized his tour.[5]

How Pevsner felt about moving into the home of a peace activist can only be imagined. In 1931 John Betjeman had satirized Hampstead Garden Suburb in a poem that begins 'O wot you why in Orchard Way / The roofs be steep and shelving? / And wot ye what the dwellers say / In garth and garden delving?'[6] Pevsner, more diplomatically, said twenty years later that the Suburb's population was 'on the whole comfortably off and ranges from true sensibility to amateur arty-craftiness'.[7] This was a rather different community from what he was used to in Göttingen: less academic and conservative, more teetotal and eccentric, more sandal-wearing, less suited.

Fletcher lived at 4 Maurice Walk. The first thing Pevsner did after settling in there was to go and see P. Gent, the general secretary of the Academic Assistance Council, which was being temporarily housed in the Royal Society's premises at Burlington House in Piccadilly. From there he went to see Constable at the Courtauld, which was also being housed in temporary accommodation in a Robert Adam house that Samuel Courtauld leased in Portman Square.

What Pevsner found at the Courtauld was an institution offering courses leading either to a BA Honours degree or an Academic Diploma in the History of Art (equivalent to an MA but without a dissertation). Constable's deputy was J. G. Mann, a specialist in the history of armour and assistant keeper at the Wallace collection. General teaching was carried out by Constable, Herbert Read, Anthony Blunt and John Alford (who moved to the University of Toronto at the end of the year and was replaced by Peter Brieger, who'd studied under Pinder, Frankl and Wölfflin). The now venerable Roger Fry was there. Others included Pevsner's friend James Byam-Shaw, the architect Sir Banister Fletcher, author of Britain's standard architectural history book 'on the comparative method', two generalists – Sir Eric MacLagan, the newly knighted director of the Victoria and Albert Museum, and Kenneth Clark, the new director of the National Gallery – and three specialists in prints and drawings, two of them Italianists – Arthur Mayger Hind and A. E. 'Hugh' Popham – and one of them a Germanist – Campbell Dodgson, a distant relative of Lewis Carroll, a member of Oscar Wilde's circle while at Oxford and one of the first historians in England to adopt the methodologies of German art history.

Pevsner's meeting with Constable was only partly successful. Constable was sympathetic to Pevsner's plight, but having just appointed all his staff, he didn't have any vacancies that needed filling. The most he could offer was a very short course of lectures over ten days in Lent term, from 12 to 21 February 1934,[8] which the Academic Assistance Council had already agreed to fund and which could be about Italian Baroque painting if Pevsner chose. With pressure from so many other foreign scholars, however, he regretted he couldn't get funding from the Council for anything more.

The tentativeness of this offer left Pevsner less sanguine about being in England than many other beneficiaries of the council's largesse. He was already uncomfortable with the fact that his presence publicly labelled him as Jewish, as defined by the Nazis, and as a victim, in a way he'd never been in Germany. (He was so uncomfortable with this that one of his children, presumably quoting him, apparently reported many years later that he'd come to England as a political refugee because he was a Socialist and that his dismissal by the Nazis had had nothing to do with his being Jewish:[9] a huge fabrication, if true.) On top of this, he was disappointed that England couldn't reproduce the academic facilities for him that it reproduced for biologists, physicists and chemists, and that the Courtauld was more inspired by 'the rapid spreading of [art history] in America' than by art history's 'well-tested existence on the Continent'[10] (though Roger Fry, in his inaugural Slade lecture of 18 October 1933, said by contrast that the Courtauld had been conceived very much in the German mould).

In addition to the paucity of opportunities in England, there were cultural difficulties. Like many newcomers to Britain, Pevsner found the English odd in the way they conducted themselves and impenetrable in their nuances and formalities. Shortly after arriving in London, he wrote home to Lola to say that 'Swimming in these waters isn't going to be easy. Each sentence, each lecture, each book, each conversation here means something completely different from what it would mean back home. The words mean something different. The wiring in the brain is different.'

Discontented in a culture without a tradition of art scholarship, it occurred to Pevsner that rather than try to adjust to a country whose principal institution was merely, in his view, trying to keep pace with the Americans, he might as well try for a job in the USA itself, which at least had a more German culture. But even that thought was not appealing. Writing about the American section of the Dresden International Art Exhibition in 1926, he'd thought it 'more interesting' than the English section as a cultural phenomenon but found the notion of American art having any artistic value so ridiculous that when he set the idea down on paper he felt he needed to add an exclamation mark. He nonetheless used his time in England to explore career options in the USA.

While familiarizing himself with the academic landscape in the USA, Pevsner was reminded that September 1933 was the fiftieth anniversary of the world's first skyscraper – Chicago's Home Insurance Building of 1883 – and wrote about skyscrapers in *Das Unterhaltungsblatt*, where he'd written about art education five months earlier. He also contacted the magazine *Art in America* and managed to sell it a translation of the piece he'd written earlier in the year for Walter Friedländer's Festschrift on 'An Unknown Early Work of the School of Caravaggio'.

Aware of the difficulties Pevsner was having, Francesca Wilson invited him to visit her in Edgbaston and offered to put him in contact with people she knew at Birmingham University while he was there. Wilson's house in Duchess Road ('on the wrong side of Hagley Road', said Pevsner, later[11]) has long since been destroyed, but for many years it seemed like a small sanctuary for the dispossessed of Europe. 'Francesca's house always had ... two-to-three adult refugees in it', remembered Jessamine Weeks, a close friend who took child refugees into her own house.

In addition to Wilson's 'waifs and strays', as others called them, one lodger between 1933 and 1935 was Constance Braithwaite, a London BSc who'd just become an assistant lecturer in the university's social study department. Braithwaite, a Quaker, had an academic interest in the voluntary sector and conducted a statistical survey while living under Wilson's roof into whether public sector provision damaged the voluntary sector. (She concluded that it didn't.)[12] In 1938 she published her results in *The Voluntary Citizen*, a study of communal philanthropy, arguing in part that charities could be more flexible and innovative than the state. She also opposed conscription, like John Fletcher, and wrote during the war about whether strikes could be reconciled with Quaker pacifism.

'When Pevsner came to England ... Francesca Wilson asked him to stay in her house as a guest', remembers Braithwaite. 'Pevsner spoke English very well and made easy contacts. I liked him very much and learned much from his knowledge and his attitudes [and] I introduced Pevsner to Florence.'

'Florence' was Philip Sargant Florence, the head of Birmingham's commerce department and chair of its social study committee, which oversaw Braithwaite's work. Born in New Jersey, Florence was educated at Rugby School and Gonville and Caius College, Cambridge, where he studied economics and was one of the founders of the Heretics, a freethinking student group. He then went to Columbia University, New York, where he wrote a doctoral paper on industrial fatigue, published as a book in 1924. In 1917 he married Lella Faye Secor, an American feminist and peace activist who'd sailed with others from Hoboken, New Jersey, on Henry Ford's Peace Ship in 1915 to try and persuade European leaders that they'd been enticed into the First World War by an international Jewish conspiracy set on making money out of armament sales. (It was this 'peace initiative' and Ford's subsequent unrelenting demonizing of Jews that inspired Hitler and led him to keep a full-size portrait of Ford in his office.)

After working for four years as a lecturer in industrial research and personnel management in New York, Florence returned to England with Lella to become a junior fellow at Magdalene College, Cambridge. There he was part of an intellectual set centred around C. K. Ogden, an intellectual dilettante who co-wrote *The Meaning of Meaning* (1923) and founded the idea of 'Basic English', both with the literary critic I. A. Richards, and who translated Wittgenstein's *Tractatus Logico-Philosophicus*.

In 1929 Florence became professor of commerce at the University of Birmingham. The university had been set up in 1900 to reverse the declining reputation of manufacturing in and around 'Brummagem' (the local name for Birmingham), once known as 'the workshop of England' but by then a synonym for shoddy goods. Two years later it had established Britain's first faculty of commerce and Florence, who had family connections in Birmingham, remained there for the rest of his career, carrying out statistical research on workplace issues and in 1933 publishing *The Logic of Industrial Organization*, a book that related industrial management to shop-floor attitudes.

At Braithwaite's suggestion, Florence invited Pevsner to Highfield, his huge house set in five acres of grounds in Selly Oak. Florence was already sympathetic to the plight of Central Europe's refugee scholars by the time of their meeting. He wrote, later:

> Many of my colleagues and I regarded as our international duty the job of caring for refu-
> gees from German and Austrian universities fleeing from Nazi persecution. A Birmingham
> University committee was formed for the purpose with [the economist] Austin Robinson
> and later Professor Duncan-Jones as honorary secretary.[13]

Florence was also sympathetic to the arts. Although his own interests concerned business, his mother had been an artist and his circle of friends in Birmingham was artistic and literary – a group often described as the West Midlands' equivalent of London's Bloomsbury Set.

When Florence and Pevsner met on 23 November 1933,[14] they probably talked about Pevsner's wish to set up a course on German art history – Kunstgeschichte – of the type he'd proposed to the University of Rome, and Florence would have been interested in this because his own department had been partly influenced by a study of commercial education in Germany.[15] Both being from overseas, they may also have exchanged impressions about what they regarded as England's peculiarities, its class distinctions and how it measured up to what each was used to abroad. In particular they would have found common ground in the disappointing quality of English manufacturing – something Pevsner would have seen in the context of his new moral mission and which he may have lamented as falling short of the ideals set by William Morris, whose centenary was coming up the following year and who'd had a connection with the Birmingham Municipal School of Art. Florence's approach to this subject would have been statistical and economic, however, and since Pevsner wasn't a statistician or an economist, there didn't seem to be anything useful he could say about manufacturing that might make him of any value to Florence's department.

In spite of this impasse, Florence was obviously impressed by Pevsner and promised to keep his predicament in mind. He subsequently reported back to the Birmingham refugees' committee that something ought to be done and a plan was hatched to invite Pevsner to give a demonstration lecture for the whole university before having to return to Germany at the end of March. Representations were duly made to the vice-chancellor, Sir Charles Grant Robertson, and thence to Walter Barrow, the pro-chancellor. Barrow, a Birmingham philanthropist related to the Cadbury family, nominated his wife Agnes to co-sponsor the event anonymously if funding could also be found from the Academic Assistance Council.

Back in London, Pevsner tried to make other academic contacts but without much success. Apart from his Courtauld lectures in mid-February and the Birmingham lecture, now scheduled for mid-March, he'd only been able to muster four other invitations before his visa to stay in England expired. One was from Borenius, to lecture at University College, London, on 23 January 1934; a second was from Armstrong College[16] in Newcastle, where Pallister Barkas had studied and through whom Pevsner was invited to talk on 26 February; a third was from Ruskin College, Oxford, two days later; and a fourth was from Fircroft College, a working-men's college in Bournville founded by the Cadbury family in 1909. It was a lot of effort for not a lot of reward.

One faint prospect offered hope. On 28 November the University of Edinburgh had advertised that the Watson Gordon Chair of Fine Art had fallen vacant and Pevsner sent off for further particulars, which were posted to him a few days later. To obtain one of the few professorships in fine art in Britain would be a coup, but he'd never visited Scotland and knew little about it, except for Charles Rennie Mackintosh and a picture by Thomas Austen Brown – born in Edinburgh – that the Dresden Gemäldegalerie possessed.[17] What he did know was that he was a newly arrived foreign academic who hadn't even achieved tenure in his own country and would be in competition not only with home-grown candidates but with a lot of other recently arrived Germans. There was therefore little likelihood of a full professorship coming his way, out of the blue.

At Christmas, understandably downcast, Pevsner took the unusual step for a refugee scholar of going back to Germany to visit his family and to see again if there were any work opportunities outside academia. He'd already contributed an article to *Das Unterhaltungsblatt* in September; over the winter holiday he looked around for other outlets. In view of the transformation in Germany's politics, he thought he might produce an article for a nakedly pro-Nazi publication in Berlin, *Kunst der Nation* – 'Art of the Nation' – about how art might respond to the new dictatorship. He wrote the piece but, aware that using his own name might be prejudicial, signed it 'Dr Peter Bernt'[18] – a contraction of one of his middle names, Bernhard – and asked his schoolfriend Helmut Meyer von Bremen to submit it for him. The editor of *Kunst der Nation*, a Herr König, returned it, assuring its author that it had been examined with great interest but couldn't be published either as a booklet or in the magazine because it was too long. König signed off 'Heil Hitler!'[19]

Pevsner must have spent the Christmas period wondering what to do next. His visit to London had come to very little, he hadn't found a job, his status was uncertain, he was away from Lola and the children, and he was living on charity. Was it really worth going back to England in the new year? Wasn't he wasting his time in this ridiculous little country with its misguided sense of its own importance and its unfathomable ways and terrible food?

Perhaps some other country might be more responsive? Perhaps Italy would at last offer him a position. Perhaps the USA would eventually respond. Or perhaps the political climate at home would change. There might still be a role for him in the new Germany when the Nazis started to feel more sure of themselves and less histrionic. He had to decide over the holidays whether he preferred to be an unwanted German in England or an unwanted Jew in Germany? Germany was shutting down his options; there was no sign of England ever opening them up. From a German perspective, England looked like an academic wasteland. Was there any point in going back?

Appendix

The second volume of this biography will look at what Pevsner decided to do after the Christmas holiday of 1933 and what followed. The purpose of this appendix is to examine the response in the press when issues raised in the first volume were first aired eight years ago.

In November 2002 the *Evening Standard*, London's evening paper, ran a double-page extract from *Pevsner on Art and Architecture*, the collection of radio talks that Sir Nikolaus Pevsner had broadcast between 1945 and 1977 and that I'd edited over the previous eighteen months. The object of the book was to fill a conspicuous gap in Pevsner's otherwise extensive literary record and show what Pevsner thought the public needed to know and how he expressed himself at a time when he was indisputably the biggest name in architectural history and simultaneously committed to advancing the cause of modern architecture.

The fact that a popular paper wanted to splash an extract across two pages looked promising. Pevsner had been dead for nearly twenty years, public awareness of him had waned and his reputation had been savaged by younger art historians and architects. Publicity in a popular newspaper, in the year of his centenary, should have been a good way to reawaken interest in him. Instead, it awoke a storm by running the extract, taken from the introduction to the book, under the sensational heading 'A Nazi in England', which is something this German-born scholar and polymath had never been.

The person who'd overseen the acquisition of the piece and its appearance on 18 November 2002 was the *Standard*'s then arts editor Norman Lebrecht, the iconoclastic chronicler of the classical music industry. Lebrecht was and is a good friend and evidently thought he'd be doing me and his paper's circulation a good turn by over-dramatizing what I'd written. On the phone the next day, he argued that all headlines tend towards overstatement and shorthand, that the headline had been written by a sub and that any other paper would have done the same. When I objected that shorthand wasn't a sufficient excuse for inaccuracy and that what subs do isn't below their editor's level of surveillance, he advised me to take the matter up with the *Standard*'s editor, Anne McElvoy. I did; she backed him up.[1]

Lebrecht tried to reassure me that the headline would attract attention. It did, but of entirely the wrong sort. The *Standard*, by its wording, had ensured I was now seen as the originator of a serious and fraudulent accusation: that a favourite English twentieth-century hero had been a Nazi in Germany and had remained a Nazi in England too.

Three days later, the *Standard* carried the first outburst in what was to become a tidal wave of protest. It was a letter from Will Vaughan, the head of the history of art department at Birkbeck College where Pevsner had once taught, denying that Pevsner was either a Nazi or a racist and accusing me of being 'mischievous and misleading'. His letter was followed the next day by two letters in *The Guardian*: one from Fred Wolsey, who'd lodged with and then become the executor of Francesca Wilson; the other from the art critic and scholar Norbert Lynton (born Norbert Casper Loewenstein in Berlin in 1927), who'd also been a German exile and who, like Vaughan, had been a student of Pevsner's at Birkbeck. Both, again, defended Pevsner against what was seen as my infamy.

A head of steam built up, not only defending Pevsner against the charge of Nazism but also accusing me of wanting to blacken Pevsner's name thereby. Papers ran counter-headlines, to challenge the *Evening Standard*'s: 'Pevsner a Nazi? Don't be so ridiculous' (*The Observer*, 8 December); 'An English gent . . . and no Nazi' (*The Sunday Telegraph*, 15 December); and 'Naughty, but no Nazi' (*Times Literary Supplement*, 28 February 2003), a strikingly crude play – via 'naughty but nasty' – on the 'naughty but nice' catchphrase that Salman Rushdie had dreamed up for cream cakes when he was an advertising copywriter. The most insidious of these counter-headlines, and the one that probably set the tone for those that followed, topped an article by Jonathan Meades in *The Times* (23 November). Meades is well known in England for wearing a trademark dark suit and dark tie on TV and what he calls 'shades'. The heading over his article ran: 'The man who helped open our eyes to architecture deserves better than this slur of guilt by association with the Nazis.'[2]

The idea that I'd called Pevsner a Nazi in order to damage him was worked up and embroidered by several reviewers. Several insisted that what I'd written was 'insulting' and a 'slur'; one accused me of a 'smear operation' (*Architects' Journal*, 9 January), adding that 'the idea that [Pevsner] remained a covert Nazi long after his move to London [was] preposterous.' The author of the *Observer* article, Ian Buruma, felt impelled to protest because only three years earlier, in his book *Voltaire's Coconuts* (1999), he'd written, uncontentiously, that Pevsner had 'arrived in Britain as an apostle of modernism, socialism and European progress'.[3] Even *The Guardian*, which had carried a laconic and prophetic commentary about the fuss just two days after the *Standard* piece came out, repeated the basic assertion that what I'd said was that 'Sir Nikolaus was a Nazi.'

The baton was picked up by *The Times*, where Simon Jenkins talked more generally about the debasement of language. In Jenkins's view, my supposed accusation was an example of the way intolerant and illiberal minds resort to cheap comparisons in order to obstruct understanding and tarnish reputations (though I would have said intolerant and illiberal minds did this because they were incapable of a better quality of analysis rather than to prevent it in others). In *The Scotsman*, Michael Pye, in an unrelentingly hostile review, conceded that when talking about Nazism, one can mean 'something quite limited', but that given what Nazism now means to us – 'the whole abominable story, camps and all' – anything one now said would be read as something larger, as if I'd wanted readers to infer, after reading the book, that Pevsner was an enthusiast for Auschwitz and Buchenwald: a contemptuous suggestion. Those and other writers argued I was guilty of callow judgementalism, the imposition of hindsight and a lack of historical empathy for Pevsner in his difficult situation as a 'racial' Jew in Germany in the 1930s.

It didn't end there. The escalating tone of outrage now triggered critics into playing catch-up with each other, because no one wanted to appear less censorious than his or her rivals. Meades, in his *Times* article, had accused me of writing opportunistic nonsense to prime the market for a forthcoming Pevsner biography that would make my fortune, suggesting I was trading on the fact that Pevsner was dead and couldn't sue. *Private Eye* went further and claimed I was taking revenge on the Pevsner family because, it was thought, they had commissioned me to write a biography of Sir Nikolaus and then cancelled the agreement: a supposition false in all its particulars. Kenneth Powell added his own bit of spite in the *Architects' Journal* two months later by suggesting I was working on the biography 'against the wishes of the Pevsner family' – another unsubstantiated supposition that the family has denied.

To their credit, all but one of the newspapers allowed me to respond, correcting what had been said and making my own position clear, though in several cases their letters editors made it equally clear to me on the phone that they were surprised to learn there was a case to answer. The one newspaper that refused me the right of reply was *The Times*, which I then still thought of – and which I dare say still thought of itself – as England's *de facto* journal of record. Instead of letting me write what I wanted, its letters editor said he'd only give me space in the paper if I let him redraft my response. He then sent a copy of the words he proposed to put into my mouth, ignoring some of my points and watering down others. When I objected, he refused to back down, and so did the paper's managing editor. I took the matter to the Press Complaints Commission which found in *The Times*'s favour, on the grounds that opinion writers must be allowed to express opinions, even if those opinions are false and malicious. As a consequence, no letter from me has ever been allowed to appear in *The Times* to refute what its two writers had said. Thus, the nation's journal of record.

None of this is to suggest there was a witch-hunt or that the book's reviewers shared a group mentality or constituted a secret cabal with an agreed agenda. Everyone who wrote about the book no doubt thought he or she was acting independently and exercising good judgement. But their independence and judgement was contaminated by events and individual writers acted like sheep without their even realizing it. What the headline in the *Standard* did was to trigger an episode of mass hysteria – stoked, as two of the subsequent reviews revealed, by myths no book review editor and no reviewer could have been immune from. To that extent, this episode was instructive as a microcosm of how a culture develops, spread by disparate actors all in their own mind acting alone and with their own goals but with no awareness of the loose connections and forces acting upon them.

The problem for the reviewers of *Pevsner on Art and Architecture* was that to attack what they'd come to believe I was saying, they had to rely on the new material I'd made available, which no one wanted to do or be seen to be doing. And so the odd situation arose where reviewers used the facts in the introduction to argue against the facts in the introduction but without attributing those facts to the introduction. This left the battlefield strewn with misrepresentations. Meades claimed, nonsensically, that Pevsner not only abhorred Nazism but regarded it mainly as an offence against style: these were 'the only grounds that really mattered to him', he ventured. He also attacked the book for arguing that Hitler's Germany shunned architectural Modernism, when the book had actually argued that opinions about Modernism among Germany's far right ranged from hostility to approval. And he floated the confusing idea that while there was no sign that Pevsner had ever been sympathetic to 'the overwhelming mainstream of Nazi architecture' (which is not something I'd written about), it would have been better if Pevsner had liked such architecture. '[Pevsner's] antipathy to creepily cute *volkisch* [sic] buildings and to neo-classical bombast is actually a shortcoming which mars *The Buildings of England*', he wrote: a fine example of having it both ways.

Simon Jenkins was just as duplicitous. He attacked the book for showing that Pevsner in his late twenties was, in Jenkins's words, 'excited by Hitler's eagerness to end the chaos of Weimar and root out corruption' – something I'd taken pains to explain objectively and put in context. But not only did Jenkins not credit me for this: he borrowed my own explanation to use against me. 'Pevsner would not have been alone in warming to the Nazis' "overpowering collective energy" as embodying the spirit of a new age', he wrote, continuing 'I might have done so too, as briefly as Pevsner allegedly did.' By that, I take him to mean that Pevsner didn't do what I said he'd done but that if he had done it, Jenkins would have done so too, for reasons that everyone except me would have understood and sympathized with.

In this remarkable case of group aphasia, writers seem to have been preconditioned to ignore the bulk of the book in favour of details they could manipulate to support their presuppositions. Those parts of the introduction that didn't have the word 'Nazi' in the vicinity didn't much figure in the reviews; the snippets that did were those that were easiest to misread and take out of context. The reason for this I can only put down to their wish to sensationalize what they'd wrongly accused of false sensationalizing and their wish to take sides in what they imagined to be a battle between Pevsner and me, or between their old Pevsner and my new one. Pevsner was an institution and, as he himself often observed, the English are conservative about institutions. I, by contrast, was a relative outsider and what I was saying didn't conform to what was usually said about him. Given the choice between retaining preconceptions and remodelling them, it was easier to pillory the new and misconstrue it.

And so much more English. There is an unpleasant tendency in England to close ranks. Pevsner suffered from it all his life. For all that he was welcomed into the country's most progressive circles and shone in them, his acceptance was found distasteful by people who regarded themselves as 'cultural Englishmen' (as Michael Pye amusingly described me in *The Scotsman*). An intriguing sidelight on this was Kenneth Powell's observation in the *Architect's Journal* that it was Pevsner's success and 'the apparent ease with which he was assimilated into the British cultural scene that fuelled the reaction against him which began before his death'. Powell had evidently not been listening carefully if he thought that that's when the hostility to Pevsner started – but that aside, it's true that although xenophobia was only part of the story, social climbers like John Betjeman and his friends did indeed exploit Pevsner's foreignness to his disadvantage.

Having observed this, though, Powell then fell foul of it himself, in a subtle way. He dated the reaction against Pevsner to the publication in 1977 of the book *Morality and Architecture*, in which David Watkin depicted Pevsner as the last in a series of social reformers who'd abused architecture to achieve ever more horrific ends. Powell, quite rightly, hadn't agreed with Watkin's analysis but gave Watkin credit, nonetheless, for having 'set out to debunk Pevsner . . . with scholarship, wit and conviction.' As it happens, Watkin's ingenious book lacked wit, its scholarship was partial and its convictions were misguided, though that was partly outweighed for Powell by other considerations. It's OK to write destructive nonsense if you do it with elegance and cite your sources. Very English.

The forces arraigned against *Pevsner on Art and Architecture* were formidable. Inevitably they attracted onlookers. An Italian design website reproduced one of the reviews from *The Times*; the *Frankfurter Allgemeine Zeitung* carried a book review that repeated slurs and innuendo that the writer had read in the British press. The only good news was that even the most hostile reviewers agreed that the talks themselves were worth reading and that the editing of them was well done. Of the few publications that admitted to being intrigued rather than offended by the introduction, one was the *Catholic Herald* (21 March 2003), where Anthony Symondson appeared to take what was written at face value; another was the Royal Institute of British Architects' *RIBA Journal* (December 2002), which found the introduction 'quite convincing'; a third was the magazine *Architecture Today*, edited by Ian Latham and Mark Swenarton, which in March 2003 ran a generous four-page excerpt from the book, under the more reasonable headline 'The Germanness of the English historian'. After that, towards the end of 2003, a paperback version of the book came out, to much less of a flurry than the hardback a year earlier. And that seemed to be that: the end of the story.

Then something very welcome happened. The book was reviewed by someone who wasn't English, didn't live in England and didn't have a position to protect in the hierarchy of English letters. Christopher Long was associate professor and chair of architectural history and theory at the University of Texas, Austin, and had a special interest in the development of architecture and design in Central Europe in the early 1900s. His review of *Pevsner on Art and Architecture* appeared in *Harvard Design Magazine* (Number 21, Fall 2004/Winter 2005), a publication of the Harvard Graduate School of Design, where Walter Gropius had taught from 1937 to 1952. Long took a refreshingly offshore position. Without any obvious axe to grind, he read the book for what it was and found the introduction 'perceptive', quoting from it to make his points and giving the example of Egon Friedell's *Die Kulturgeschichte der Menschheit* (1927) when discussing the overfrequent 'elasticity' of German scholarship 'for those engaged in *Geisteswissenschaften*' before the war. Suddenly the subject of Pevsner and the nature of his thought was being looked at dispassionately and responsibly by a historian who didn't feel he had either to build Pevsner up or knock him down in order to say something useful about him.

The fact that Long was able to write as he did for an American readership exposed how sacred Pevsner's memory must still be to the English and the extent to which new literature about him was expected to pay homage to old literature about him. In Britain, Pevsner was evidently still an icon. In spite of my expectations, there was an unspoken understanding that he merited special treatment and, as a wide cross-section of the press had demonstrated, that the difficulties and incongruities he gave rise to were not a proper subject for public airing. It seemed that only overseas could one find the independence of thought and professionalism that were needed to see him in any other terms.

Since then there's been a slight thaw. In the summer of 2006, almost four years after the book's first publication, a review appeared in one of the UK's leading scholarly journals, *Visual Culture in Britain*, that saw *Pevsner on Art and Architecture* quite differently from what had been written about it in the UK until then. In the course of an assessment of where Pevsner now stood, prompted by the publication of three new Pevsner-related books, Richard J. Williams, senior lecturer and director of the Graduate School of Arts, Culture and Environment at the University of Edinburgh, spoke of the introduction as 'brilliant'. That was gratifying; but what was also significant was that Williams wrote as if the book's mauling by the press was now part of the story of Pevsner's reception and something that required comment. He said:

> When originally published, Games was widely criticized for misrepresenting Pevsner, specifically accusing him of being a Nazi when his politics and his morality were nothing of the kind. Several reviews were hysterically anti-Games (in the *Observer* in December 2002, Tim Adams describes the Games introduction as a 'cheap shot', then a 'scurrilous attack', no more than a means of increasing the volume's notoriety and therefore a means of increasing sales). What Games actually says is mild and, to this reviewer at least, sensible

...What Games explicitly does not do is claim Pevsner was a Nazi. Even a cursory reading
of the text makes this clear.

It's because *Pevsner on Art and Architecture* and its aftermath may have become
part of Pevsner's story that I've offered the foregoing account of it. It raises the
question, however, of what there was in the book that could have been miscon-
strued by a slovenly reader, especially one who'd been prejudiced by the furore
the *Evening Standard* had triggered. What I'd tried to say, and I don't think my
attempt was too clumsy, was that in his younger life at least, Pevsner wasn't the
Hampstead liberal that England later took him for. He wasn't a Socialist (at a
time when all intellectuals in England were thought to be Socialists), he wasn't
an internationalist and – certainly when he arrived in England – he wasn't an
anglophile. His mother had been all these things. He'd seen what it meant to
be an activist on that side of the political spectrum but he hadn't followed his
mother's lead. What he did do, and how he came to do it, is what *Pevsner – The
Early Life: Germany and Art*, the first part of Pevsner's biography, now goes into
in more detail, and detail is needed if the misapprehensions readers read into
the last book are at last to be disposed of. I hope the urge to reduce criticism to
the application of ugly labels doesn't happen again. We talk about what people
do, not what they are.

That said, the book doesn't take the line that those closest to Pevsner have
always taken: that he either wasn't political or didn't understand politics. This
answer – 'he was really obviously in some ways politically very naïve' – was
offered by Dieter Pevsner, his younger son, in the BBC radio documentary I
made about Pevsner on his eightieth birthday, and it's understandable that he
would say that.[4] It was repeated, however, twenty years later by Bridget Cherry,
a contributor to and later editor of Pevsner's *Buildings of England*, and by a
handful of others who were privately aware that Pevsner's past wasn't what they
would like it to have been. It was even followed by a disingenuous but otherwise
well-informed reviewer of *Pevsner on Art and Architecture* in the *Times Literary
Supplement*, someone who not only had access to all the written materials I had
but more besides. In short, there are matters here that have been consciously
wished away in order not to complicate the reputation of a man whom the
English, for good reason, had taken to their hearts.

Misapprehensions about Pevsner are understandable. For many years, the
English have burnished the view that Pevsner had somehow magically arrived
in England from Germany as a fully fledged Englishman. It's a view that was
promoted by the novelist and counter-culturalist Colin McInnes, referred to
at the start of the present book, whose mother, the novelist Angela Thirkell,
was a cousin of Rudyard Kipling and Stanley Baldwin and a granddaughter of
the painter Edward Burne-Jones. In 1960 McInnes had written an essay in the
magazine *The Twentieth Century* titled 'The Englishness of Dr Pevsner', a pun on
the title of Pevsner's 1955 Reith Lectures 'The Englishness of English Art'. In

that essay, republished by Penguin in 1961,[5] McInnes argued that Pevsner was 'a thoroughly inside outsider' whose 'rare and enriched dual vision' had given him an insight into the English that most English people were incapable of and that put him on a par with Defoe, Dickens, Mayhew and Firbank as essential, but also essentially English, reading. McInnes was writing here with the aim of finding an exoticness in the London of the 1950s, otherwise 'so formless and so hideous, [offering] no meaning or shape', in contradistinction to what he called 'the truly dreadful 1930s'. To that extent Pevsner served his purpose. But the estimation of Pevsner as more English than the English stuck, helped by his very light Saxon accent, the rhythm of which made him sound as if he was simply being precise rather than German, by contrast with Ernst Gombrich, for example, whose accent was so strong that the BBC regarded him for many years as unbroadcastable.

Pevsner wasn't English. Before he arrived in England at the age of thirty-one, he was German, had been born German, was raised German, thought of himself as German, believed in Germany, wanted Germany to succeed and had ambitions to become great in Germany. Beneath that Germanness, however, there were tensions. It's those tensions that *Pevsner on Art and Architecture* gave attention to eight years ago and that the first volume of the biography now looks at in more detail.

Notes

Notes to Introduction

1 Mowl, 2000.

2 Betjeman, 1952.

3 Jencks, 2009.

4 In my own case, by the American designer Bob Gill, who taught at the Central School while I was there.

5 Gombrich didn't credit Pevsner with being already industrious, as those who have subsequently quoted this story invariably say.

6 Other contributors included Sir James Richards, who'd employed Pevsner at the *Architectural Review* in the mid-1930s and then handed him his editorial seat during the war; the American architect Philip Johnson, who'd found Pevsner's view of modern architecture too inflexible by the 1960s; the English architects Sir Denys Lasdun and Sir Hugh Casson; Hans Schmoller (Penguin's typographer); Jane Fawcett (Secretary at the Victorian Society and a student of Pevsner's at Birkbeck College); John Newman (a PhD student of Pevsner's at the Courtauld Institute and subsequently the author of two books in Pevsner's *Buildings of England* series) and Pevsner's younger son, the publisher Dieter Pevsner.

7 Designed by Walter Gropius's great-uncle Martin Gropius and completed, after his death, by Heinrich Schmieden.

8 On 'Die Internationale Kunstausstellung Dresden 1926 unter besonderer Beruecksichtigung der Besprechungen von Nikolaus Pevsner und Will Grohmann'.

Notes to Chapter 1: Home

1 In the early 1980s a vast hoard of money was found in Frege's own house, including tokens of exchange from different countries and different ages.

2 In north-west London, Thomas ARNold (North Wembley); William Henry DRUmmond (also North Wembley); John DRYden (Kingsbury); William WORdsworth (Kenton); Lord BYRon (South Harrow). In north London, John KEAts (Enfield).

3 The house next door, number 29, had a glass fanlight over the front door depicting wispy trees with huge leaves and, looking as if they'd been carved into the bark of the trees with a penknife, the initials WM and the year 1900, below little hearts in the style of Charles Rennie Mackintosh.

4 The university quarter of Kensington built around Imperial College, the Royal College of Music, the Royal College of Art and the museums was inspired by Prince Albert, the younger son of the Duke of Saxe-Coburg-Gotha, and at one time known whimsically as 'Albertopolis'.

5 Michel, October 1984.

6 Pevsner, *Outline*, 1948, p. 205.

7 From Pevsner, June 1939.

8 Dr Hella Wenskus, 22 May 1984.

9 Alec Clifton-Taylor, 1981.

10 Ernst Ullmann, 1984.

11 The claim that Schwägrichenstraße overlooks the Johanna Park (see Paul Crossley, Introduction, *Reassessing*, 2004, p. 1) is wrong. The street lies one road back.

12 Inappropriately called the Herrenzimmer.

13 Heinrich Pollack, 2007.

14 Dreessen, 1983.

15 Ibid.

16 Pevsner, 1954.

17 Michel, December 1984.

18 Draft, Pevsner, *Family History*, 1954.

19 Michel, October 1984.

20 Pevsner, letter, 20 January 1975.

21 Ibid.

22 Published in a collection of short stories called *Wetterleuchten im Herbst*, Reclam, 1922.

23 Confirmation of Pevsner's absence from home between 22 August 1905 and 8 January 1906 is noted in the Führungszeugnis of the Polizeipräsidium, Leipzig, and in the records of the Dresden Gemäldegalerie, and coincides with identical annotations in his parents' Einwohnermeldekarte, now housed by the Sächsisches Staatsarchiv.

24 The German historian Heinrich Dilly commented at the V&A's Pevsner Conference in 2001 that it was very modern of the Pewsners to have only two children in the early 1900s, but it's possible that Annie was unhappy because she wasn't able to have more children.

25 Auguste Forel (1848–1931).

26 Forel, 1905.

27 This must be a mistake. Pevsner would have been too young to remember his mother seeing Forel at Morges.

28 Games, 1982.

29 Forel, 1912, wrote: 'Smaller than the typical type [of Crematogaster]. The scape [i.e., the long basal joint of the antennae] does not completely reach the back of the head, whereas in the typical form it goes beyond it a bit, varying more or a little less according to the individuals. The head is at least as long as it is broad (a little broader than long, typically).' The ant is now known more simply as 'Crematogaster distans', following a revision of names, and I am grateful to Christiana Klingenberg of the Museum für Naturkunde in Karlsruhe and Donat Agosti of the American Museum of Natural History in New York for tracking the little fellow down for me. For more information, see antbase.org.

30 The first German Women's Conference was held in Leipzig on Sunday, 15 October 1865 at 6.30 in the evening, in a room at the Leipzig book dealers' exchange. Louise Otto-Peters, a poet and pioneer of women's rights, opened the meeting. Annie's headmistress at the Leipzig State High School for Girls, Auguste Schmidt, became its pioneering figurehead. Two weeks after Schmidt's death on 10 June 1902, the July edition of the General German Women's Association's publication *Neue Bahnen* ('New Ways') announced that eight German women's groups had agreed to build a house in Auguste Schmidt's name in Leipzig. A commemorative service was held at the State High School, at which speeches were made and local schoolgirls sang songs. So although Pevsner thought his mother was involved in launching the Auguste Schmidt Haus, the launch took place several years before Forel's treatment. Even then, the person whose name appears on the records as running the café at the Auguste Schmidt Haus was Hedwig Dettloff, who remained there until 1911 when an expansion programme began. Dettloff then went off to start a café of her own, Café Dettloff, in Nikolaistraße. From 1912, the Auguste Schmidt House, briefly at both Inselstraße and Dresdnerstraße, as Pevsner says, started housing more and more women's groups. First there was the Auguste Schmidt Society, then from 1915 the Auguste Schmidt Reform Inn, the Leipzig Women's Teachers Association,

the Mothers' Shelter Club, the Association for Female Post and Telegraph Workers, the General German Women's Association Town Group, and the Mercantile Society for Female Employees.

31 Pevsner, 1954.

32 Ibid.

33 Unsalaried university lecturer, independently funded or paid privately by students.

34 The competition was held by the Académie des Sciences Morales et Politiques within the Institut de France. Guyau's submission ran to 1,300 pages.

35 Augustine Guyau didn't marry Fouillée until 1885, following the reintroduction of divorce laws into France under the Third Republic in 1884. She had parted from her first husband after finding him violent and intellectually disappointing.

36 Guyau, mainly forgotten now, is one of the many thousands of historical figures whose writings, though tantalizing at the time, led to dead-ends or ran out of steam or were too complicated to lend themselves for adaptation by later generations – a fascinating case study of extinction in the evolution of ideas. By that token, Guyau is fascinating because he takes us back to a world of ideas that's no longer familiar to us and no longer has a place within what is normally taught as philosophy. Guyau's public recognition, for example, brought him numerous encounters with other academic figures of his day, including the religious historian Ernest Renan and the historical researcher Hippolyte Taine, with whom he shared an interest in artistic phenomena. He also published widely. His main interests were aesthetics, ethics and religious theory, and in all three areas he put critical appraisal of conventional teachings alongside his own ideas. Guyau's main concern lay with what he saw as the damaging impact of science on traditional existential thinking. He felt that contemporary life in the second half of the nineteenth century needed to embrace empiricism rather than doctrine, though he was also an advocate of vitalism, a now-discredited nineteenth-century philosophy that saw evolution as a creative process unrestrained by normal science. This led Guyau in the early 1880s to tackle the origins of art and literature, the results of which he published in 1884 under the title *Les problèmes de l'esthétique contemporaine*. There then followed *Esquisse d'une morale sans bond ni sanction* in 1885, an attempt to find a scientifically based system of ethics and to examine ideas about social self-restraint. The last book to appear during his lifetime, *L'irreligion de l'avenir*, came out in 1887 and speculated on religion being supplanted by social idealism. Guyau wrote most of his work in the village of Menton, in the Maritime Alps, which became his habitual retreat. There, in 1882, he married Barbe Marguerite André, an author who, like Guyau's own mother, Augustine Tuillerie, published mainly children's books and, like his mother, used a pseudonym: 'Pierre Ulric'. In December 1883, they had a child whom they named Augustin, after Guyau's mother, and who also eventually became a philosopher, publishing in 1913 *La philosophy et la sociologie d'Alfred Fouillée*, in memory of his great uncle who'd died the year before. Augustin volunteered for the front and was killed in July 1917 on the banks of the Maas in Belgium, aged thiry-four. Jean-Marie Guyau had died at about the same age nearly thirty years earlier. After an earthquake hit the Riviera early in 1888, he became afraid to sleep indoors. As a result, he caught a cold that proved fatal. He died, aged thirty-three, on Good Friday, 31 March 1888, and was buried on Easter Sunday in Menton cemetery. A road was named in Menton in his honour.

37 Vol. 1: *Einleitung: Die Philosophie Guyaus*, by Dr Ernst Bergmann; *Verse eines Philosophen*. German translation by Udo Gaede; *Die ästhetischen Probleme der Gegenwart*, transl. by Ernst Bergmann (Leipzig, 1912). Vol. 2: *Sittlichkeit ohne Pflicht*, transl. by Elisabeth Schwarz (Leipzig, 1912). Vol. 3: *Die Irreligion der Zukunft. Soziologische Studie*, transl. by Marie Kette (Leipzig, 1912). Vol. 4: *Die Kunst als soziologisches Phänomen*, transl. by Paul Prina and Dr Guido Bagier (Leipzig, 1912). Vol. 5: *Erziehung und Vererbung. Eine soziologische Studie*, transl. by Elisabeth Schwarz and

Marie Kette (Leipzig, 1913). Vol. 6: *Die englische Ethic der Gegenwart*, transl. by Annie Pevsner (Leipzig, 1914). (In English: Vol. 1: *Introduction; Verses of a Philosopher; Problems of Contemporary Aesthetics*; Vol. 2: *Morality without Obligation*; Vol. 3: *The Irreligion of the Future*; Vol. 4: *Art as a Sociological Phenomenon*; Vol. 5: *Education and Heredity*; Vol. 6: *Contemporary English Ethics*.)

38 Alfred Kröner Verlag also welcomed female translators. Of the thirty-seven titles in Kröner's 1914 catalogue, all but seven were translations and three – ten per cent – were by women.

39 Guyau, 1887.

40 Bergmann, 1912.

41 The excitable tone of Bergmann's lectures is hinted at in his writing in *In the Grip of Illusion* in which he says, for example: 'JEAN-MARIE GUYAU – at nineteen, the author of an unusual, brilliant prizewinning work on utilitarian morality; at thirty three, dead! That one who was snatched away early by consumption could write a philosophy of life! A positivist out of the school of COMTE and SPENCER who got drunk on AUGUSTINE! Convinced of the destruction of the world and the mind, but living and acting as if both would last forever. One can think of no greater contrast fused together in one breast . . .'

42 Nietzsche had described Christianity as 'the one great curse, the one enormous and innermost perversion . . . I call it the one immortal blemish of mankind . . . This Christianity is no more than the typical teaching of the Socialists.'

43 *Die 25 Thesen der Deutschreligion* ('Twenty-Five Points of the German Religion').

44 Peters, acc. Gordon A. Craig.

45 Of this, Peter Kratz of the Berliner Institut für Faschismus-Forschung und Antifaschistische Aktion, remarks: 'Such insights, comments [Carl] Peter in the foreword, are Bergmann's contribution to the spiritual construction of the Reich, in loyal obedience to the Fuehrer.'

Notes to Chapter 2: Family

1 School report (Berichte), Thomasschule, Städtisches Gymnasium zu Leipzig, in the library of the Leipzig Municipal Museum (Bibliothek der Stadtgeschichtlichen Museums Leipzig.)

2 Michel, 8 December 1984.

3 Ibid.

4 There were twenty classes in the school altogether, spread across nine years. There were two classes – A and B – at entry level (*Sexta*) and two in each of the next six years (*Quinta, Quarta, Unter-Tertia, Ober-Tertia, Unter-Sekunda* and *Ober-Sekunda*). Each of these classes had about thirty boys in it. The top two years – *Unter-Prima* and *Ober-Prima* were streamed into three classes, with about twenty boys in each.

5 Michel, 8 December 1984.

6 Pevsner, letter, 20 January 1975.

7 Franz Kockel, 1984.

8 Drücker, 1998.

9 Leipzig city archives, file 1P463.

10 Dreessen, 1983.

11 The year 1901 should have been an auspicious one for the fur business, because it saw the opening of the Trans-Siberian railway, which reduced the cost of importing pelts from across Russia's thirteen time zones. Pevsner may have meant 1903, the year of Germany's great economic slump, when a savage and widespread economic downturn injured the fur trade particularly badly. Another family source, Heinrich Pollack, however, believes the bankruptcy took place many years earlier, which is more likely because it allows more time for the events that followed to take place.

12 In Sumatra Road, then at 66 Solent Road, NW6. (See *Jewish Chronicle*, 16 January 1916, pp. 14–15.)

13 Pevsner made no reference to being accompanied by his father in his account of this journey, but he recorded elsewhere that his parents once went to England together, and since they rarely travelled together, this visit may have been the one he was referring to. If that's the case, it's unlikely they didn't take their older son as well.

14 Pevsner, 1954.

15 Published in German as *Eine neue Hamlet-Auffassung*, 1909; in English as *Hamlet – an Actor*, 1913.

16 Dreessen, 30 November 1983.

17 Pollack, 2007.

18 Pevsner, 1954.

19 Vladimir, noted Pevsner, was the first example of a truly Russian name in his family. 'Until then they had all been names of the ghetto.' In fact, none of Pevsner's family had lived in a ghetto; he simply means the traditional 'child, son-of-father' type of name that was used in the East European pale of Jewish settlement, from the Baltic to the Black Sea, until surnames were made compulsory for Jews in Posen in 1833.

20 The name is not distantly but directly connected with Posen.

21 I have replaced the mention of Antoine Pevsner that appears at this point in the text with another ('that mysterious . . . do with us') that occurs elsewhere in the same family history.

22 G in Russian is a transliteration of what in other languages would be H. Thus, Russians write Holland as Gollandia and The Hague as Gaaga. Pevsner seems not to have known this.

23 The building was destroyed by Allied bombing during the Second World War, as most of the commercial centre of Leipzig was.

24 Pevsner, 1954.

25 Treitschke, 1879.

26 Bernhard Prince von Bülow, Reich chancellor (1900–1909).

27 The Hungarian conductor Arthur Nikisch (1855–1922) was musical director of the Leipzig Gewandhaus orchestra and an international celebrity. His wife Mitja died young.

28 Pevsner family, 1954.

Notes to Chapter 3: Friends

1 Marianne Kockel, 1984.

2 Also known as Ernest Thompson Seton, Ernest Seton Thompson and Ernest E Thompson.

3 Undated personal note, NP.

4 Ibid.

5 Marianne Kockel, 1984.

6 Helmut Meyer von Bremen, letter of recommendation, 27 November 1938. In the possession of Heinrich Günter-Pollack.

7 Another reference puts it at thirty-five pages over three days.

8 The ancestor table was first developed in the seventeenth century by the Spanish genealogist Jerome de Sosa. It is therefore sometimes called the Sosa-Stradonitz system.

9 Pevsner wrongly transcribed his name first as Philip Johann Christoph and later as Johann Christoph Philip.

10 Senior civil servant.

11 Privy Councillor.

12 Expert Councillor.

13 Provincial high court and court of appeal.

14 High Privy Councillor.

15 Excellency.

16 Privy Councillor.

17 Legal intern or clerk.
18 Helmut's uncle, Pastor Ludwig Schneller, was well known in the 1930s as the director of the German Protestant 'Syrian Orphanage' in Jerusalem. Cf. Helmut Meyer von Bremen, letter of recommendation, 27 November 1938.
19 Michel, 8 December 1982.
20 Ibid.
21 Sensitivity to rank may seem offensive and calculating. It survives, today, in the self-imposed law of the Hohenzollerns, the former ruling family of Prussia, who still require the head of the family either to marry a woman of equal rank or surrender his position, a restraint upheld by Germany's Supreme Court in 1998 after being dismissed by two lower courts as 'immoral'.
22 Marianne Kockel, 1984.

Notes to Chapter 4: Death

1 Pevsner, 1919.
2 A coastal village just outside Helsingør in Denmark.
3 Neisser, 1983. According to Neisser, Pevsner recalled having only met Mann on the one occasion in Frankfurt, but Pevsner's remarks in his family history, as well as items of correspondence and other notes, suggest they may have met earlier, at Annie's salons, as well.
4 Jelavich, 1999.
5 Riksarkivet.
6 In the view of Ulrich Michel, Hugo may also have found a way of obtaining or reobtaining a Russian passport, something he wouldn't have needed before the war when border controls were more relaxed, if he needed to reach suppliers in Russia. Michel, December 1984.
7 This is all implicit from a comparison of Pevsner's own notes of 1954 about his brother and details of his father's movements in the records of the Swedish National Archive.
8 Dreessen, 1983.
9 Pevsner, 1954.
10 Ibid.
11 Author's translation.
12 Pevsner, Gernsheim, 1949.
13 Berger, 1919.
14 Pollack, 2007.
15 Riksarkivet.
16 Ibid.
17 Dreessen, 1983.
18 Marianne Kockel, 1984.
19 Gay, 1967.
20 Pevsner, 1954.
21 Pollack, 2007.

Notes to Chapter 5: History

1 Michel, 8 December 1984.
2 Pollack, 2007.
3 See Pevsner, 1942. 'Yet this is how our civilization began, and how all civilizations begin – in the darkness of tribal barbarism' (p. 17). And 'Yet during these dark and troubled years the foundations of medieval civilization were laid' (p. 21).
4 A phrase undermined by new archaeological finds, new attitudes and new historical methodologies.
5 *Newnes*, 1933, p. 81.

6 The Merovingian dynasty of Frankish kings descends from the family of Meroveus and proceeds through Childeric I in 456 to Childeric III, 'King of all Kingdoms', who was deposed in 751. Of special interest in this narrative is Clovis I (c. 466–511), the son of Childeric I, who united the Franks for the first time by conquering Austrasia, Neustria, Burgundy and Aquitaine. The Franks were credited with developing a civil service and creating a court school for training young noblemen in the art of war and courtly ceremony: evidence of the importance of militarism and social formality.

7 The name Louis is a variant of the Merovingian name Clovis, the initial C being dropped.

8 The oscillations of that conflict, shaped by the emergence of nation-statehood and the Reformation, became especially violent during the Thirty Years War (1618–1648) which was played out mostly on German territory, halving its population and leaving it in fragments, while Bourbon France went on to become the most powerful nation in Europe. In the Napoleonic Wars at the beginning of the nineteenth century, France overran most of the Continent and the Mediterranean basin, invading Germany and reforming its moribund political system. Then, during the Franco-Prussian War (1870–1871), Germany captured Paris, regained Lorraine and billed France £200 million for its costs. In the First World War, Germany almost succeeded in invading France and dispossessing it of its colonies only to be punished after the war by being stripped of its acquisitions of the previous hundred years, including Lorraine. In the 1920s, France reoccupied the Ruhr on the pretext of Germany's failure to make timely reparation payments as required by the Treaty of Versailles. In the Second World War, Germany held France for four years. The symbolic headquartering of the Council of Europe in Strasbourg, Lorraine's main town, in 1949 illustrates the extent to which attempts to unify Europe after the Second World War were targeted specifically at the historic conflict between France and Germany rather than between other disputants.

9 The electoral college of the Holy Roman Empire consisted of three German archbishops (of Mainz, Trier and Cologne), the three rulers of the Palatine of the Rhine, Saxony and Brandenburg, and an outsider – the King of Bohemia.

10 Hence the sonorous rhetoric about empires lasting a thousand years in the speeches of both Churchill and Hitler in the Second World War.

11 Backbourn, 1997, quotes Frosch in Part I of Goethe's *Faust* beginning his drinking song with the couplet 'Das liebe heil'ge röm'sche Reich, Wie hält's nur noch zusammen?' – 'The dear old Holy Roman Empire, what holds it all together?'

12 The *Lex Aron*.

13 Bruno Gebhardt (1858–1905).

14 Karl Hampe (1869–1936).

15 Heil (1903).

16 Karl Lamprecht (1856–1915).

17 Pevsner, 19 October 1952.

18 Ibid.

19 The emphasis Pevsner gave to Burckhardt would not be followed by many historians today, who credit Burckhardt more as relating art to its cultural environment, in distinction to the more abstract empathetic approach of Wölfflin.

20 Pevsner, 1970, p. viii.

21 Pevsner, 19 October 1952.

22 For this reason, the words have been reintroduced into the text of this talk in *Pevsner on Art and Architecture*.

23 Pevsner, 1969.

Notes to Chapter 6: University

1 'Perioden der Kunstbetrachtung'.
2 Spengler, 1918. Ernst Kitzinger (Kitzinger, February 1984) credits Winckelman (1717–1768) as the originator of the concept of cultural decay.
3 At this point Annie added a note: 'Then how could Spengler have done so?'
4 Alois Riegl (1858–1905).
5 *Das Verhältnis der Einzelstaaten zum Reich innerhalb der deutschen Geschichte.*
6 See 'Heinrich Wölfflin' in *Dictionary*, 2000.
7 See 'Rudolf Wittkower' in *Dictionary*, 2000.
8 Wilhelm Waetzoldt, quoted in Kultermann, 1993, p. 179.
9 Dehio and von Bezold (1892–1901).
10 Émile Mâle (1862–1954).
11 Mâle, 1908.
12 Goldschmidt, 1910.
13 Pollack, 16 August 2009.
14 Pollack, 3 September 2009.
15 Pevsner, 1954.
16 Ernst Gombrich talked frankly about his own negativity towards East European Jews in an interview with the author in 1999.
17 Marianne Kockel, 1984.
18 Berger, 2005.
19 Marianne Kockel, 1984.
20 Klemperer, 1998, p. x.
21 Kitzinger, February 1984.
22 Pinder, 1927.
23 Gundersheimer, April 1984.
24 Dreessen, 1983.

Notes to Chapter 7: Leipzig

1 Theodor Mommsen, who taught law at Leipzig from 1848, was forced to resign in 1851 for criticizing the government of Saxony for its conservatism. It was argued that he'd compromised his job as editor of Saxony's official newspaper.
2 See Chickering, 1993.
3 See Blumenthal, 1998.
4 *Das Institut für Kultur- und Universalgeschichte an der Universität Leipzig.*
5 Chickering, 2000.
6 Hellmann, 1920.
7 Ludo Moritz Hartmann (1865–1924) taught at Vienna University from the age of twenty-four but didn't become professor until after the First World War, having been the first Austrian envoy in Berlin after the First World War. As a historian and Mommsen's pupil, he was a campaigning modernizer in the field of national education. He helped pioneer the establishment of university extension courses in 1895, partly financed the building of a home for the Viennese National Education Association, was deputy chairman of a women's educational group and in 1905 established some of the first adult education evening classes in Europe.
8 See 'Hellmann' in *NDB*.
9 See Hoffmann, 1991, p. 163, quoting ASPSL.
10 Colloquium at Leipzig's Karl-Marx Universität, October 1973, on the centenary of the founding of the chair of art history.
11 Craig, 1981, p. 199 (translated).

12 The remark, about Springer's *Geschichte Österreichs seit dem Wiener Frieden 1809*, published in 1865, was made by Sir Lewis Namier in his Raleigh Lecture on History at the British Academy. See Namier, 1944.

13 In choosing Springer rather than Schnaase, Leipzig was specifically preferring an anti-Hegelian to a Hegelian theorist. Springer had begun his career strongly opposed to Hegel, whom he saw, in the light of the French Revolution, as Germany's Robespierre: an aloof, unsmiling tyrant for whom reason was a force for repression rather than liberation. In his student dissertation, Springer had attacked Hegel's critical exclusivity and his idea of art (the developing way that the individual artistic mind in particular and the supreme thinking mind or 'spirit' or 'idea' in general sought to express itself in every age), which he found artificial and repulsive. He saw Hegel as intolerant of inconvenient facts, just as Hegel's ideal state and ideal religion were intolerant of inconvenient people and practices. According to Springer, historians and philosophers gained no special detachment or authority from living in the present and in Protestant Prussia, as Hegel thought. They and their ideas were equally a part of history and should be recognized as such. As for art, its function lay not in its idealism but in its bridging of the mundane and the infinite, and of the contradictions of body and mind. But Springer, not being an absolutist, was not rigid in his rejection of Hegel; he saw a limited role for Hegelianism, but stripped of its religious overtones.

14 Schmarsow's writings include *Leibniz und Schottelius* (1877), *Der Wert der drei Dimensionen im menschlichen Raumgebilde* (1893), *Das Wesen der architektonischen Schöpfung* [The Essence of Architectural Creation] (1894), the three-volume *Beiträge zur Aesthetik der bildenden Künste*, made up of Vol. I: *Zur Frage nach dem Malerischen* (1896); Vol. II: *Barock und Rokoko* (1897); and Vol. III: *Plastik, Malerei und Reliefkunst* (1899) and *Grundbegriffe der Kunstwissenschaft* (1905).

15 Pevsner seems to have forgotten that in 1928 he claimed – more generously than there seems evidence for – that 'the entire scientific method' of his doctoral thesis rested on Schmarsow and that Schmarsow was the fundamental reason for his having enjoyed his education. See Pevsner, *Leipziger*, 1928.

16 Pevsner, 1948.

17 Quoted in Kultermann, 1993.

18 Ibid.

19 'The Nature of Architectural Creation'.

20 Quentin Massys's names can also be spelled Quinten and Matsys or Metsys.

21 Pevsner greatly admired Dvořák's 'comprehensive and learned papers on painting of the fourteenth century in Bohemia (1902), his *Rätsel der Brüder van Eyck* (1904), his *Idealismus und Naturalismus in der gotischen Skulptur und Malerei* (1918), and especially his *Kunstgeschichte als Geistesgeschichte* essays collected in 1924 and including "Greco und der Manierismus"'. See Pevsner, 1969, p. ix.

22 Kautzsch's directorship also involved him in some teaching at Leipzig. In the winter semester of 1900–1901 he lectured on the history of mediaeval architecture and conducted research seminars in the same area.

23 In the winter semester of 1907–1908, for example, Vitzthum taught a course on ancient Carolingian and Ottoman art and held a seminar on aspects of mediaeval art. Schmarsow, meanwhile, held lectures on nineteenth-century art history (with slides) and dealt with Rembrandt's drawings in his seminar.

Notes to Chapter 8: Pinder

1 Pinder, 15 July 1930.

2 Pinder, 1943.

3 König, 1984.

4 Kitzinger, February 1984.

5 Wölfflin became professor of art history at Munich in 1912. In 1924, he took up the chair at Berlin, returning to Zurich in 1934.

6 Wolfgang Hermann, July 1985.

7 According to Peter Guth, Pinder took some time to prove himself in Leipzig's more established academic circles. Renate Drücker adds that Schmarsow and, from 1923, Theodor Hetzer (1890–1946) still attracted more attention and were regarded as more profound.

8 Ullmann, 1984; Holt, 1984.

9 Drücker, 1984.

10 Degenhardt, May 1984.

11 Kitzinger, op. cit.

12 Paatz, July 1984.

13 Mütherich, April 1984.

14 Ibid.

15 Holt, April 1984.

16 Kitzinger, op. cit.

17 It's hard to know if Pinder's expressive awkwardnesses were natural or contrived and whether they masked a clumsiness of thought. A similar question can be asked of writers, musicians and artists of the time. Of Expressionist playwrights, Peter Gay has written: 'Prolific and hostile – to the rules, to the audience, often to clarity – they poured out plays eccentric in plot, staging, speech, characters, acting and direction . . . Speech rose to declamation and, often, sheer yelling, as far removed from ordinary manner as possible.' Gay, 1992, p. 115.

18 Known in Germany at the time as 'Revel'.

19 Clemen, 1919.

20 Maurice, Count Maeterlinck (1862–1949), Belgian playwright, poet and essayist who wrote in French.

21 Emile Verhaeren (1855–1916), Belgian poet who wrote in French.

22 Quoting from Dehio, 1909.

23 Bondi, 1984.

Notes to Chapter 9: Dissertation

1 See Fergusson, 1975.

2 Ibid.

3 Wolfgang Hermann, 18 July 1985.

4 Margarete Kurlbaum-Siebert (1874–1938), best known for her novel *Maria Stuart in Schottland* (1911), published in English as *Mary Queen of Scots* (1928).

5 Pevsner, 1954.

6 Pevsner remembered it as 1906. In fact it was 1900. He may have been recalling the date of her book on mediaeval Dutch art.

7 Pevsner, 1954.

8 Ibid.

9 Wolfgang Hermann, 4 August 1985.

10 Ibid.

11 Author's translation. Original in GRI.

12 Pevsner, 1954.

13 Margarete Siebert died in 1938. Her adopted daughter, Lotte Johne, went on to be a doctor in Berlin.

14 Marianne Kockel, 1984.

15 Ibid.

16 Ibid.

17 Repeated by Franz Kockel, 1984.

18 Marianne Kockel, 1984.

19 Pevsner, 1942, p. 99. Pevsner also stresses (p. 97) that 'the Rococo is not a separate style. It is part of the Baroque, as Decorated is part of the Gothic style'.

20 'Leipzig could not boast to have been the home of some genius and the same was true of its buildings, if we overlook the Völkerschlacht Denkmal, erected to remember the victory over Napoleon – an atrocity. The remaining old buildings: the marketplace with the old Rathaus and the old stock exchange at the back; the three or so cellar-restaurants with the Augustiner Keller of Offenbach fame; the Augustplatz, large enough for the whole German army to parade on it, with the opera on one side, the Grassi Museum on the other and the old university building on the third; the modern railway station – interesting as it was one of the few stations in Germany built as a terminus with twenty-six platforms.' Michel, 8 December 1984.

21 Pevsner, 1942, p. 133.

22 Pevsner, 1948, p. 120.

23 Banham, 1981; Games, 1982.

24 Pevsner, 1966.

25 Die Baukunst der Barockzeit in Leipzig.

26 Pevsner, Leipziger, 1928. It's not clear from the text whether Pevsner was saying that Leipzig had more Baroque houses in the past or that more had survived to the present day.

27 Ibid.

28 By the 1750s, the fairs were said to be attracting between 6,000 and 10,000 visitors a year.

29 'What irks me particularly now is that no consideration was given at all to the peculiar, indeed unique, function of the high merchants' houses. They contained shops and flats and were regularly cleared of domestic tenants for the Leipzig fairs, in order to become exhibition premises to show and sell samples of merchandise. No social history then for me in 1923–1924.' Pevsner, 1969, p. ix.

30 Pevsner, Leipziger, 1928, p. 184.

31 Ibid, p. 4.

32 Dresden in 1852 had been the third German town to reach a population of 100,000 but then grew at only half Leipzig's rate.

33 In Games, 1982.

Notes to Chapter 10: Mannerism

1 Now the Staatliche Gemäldegalerie.

2 Epple, 2009.

3 Posse lived in Pavilion J between 1914 and 1938 or 1939, sharing part of it between 1919 and 1923 with the painter Oskar Kokoschka (see Kokoschka, 1971). See also Wuchrer/Baernighausen, 2006; and Bischoff, 1996. I am indebted to Annegret Karge for this information.

4 'In 1924 the institute organized, under Bodmer's supervision . . ., a "campagna fotografica" . . . which aimed at a complete documentation of Bolognese baroque painting. Since Pevsner hints at this initiative in the preface to his Handbuch der Kunstwissenschaft volume, some sort of contact [between him and the institute] may not be excluded. It is also true that Bodmer himself was working in those years on L. Carracci and that in 1925 Posse's monograph on the baroque painter Sacchi was published as a volume of the institute's series Italienische Forschungen. All these facts must have aroused Pevsner's interest in the institute's activities. But I cannot find any proof of that.' Tigler, 1984.

5 Andrea Sacchi (1599–1661).

6 Other pre-nineteenth-century artists whose work the Gemäldegalerie acquired during Pevsner's time included Jan Lys, Füssli, de Marées, Rotari and Thiele.

7 See Annual Reports of the Gallery, written by Posse.

8 In *Der Cicerone*.

9 In *Kunstwanderer*.

10 In *Chronache D'Arte*.

11 Pevsner, 1954.

12 Marianne Kockel, 1984.

13 Pevsner, 1954.

14 Wolfgang Hermann, July 1985.

15 Marianne Kockel, 1984.

16 GRI notes.

17 Not *Handbuch für Kunstwissenschaft*, as misquoted by other writers.

18 See 'Fritz Burger' in *Dictionary*, 2000.

19 Propyläen eventually published twenty-five volumes between 1923 and 1935.

20 'Da können Sie sich Ihren Ruhm gleich an der Wurzel abgraben.'

21 'Die Darstellung wird ... immer von der ausführlichen Analyse des einzelnen Bildes ausgehen und erst von ihr aus zum Stil des Künstlers, zum Stil seiner Heimat, seiner Zeit und schließlich zu den geistesgeschichtlichen Grundlagen vordringen.' Foreword, Pevsner, *Handbuch*, 1928.

22 See Pevsner, 1964, p. 279.

23 It was this dispute that Pevsner would refer to in his radio talk on art history (Pevsner, October 1952), when he recalled arguing about works of art in museums and then not remembering what they depicted.

24 Pevsner had read Dvořák's *Das Rätsel der Kunst der Brüder van Eyck* in December 1920.

25 Pevsner, 1964, p. 279.

26 Pevsner, 1948, p. 136.

27 Siebert, 1906.

28 Pevsner, *Handbuch*, 1928, p. 238, fn.29.

29 Ibid, p. 98.

30 *Jahrbuch der preußischen Kunstsammlungen*.

31 Pevsner, January 1952.

32 Pevsner's question was changed to 'Can he therefore *not* ...' in the final script.

33 Pevsner, *Handbuch*, 1928, p. 99.

34 Pevsner, October 1952. This story was told by Pevsner with the intention of criticizing Wölfflin (and Roger Fry) but it self-evidently goes further than that because he's talking about his own tendency and he wasn't a Wölfflinite.

35 Weisbach, 1921.

36 In Pevsner, Weisbach, 1925.

37 Ibid; Pevsner, 1968.

38 At one point in his essay, Pevsner complimented Ranke on his 'superb description' of St Philip Neri, revealing that the quality of Ranke's writing was at least as appealing to him as its accuracy.

39 Pevsner, *Handbuch*, 1928, p. 98.

40 Pevsner, Revision (1927–1928).

41 'Caravaggio is the first representative of the type of progressive modern artist whose works, in defiance of the existing standards of taste, bring about a violent taking sides with the art world ... How obvious are ... the parallels ... to the personalities and the history of the great art movements of recent times. Like so many of the moderns whom I need not specify, Caravaggio, too, had the strongest possible belief in his mission and contempt for other forms

of art . . . For the first time do we hear of people refusing to accept pictures they had ordered, on account of their being shocked by the artist's treatment of the subject.' Borenius, 1925.

42 Pevsner, *Der Cicerone*, 1926.
43 Pevsner, *Kunstwanderer*, 1925.
44 Pollack, 2007 and 16 August 2009.

Notes to Chapter 11: Dresden

1 On Hähnelstraße in Johannstadt, just east of the Gemäldegalerie, in a miniature art district that mirrored the Musikviertel in Leipzig. Hähnelstraße was named after Ernst Hähnel (1811–1891), a Dresden sculptor who'd taught at the city's Art Academy. Canalettostraße, Holbeinstraße and Dürerstraße were nearby, as well as Wallotstraße, named after the architect of the Reichstag in Berlin.

2 The other was the *Dresdner Neueste Nachrichten*.

3 In 1925 he wrote about exhibitions of work by Kolbe, Meidner, El Lissitzky, Thoma, Edmund Möller, Holder, Huf, Kirchner, Hofer, Felixmüller, Böckstiegel, Pechstein, Beckmann and Jawlensky; in 1926, about Hettner, Slevogt, Zrzavý, Oppenheimer, Feldbauer, Utrillo, Dix, Klee and the photographers Erfurth and Jonas; and in 1927, about Kretzschmar, Liebermann, von Hoffmann (twice), Munch, Dix again, Nolde, Scholtz, Schmidt-Rotluff and the photographer Gertrud Riess. This is in addition to his writings on group shows and special collections (the Rhenish Millennium exhibition; Japanese woodcuts; German applied arts abroad; model housing in the Dresden Annual Exhibition, the Dresden Academy Annual Show; contemporary art of Saxony; international applied art; the Leipzig International Exhibition of the art of the book; the Gert von Dietel Collection), historical art (the cathedral sculptures of Strasbourg, Bamberg and Naumburg; and old masters at the Berlin Academy of Arts) and figures of note in museology.

4 Pevsner, 7 July 1925.

5 Pevsner, 9 July, 1925. Herbert Read made this connection in a satirical account of the phases of Picasso's work. See Read, 1968, p. 149.

6 See Craig, 1981, pp. 502–504, with many references to contemporary sources.

7 Albiker, Hofmann, Rösler and Gußmann were on the exhibition committee, Tessenow was its resident architect and Sterl had until recently been its executive director.

8 See Maciuika, 2005.

9 Ibid.

10 The first Annual Show was held in 1922 and featured porcelain, ceramics and glass. The second, in 1923, was on play and sport. The third, in 1924, concentrated on textiles. The fourth, in 1925, was on houses and housing estates.

11 Foreword, *Catalogue*, Dresden International Exhibition, 1926.

12 The first building on the 140-hectare site that Schmidt had assembled from parcels of land acquired from seventy-three local farmers was the Deutsche Werkstätten für Handwerkskunst.

13 I am grateful to Annegret Karge for this information.

14 Ibid.

15 Box 105, Folder of notes on Pevsner's foreign trips, GRI.

16 I am grateful to Annegret Karge for this information.

17 'Ein eifriger und unermüdlicher Helfer.'

18 The countries of North, Central and South America absented themselves on the grounds, variously, that participation after a costly war was inappropriate, costly and frivolous.

19 Pevsner, 1937, p. 27.

20 See Chandler, 1988.

21 Late nineteenth-century manufacturing output at Dessau included farm tools, farm machines, cement, chemicals, gas equipment, gas-powered vehicles and sugar refining.

22 Kutschke, 1981.

23 At the time of writing, Annegret Karge has just completed an MA thesis on Dresden in the 1920s.

24 Grohmann wrote two monographs on Kandinsky and Klee in 1924 and several other articles about Bauhaus artists. He also wrote an extensive article about the exhibition in a special edition of *Cicerone*, suggesting he had particular knowledge of it. Karge therefore thinks he's most likely to have been the person who gave Posse the names and addresses of potential participants.

25 In 2002, I came across information that suggested Pevner had visited the Bauhaus in 1925. I now suspect this information was wrong. In addition I was told in 1984 by Thomas Topfstedt in Leipzig that Pevsner had told him while on a visit to Leipzig in 1978 that he'd just seen the Bauhaus in Dessau for the first time.

26 As it happens, neither Gropius nor any other architects involved with the Bauhaus had been invited to exhibit at the Jahresschau and it's possible they were seen as too political to be able to fit easily into a commercial show, since those architects who did take part had to find developers to pay for their designs to be built, which meant that all the new designs had to have been judged as commercially viable by at least one private sponsor.

27 Bruno Paul was the head of the Vereinigte Staatsschulen für freie und angewandete Kunst (the United State Schools for Fine and Applied Art) in Berlin, which Pevsner thought superior to the Bauhaus.

28 Pevsner, 21 July 1925. Architects whom Pevsner singled out for criticism included Hempel, Höntsch, Mund, Fimmen, and the partnership of Uhlemann and Rößler. He also accused Bruno Taut and Kurt Lüdecke of 'throwing the baby out with the bathwater' in their Modernism, but thought that Lüdecke was young enough to come to his senses and moderate his extremism.

29 A woodcut by Lyonel Feininger, originally titled 'The Cathedral of Socialism', was used as the cover design of the first Bauhaus manifesto by Gropius in 1919, and the phrase was repeated in the exhibition pamphlet that Oskar Schlemmer prepared in the summer of 1923 while Gropius was on holiday, though Gropus himself is said – in the USA – to have objected to it. See Isaacs, 1991, p. 102.

30 From Pevsner, 1961.

31 That passing reference described the Bauhaus as 'this hopeful and important nursery of modern architecture in Germany' in the course of describing some of its artists (Kandinsky, Klee, Jean Paul, Moholy-Nagy, Lissitzky and Feininger) but treated the artists as individuals who happened to find themselves at the Bauhaus by chance and didn't elaborate on the school as an institution. See Pevsner, 14 August 1926.

32 Germany, Austria, France, Spain, Italy, Belgium, Holland, Switzerland, Sweden, Norway, Denmark, Finland, Russia, England, America, Hungary, Czechoslovakia, Poland and Japan.

33 Including Archipenko, Braque and Picasso, Carrà, Chagall, De Chirico, Robert Delaunay, Derain, Dufy, Gabo, Gris, Kokoschka, Klee, Léger, Modigliani, Moholy-Nagy, Mondrian, Morisot, Rouault, Severini and Vlaminck.

34 Including Cézanne, Monet, Renoir, Rodin, Pissarro, Maillol, Utrillo, Munch, Hodler, Toorop, van Gogh, Gauguin, Modersohn-Becker, Signac, Sisley, Klimt and Schiele.

35 Pevsner named just six American artists and was amused at how un-American they were. The best three were Maurice Stern and Joseph Stella, the one living in Italy, the other born there, and Jules Pascin, born in Romania and educated in Germany and France. His runners-up were Rockwell Kent, Samuel Halpern and Max Weber.

36 Die Brücke: Heckel, Kirchner, Schmidt-Rottluff, Müller, Nolde and Pechstein.

37 Neue Künstlervereinigung München: Adolf Erbslöh, Wassily Kandinsky and Alexander Kanoldt.

38 Der Blaue Reiter: Lyonel Feininger, Natalie Goncharova, Alexej von Jawlensky, Wassily Kandinsky, Paul Klee, August Macke (died 1914) and Franz Marc (died 1916).

39 That gap was filled instead by members of the 'Dresden Secession Group 1919', the main members of which included Conrad Felixmüller, Otto Dix, Wilhelm Heckrott, Bernhard Kretzschmar, Otto Schubert, Lazar Segall and Constantin von Mitschke-Collande, and they, with the exception of Dix who had by then decamped to Berlin, were more positive and unironic, looking for consolation from the world – albeit angular and restless – rather than treating it with derision, as the Dadaists did.

40 The model was Leo Michelson. See Max Michelson's autobiography, 2004.

41 Bettina Feistel-Rohmeder.

42 Such a complaint is mischievous because it was normal in German art history to use the word 'neu' and 'young' in the sense of later or more recent. Hence 'mittelalterliche und neuere Kunstgeschichte': mediaeval and more recent art history; 'die jüngste Vergangenheit und die Gegenwart': the most recent past and the present.

43 For a fuller account of the Deutsche Kunstgesellschaft, see Clinefelter, 2005.

44 Lola.

45 Bernhard Bleeker (1881–1968), German sculptor.

46 Pevsner, 1954.

Notes to Chapter 12: Göttingen

1 Stechow, 1946.

2 König, 1984.

3 Elisabeth Paatz's name is often wrongly spelled with a 'z' instead of an 's' in her first name. In letters to the author, she signs her name with an 's'.

4 Paatz, 1984.

5 Schmidt-Jüngst, 1984.

6 *Barockmalerei in den romanischen Ländern*. See Pevsner, *Handbuch*, 1928.

7 And not in 1928, as stated in Barr, 1970. Confirmation that Pevsner had begun teaching before the first of his courses that were included in the university's register can be found in the joint application by Vitzthum and Hecht for a salaried post for him.

8 Ratcliff, letter, 8 April 1932.

9 The Hechts lived at Hainholzweg 60.

10 Ratcliff, letter, 17 April 1932.

11 Ratcliff, letter 15 May 1932.

12 König, 1984.

13 Schmidt-Jüngst, 1984.

14 Ursula Stechow, 1984.

15 Außerplanmäßiger Assistent.

16 Karl Arndt, 1984.

17 König, 1984.

18 Gerson, 1975.

19 'I was the only lecturer in Germany who got students out of the house quite a lot and we made expeditions together,' Pevsner recalled years later. (Pevsner in interview with Frank Herrmann, 24 June 1976.) In fact, as shown, several lecturers took students on visits.

20 Unpublished but lodged in the University Library at Göttingen. Pevsner had also written an essay for *Kunstchronik und Kunstliteratur* about a Rococo exhibition that he'd seen in Venice in 1929.

21 For 'Gurtchenbroder me pinxit Hezoldus' – 'Hezold of Gurtchenbroder painted this'.

22 Presumably Hilde Kurz.

23 Pevsner, 'Beiträge', 1928.

24 Hans Erich Freiherr von Campenhausen.

25 Von Campenhausen, letters and interview, 1984.

26 Pevsner, 21 January 1929.

27 Annegret Karge says discussions over what work should go into the Dresden section of the International Exhibition led to another fight within the Künstlervereinigung, with the artist Bernhard Kretzschmar also complaining about the arrogance and stupidity of the 'radicals' and naming Conrad Felixmueller, Otto Lange and others.

28 Behrens, 1922.

29 Thus Gropius could speak mediaevally of a unity of crafts that would 'one day rise to heaven from the hands of a million workers', but could also turn down the offer of an honorary professorship at the Bauhaus in 1919 on the grounds that it was important to be free of 'ridiculous trifles that no longer belong to our time.' See Gropius, 1919. Quoted in Isaacs, 1991.

30 Pevsner, 1969.

31 Ibid.

32 There's no record of whether Vitzthum welcomed this change of direction by Pevsner but it indicates how little control he exerted over his small department, since it flew in the face of what he'd wanted.

33 From Pevsner, 1942.

Notes to Chapter 13: Interlude

1 Frank Hermann, 1976. Pevsner would always refer later to what he taught as if it had been an art-history topic and one he'd initiated himself.

2 Preußisches Ministerium für Wissenschaft, Kunst und Volksbildung (Prussian Ministry of Science, Art and Public Education).

3 Cope, 1989.

4 Ibid.

5 Pevsner was also quoted as saying that those who fell outside this moral chain included the French Impressionists, who cut themselves off from society and glamorized the isolation of the artist, to the despair of Renoir; the philosophical van Gogh; and the German Expressionists, whom van Gogh inspired but who'd had no impact on the social arts of architecture and design.

6 Pinder, 1935.

7 Pevsner spent a lifetime confronting criticism of his moral chain argument. In 1960, he wrote of having to do a 'securing job' in a new edition of the book based on this argument, and was only troubled that what seemed right to him was thought wrong by others. See Foreword to Pevsner, 1960.

8 Frank Hermann, 1976.

9 In Wiltshire, south of Salisbury.

10 Pevsner, 1954.

11 The Durning-Lawrence Professor of Art.

12 Tarkowski, 2009.

13 Borenius also reintroduced Pevsner to Swedish, which, like most Finns from the south of the country, he spoke in preference to Finnish and which belongs to the Germanic family of languages, while Finnish relates only to Hungarian.

14 Three out of four courses on English art; six out of eight courses on European art.

15 Frank Herrmann, 1976.

16 According to the university register, Pevsner had so far only taught four semesters, so Vitzthum was probably including teaching that Pevsner had carried out in the summer of 1929, after the register had gone to press.

17 Habicht, 1931.

18 Pevsner, 'Wandlung', 1932.

19 Pevsner, 'Gegenreformation', 1925.

20 Viz., the 'subordination' of the human figure 'to something external, the way in which the legs are cut by the edge of the picture, or the strange insecure shifting between the vertical of the figure and the vertical of the picture plane ...'

21 Ibid.

Notes to Chapter 14: Modernity

1 Foreword, Pevsner, 1956.

2 Bauhaus, 1923.

3 Gropius's resignation from the Bauhaus took place in February 1928. It was caused by political difficulties, funding problems and overwork.

4 From Pevsner, BBC, 1949.

5 From Chapter 1, Pevsner, 1936.

6 Pevsner now accepted that Gropius had been able to synthesize, or blur, the two ideas that had split the Werkbund: van de Velde's belief in artistic individuality and Hermann Muthesius's belief in anonymous standardization. 'Only by standardization can we recover that universal importance that architecture and design possessed in ages of harmonious civilization', Muthesius had said at the Werkbund conference in July 1914. Pevsner would later respond 'But standardization cannot be the only remedy for our worries and thank God for that' (see Pevsner, BBC, 1949), but he accepted standardization because Gropius had persuaded him that his goal for the Bauhaus was to be 'a laboratory for handicraft and for standardization; a school, and a workshop' (Chapter 1, Pevsner, 1936).

7 Chapter 1, Pevsner 1960. In 1936, Pevsner's wording was 'a genuine and adequate style of our century'. See Pevsner, 1936.

8 Preface, Pevsner, 1968.

9 Pevsner, *Dictionary*, 1966.

10 Pevsner, 1968.

11 Foreword, Pevsner, 1936.

12 Pevsner, 1976; Barr, 1970.

13 How accurate Pevsner was being in these descriptions of his output is hard to know. Göttingen's records of its lectures from this period are still intact but nothing quite matches up with what he described. It's probable he was including the teaching he was doing for Hecht, which didn't appear in the university records. Imprecision in details of his own life is not uncommon with Pevsner, however. In the foreword to a book he published in 1956, he wrote of a particular period in his own life as 'not much longer than thirty years' when in fact it was just over twenty.

14 Pevsner, 'Gemeinschaftsideale', 1931.

15 Pevsner, 'Geschichte', 1932.

16 *Le Corbusier und Jeanneret*, 1930.

17 Individual architects weren't responsible for the use of iron and ferro-concrete, he said: it was a chain of engineering achievements the Swiss art historian Siegfried Giedion had identified – in iron, from the Paris Grain Hall of 1811 via Labrouste, Horeau, Baltard, Eiffel and the Hall of the Machines at the Paris World Fair of 1889, and in ferro-concrete from Anatole de Baudot via Perret, Garnier, Freyssinet and then Le Corbusier. This didn't make architecture's origins any

less French, however, so he moved the argument to which country had made more progress in the early 1900s. Here again he had to concede that skeleton construction – structural columns with non-loadbearing screen walls between them – was due entirely to Perret and could be seen as early as 1903 in his house in the Rue Franklin, Paris. It wasn't until Peter Behrens's turbine hall for AEG in Berlin in 1909 that Pevsner could show that Germany was even level-pegging, but having done so he went on to criticize Le Corbusier for not admitting he'd worked in Behrens' office for a few months during 1911–1912 and thereby not admitting his indebtedness to Germany. For skeleton construction, he credited cantilevers and the use of window walls to Frank Lloyd Wright in America (1906) and again to Behrens in the turbine hall, concluding that this element first gained its 'fullest artistic effect in twenty-eight-year-old Walter Gropius's factory for Fagus' at Alfeld an der Leine (1911–1913) – Gropius was in fact thirty-two in 1911. The grouping of simple cubic forms he credited to the Austrians Otto Wagner, Josef Hoffmann and Adolf Loos as much as to Behrens and Wright, around 1905. For flat roofs he quoted Wright and Behrens.

18 Where Le Corbusier had said the 'new style of today' was coming together in the same years as Picasso and Derain and Matisse and the Fauves in Paris, between 1903 and about 1908, Pevsner argued it was also the period of Kokoschka, of Nolde's first religious masterpieces, and of the young artists of Die Brücke in Dresden.

19 See Pevsner, 1936, Foreword.

20 Sigfried Giedion (1888–1968) was a Swiss art historian, trained under Wölfflin, who taught art history and promoted modern architecture. He was the first Secretary-General of the Congrès International d'Architecture Moderne.

21 See Hitchcock and Johnson, 1932.

22 Ibid.

23 See Pevsner, 1936. The half-paragraph reference to the Bauhaus in the introductory chapter of this book deals only with the theory of what Gropius intended to take place there and not the facts of its more complicated history.

24 Pevsner, 1936. In his revision of this book in 1960, Pevsner said instead: 'France at this moment can disappear from our stage. Between 1904 and 1921, the year of Le Corbusier's Citrohan designs, she did not contribute anything of international significance. Le Corbusier (born in 1887) is Swiss, but has spent nearly his whole working life living in Paris. If his work before 1921 is not considered in this book, the reason is that he cannot be considered in the same category of pioneers as the architects to whom it is devoted, though he has tried in his writings to make himself appear one of the first-comers. His designs for an estate called Domino, which was to be built entirely in concrete, are certainly very progressive, and they date from 1915; but in 1916 Le Corbusier could still build a private house that does not go beyond the stage reached by Perret or van der Velde before the war.' Pevsner, 1960.

25 From Pevsner, 'Reynolds', 1955.

26 From Pevsner, 'Anti-pioneers', 1966.

Notes to Chapter 15: Hitler

1 Mühlberger, 1991.

2 Allen, 1984.

3 Göttingen University website, numerous quoted sources. See also Göttingen, 1983.

4 Göttingen University website.

5 Ibid.

6 Dahms, 1984.

7 Ratcliff mistakenly uses Burgenschaft and Burschenschaft interchangeably. A Burgenschaft is a sort of parliament. The words 'Burschenschaft' and 'Corps' can, however, be interchanged.

8 Ratcliff, 15 May 1932, quoted in Ratcliff, 15 October 1983.

9 Ratcliff, 8 May 1932.

10 Ratcliff, 1 May 1932.

11 Ratcliff, 15 October 1983.

12 'Hitlertag Göttingen'. See Stadtarchiv Göttingen.

13 Schutzstaffel (Protective Squadron).

14 See Allen, 1984, pp. 123–125.

15 Ibid.

16 Von Campenhausen, 1984.

17 Max Wien (1866–1938) was director of the Institute of Physics at the University of Jena. Erwin Schrödinger (of the Schrödinger principle) called Wien 'moderately anti-Semitic' in his autobiography.

18 The *Vossische Zeitung* was a liberal newspaper brought out by Ullstein Verlag, a Jewish publisher, that from January 1933 was harassed into extinction. In April 1934, Ullstein Verlag was 'Aryanized'. See: Bender, 1972.

19 Uta von Ballenstedt was an eleventh-century beauty whose effigy – an exceptional example of thirteenth-century Gothic portraiture in stone – had for many years been venerated in Germany and in the 1930s became a shrine to German womanhood (becoming, in turn, a shrine to Communist womanhood in the 1950s). The choice of Uta von Ballenstedt must have felt very personal for the Pevsners in view of the fact that the effigy was housed near Alfred Kurlbaum's country estate in the cathedral at Naumburg, which von Ballenstedt had been one of the twelve founders of – a cathedral famous also for its symbolic sculptures of 'Ecclesia', representing heroic Christianity, and 'Synagoga', shown wearing a blindfold and with her crown slipping off, to represent defeated Judaism. These sculptures, similar to ones that can be found in Gothic cathedrals all over Europe, and that of Uta (remarkable also for being a secular effigy and not a saint) were set off in Naumburg by the west choir screen of c. 1249–1255, which was made up of a sculptural group of grotesque Jewish caricatures commissioned by the Bishop of Wettin.

20 By coincidence, the Bishop of Wettin referred to above was called Dietrich, but there's no evidence to suggest this was the person Nikolaus and Lola named their younger son after.

21 Priestman, 6 March 1984.

22 Ratcliff, 15 May 1932, quoted in Ratcliff, 4 October 1983.

23 König, 1984.

24 Ratcliff, 11 September 1983.

25 Ratcliff, 4 October 1983.

26 Priestman, 6 March 1984.

27 Ibid.

28 Ibid.

29 Rheins, 1978.

30 Klemperer, 1998.

31 Priestman, 2009.

32 Pevsner, 1936.

33 Pevsner, 'Beiträge', 1928.

34 Pinder, 1935.

35 Pevsner, 1936.

36 The sequence of failure included Papen's idea of a new type of state run by the aristocracy; the replacement of Papen by Schleicher; Schleicher's idea of a Spenglerian workers' coalition; Schleicher's attempt to promote the Nazis' Prussian leader, Gregor Strasser, over the head of Hitler; and finally Schleicher's resignation.

37 'Gesetz zur Wiederherstellung des Berufsbeamtentums, 7 April 1933' or 'Berufsbeamtengesetz' for short.
38 Thomas Pevsner, 1984.

Notes to Chapter 16: Dismissal

1 Quoted in Scholzel, 2003.
2 Dahms, 1983.
3 See Craig, 1981, p. 579.
4 'Beurlauben' is the usual German word for being granted leave of absence or being suspended from a job. Its root form is 'Urlaub' – 'holiday' or 'vacation'.
5 Paatz, 1984.
6 Priestman, 6 March 1984.
7 The 1929 May Day ban had led to protest demonstrations and the firing of 10,000 rounds of ammunition by the police, killing thirty-two. Hitler restored May Day, supposedly to symbolize the new unity between the state and the people, but banned trade unions the next day, sequestering their funds and putting their leaders in prison.
8 Wilson withheld the name of Göttingen and of her interviewees to protect their identities.
9 Wilson, May 1933.
10 Priestman, 2009.
11 Wilson, May 1933.
12 Ibid.
13 Marianne Kockel, April 1984.
14 Quoted in 'Book', 2002. See also the author's response in 'Cherry', 2002.
15 The view is faulty also because it's impossible to distinguish between the second and third categories (everyone, after the event, could claim to have been duped) and because such a definition could only be made in hindsight, after the consequences of supporting the extreme right were fully known: after it was realized that Nazism meant abusing, then delegitimizing, then shooting, and then deporting and industrially killing undesirables in their millions.
16 Thus Karl Lueger, Mayor of Vienna, said 'Wissenschaft is' wos a Jud' vom andern abschreibt' (Science is what one Jew copies from another); and Rudolphe Tomaschek: 'Modern physics is an instrument of Jewry for the destruction of Nordic science. . . . True physics is the creation of the German spirit.' Widely quoted and misquoted: 'Kultur is' . . .', 'Literatur is' . . .', etc.
17 'Bekenntniss der Professoren an den deutschen Universitäten und Hochschulen zu Adolf Hitler und dem nationalsozialistischen Staat'.
18 Klemperer, 1998.
19 In 1925 Alfred Hessel published *Geschichte der Bibliotheken*, a short survey of libraries from ancient Alexandria to the early twentieth century.
20 Priestman, 1984.
21 Deutschen Volkspartei.
22 Graf Georg Vitzthum von Eckärt, letter, Göttingen University archives.
23 Romanell, 1965.
24 Pevsner also canvassed support from Pietro Toesca (1877–1962), who specialized in mediaeval art and had been chair of art history at Turin, Florence and since 1926 Rome; and Arturo Farinelli (1867–1948), Professor of German literature at Turin.
25 Priestman, 2009.
26 Later Lord Beveridge (1879–1963).
27 He also wrote an article with strong Germanic overtones about the building activity of Bishop Gotthard (960–1038) at Hildesheim Cathedral. See Pevsner, 'Bautätigkeit', 1933.

28 This letter was sent to the publishing house of Eugen Diederichs, the publisher of, among others, Nietzche and Ruskin. Diederichs died in 1930 and his sons took over the company, navigating the demands of the Nazis with less difficulty than other publishers, partly because their imprints already had a nationalist-conservative thrust.

29 Letter to Pevsner, 9 April 1933. GRI.

30 Pevsner, 'Randbemerkung', 1933.

31 Ibid.

32 Ibid.

33 The name of the third was Farinelli.

34 Capristo, 2001.

Notes to Chapter 17: England

1 Priestman, 1984. The two sentences starting 'My father still . . .' are from Priestman, 2009.

2 Priestman, 1984.

3 Ibid.

4 The cultural historian Samson Knoll, who left Germany in 1934, thinks the invitation to Pevsner would have come directly through Wilson, and that she herself had started a programme to bring over German emigrés based on a similar programme she'd started after the First World War.

5 Library of the Society of Friends: *Dictionary of Quaker Biography* (unpublished).

6 See Betjeman, 2009, p. 172.

7 Pevsner, *Middlesex*, 1951.

8 Pevsner, 12 February 1934.

9 Waterson, 1984.

10 Pevsner, October 1952.

11 Wolsey, 1984.

12 See Finlayson, 1994.

13 Ref. in Barbara Florence, 1984.

14 Philip Sargant Florence's diary. Ref. in Barbara Florence, 1984.

15 Birminhham's first professr of commerce, William Ashley, wrote about German educational experiments at trade schools in Berlin and Cologne in *The Times*, 2 April 1903.

16 Later amalgamated into Durham University.

17 In all Pevsner's writing to date, he followed foreign custom – and occasionally English custom too – in saying 'England' whether he meant England or the whole of Britain, an insensitivity he would at the time have been unaware of but that couldn't please the Scots.

18 Pevsner often used pseudonyms. In a novella he'd written as a schoolboy, he signed himself 'Bernud'. He'd use other *noms-de-plume* in later life.

19 Pevsner, 21 February 1934.

Notes to the Appendix

1 Norman and I have discussed my intention to write about these events and he's kindly indicated that he doesn't have any objection to my doing so or to my naming him. I appreciate his understanding of my predicament.

2 A review in *The Scotsman* (4 January 2003) headed 'Voice of a missionary' carried the subtitle 'An engaging collection of Nikolaus Pevsner's broadcasts is poisoned by the accusation that he was a closet Nazi'.

3 Quoted in Bradley and Cherry, 2001.

4 See Games, BBC, 1982. The programme was wrongly titled (twice) and wrongly dated by Paul Crossley in citations in his introduction to *Reassessing Nikolaus Pevsner*, ed. Peter Draper

(Ashgate, 2004), confusing it with a book by Ernst Fischer. The presenter was also wrongly identified as the programme's director.

5 McInnes, 1961.

References

PRINCIPAL MEMBERS OF PEVSNER'S FAMILY CITED

Pevsner	Nikolaus Bernhard Leon, born Nikolai Bernhard Leon Pewsner
Pevsner	Carola ('Lola'), née Kurlbaum. Pevsner's wife
Pewsner	Hugo (Gilel). Pevsner's father
Pewsner	(Sara) Anna ('Annie'), née Perlmann. Pevsner's mother
Pewsner	Heinrich ('Heinz') Wolfgang. Pevsner's older brother
Kurlbaum	Alfred Adolf. Carola's father
Kurlbaum	Paula, née Neisser. Carola's mother
Perlmann	Saveli Maximovich. Pevsner's mother's father
Perlmann	Jeannette, née Blidin. Pevsner's mother's mother
Perlmann	Ida ('Idittchen', 'Iditta', 'Idchen'). Pevsner's mother's sister
Pevsner	Uta Hodgson. First child of Nikolaus and Carola Pevsner
Pevsner	Thomas. Second child of Nikolaus and Carola Pevsner
Pevsner	Dietrich ('Dieter'). Third child of Nikolaus and Carola Pevsner
Kockel	(Edith) Marianne, née Kurlbaum. Sister of Carola Pevsner
Kockel	Franz. Son of Marianne Kockel
Pollack	Heinrich. Pevsner's first cousin. Son of Ida Perlmann, Pevsner's aunt
Dreessen	Ellen, née Perlmann. Daughter of George Perlmann, Pevsner's uncle

ABBREVIATIONS AND SPECIAL TERMINOLOGY

AAC	Academic Assistance Council
Abitur	School graduation certificate, gained by examination and qualifying the holder for a university place
ASPSL	Archives of the Society for the Protection of Science and Learning, Bodleian Library, Oxford, 498/2. Quoted in Hoffmann, 1991, p.163
CUP	Cambridge University Press
GRI	Getty Research Institute, Brentwood, Los Angeles, CA
Habilitationsschrift	Postdoctoral academic paper submitted to a university to gain a teaching position
Kurator	University registrar
NDB	*Neue Deutsche Biographie*
OUP	Oxford University Press
Privatdozent	Unsalaried university lecturer, independently funded or paid privately by students
Riksarkivet	Swedish National Archives
SPSL	Society for the Protection of Science and Learning
Venia legendi	University teaching certificate.

1. PEVSNER PUBLISHED WORKS CITED

1924	'Regesten zur Leipziger Baukunst der Barockzeit', in: *Neues Archiv für Sächs. Gesch. und Altertumskunde*, 45, Dresden, pp. 104–120.
1925, July 7	'Dresdner Künstlervereinigung I: Zum Dresdner Künstlerstreit', in: 'Kunst and Wissenschaft', *Dresdner Anzeiger*.
1925, July 9	'Dresdner Künstlervereinigung II: Sommer-Ausstellung in der Lennéstraße', in: 'Kunst and Wissenschaft', *Dresdner Anzeiger*.
1925, July 21	'Hausmodelle auf der Jahreschau II', in: 'Kunst and Wissenschaft', *Dresdner Anzeiger*.
1925, November	Review: Voss, 1925, in: *Kunstwanderer*, Vol. 7.
1925	'Leipziger Barockhäuser', in: *Mitteilungen des Landesvereins Sächsischer Heimatschutz*, 14 (1/2), pp. 252–66.
1925	'Giovanni Battista Crespi', in: *Jahrbuch der prüssischen Kunstsammlungen*.
1925	Review: Weisbach, 1921, in: 'Gegenreformation und Manierismus', *Repertorium für Kunstwissenschaft*, XLVI, 1925. Reprinted in Pevsner, 1968.
1926, August 7	'Internationale Kunstausstellung: Die ältere deutsche Malerei', in: 'Kunst and Wissenschaft', *Dresdner Anzeiger*.
1926, August 14	'Internationale Kunstausstellung: Die deutsche Malerei der Gegenwart', in: 'Kunst and Wissenschaft', *Dresdner Anzeiger*.
1926, Jan-Feb	Review: Posse, 1925, in: *Chronache D'Arte*, Vol. 3, p. 54.
1926	Review: Lang, 1924, in: *Der Cicerone*.
1927–1928	'Eine Revision der Caravaggio-Daten', *Zeitschrift für bildende Kunst*, Vol. 61, pp. 386–92.
1928, November	Review: Nisser, 1927, in: *Kunstchronik*, Vol. 62, p. 97. Supplement to *Zeitschrift für bildende Kunst*.
1928	'Beiträge zur Stilgeschichte des Früh- und Hochbarock, in: *Repertorium für Kunstwissenschaft*, Vol 49, pp. 225–246. Reprinted in Pevsner, 1968.
1928	*Leipziger Barock: die Baukunst der Barockzeit in Leipzig*, Wolfgang Jess. Reprinted 1990, Seemann: Leipzig.
1928	*Handbuch der Kunstwissenschaft*, Akademische Verlagsgesellschaft Athenaion.
1929, January 29	'Über Dresdens Zukunft als Kunststadt, I and II', in: 'Kunst and Wissenschaft', *Dresdner Anzeiger*.
1929, October	Rokoko Austellung, in: *Kunstchronik und Kunstliteratur*, Vol. 63, pp. 73–79.
1931 Aug-Sept	Review: Habicht, 1930. In *Kunstkronik*, Vol. 65, p. 55. Supplement to *Zeitschrift für bildende Kunst*.
1931	'Gemeinschaftsideale unter Kunstlern des 19 Jahrhunderts', in: *Deutsche Vierteljahresschrift für Literatur*.
1932	'Die Wandlung um 1650 in der italienischen Malerei', *Wiener Jahrbuch für Kunstgechichte*, Vol. 8, ed. 22, pp. 69–92. Reprinted in Pevsner, 1968.
1932	'Geschichte des Architektenberufs', *Kritische Berichte zur Kunstliteratur*.
1933, September 24	'Randbemerkung zum Briefwechsel Furtwängler-Goebbels', in: *Das Unterhaltungsblatt*, Berlin.
1933	'Die Bautätigkeit des Heiligen Godehard am Hildesheimer Dom', in: *Die Denkmalpflege: Zeitschrift für Denkmalpflege und Heimatschutze*.
1936	*Pioneers of the Modern Movement*, CUP.
1937	*An Enquiry into Industrial Art in England*, CUP.
1939, June	'A plea for contemporary craft', in: *DIA News*, Vol. 3, No. 5.
1942	*Outline of European Architecture*, 1st ed., Penguin.

1946	'The architecture of Mannerism', in: *The Mint*, ed. Geoffrey Grigson, Routledge.
1948	*Outline of European Architecture*, hardback, John Murray.
1949, March 6	*From William Morris to Walter Gropius*, BBC Third Programme. Reprinted in Pevsner, 2002.
1949	Foreword, Helmut Gernsheim, *Focus on Architecture and Sculpture*, Fountain Press: London, 1949.
1951	*The Buildings of England: Middlesex*, Penguin.
1952, January 6	'Modern architecture and the Church', in: *Prospect*, BBC Third Programme.
1952, October 19	'Reflections on not teaching art history', BBC Third Programme. Reprinted in Pevsner, 2002.
1955, October 30	'Reynolds and detachment', *The Englishness of English Art*, Reith Lectures, BBC Third Programme. (Repeated, BBC Home Service.) Reprinted in Pevsner, 1956 and Pevsner, 2002.
1956	*The Englishness of English Art*, Architectural Press. Original version of the BBC talks (1955) reprinted in Pevsner, 2002.
1960	*Pioneers of Modern Design*, Pelican.
1961, February 11	'The return of Historicism', BBC Third Programme. Reprinted in Pevsner, 2002.
1964, February 21	'Mannerism and Elizabethan architecture', Part I, BBC Third Programme. Reprinted in Pevsner, 2002.
1965	'Möglichkeiten und Aspekte des Historismus', in: *Historismus und bildende Kunst: Vorträge und Diskussion im Oktober 1963 in München und Schloß Anif*, Prestel.
1966, December 3	'The anti-pioneers', BBC Third Programme. Reprinted in Pevsner, 2002.
1966	*A Dictionary of Architecture*, co-authors John Fleming and Hugh Honour, Penguin.
1968	*Studies in Art, Architecture and Design*, Thames and Hudson.
1969	Foreword, Barr, 1970.
1976	*A History of Building Types*, Thames and Hudson.
2002	*Pevsner on Art and Architecture: The Radio Talks*, ed. Stephen Games, Methuen: London. Revised (paperback), 2003.

2. PEVSNER UNPUBLISHED WRITINGS CITED

1919	*Die letzte Stunde* (draft: July 31; revision: August 15).
1934, February 12	Letter to the AAC. (SPSL archive, Bodleian Library).
1954, August	*Family History* (unpublished), Germany/Fedaia/Venice.
1975, January 20	Letter to Herr Stresow, Prestel Verlag (GRI, Box 4).

3. CORRESPONDENCE WITH THE AUTHOR CITED

1983, September 11	John Ratcliff, Richmond, Surrey.
1983, October 4	John Ratcliff, Richmond, Surrey.
1983, October 15	John Ratcliff, Richmond, Surrey.
1984, January 4	Hans Erich Freiherr von Campenhausen, Heidelberg.

1984, March 14	Barbara Florence (daughter-in-law of Philip Sargant Florence), New Mexico.
1984, March et seq.	Elizabeth Gilmore Holt, Washington.
1984, April 18	Florence Mütherich, Munich.
1984, April 18	Herman Gundersheimer, Philadelphia.
1984, April 21	Ursula Stechow (widow of Wolfgang Stechow), Ohio.
1984, April 29	Edeltrud König, Göttingen.
1984, May 22	Dr Hella Wenskus, Leipzig.
1984, May 29	Bernhard Degenhart, Munich.
1984, August 22	Dr Peter Tigler, Kunsthistorisches Institut, Florence.
1984, October 31	Dr Ulrich A. Michel, Amersham.
1984, December 08	Dr Ulrich A. Michel, Amersham.
1984, September 15	Ilse Gerson, Groningen.
1998, December 16	Renate Drücker, in Leipzig.
2009, March-Oct	Sabine Epple, Curator, Modern Collection, Grassi Museum für Angewandte Kunst, Leipzig.
2009, August 16	Heinrich Pollack, Haifa.
2009, September 3	Heinrich Pollack, Haifa.
2009, November 11	Charles Jencks, London.

4. INTERVIEWS/CONVERSATIONS WITH THE AUTHOR CITED

1981	Reyner Banham, in London.
1981	Sir Alec Clifton Taylor, in London.
1983, November 30	Ellen Dreessen, in London.
1984	Fred Wolsey, in London.
1984	Jenny Waterson, by telephone.
1984	Trude Bondi, in London.
1984, February	Ernst Kitzinger, in Oxford.
1984, March 6	Rosalind Priestman, in London.
1984, March 26	Thomas Pevsner, in London.
1984, April 27	Elizabeth Gilmore Holt, in London.
1984, April	Franz Kockel, in Bochum.
1984, April	Marianne Kockel, in Marburg.
1984 July	Edeltrud König, in Göttingen.
1984 July	Karl Arndt, in Göttingen.
1984, July	Peter Guth, in Leipzig.
1984 July	Hans-Joachim Dahms, in Göttingen.
1984, July	Renate Drücker, in Leipzig.
1984, July	Ernst Ullmann, in Leipzig.
1984, July	Thomas Topfstedt, in Leipzig.
1984, July	Elisabeth Paatz, in Heidelberg.
1984, July	Agnes Schmidt-Jüngst, in Germany.
1985, July 18	Wolfgang Hermann, in Hampstead.
1985, August 4	Wolfgang Hermann, in Hampstead.
2009, June	Ursula Tarkowski, in Oxford.

5. OTHER WORKS CITED

1812	Johann Wolfgang von Goethe, *Dichtung und Wahrheit*, Part II, Book 6.
1824	Leopold von Ranke, *Die Geschichte der romanischen und germanischen Völker.*
1861–1863	Gottfried Semper, *Der Stil.*
1873	Robert Vischer, *Über das optische Formgefühl.*
1879	Treitschke, 'Unsere Aussichten', published in *Preußichen Jahrbüchern*, which Treitschke also edited.
1887	Jean-Marie Guyau, *L'irreligion de l'avenir.*
1891–1893	Karl Lamprecht, *Deutsche Geschichte.*
1892–1901	Georg Dehio and Gustav von Bezold, *Die kirchliche Baukunst des Abendlandes.*
1901	Bruno Gebhardt, *Handbuch der deutschen Geschichte.*
1903	B. Heil, *Die deutschen Städte und Bürger im Mittelalter*, Leipzig (4th edn, 1921).
1905	Auguste Forel, *Die Sexuelle Frage.*
1906	Margaret Siebert, *Die Madonnendarstellung in der altniederlandischen Kunst von Jan van Eyck bis zu den Manieristen* in *Zur Kunstgeschichte Des Auslandes*, Heft XLI, Heitz & Mündel.
1908	Émile Mâle, *L'art religieux de la fin du moyen âge en France*, Librarie Armand Colin.
1909	Karl Hampe, *Deutsche Kaisergeschichte in der Zeit der Salier und Staufer.*
1909	Georg Dehio, *Italien.*
1910	Adolf Goldschmidt, *Das Evangeliar im Rathaus zu Goslar.*
1912	Auguste Forel, 'Formicides Néotropiques Part III', *Extrait des 'Memoires des Société Ontomologique de Belgique'*, Tome XIX.
1912	Ernst Bergmann, *Die Philosophie Guyaus*, Leipzig.
1918	Oswald Spengler, *Der Untergang des Abendlandes.*
1919, March 31	Walter Gropius, Letter to his mother, Berlin.
1919, July 4	Letter from Max Berger to Annie Pevsner, in: Pevsner Archive, GRI.
1919	*Protection of Art during War: Reports concerning the Condition of the Monuments of Art at the Different Theatres of War and the German and Austrian Measures taken for their Preservation, Rescue and Research, in Collaboration with Gerhard Bersu, Heinz Brau and others*, ed. Paul Clemen, Seeman.
1920	Siegmund Hellmann, *Das Mittelalter bis zum Ausgange der Kreuzzüge*, in: *Weltgeschichte*, Band IV, ed. Ludo Moritz Hartmann. (Facsimile edition, 1969.)
1921	Werner Weisbach, *Der Barock als Kunst der Gegenreformation*, Cassirer.
1922	Franz Adam Beyerlein, 'Wie eine Feder im Winde', published in a collection of five short stories called *Wetterleuchten im Herbst* [*Autumn Lightning*], Reclam.
1923	*Idee und Aufbau des Staatlichen Bauhauses*, Bauhaus: Weimar.
1923	Peter Behrens, 'Die Dombauhütte'. Quoted in Anderson, 2008.
1924	Ludwig Lang, *Was ist Barock?*, Montana: Stuttgart.
1924	Philip Sargant Florence, *Economics of Fatigue and Unrest and the Efficiency of Labour in English and American Industry*, Holt: New York.
1925, 1926, 1927	Hans Posse, annual reports of the Gemäldegalerie Gallery: Dresden.

1925, July–December Tancred Borenius, 'An early Caravaggio re-discovered', *Apollo*: London,
                      Vol. 2.
1925   Hans Posse, *Der römische Maler, Andrea Sacchi*, Seemann: Leipzig.
1925   Herman Voss, 1925, *Die Malerei des Barock in Rom*, Propyläen.
1926   Foreword, *Catalogue*, Dresden International Exhibition.
1926   Wilhelm Pinder, *Das Problem der Generation in der Kunstgeschichte Europas*,
                      Frankfurter Verlaganstalt: Berlin.
1927   Wilhelm Nisser, *Michael Dahl and the Contemporary Swedish School Painting
                      in England*, John Lane: The Bodley Head, Uppsala. Also Almquist &
                      Wilsells.
1930, July 15   Wilhelm Pinder to Nikolaus Pevsner, Letter from Munich (Pevsner
                      Archive, GRI).
1930   *Le Corbusier und Jeanneret, Pierre, Ihr gesamtes Werk von 1910 bis 1929*, ed.
                      and trans. O. Stonorov and W. Boesiger, Girsberger: Zurich.
1930   Victor Curt Habicht, *Niedersächsische Kunst in England*, Edler & Krische:
                      Hannover.
1932   Henry-Russell Hitchcock and Philip Johnson, *The International Style*,
                      Norton: New York.
1932, April 8   John Ratcliff, Letter to his mother. Quoted in Ratcliff, 15 October 1983.
1932, April 17   John Ratcliff, Letter to his mother. Quoted in Ratcliff, 15 October 1983.
1932, May 1   John Ratcliff, Letter to his mother. Quoted in Ratcliff, 15 October 1983.
1932, May 8   John Ratcliff, Letter to his mother. Quoted in Ratcliff, 15 October 1983.
1932, May 15   John Ratcliff, Letter to his mother. Quoted in Ratcliff, 4 October 1983
                      and 15 October 1983.
1933, April 9   Letter to Nikolaus Pevsner. (Pevsner Archive, GRI.)
1933, May   Francesca Wilson, 'German University Town: After the Celebrations of
                      May Day', *Birmingham Post*.
1933   *Newnes Pictorial Knowledge*, 2nd ed., Vol. 2.
1935   Wilhelm Pinder, 'Architektur als Moral', in: *Heinrich Wölfflin: Festschrift
                      zum siebzigsten Geburtstag*, Jess, pp.145–51.
1942   Wilhelm Pinder, Richard Graul appreciation.
1943, June 5   Wilhelm Pinder, filmed interview, *Filmarchivs der Persönlichkeiten*, ed.
                      Gerhard Jeschke, in: *Encyclopaedia Cinematographica*, ed. G Wolf, Göttingen,
                      1957.
1944   Lewis Namier, *1848: The Revolution of the Intellectuals*, from *The Proceedings
                      of the British Academy*, Vol. XXX, OUP: London.
1946   Wolfgang Stechow, 'Vitzthum Obituary Notice', *Oberlin College Art
                      Journal*.
1952   John Betjeman, *First and Last Loves*, John Murray.
1960   W. L. Shirer, *The Rise and Fall of the Third Reich*, Simon & Schuster: New
                      York, Ch. 8.
1961   Colin McInnes, *England, Half English*, Penguin.
1965   Patrick Romanell, 'Translator's Introduction', Benedetto Croce, *Guide
                      to Aesthetics*, tr. Patrick Romanell, The Library of Liberal Arts, Bobbs-
                      Merrill.
1967   Peter Gay, *Weimar Culture*, Secker & Warburg.
1968   Herbert Read, *A Concise History of Modern Painting*, Thames and
                      Hudson.
1970   John R. Barr, *Sir Nikolaus Pevsner: A Bibliography*, The American

	Association of Architectural Bibliographers, Papers, Vol. VII, ed. William O'Neal, University Press of Virginia: Charlottesville.
1971	Oskar Kokoschka, *Mein Leben.*
1972	Klaus Bender, 'Die Vossische Zeitung', *Deutsche Zeitungen des 17. bis 20. Jahrhunderts*, ed. Fischer, H.-D., Pullach.
1975, June	Horst Gerson, 'Wolfgang Stechow', *Kunstchronik*, Vol. 28.
1975	Adam Fergusson, *When Money Dies*, William Kimber.
1976, June 24	Nikolaus Pevsner in private interview with Frank Hermann.
1978	Carl J. Rheins, *German Jewish Patriotism 1918–1935*, State University of New York, Stony Brook, doctoral thesis.
1981	Christine Kutschke, *Bauhaus Buildings of Dessau*, doctoral thesis, Weimar.
1981	Gordon A. Craig, *Germany 1866–1945*, OUP.
1982, January 30	Stephen Games, *Pevsner: The Necessary Art*, BBC Radio Three. (Extract published: *The Listener.*)
1983, December 1	Remembered by Jerry Neisser, a relation of Carola Pevsner. Quoted by Lu Fenton, New York, in: Letter to Dieter Pevsner, 1 December 1983.
1983	Hans-Joachim Dahms, *Göttingen Unterm Hakenkreuz*, Göttingen University.
1984	William Sheridan Allen, *The Nazi Seizure of Power: Revised edition*, Franklin Watts: New York.
1988	Arthur Chandler, 'The art deco exposition', *World's Fair*, Vol. VIII, No. 3.
1988	Heinz-Joachim Müllenbrock and Theodor Wolpers, *Englische Literatur in der Göttinger Universitätsbibliothek des 18. Jahrhunderts*, Vandenhoeck und Ruprecht: Göttingen.
1989	Kevin Cope, Review of Müllenbrock and Wolpers, 1988, in *South Atlantic Review*.
1991	Detlef Mühlberger, *Hitler's Followers: Studies in the Sociology of the Nazi Movement*, Routledge: New York.
1991	Christhard Hoffmann, 'The contribution of German-speaking Jewish immigrants to British Hhstoriography', *Second Chance: Two Centuries of German-Speaking Jews in the United Kingdom*, co-ed. Julius Carlebach and Werner E. Mosse. In the 'Schriftenreihe wissenschaftlicher Abhandlungen des Leo Baeck Instituts', Vol. 48, Mohr: London and Tubingen.
1991	Reginald Isaacs, *Gropius*, Bullfinch Press.
1992	Peter Gay, *Weimar Culture*, Penguin.
1993	Roger Chickering, *Karl Lamprecht: A German Academic Life*, Brill.
1993	Udo Kultermann, *The History of Art History*, Abaris Books.
1994	Geoffrey Finlayson, *Citizen, State, and Social Welfare in Britain 1830–1990*, OUP.
1996	Ulrich Bischoff: 'Hans Posse und Kokoschka', in: *Kokoschka und Dresden* (exhibition catalogue), Staatliche Kunstsammlungen Dresden, pp. 76–80.
1997	David Backbourn, *The Long Nineteenth Century*, OUP.
1998	R. J. W. Evans, *The Language of History and the History of Language: An Inaugural Lecture delivered before the University of Oxford on 11 May 1998*, Clarendon Press.
1998	Victor Klemperer, *I Shall Bear Witness*, Weidenfeld and Nicolson.
1998	Arthur L. Blumenthal, 'Leipzig, Wilhelm Wundt and Psychology's Gilded Age', *Portraits of Pioneers in Psychology* Vol. III, ed. Gregory A. Kimble and Michael Wertheimer, Taylor & Francis.

1999	Peter Jelavich, 'German culture in the Great War', *European Culture in the Great War*, ed. Aviel Roshwald and Richard Stites, CUP.
2000	*Dictionary of Art Historians*, ed. Lee Sorensen. (www.dictionaryof arthistorians.org).
2000	Roger Chickering, 'The Lamprecht Controversy', *Historikerkontroversen*, ed. Hartmut Lehmann, Wallstein.
2000	Timothy Mowl, *Stylistic Cold Wars: Betjeman versus Pevsner*, John Murray.
2001	*The Buildings of England: A Celebration*, ed. Simon Bradley and Bridget Cherry, Penguin Collectors' Society.
2001	Annalisa Capristo, 'The exclusion of the Jewish scholars from the Accademia d'Italia', *La Rassegna mensile di Israel*, Vol. 67, No. 3, pp. 1–36.
2002, November 18	Stephen Games, 'A Nazi in England', *London Evening Standard*.
2002, November 29	'Book connects Pevsner to Nazis', *Building Design*, p. 2.
2002, December 13	'Cherry picking', Letters, *Building Design*, p. 6.
2003	Christian Scholzel, 'Fritz Rathenau: On Anti-Semitism, Acculturation and Slavophobia', *The Leo Baeck Institute Yearbook*, Vol. 48.
2003	Gauvin A. Bailey, *Between Renaissance and Baroque: Jesuit Art in Rome, 1565–1610*, University of Toronto Press.
2004	*Reassessing Nikolaus Pevsner*, ed. Peter Draper, Ashgate.
2004	Max Michelson, *City of Life, City of Death* (autobiography), University of Colorado Press.
2005	Manfred Berger, *Kirchenlexikon*, Vol. XXV, Columns 1583–1600.
2005	John V. Maciuika, *Before the Bauhaus*, CUP.
2005	Joan L. Clinefelter, *Artists for the Reich*, Berg Publishers.
2007	Viktoria Wuchrer/Hendrik Baernighausen, 'Der Kunsthändler Herrmann Holst, der Galeriedirektor Hans Posse und der Maler Oskar Kokoschka als Bewohner des Pavillon J im Grossen Garten in Dresden', in: *Jahrbuch des Schlösserlands Sachsen*, Staatliche Schlößer, Burgen und Gärten, Band 14/2006, Dresden, pp. 129–42.
2007	Heinrich Pollack, *Deine Treue ist groß*, Aussaat.
2007	Mark A. Russell, *Between Tradition and Modernity*, Berghahn Books.
2008	Ross Anderson, 'The medieval masons' lodge as paradigm in Peter Behrens's Dombauhütte in Munich, 1922, in *Art Bulletin*, 90, pp. 441–65.
2009	Rosalind Priestman, *A Thread through my Memories*. (Privately printed.)
2009	John Betjeman, *Betjeman's England*, ed. Stephen Games, John Murray.

Index

Academic Assistance Council
  (London) 192, 193, 201, 204
archaeology 69, 81, 97
architecture 7, 11, 93, 111–12
  architectural writing 3,
    6, 81
  in England 22, 56, 111,
    123, 159, 160
  German 10, 22, 24, 111,
    112–13, 116–17, 168, 169
  Modern Movement 3,
    168–72
  as mother of the arts 3
  as shaping society 7
art history 3–4, 73–4, 111,
  121–2, 157, 164
  in Britain 160, 193–4, 201,
    202
  as ending in 1914 172, 173
  in Germany 13, 73, 75, 76,
    77–8, 79, 81, 90, 91–3,
    96, 97, 98, 99, 100, 101,
    103–5, 111, 119, 123,
    128, 147, 161, 163, 179
  in Italy 192
Asenijeff, Elsa 24

Banham, Reyner 3, 5, 112, 114
Barkas, Palliser 180, 187, 192,
  193, 200, 205
Barrow, Walter 204
Bauhaus, the 135–6, 138, 151,
  156, 166, 168
Behrens, Peter 151, 169
Below, Georg von 87
Benjamin, Elia 38
Bergmann, Ernst 29, 30–1, 55
Betjeman, John 1–2, 15, 35,
  201, 211
  First and Last Loves 2
Betjeman's England (Games) 15
Beveridge, Sir William 192–3
Bezold, Gustav von 101, 102
Birmingham 203
Bismarck, Otto von 42, 51, 71
Blidin, Leib (NP's great-
  grandfather) 36, 38

Bodmer, Heinrich 117, 126,
  192
Borenius, Tancred 127, 160,
  162, 193, 194, 199, 205
Braithwaite, Constance 203
  The Voluntary Citizen 203
Brandenburg, Erich 85, 88
Bremen, Alexander von 46
Bremen, Helmut Meyer von
  36, 45–7, 50, 52, 203
Briggs, Martin
  The Architect in History 163
Brinckmann, Alfred 93, 121
Brückwald, Otto 24
Bruhns, Leo 85, 111, 126, 179
Büchting, Dora 149
Burckhardt, Jacob 122
  History of the Renaissance 74
Burger, Fritz 120, 121
Buruma, Ian 4
  Voltaire's Coconuts 208
Byam-Shaw, James 158

Campenhausen, Hans von 150,
  178, 190
Carravagio 127
Catholic Church 125–6
Central School of Art
  (London) 3
Cerano (Giovanni Battista
  Crespi) 123, 124
Charlemagne 70–1
Cherry, Bridget 189, 213
cinema 151, 164
Clemen, Paul 104–5
Clifton-Taylor, Sir Alec 5, 24
Constable, W. G. 193, 199, 201
Courant, Gertrud 182
Courant, Richard 182, 186
Courtauld Institute of Art
  (London) 193, 201, 202
Croce, Benedetto 192
Curtius, Ludwig 140, 144

Dahms, Hans-Joachim 185
Däubler, Theodore 65
Degenhardt, Bernhard 99–100

Dehio, Georg 6, 98, 101, 102,
  103, 104, 105, 116
  *Geschichte der deutschen
    Kunst* 101
  *Handbuch der deutschen
    Kunstdenkmäler* 101
design 3, 132
Deutscher Werkbund 10, 171,
  190–1
Dilthey, Wilhelm 87
Döring, Christian 113
Dostoyevsky, Fyodor 54,
  111
Dragendorff, Hans 81
Dreessen, Ellen (née
  Perlmann) 25, 36, 58, 62, 84
Dresden 111, 129
  architecture of 117
  contemporary art in 130–1,
    133, 150–1
  International Exhibition
    of 1926 131–4, 136–7,
    138–9, 151, 202
  Staatliche Gemäldegalerie
    116, 118–19, 155
Dvořák, Max 92–3, 122
Dybbuk, The (Ansky) 38–9

England
  and anti-Semitism 41
  art in 155–6
  as home for notable
    Germans 1
  living standards in 23
  as model for some
    Germans 56
  and refugees 201, 202–3,
    204, 205

fascism 192, 194
First World War 43, 52, 56–7,
  96, 200
  destruction of monuments
    in 103–4, 143
  German Jews and 51
  and Germany 2, 45, 51,
    56–7, 103

First World War (*continued*)
and (German) nationalism
35, 56
Fletcher, John 200, 201, 203
Florence, Philip Sargant 203–4
*The Logic of Industrial
Organization* 204
Ford, Henry 203
Forel, Auguste 5, 27–8, 29, 42,
87
Fouillée, Alfred 29
France
and culture 55, 56, 134–5,
151, 166, 170, 181–2
Franck, James 185
Franco-Prussian War 91, 134
Frick, Wilhelm 177, 183
Friedell, Egon
*Die Kulturgeschichte der
Menschheit* 212
Friedländer, Walter 126
Froshaug, Anthony 3
Fry, Roger 201, 202
Fuchs, Johann Gregor 113
Furtwängler, Wilhelm
dispute with Goebbels 194,
196

Gabetti, Giuseppe 192
Games, Stephen 2–17
and controversy over
Pevsner 207–11, 212–13
Gebhardt, Bruno
Handbook of German History
73, 88
Gentile, Giovanni 192
German Art Society (Deutsche
Kunstgesellschaft) 139
Germany 22, 23, 28, 54, 84,
159
anti-Semitism in 41–2, 46,
51, 82, 175, 176, 178, 184,
185, 188, 190, 191, 195,
196, 198, 199
craze for the past 151
East Germany 9–11
political collapse and
Weimar Republic 2, 42,
57, 64–5, 67, 79, 80, 83,
103, 106–7, 109–10, 131,
150, 151, 152, 174, 182–3
Prussian militarism in 50–1,
86
and Thirty Years War 125
and Versailles Treaty 67
West Germany 9

see also First World War;
Judaism; Nazism
Gerson, Horst 148
Getty organization 11–12, 13
Goebbels, Joseph 185, 194,
196, 197
Goethe, Johann Wolfgang von
65, 112, 114, 116
Goldschmidt, Adolph 76, 81,
111, 123
*The Gospels in Goslar Town
Hall* 81
Gombrich, Ernst 5, 27–8, 214
Göring, Hermann 183
Gothein, Eberhard 123, 125
Göttingen 11, 146, 154–5
Göttingen University 143,
146–7, 150, 152, 154, 155,
157, 162, 175–6, 179, 180,
187–8, 191, 198
and the Nazi Party 174–5,
176, 177–8, 185–6, 187–8,
191
Graul, Richard 102, 118
Grimm, Hermann 161
Grohmann, Will 130, 137, 139
Gronau, Carmen 148, 178
Gropius, Walter 2, 3, 10, 135,
136, 137, 166–8, 169, 170–2,
182, 212
Grote, Ludwig 136
Gundersheimer, Herman 84
Gurlitt, Cornelius 113, 114,
132
Guyau, Jean-Marie 29, 30

Hampe, Karl
*German Imperial History
. . .* 73
Handbuch der Kunstwissenschaft
(encyclopaedia) 96, 101,
120–1, 124
Hartmann, Ludo Moritz 88
Hauttman, Max 79, 111
Hecht, Hans 146, 154, 162,
176, 179, 180
Hecht family 146, 176
Hegel, Georg 86
Heil, Bernhard
*German Towns and Citizens
in the Middle Ages* 73
Heimpel, Hermann 88, 90
Heinze, Richard 33
Hellmann, Siegmund 85, 118
*The Middle Ages to the End
of the Crusades* 88–90

Hemingway, Ernest 106
Hermann, Wolfgang 99, 107–8,
110, 120
Hessel, Alfred 173, 191
history (as discipline)
in England 88–9
in Germany 69–73, 86,
87–90, 92
and the Holy Roman
Empire 71, 72
and the Roman Empire
69, 89
History of Witchcraft (Soltan)
126
Hitchcock, Henry-Russell 3,
171, 172
Hitler, Adolf 80, 174, 176, 177,
178, 181, 182, 203
as chancellor 183, 185, 186,
187–8, 190, 199
Mein Kampf 180
Hollis, Richard 3
Holzhausen, Walter 156
Humboldt, Wilhelm von 86

Isermeyer, Adolf 148, 149, 178,
179
Italian Encyclopaedia 192

Jähnig, Karl 119
Jencks, Charles 2, 12, 17
Jenkins, Simon 208, 210
Jess, Wolfgang 141, 144
Johnson, Philip 171, 172
journals
Architect's Journal 209, 211
Architectural Review 5, 11
Art in America 202
Der Sammler 141
Harvard Design Magazine
212
Jewish Chronicle 37
Kunst der Nation 205
Göttingsche gelehrte Anzeigen
150, 169, 191
RIBA Journal 211
Times Literary Supplement
213
Visual Culture in Britain 212
Zeitschrift für bildende Kunst
118
Judaism
and anti-Semitism 41–2,
181, 185, 203
culture and customs 37,
40–1

German Jews 41, 42, 82–3, 123, 178, 180–1
Jewish immigrants in Germany 82–3, 181, 188

Karge, Annegret 136
Kautzsch, Rudolf 76, 85, 94, 98, 111
Kehrer, Hugo 79
Kitzinger, Ernst 84, 98–9, 100, 101
Klemperer, Victor 84, 181, 190
Knauth, Liez 26
Kockel, Marianne (née Kurlbaum; NP's sister-in-law) 34, 44, 45, 52, 62, 83, 107, 109, 110, 120, 121, 129, 138, 141, 142, 188
König, Edeltrud 143, 147–8, 149, 178–9
Kötzschke, Rudolf 85, 88, 97
Krause, Anna 25, 45
Kummer, Friedrich 129
Kunstgeschichte (encyclopaedia) 121
Kunsthistorisches Institut (Florence) 117, 126, 140, 192
Kurlbaum, Alfred (NP's father-in-law) 31, 50, 51–2, 107, 108, 109, 110, 141, 175
Kurlbaum, Dieter 45
Kurlbaum, Eduard 48
Kurlbaum, Ferdinand 51
Kurlbaum, Paula (née Neisser) 51–3, 65, 83

Lamprecht, Karl 87, 88, 98
German History 73
Landau, Edmund 185
Lang, Ludwig 127
Lebrecht, Norman 207
Le Corbusier 135, 137, 169–70, 171, 172
Collected Works 169
Vers une architecture 137
Leipzig 10, 28, 87, 114
architecture of 10, 22, 24, 111, 113–15, 116–17
commerce in 113
(musical) culture in 21, 25, 68
after First World War 67, 109–10
Leipzig University 86–7, 90, 92–4, 99, 100, 121
Pevsner's view of 114

religious affiliations in 32, 46, 50
the Thomasschule 32–3, 35, 67
Liebermann, Max 139
Long, Christopher 212
Luther, Martin 41
Lynton, Norbert 208

MacCormac, Sir Richard 4
McElvoy, Anne 207
McInnes, Colin 1, 213–14
Mâle, Émile
Religious Art 81
Mann, Thomas 54–5, 65, 79, 111, 151
The Magic Mountain 54
Reflections of an Unpolitical Man 55
Marchand, Hildegard 119
Meades, Jonathan 208, 209, 210
Melnikov, Konstantin 135
Mendelssohn, Moses 41
Meyer, Bruno 161
Michalski, Ernst 107, 119, 121, 124
Michel, Ulrich 22, 25, 26, 32, 34, 50, 67, 110, 114
Middleton, Robin 4
Mises, Ludwig von 192
Mommsen, Theodor 88, 91
Montefiore, Sir Moses 38
Morris, William 156, 167, 204
Mussolini, Benito 192, 194
Mütherich, Florence 100
Muthesius, Hermann 134
The English House 56

Napoleon Bonaparte 41
Naumann, Max 181
Nazism 2, 31, 56, 79, 80, 90, 174–5, 176, 181–2, 183, 202, 234 n. 15
concentration camps 191
education policy of 194, 199
and Gleichschaltung 190, 197
Nazis in power 177, 183–4, 185–8, 190, 196, 198, 199, 205
Neisser, Julie 109
Neisser, Max 51
newspapers
Birmingham Post 9, 186–8
Catholic Herald 211

Das Unterhaltungsblatt 195, 202, 205
Die Vossische Zeitung 178, 195
Dresdner Anzeiger 129, 131, 138, 150, 151, 156
Dresdner neueste Nachrichten 156
Evening Standard 207–8, 209, 213
Frankfurter Allgemeine Zeitung 211
Göttinger Tageblatt 186, 190
Guardian 208
Observer 208
Private Eye 209
Scotsman 208–9, 211
The Times 208, 209
Nietzsche, Friedrich 51, 54, 111
Nikisch, Arthur 21, 26, 33, 42, 65, 196
Nikisch, Mitja 42
Noack, Ferdinand 81
Noorden, Carl von 86

Paatz, Elisabeth 100, 143, 186
Panofsky, Erwin 84
Paris International Exhibition 134–5, 170
Pastor, Ludwig
History of the Popes 125
Perlmann, Bernhard (NP's uncle) 35–6
Perlmann, Paula (NP's aunt) 160
Perlmann, Saveli (NP's grandfather) 36, 37, 38
Einiges über China 37
The Jews in China 37
Perlmann, Taube 'Jeanette' (née Blidin; NP's grandmother) 36, 38, 65, 81, 160
Peter, Carl 31
Ernst Bergmann und seine Lehre 31
Pevsner, Carola 'Lola' (née Kurlbaum; NP's wife) 23, 45, 46–7, 52, 199
family of 48, 49–50, 51, 52
influence on NP 83
Jewish 51, 52, 178
married life 107, 108, 138, 148, 180, 191, 192
at university 83, 85, 106

Pevsner, Dieter (son of NP)
178, 213
**Pevsner, Nikolaus Bernhard
Leon 'Nika' (born Nikolai
Bernhard Leon Pewsner)**
  formative influences 2
    architectural guidebooks
      24
    architecture in Leipzig
      22
    art historian Wilhelm
      Pinder 76, 84, 85, 105,
      121, 122, 126, 127,
      147, 159, 189
    art historian August
      Schmarsow 92–3,
      224 n. 15
    childhood household
      and circle 25–6, 33, 44,
      46, 50, 62, 65, 73
    historian Siegmund
      Hellmann 90
    literature 54, 79, 80, 111
    school 46, 62
  general and private life
    Alzheimer's disease 4
    applies for posts outside
      Germany 192, 193,
      198
    birth 2, 9, 21, 23
    character 5, 26, 28, 44–5,
      46–7, 62, 108, 109,
      111, 118, 120, 178
    childhood and youth in
      Leipzig 9, 10, 12, 22,
      23–5, 27, 44, 45–7, 54,
      55–6, 65
    chooses not to study
      English at school 33,
      56
    decides to become an
      art historian 65
    early contacts in
      England 200, 201, 203,
      204, 205
    education at the
      Thomasschule 10, 32,
      33, 68, 73, 74, 76, 79
    engagement to Lola
      83, 106
    in England as political
      refugee 200–5
    explores options in USA
      202
    family and background
      10, 14, 21, 23–5, 28–9,

33–4, 35–40, 42,
49–50, 58–9, 61–2,
68, 81
    family circle and
      connections 21, 26,
      28, 33, 42, 45, 46, 80,
      196
    family holidays 27, 42,
      52, 67, 118, 141, 180
    as father 117, 200
    and (aftermath of) First
      World War 44, 56,
      61–2, 64, 67, 109–10,
      159
    friendships 11, 24, 26,
      45–6, 50, 52, 65, 107,
      119, 124, 147, 189,
      205
    illness 80
    impractical 110, 189
    interests 44, 46, 54, 73,
      74–5, 109, 111, 148
    living away from home
      80, 109
    married and family life
      110, 129, 140, 145,
      147, 155, 178–9, 189,
      205
    meeting and fascination
      with future wife Lola
      45, 46–7, 50, 52, 68,
      83, 109
    nationalism of 81, 116,
      124, 135, 155, 170,
      178, 187
    physique 178, 179
    relations with mother
      43, 45, 56, 76, 77,
      81, 84
    reputation in England
      1–2, 5–6, 7, 9, 114,
      116, 189, 207, 210–11,
      212, 213
    response to being Jewish
      36, 39, 40, 42, 43, 49,
      82, 84, 178, 181, 201
    return (visit) to
      Germany 205–6
    sense of being unloved
      45
    as subject of radio
      programme 2, 5, 6,
      27, 213
    talents 43, 44, 47, 120,
      130, 203
    travel 5, 149

    view of and relations
      with father 33–4, 40,
      44, 58, 62, 84, 117,
      149, 158
    visits England as a child
      9, 155
    wedding and
      honeymoon 106,
      107–9
  ideas and opinions
    on architecture 22–3,
      92, 116
    England and its art 155,
      158–9, 166, 202, 204,
      205
    on ethics of working in
      territory not of one's
      background 123–4
    on history 90, 151–2
    on Le Corbusier 137,
      169–70
    modern art in Germany
      130–1, 137, 138, 139,
      151, 156
    on the modern world
      116–17, 152
    moral chain argument
      156–7, 230 n. 7
    political views 4, 137,
      178, 180, 181, 182,
      187–8, 189, 197, 213
  identity and nationality
    181
    as citizen of Saxony, thus
      Germany 2, 35, 36,
      187, 214
    conversion to Lutheran
      (Evangelisch) Church
      82, 83, 84, 123, 124,
      181, 184
    discomfort over parents'
      Russian-Jewish origins
      33–4, 35, 36, 39, 46,
      49, 82, 108, 115
    and Englishness of 1,
      213–14
    sense of having German
      roots and pedigree
      through Lola 50
  publications and writing
    academic essays, reviews,
      articles 113, 116, 119,
      120, 123, 124–5, 127,
      129, 141, 150, 163–5,
      168–70, 182, 191, 192,
      194, 195–7, 202, 205

autobiographical essay 92

Baroque Painting in South-Western Europe 144

The Buildings of England (editor) 5, 11, 22, 23, 113, 189, 210

diaries 44, 46–7, 65, 80, 109

Dictionary of Architecture 112

drafts short stories 54

family history 27, 33–4, 36, 37, 38–9, 43, 47, 48–50, 52–3, 62

foreign editions of books 8

Handbuch der Kunstwissenschaft (encyclopaedia vol.) 121–3, 127, 144, 145, 156, 163, 170, 189

A History of Building Types 11

New Archive for Saxon History and Archaeology 113

An Outline of European Architecture 3, 5, 13, 90, 92, 112, 113

Pelican History of Art (editor) 5, 14

Pioneers of Modern Design 2, 3

Pioneers of the Modern Movement (begun in Germany) 90, 168, 169, 172

schoolboy essay on van Gogh 62–4, 73

writing technique and quality 113, 127, 164–5, 182

university studies

Berlin: archaeology, philosophy, art history 81, 109, 120, 123

doctoral dissertation on Leipzig architecture 10, 85, 106, 110, 112–15, 117, 118, 132, 152

Frankfurt am Main: art history, archaeology, architecture 85

Leipzig: art history, history, aesthetics 9, 68, 69, 83–4, 85–6, 88

Munich: history and art history 76, 79–81, 107

work in England

as academic 4, 5, 14, 208

as art historian 2, 3, 4, 14, 73–4, 92

associates and students 5, 14, 112, 114, 189, 208

correspondence 8, 11, 14

as critic 4

as editor 4, 5, 11, 14

expert adviser in planning disputes 116

as historian of design 3

as interpreter of Englishness 2, 3, 56

involvement with institutions 4, 8–9, 12

lectures abroad 12

radio talks 4, 5, 12, 14, 73, 74–5, 84, 92, 123–4, 194, 207

Reith Lectures of 213

work in Germany

approach to art history 124–5, 126, 145

art reporter in Dresden 129–31, 133, 137, 138, 139–40, 150, 155

change of professional interests 149, 150, 152, 154, 156, 157–8, 166–7, 168–71

as collector of visual material 161–2

contributes to the Thieme-Becker artists' lexicon 149–50

dealings with publishers 120, 121, 141, 144, 145

first book project: Mannerism 120, 121–4, 126, 131, 141, 163

(unpaid) internship in Dresden 12, 116, 119, 121, 123, 128, 129, 131, 133–4, 138, 140–1, 142

learning about the art world 134

prepares doctoral thesis for publication 141

professional manner 127, 147, 150

reception and standing of 126, 127, 144, 145, 149, 156, 162, 163, 170, 179, 193, 195

and research trips 129, 133, 134, 136, 157, 158–61, 163, 166, 168, 192, 200

suspension of courses, then dismissal 191–2, 195, 198

as teacher (Privatdozent) at Göttingen University 9, 145, 147–50, 152, 154, 155–6, 161, 162, 163, 164, 168, 173, 174, 178, 179, 186, 188–9

working method when travelling 159–60, 161

Pevsner, Thomas (son of NP) 178, 180, 184, 200

Pevsner, Uta (later Hodgson; daughter of NP) 117, 178, 180, 187, 200

Pevsner archive (Getty Research Institute, Los Angeles) 11–12, 13–14, 44

Pevsner on Art and Architecture (ed. Games) 14–15, 210, 211–12

controversy over 207–9, 212–13

Pewsner, (Sara) Annie (née Perlmann; NP's mother) 24, 25, 27, 36, 42, 43, 58, 182

as alien (Russian) in Leipzig 34, 35

as anglophile and pacifist 29, 51, 56, 155

attempts suicide 62

illnesses/depression 27, 28, 43, 62

interest in art and music 25, 44, 45, 65, 76, 78–9

involvement in politics 64, 65, 213

involvement in social work 28, 35, 200, 213

Jewish 36, 37, 42

as parent 43, 44, 62, 79, 107

Pewsner, (Sara) Annie
(*continued*)
  as society hostess 10, 26,
    29, 65
  as translator 29, 30–1, 74
Pewsner, Heinrich 'Heinz'
  (NP's brother) 10, 25, 32, 33,
  36, 44, 45, 54
  and First World War 59
  intelligence of 58–9
  suicide 61, 64
Pewsner, Hillel Benjamin
  'Hugo' (NP's father) 10, 23,
  25, 29, 39, 57–8, 68, 107,
  108, 134
  absences on business 42–3,
    44, 51, 58, 59, 61–2, 67
  as alien (Russian) in Leipzig
    34–5
  in business as fur trader 10,
    32, 33–4, 40, 42, 57–8,
    65–6, 67, 76, 110, 114–15,
    158
  contracts tuberculosis 27,
    48
  Jewish 38, 39, 40
  supports NP 149, 158
Pewsner, Shmuel Shmelkin
  (NP's grandfather) 39
  philosophy 6, 86, 87
Pinder, (Georg Maximilian)
  Wilhelm 96, 98, 100–1, 102,
  111, 121, 155, 157, 164,
  175
  character of 97, 98, 99
  Collected Writings 85
  German Baroque 127
  as head of art history at
    Leipzig 76, 77, 78, 79, 81,
    85, 97, 99–100, 118
  and Pevsner 76, 118, 143,
    144, 189–90, 192, 193
  and politics 84, 101, 102–3,
    105, 190
Pollack, Heinrich 24–5, 27, 65,
  68, 81, 82, 109, 128
Pollack, Ida (née Perlmann;
  NP's aunt) 25, 65, 109
Pollack, Walter 82
Posnen, Reb Gershen Tanchum
  (NP's great-grandfather) 38
Posse, Hans 116, 118, 121, 131,
  133, 140
Powell, Kenneth 209, 211
Priestman, Rosalind 9, 180,
  182, 186, 191, 199–200

Pugin, Augustus 3, 7
Pye, Michael 208–9, 211

Ranke, Leopold von 72, 86,
  87, 127
  History of the Popes 125
  *History of the Latin and
    Teutonic Nations* 70
Ratcliff, John 146, 155, 175–8,
  179
Rathenau, Fritz 185
Religious Architecture of the West
  (Dehio and von Bezold) 81
Rheins, Carl 181
Rhode, Carl Ferdinand 21
Riegl, Alois 74, 78, 92
Rörig, Fritz 85, 88
Rose, Hans 79, 111, 163

Sabersky, Heinrich 109, 120
Sauerlandt, Max 85
Schatz, David 113
Schmarsow, August 74, 92–3,
  97, 98, 99, 113, 117, 144, 145
Schmidt, Karl 131, 133
Schmidt-Jüngst, Agnes 144,
  147
Schöne, Wolfgang 149, 179
Schrader, Hans 85
Schumacher, Fritz 190
Schwägrichen, Christian
  Friedrich 21
Secor, Lella Faye 203
Semper, Gottfried
  Der Stil 168
Siebert, Margarete 107, 108,
  109, 122
  *The Representation of the
    Madonna . . .* 122–3
Spengler, Oswald 13, 76–8, 182
  The Decline of the West 76–7
Spranger, Wilhelm 81
Springer, Anton 90–2, 101
  History of Austria 91
Stechow, Wolfgang 145, 147,
  148, 163, 178, 191, 198
Stradonitz, Stephan Kekulé
  von 47
Studniczka, Franz 85, 94, 97,
  98, 118
Sturm, Leonhard Christoph
  113
Summerson, John 3
Sutcliffe, Thomas 5, 6
Symondson, Anthony 211
Szilárd, Leó 192

Tarkowski, Ursula 160
Treitschke, Heinrich Gotthard
  von 42

Ullmann, Ernst 24
USA
  art and architecture in 202

Valentiner, Justus Theodor 186,
  191, 198
van der Rohe, Mies 197
van de Velde, Henri 131, 136,
  156, 166
van Gogh, Vincent 62–4, 197
Vaughan, Will 208
Vischer, Friedrich Theodor
  92
Vischer, Robert 92
Vitzthum, Georg 94–5, 100,
  143–4, 145, 147, 150, 156,
  157, 162, 191, 198
Volkelt, Johannes 85
Vollmer, Hans 149, 150
Voss, Herman
  Baroque Painting in Rome
  127

Waitz, George 102, 105
Watkin, David 3–4, 8
  Morality and Architecture 6–7,
  211, 214
Watzdorf, Erna von 119
Weber, Ernst Heinrich 87
Weeks, Jessamine 202–3
Weisbach, Werner 81, 92,
  124–5, 127
  *Baroque as the Art of the
    Counter-Reformation* 124
Wickhoff, Franz 92
Wilde, Oscar 196, 201
Wilhelm I of Prussia 51, 71
Williams, Richard J. 212
Wilson, Francesca 186–8, 200,
  202, 203, 208
Wittkower, Rudolf 79
Wölfflin, Heinrich 74, 76,
  79–80, 92, 99, 113, 144, 161
  *Italy and the German Sense of
    Form* 101
  Renaissance and Baroque
  111
Wolsey, Fred 9, 208
Wulff, Oskar 81, 93
Wundt, Wilhelm 87, 88, 92,
  98, 100
Wustmann, Gustav 113